SUPERMAN BATMAN
SUPERGIRL

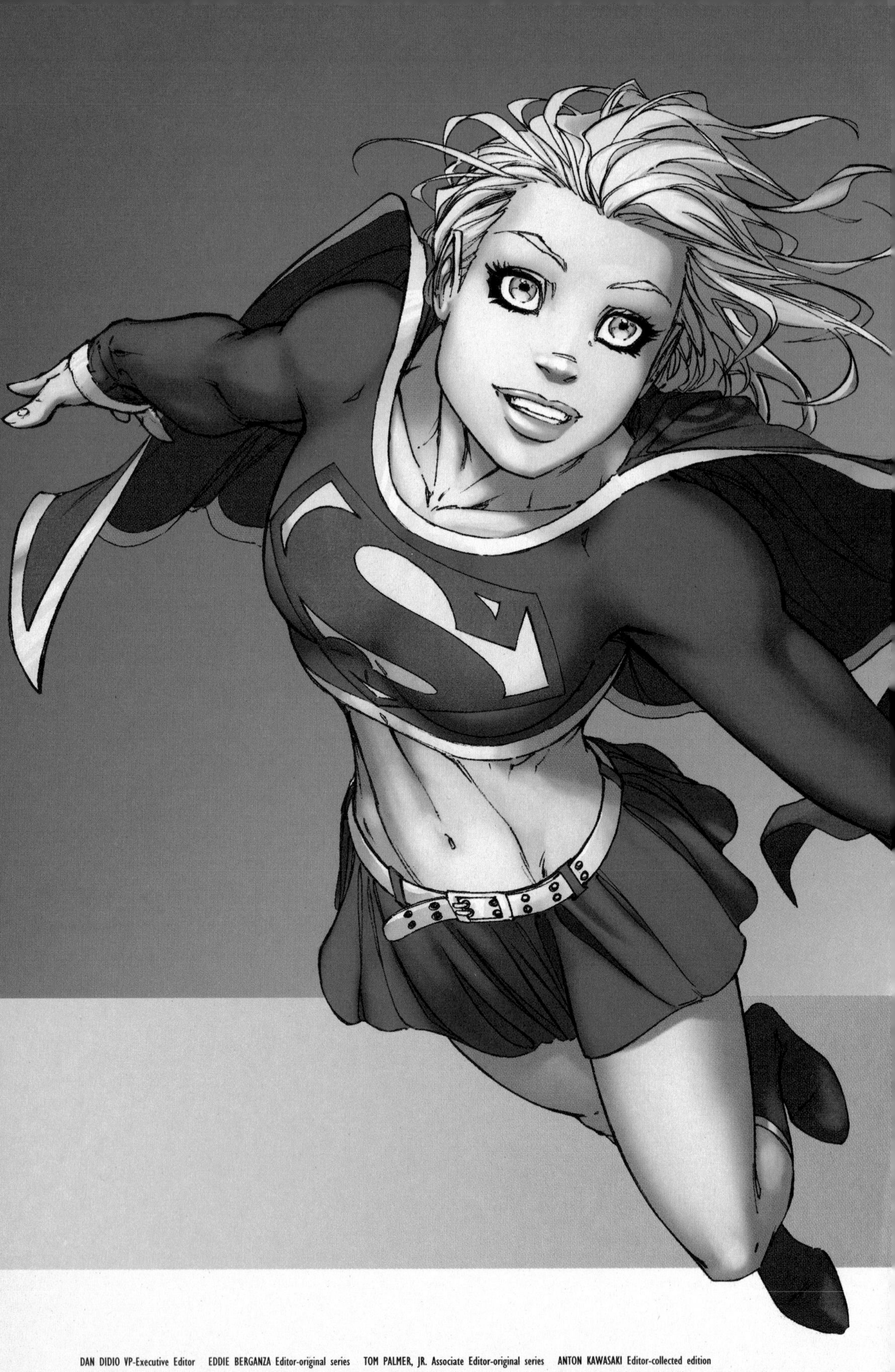

DAN DIDIO VP-Executive Editor EDDIE BERGANZA Editor-original series TOM PALMER, JR. Associate Editor-original series ANTON KAWASAKI Editor-collected edition
ROBBIN BROSTERMAN Senior Art Director PAUL LEVITZ President & Publisher GEORG BREWER VP-Design & Retail Product Development RICHARD BRUNING Senior VP-Creative Director
PATRICK CALDON Senior VP-Finance & Operations CHRIS CARAMALIS VP-Finance TERRI CUNNINGHAM VP-Managing Editor ALISON GILL VP-Manufacturing RICH JOHNSON VP-Book Trade Sales
HANK KANALZ VP-General Manager, WildStorm LILLIAN LASERSON Senior VP & General Counsel JIM LEE Editorial Director-WildStorm DAVID MCKILLIPS VP-Advertising & Custom Publishing
JOHN NEE VP-Business Development GREGORY NOVECK Senior VP-Creative Affairs CHERYL RUBIN Senior VP-Brand Management BOB WAYNE VP-Sales & Marketing

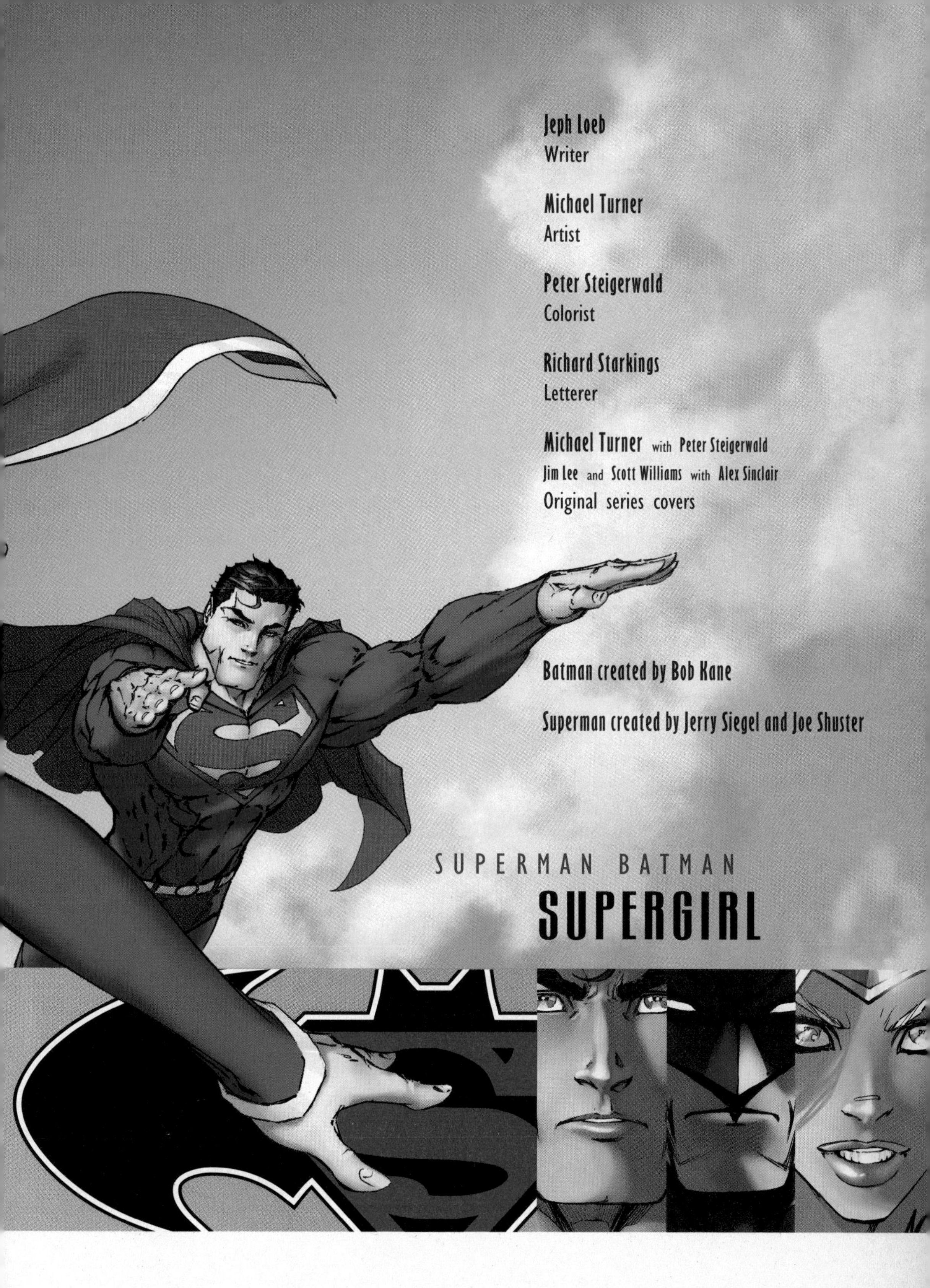

Jeph Loeb
Writer

Michael Turner
Artist

Peter Steigerwald
Colorist

Richard Starkings
Letterer

Michael Turner with Peter Steigerwald
Jim Lee and Scott Williams with Alex Sinclair
Original series covers

Batman created by Bob Kane

Superman created by Jerry Siegel and Joe Shuster

S U P E R M A N   B A T M A N
SUPERGIRL

SUPERMAN/BATMAN: SUPERGIRL
Published by DC Comics. Cover, introduction and compilation copyright © 2005 DC Comics. All Rights Reserved.
Originally published in single magazine form in SUPERMAN/BATMAN: SUPERGIRL #8-13. Copyright © 2004 DC Comics. All Rights Reserved. All characters, their distinctive likenesses and related elements featured in this publication are trademarks of DC Comics. The stories, characters and incidents featured in this publication are entirely fictional. DC Comics does not read or accept unsolicited submissions of ideas, stories or artwork.
DC Comics, 1700 Broadway, New York, NY 10019. A Warner Bros. Entertainment Company. Printed in Canada. Second Printing.
ISBN: 1-4012-0250-0. ISBN 13: 978-1-4012-0250-7.
Cover art by Michael Turner with Peter Steigerwald.

ON THE ROLLER COASTER

OR, HOW SUPERGIRL RETURNED TO THE DCU
FOR THE FIRST TIME

It was on a roller coaster that it all happened. Dan Didio, the big Muckity-Muck at DC, and a Pal of all things Good, had been on the Superman roller coaster at one of the amusement parks that has such a thing.

When he got off, he looked up to see a spectacular billboard of SUPERMAN and a short bio. Superman was from the planet Krypton, he's disguised as Clark Kent, he loves Lois Lane — you know the drill.

Next to that was an equally spectacular billboard of SUPERGIRL and an equally short bio that went something like this: An ectoplasmic being from a parallel dimension, she came to this world and bonded with an Angel... and... At that point I think Dan had what we like to call "a moment where his cable went out." Static. Snow. When Dan sees static, he sees a problem.

I don't know if this story is true, but as a fan of "Liberty Valance," I do believe that when the legend becomes the truth, print the legend.

Some quick background for you non-regular comic-book readers. There has always been a Supergirl since about 1958. She was, yes, you remember correctly, Superman's cousin. Some people think of her as Superman's little sister and for me, that's close enough. Then came 1986 and something called CRISIS ON INFINITE EARTHS.

CRISIS rebooted the DCU (The DC Universe) and in order to do so, there was, well, a crisis. During that epic tale, Supergirl — the one you think you remember — died a heroic and truly emotional death. George Pérez's cover of Superman holding her lifeless body is one of the true milestones in Comic Book History.

After the reboot, there was no Supergirl. Superman was the last survivor of Krypton and that was the end of it.

But a good idea is a good idea, and Supergirl was a great idea and those simply can't and shouldn't stay dead. With the help of some very talented writers and artists, Supergirl was reintroduced as a... well, an ectoplasmic being who — you get the picture. There are fans of those incarnations (there were others too) and all of them were wonderfully inspired moments in comic-book lore.

However, Dan, like me, remembered Supergirl as Superman's cousin. It was clean, simple and easy to relate to. Now, all he had to do was make that happen. Not so clean, simple or easy to do. But, the roller coaster had left the station. The ride had begun.

Meanwhile, I was writing the monthly SUPERMAN. Eddie Berganza, the Muckity-Muck in the Superman office and Keeper of all things Good, and I had developed a working and personal friendship. One day we talked about this giant meteor that was a fragment of Krypton and somehow that got around to "what if there were something IN that meteor." Something... Good. SomeONE... Good.

We giggled like the two idiots we are and decided nobody would let us do it and put it back to bed.

When DC and I got together to give birth to a new title called SUPERMAN/BATMAN, the premise was to have Superman and Batman in stories that were huge in scope with rotating A-plus star artists. To our delight it worked. It really worked!

The first six-part tale dealt with Lex Luthor and is collected in SUPERMAN/BATMAN: PUBLIC ENEMIES — it was probably right next to this collection in your store. In that storyline, a giant meteor was coming toward Earth that had been part of the Planet Krypton. Yes, Eddie and I had decided to hatch our mad scheme. The roller coaster was going up that first big hill.

Intersecting that insidious plot was Dan D. out with his Supergirl quest. That's when peanut butter met jelly and this story was given the green light... with one big giant problem: I can't draw, and my Supergirl would look like Scribble Girl. Simply put, we had to have the right artist. The Perfect Artist.

Michael Turner and I have known each other for years. We were like two dogs on the street corner sniffing around, wondering when and if we could ever work together. Mike made his name on his creations *Witchblade* (which became a hit television series) and *Fathom* (which is being developed as a major motion picture). Two giant hits right out of the box. And he's the nicest guy to boot!

Mike had never done any super-hero work before. The characters he previously created existed in the "real" world. He didn't know from Capes and Kryptonite.

What Mike knew, however, was that working with the Icons would be a massive charge, and there are none bigger than Superman and Batman. He could really get into that!

In turn, what I knew was that Mike had not only made his name from clever, imaginative concepts that flew out his head as easy as Cheerios pour out of a box — he drew the darndest sexiest women in comics. What made them sexy wasn't the typical pinup shot of adolescent male fantasies. Mike imbues all his female characters with a strength, both externally and internally — and that, more than anything, made me certain he was our guy.

Once again, enter Dan D. While I was thinking what I was thinking, Dan was making it happen. In one of the most successful collaborations between an artist and a comic-book company, Dan brought Mike, along with Mike's production company Aspen, to the DCU.

Then, Dan brought us together and said, "What do you think of bringing back Supergirl?" The roller coaster was tearing down the first hill and folks were screaming!

What followed was startling. Mike immersed himself in the lore of the DCU. When we started, he didn't know Lex Luthor from Krypto, but by the time his studies were done, he was saying things like "Well, if we're going to use Harbinger, don't forget that she can..." and I was giggling with joy. I had found a real partner for this epic. The roller coaster was flying around hairpin turns!

Mike took my extremely detailed script and added his magic to it. Every corner, every page had some new spin on the DCU that nobody had ever seen before. The look of the artwork was simply astonishing.

His Kara Zor-El (Supergirl's Kryptonian name) was spot-on both in innocence and strength. His Wonder Woman — who plays an important role in what follows — was breathtaking and commanding. His Superman displayed the sheer awe of the character. But, his Batman... well, when you see him come out of the water in the opening of the first chapter, you'll see what cool is.

Mike's partner in crime throughout this adventure is something of a magician himself. Peter Steigerwald is the — well, there's no other word for it — *genius* behind the color and effects you see in this collection. Quite simply, Peter has an understanding of color and how to make it dazzling that those of us who are mere mortals can never touch. I suspect there's some Kryptonian blood in him, but we'll never know for sure. The roller coaster hit that second monster hill and shot around like a rocket!

Any project I take on, I cannot do without my good luck charm, Richard Starkings and his Comicraftsmen at Comicraft. Richard takes my words and puts them into the balloons and captions you read (as well as all the sound effects) in such a way that he actually makes the writing better! Richard is to lettering what Babe Ruth is to baseball. He makes what he does seem so effortless and yet — trust me on this — it's the hardest thing in the world to get right, and Richard does it right every time. The roller coaster went for that extra surprise turn that catches you every time and makes you scream!

None of this would have been possible without the fantastic imaginations of dozens of writers and artists who have worked with any incarnation of The Girl of Steel (she was once called The Maid of Might... but, I think we'll retire that!). I'm proud to be added to that list.

On the DC side of things, it's pretty obvious that without Dan D. and Eddie we never would have gotten off the ground, and for them I am so truly grateful. Thanks to everyone who supported this project from Paul Levitz to Terri, Jack, Bob W., Patti J., Matt K. and Tom Palmer Jr. and Jeanine and everybody in production (Thanks, Alison!) and in the entire building because this was such a labor of love.

Behind the scenes, everybody at Michael Turner's company, Aspen (Hey, Frank!) made the production seamless. Thanks, gang!

Two special acknowledgments have to be made just because it's what Superman and Batman would want me to do. Geoff Johns and I share a studio together. He is the brightest new star on the writing scene in comics, and he guided me through this story with an infectious enthusiasm that I tried my best to capture on the page. Walter Simonson, friend and gentleman, became my midnight Obi Wan Kenobi — who took every phone call, and as a Maker of all things Good, was my professor in the world of Apokolips and Darkseid (who you will meet inside). It is said that your hero is only as good as your villain, and Jack Kirby's creation, Darkseid, is one of the best. Geoff and Walter, I owe you guys, big time!

So, here is Supergirl, together again for the first time (I've always wanted to say that!) with Superman, Batman and Wonder Woman! The roller coaster has just pulled into the station. You've bought your ticket and hold on tight. And don't be surprised if you want to go on it again and again.

JEPH LOEB
LOS ANGELES 2004

P.S. During this experience, I fell in love with Kara Zor-El. From her first moment of terrified innocence to her surprising turn in — ulp, you'll see — she has been a delight. In so many ways, Kara reminded me of my daughter, Audrey, who has shown me in some of the darkest times there can be joy and to never forget that there is hope. I'm in awe of her strength and helpless before her laughter. *This one's for you, Boo.*

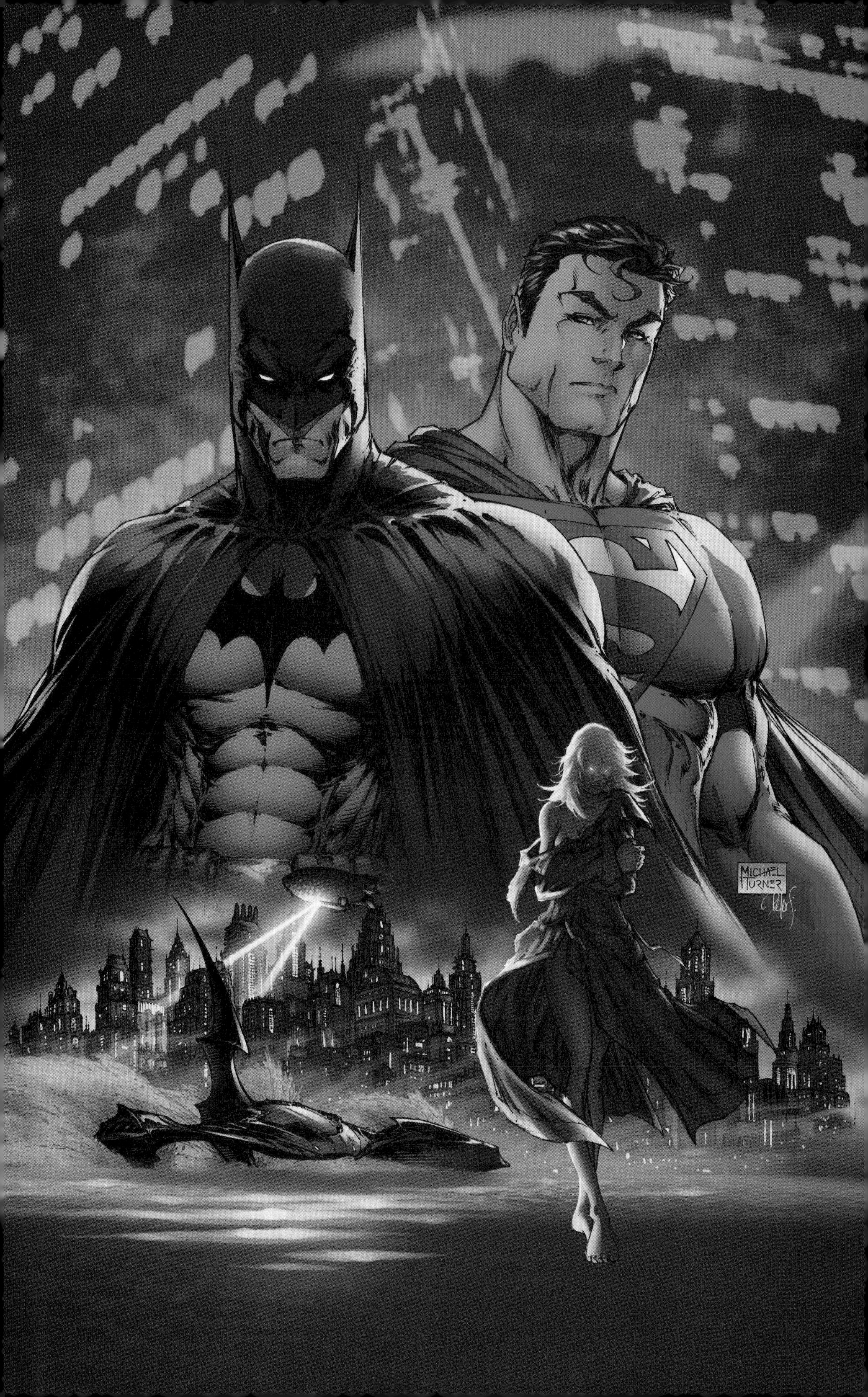
MICHAEL TURNER

ALONE

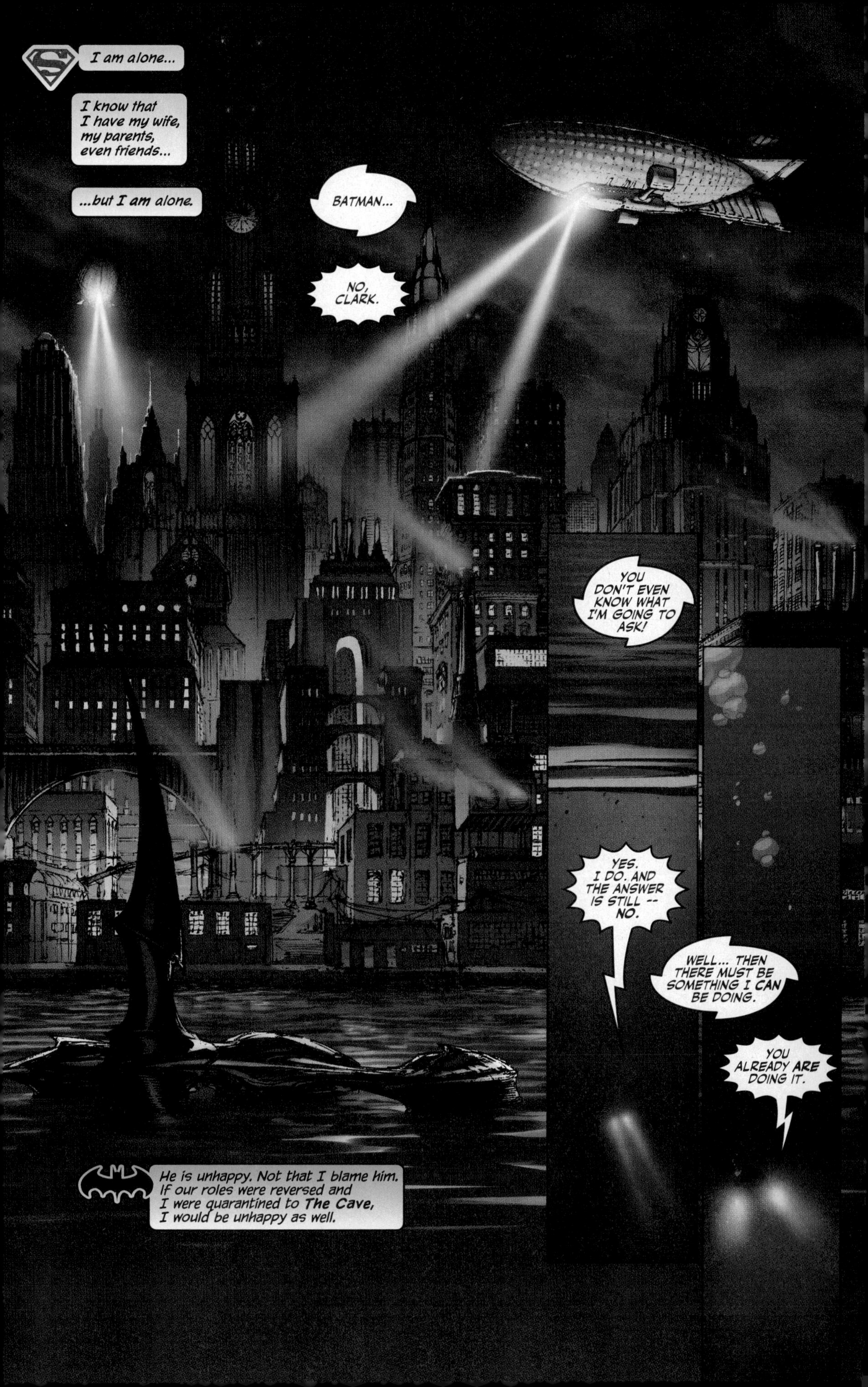
I am alone...
I know that I have my wife, my parents, even friends...
...but I am alone.
BATMAN...
NO, CLARK.
YOU DON'T EVEN KNOW WHAT I'M GOING TO ASK!
YES. I DO. AND THE ANSWER IS STILL -- NO.
WELL... THEN THERE MUST BE SOMETHING I CAN BE DOING.
YOU ALREADY ARE DOING IT.
He is unhappy. Not that I blame him. If our roles were reversed and I were quarantined to The Cave, I would be unhappy as well.

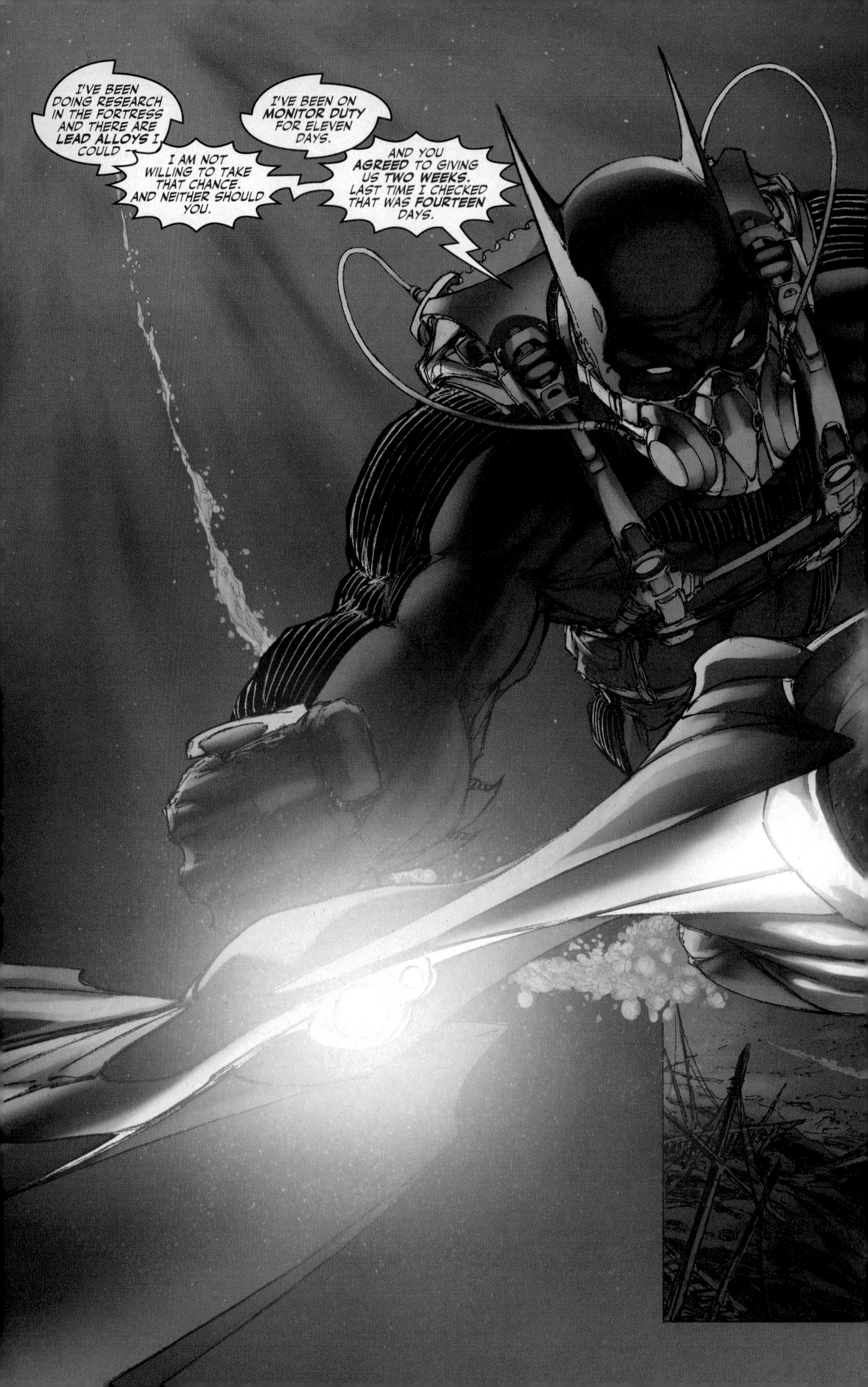
I'VE BEEN DOING RESEARCH IN THE FORTRESS AND THERE ARE LEAD ALLOYS I COULD --
I AM NOT WILLING TO TAKE THAT CHANCE. AND NEITHER SHOULD YOU.
I'VE BEEN ON MONITOR DUTY FOR ELEVEN DAYS.
AND YOU AGREED TO GIVING US TWO WEEKS. LAST TIME I CHECKED THAT WAS FOURTEEN DAYS.

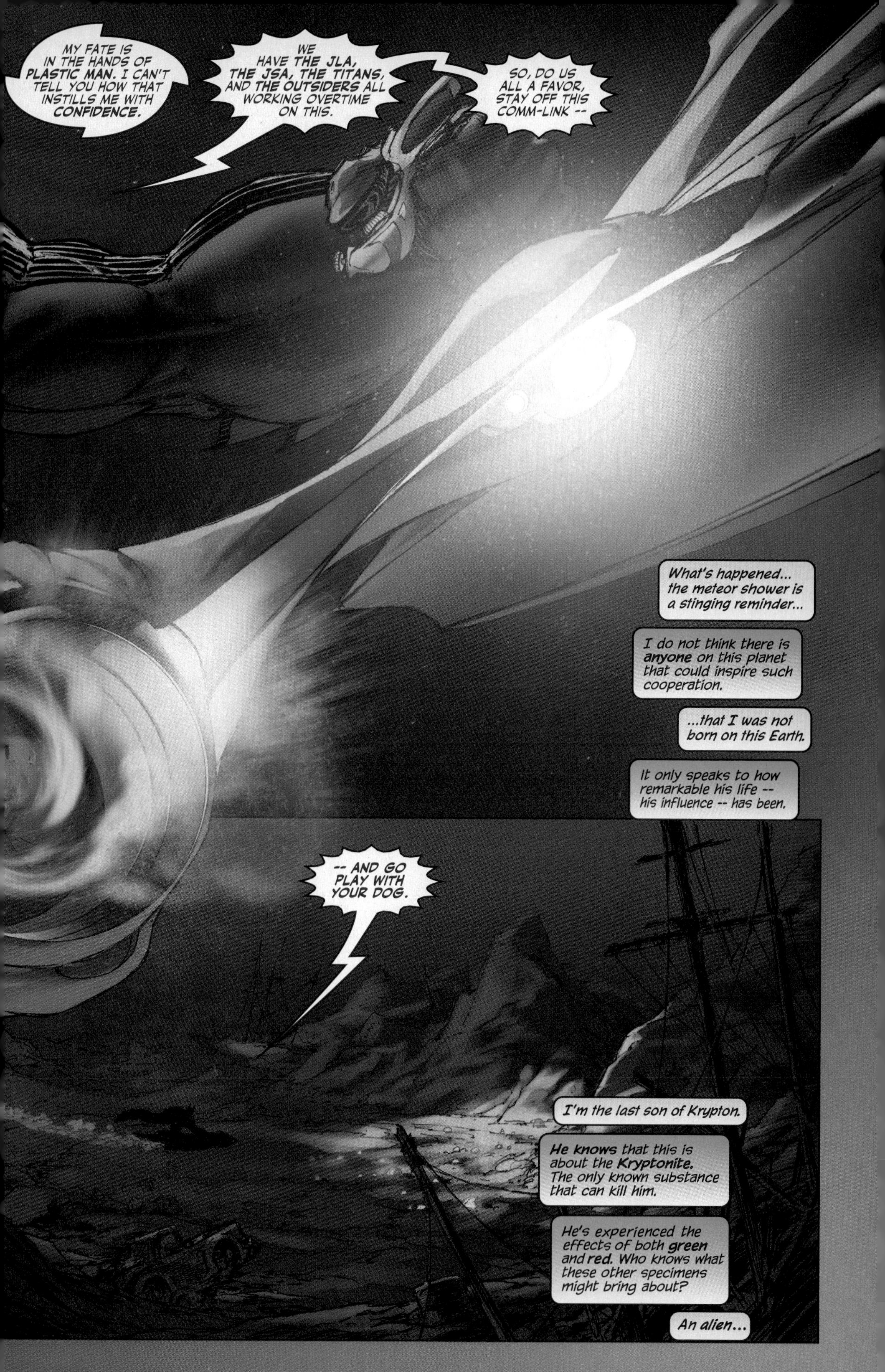
MY FATE IS IN THE HANDS OF PLASTIC MAN. I CAN'T TELL YOU HOW THAT INSTILLS ME WITH CONFIDENCE.
WE HAVE THE JLA, THE JSA, THE TITANS, AND THE OUTSIDERS ALL WORKING OVERTIME ON THIS.
SO, DO US ALL A FAVOR, STAY OFF THIS COMM-LINK --
What's happened... the meteor shower is a stinging reminder...
I do not think there is anyone on this planet that could inspire such cooperation.
...that I was not born on this Earth.
It only speaks to how remarkable his life -- his influence -- has been.
-- AND GO PLAY WITH YOUR DOG.
I'm the last son of Krypton.
He knows that this is about the Kryptonite. The only known substance that can kill him.
He's experienced the effects of both green and red. Who knows what these other specimens might bring about?
An alien...

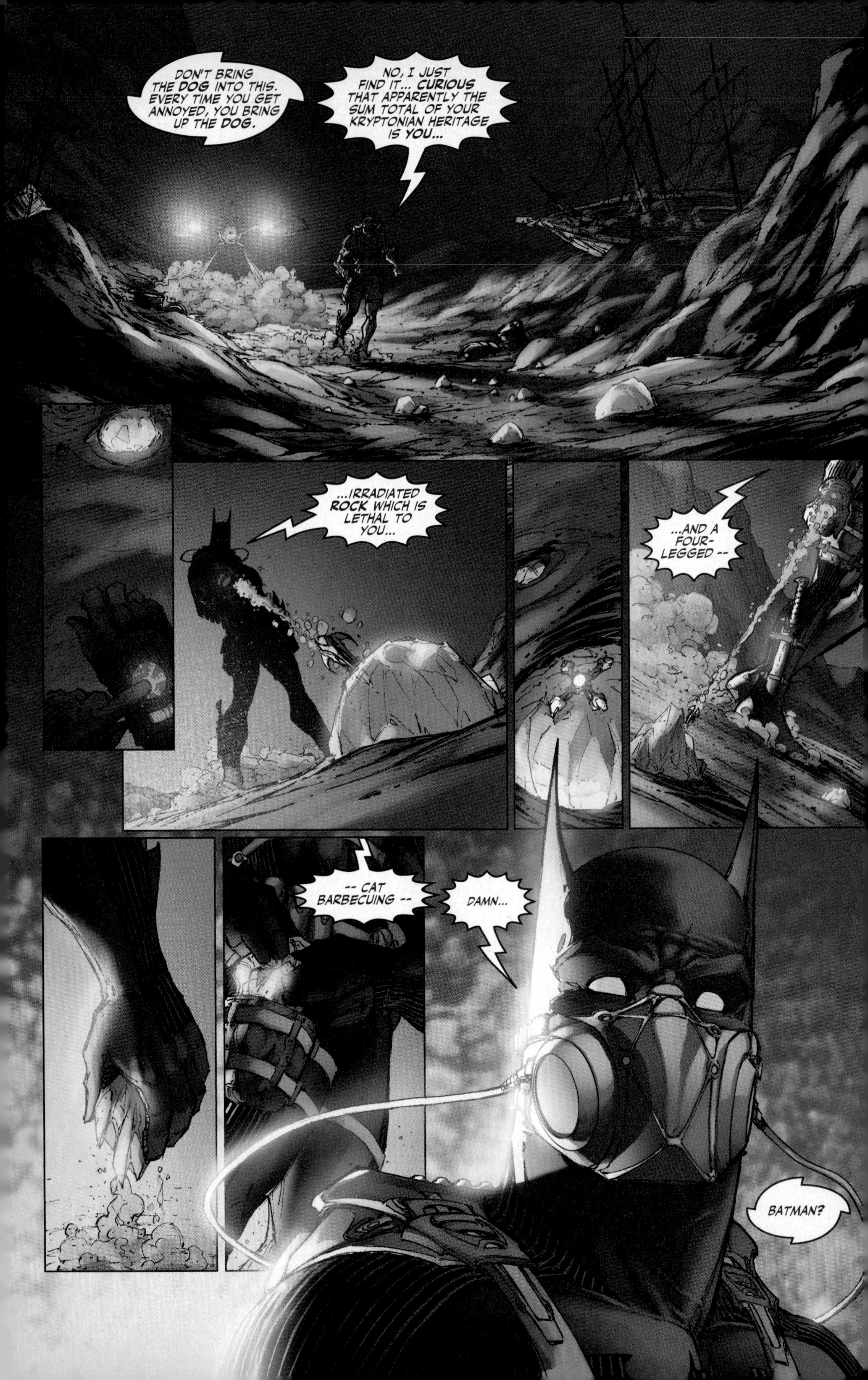
DON'T BRING THE DOG INTO THIS. EVERY TIME YOU GET ANNOYED, YOU BRING UP THE DOG.
NO, I JUST FIND IT... CURIOUS THAT APPARENTLY THE SUM TOTAL OF YOUR KRYPTONIAN HERITAGE IS YOU...
...IRRADIATED ROCK WHICH IS LETHAL TO YOU...
...AND A FOUR-LEGGED --
-- CAT BARBECUING --
DAMN...
BATMAN?

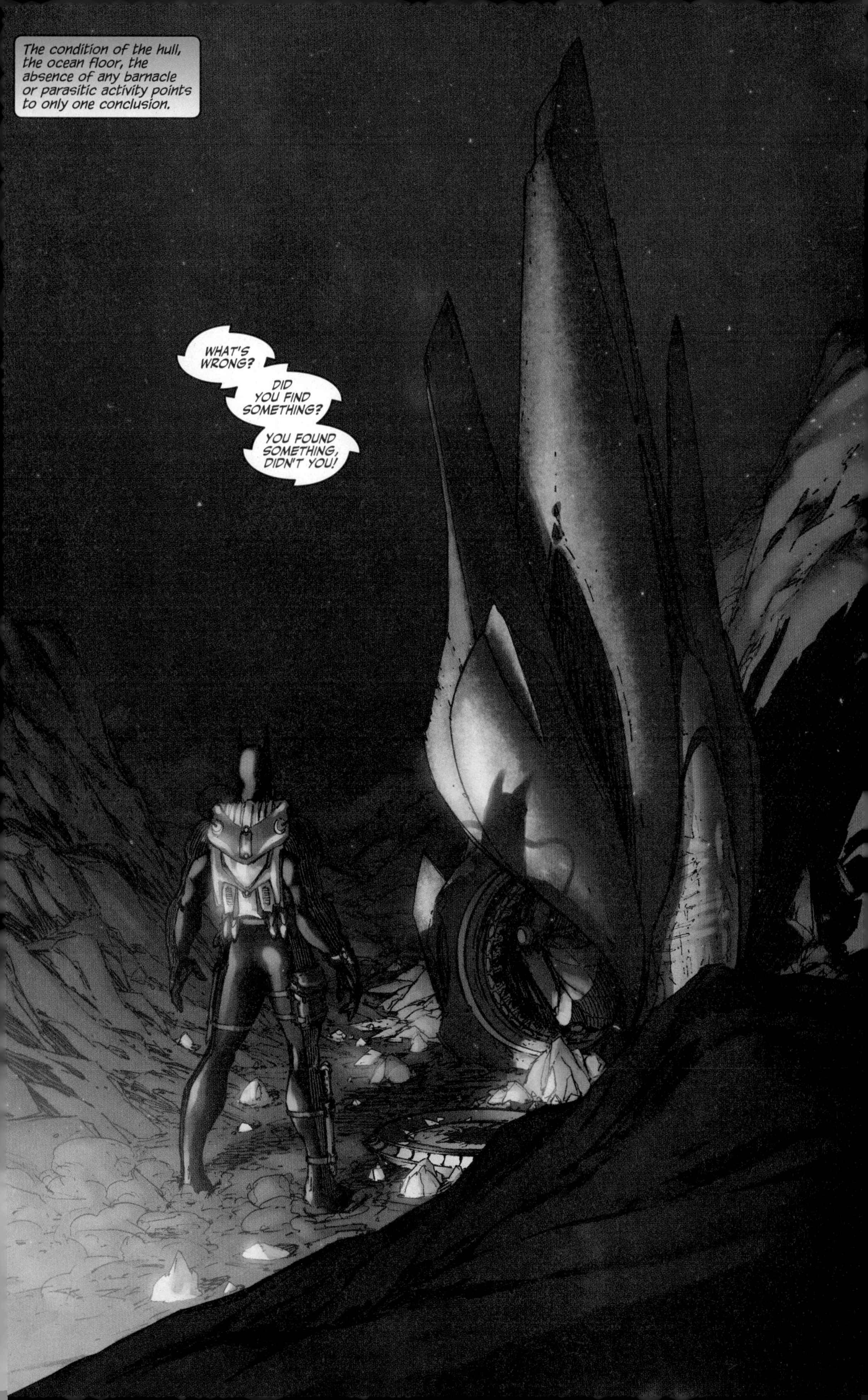
The condition of the hull, the ocean floor, the absence of any barnacle or parasitic activity points to only one conclusion.
WHAT'S WRONG?
DID YOU FIND SOMETHING?
YOU FOUND SOMETHING, DIDN'T YOU!

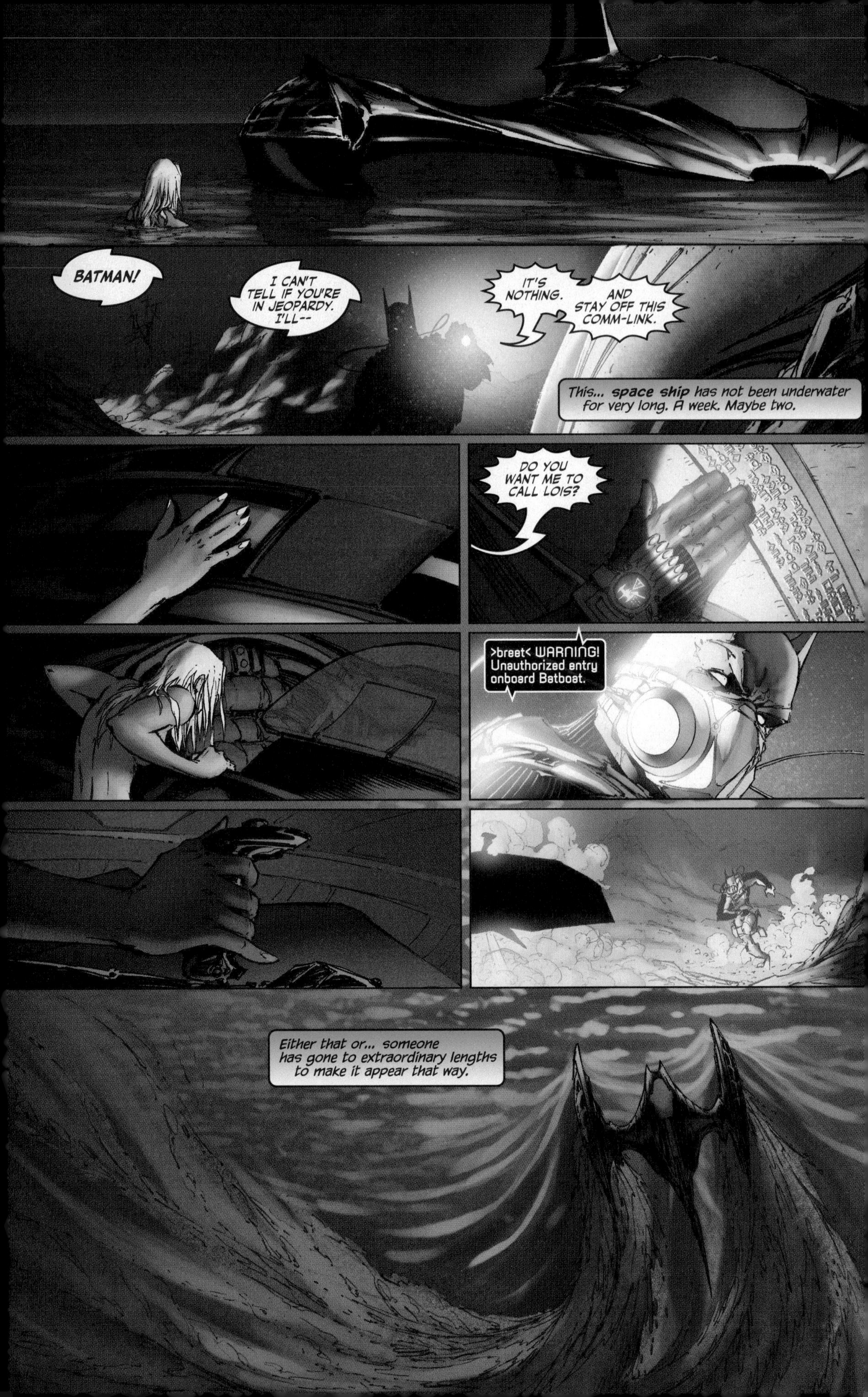
BATMAN!
I CAN'T TELL IF YOU'RE IN JEOPARDY. I'LL--
IT'S NOTHING.
AND STAY OFF THIS COMM-LINK.
This... space ship has not been underwater for very long. A week. Maybe two.
DO YOU WANT ME TO CALL LOIS?
>breet< WARNING! Unauthorized entry onboard Batboat.
Either that or... someone has gone to extraordinary lengths to make it appear that way.

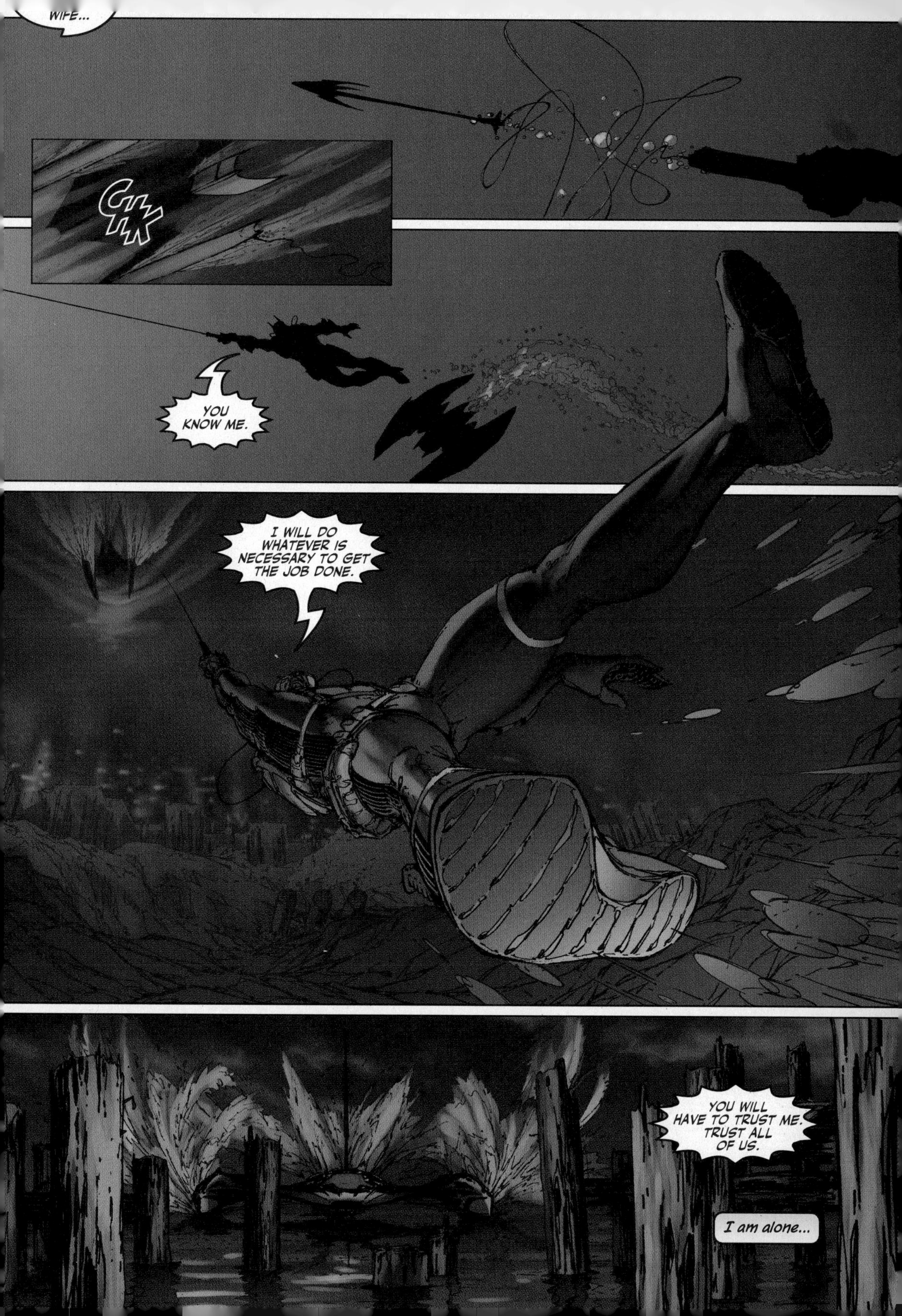
WIFE...
GAK
YOU KNOW ME.
I WILL DO WHATEVER IS NECESSARY TO GET THE JOB DONE.
YOU WILL HAVE TO TRUST ME. TRUST ALL OF US.
I am alone...

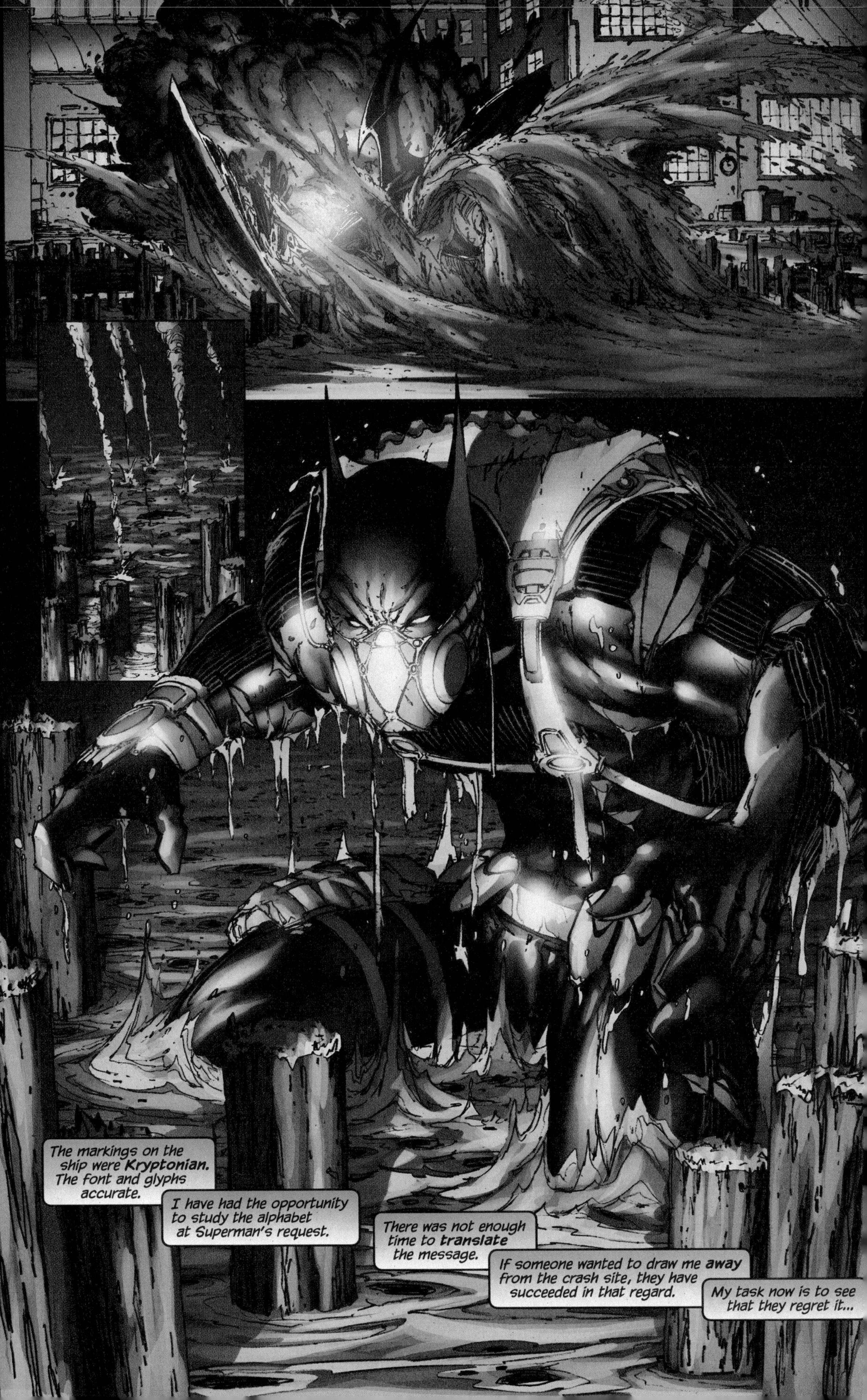
The markings on the ship were **Kryptonian.** The font and glyphs accurate.
I have had the opportunity to study the alphabet at Superman's request.
There was not enough time to **translate** the message.
If someone wanted to draw me **away** from the crash site, they have succeeded in that regard.
My task now is to see that they regret it...

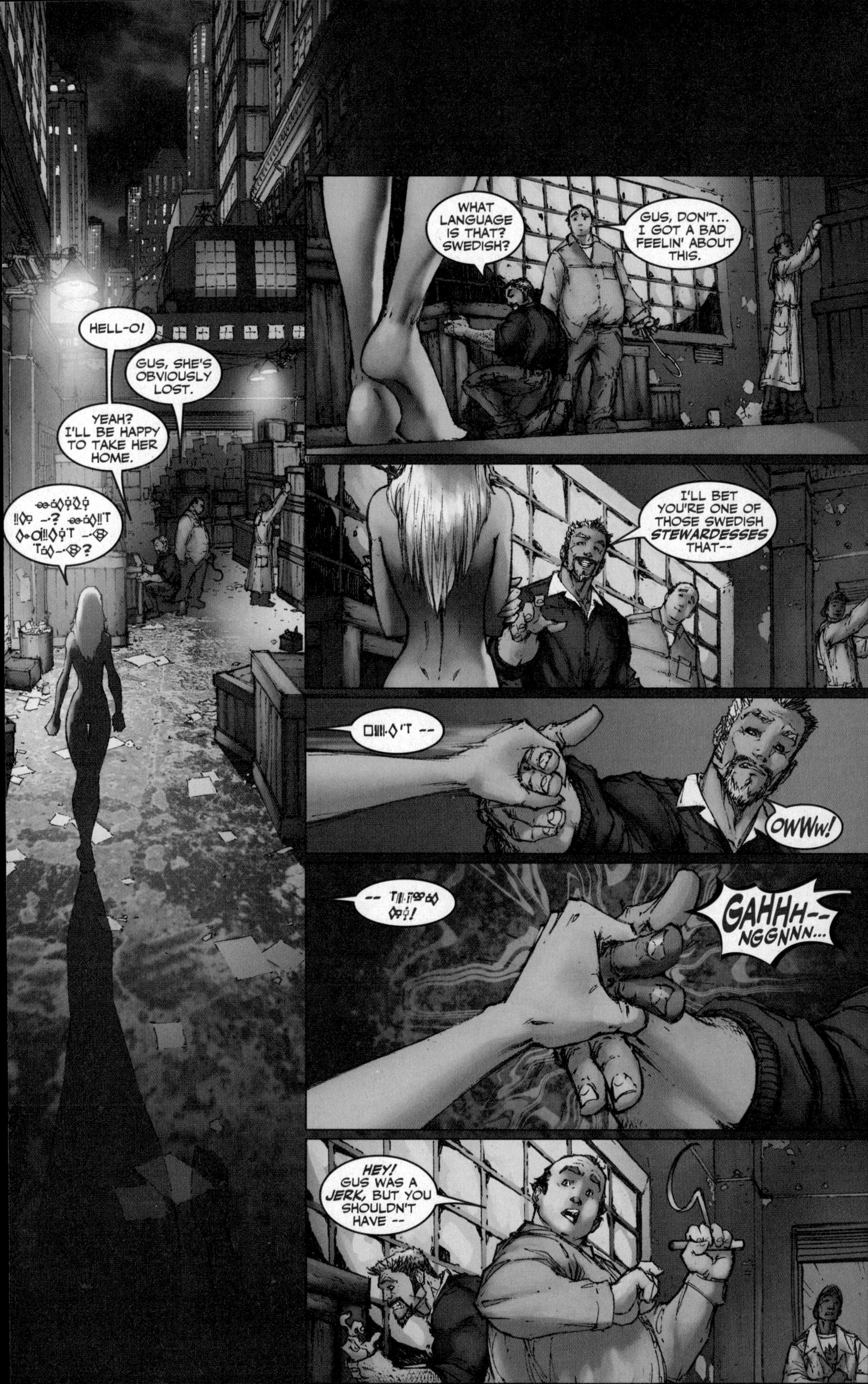
HELL-O!
GUS, SHE'S OBVIOUSLY LOST.
YEAH? I'LL BE HAPPY TO TAKE HER HOME.
WHAT LANGUAGE IS THAT? SWEDISH?
GUS, DON'T... I GOT A BAD FEELIN' ABOUT THIS.
I'LL BET YOU'RE ONE OF THOSE SWEDISH STEWARDESSES THAT--
OWWw!
GAHHH--NGGNNN...
HEY! GUS WAS A JERK, BUT YOU SHOULDN'T HAVE --

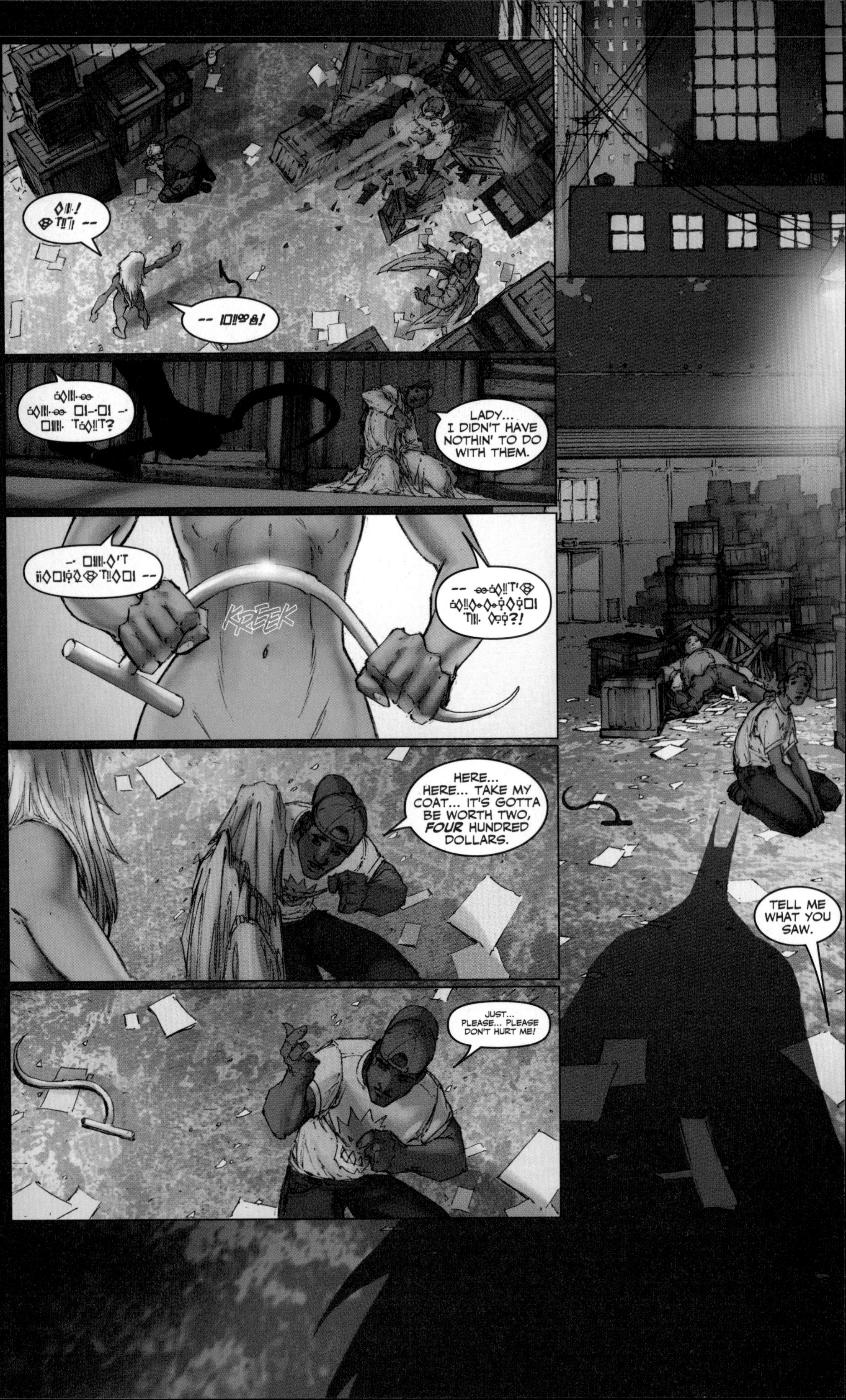
LADY... I DIDN'T HAVE NOTHIN' TO DO WITH THEM.
KREEK
HERE... HERE... TAKE MY COAT... IT'S GOTTA BE WORTH TWO, FOUR HUNDRED DOLLARS.
JUST... PLEASE... PLEASE DON'T HURT ME!
TELL ME WHAT YOU SAW.

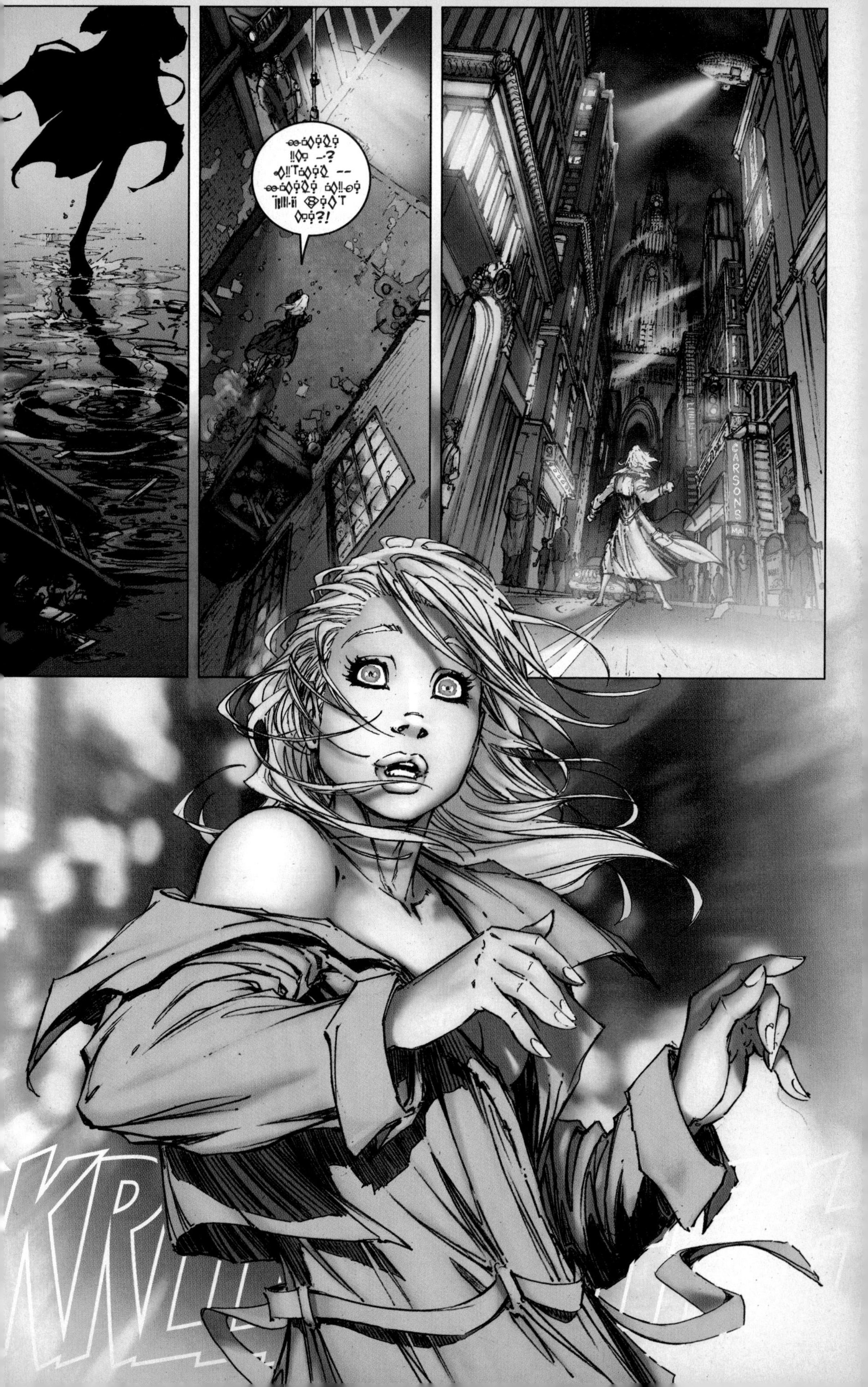
GARSONS

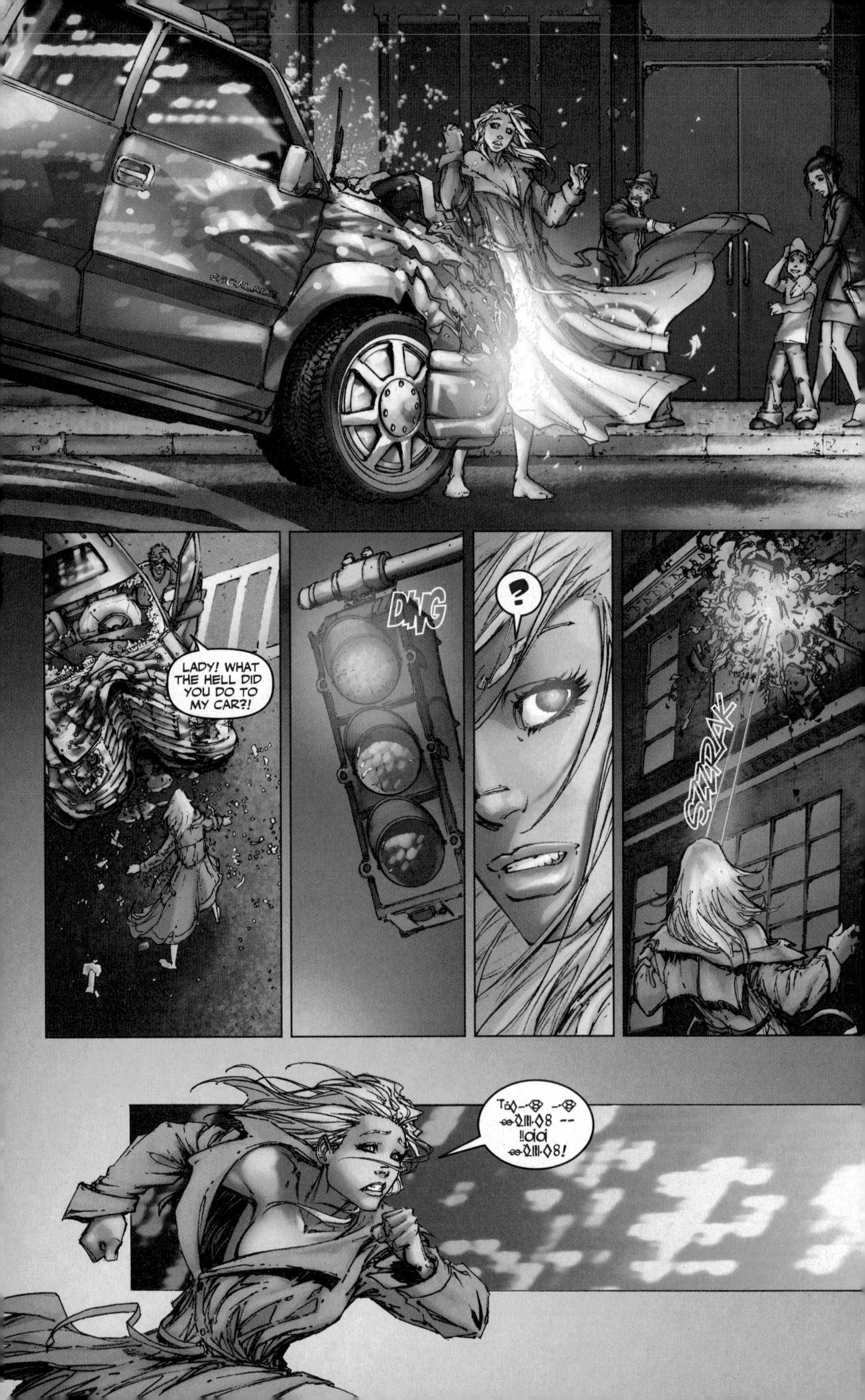
ESCALADE
LADY! WHAT THE HELL DID YOU DO TO MY CAR?!
DING
?
SZZRAK

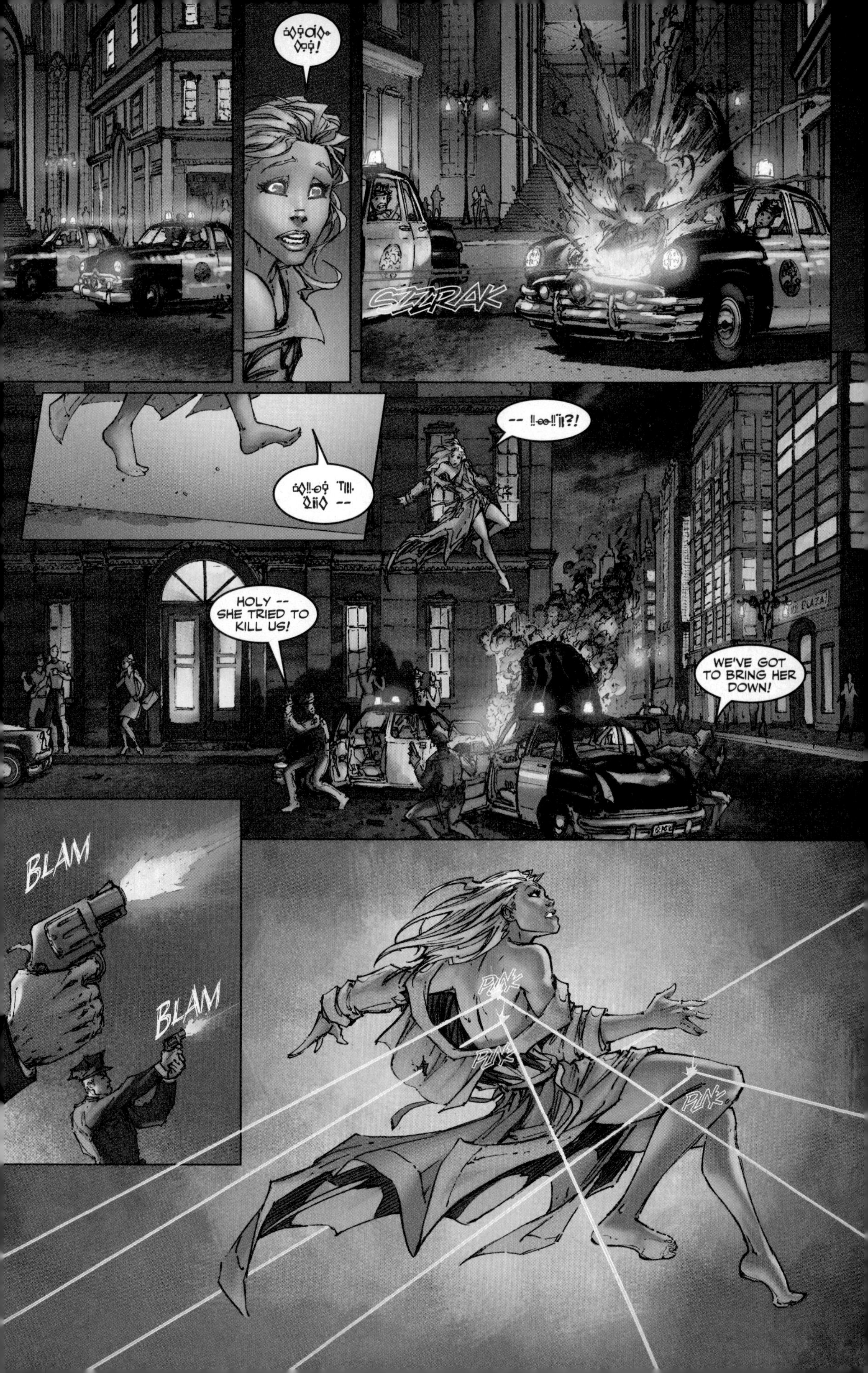

SZZRAK
-- !!?!
HOLY -- SHE TRIED TO KILL US!
WE'VE GOT TO BRING HER DOWN!
PLAZA!
BLAM
BLAM
PLINK
PLINK
PLINK

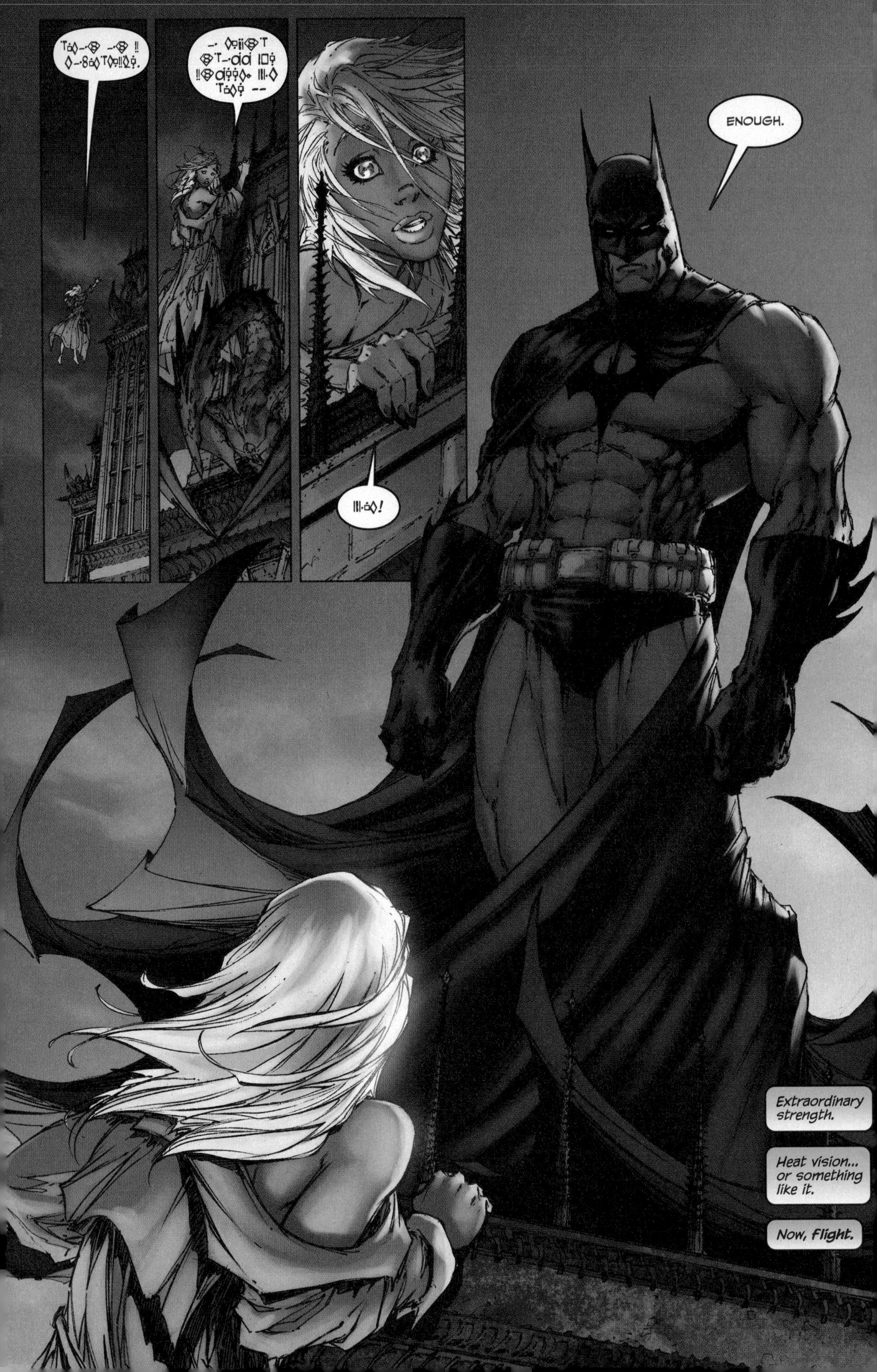
ENOUGH.
Extraordinary strength.
Heat vision... or something like it.
Now, Flight.

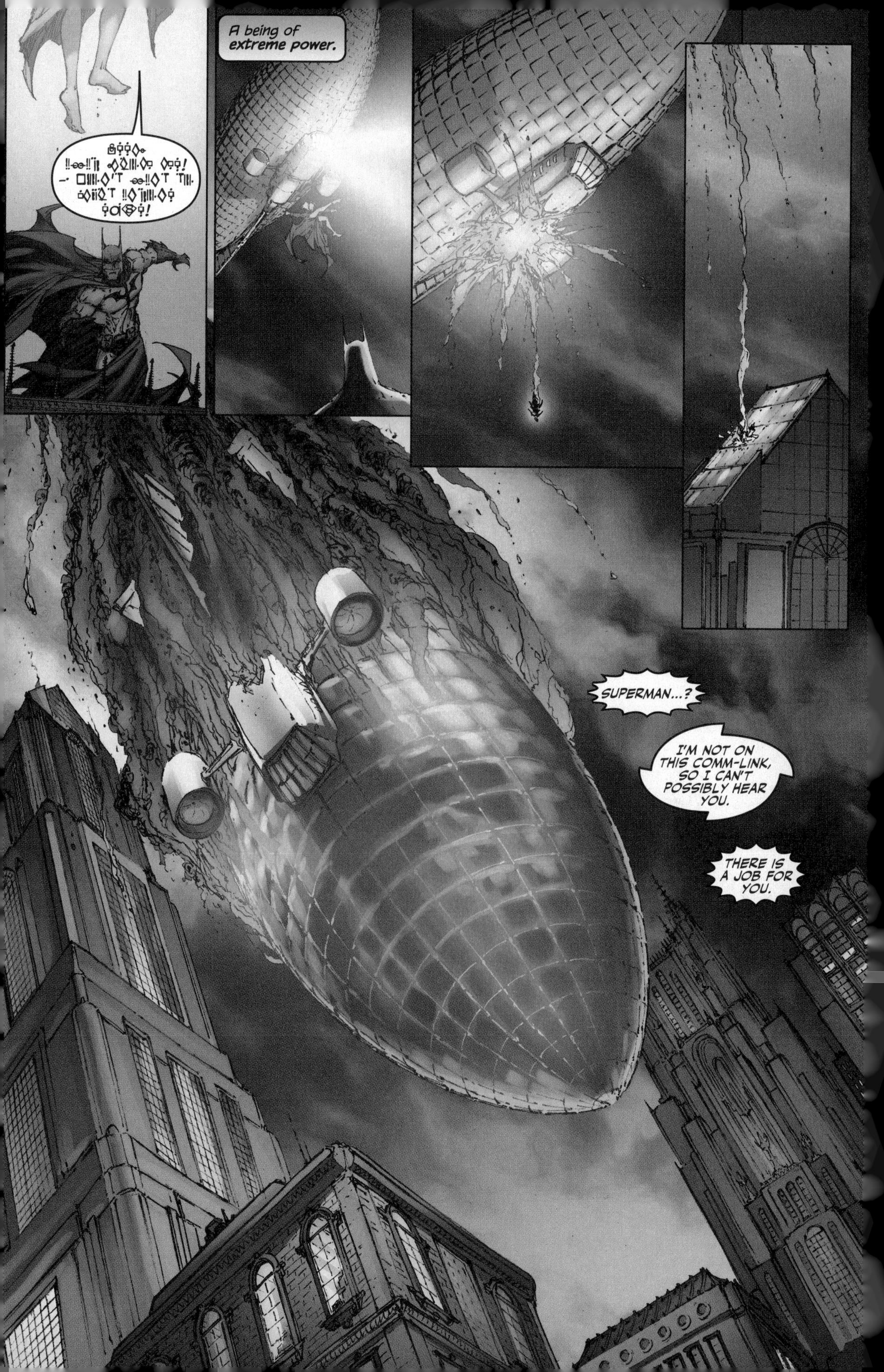
A being of extreme power.
SUPERMAN...?
I'M NOT ON THIS COMM-LINK, SO I CAN'T POSSIBLY HEAR YOU.
THERE IS A JOB FOR YOU.

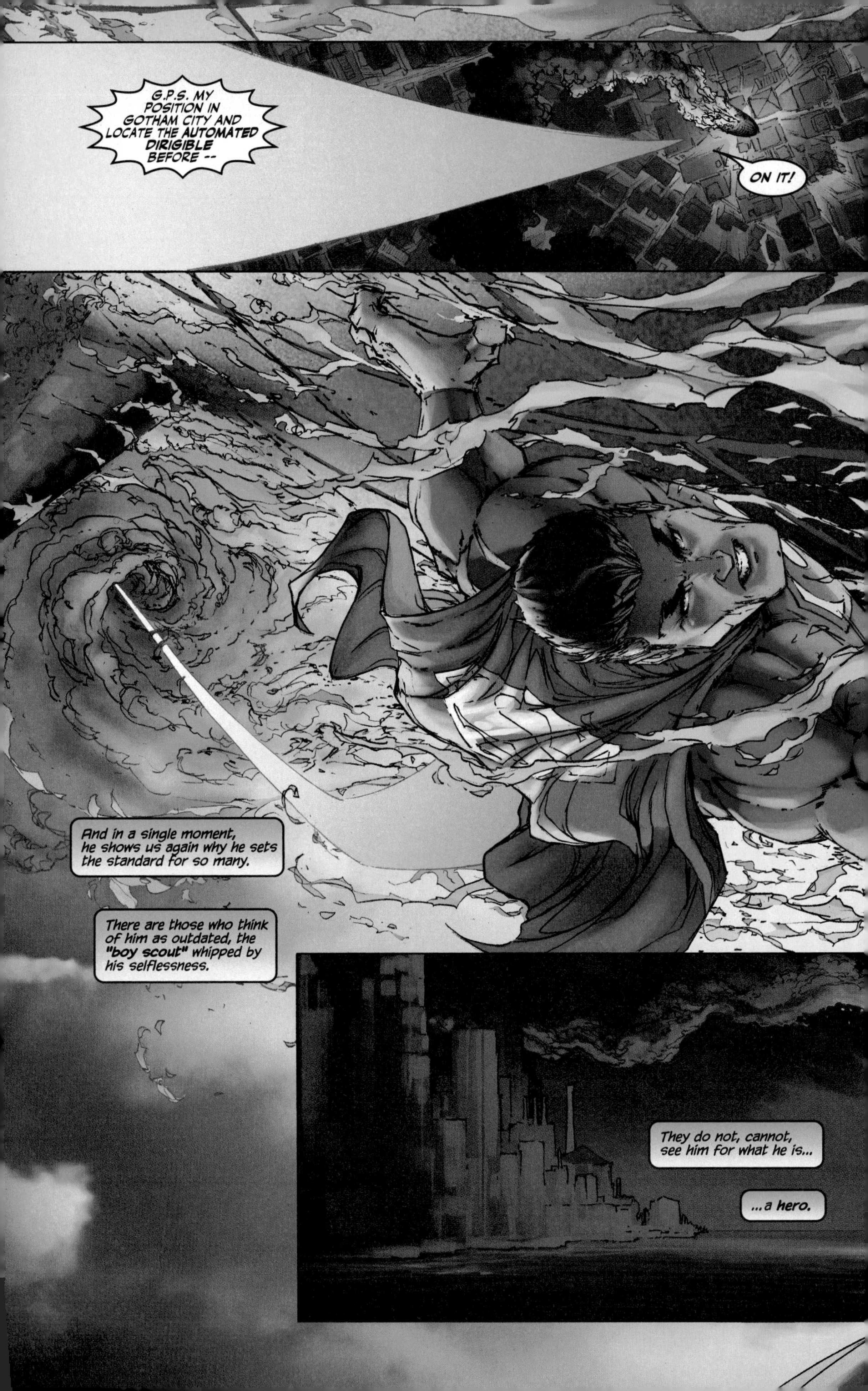
G.P.S. MY POSITION IN GOTHAM CITY AND LOCATE THE AUTOMATED DIRIGIBLE BEFORE --
ON IT!
And in a single moment, he shows us again why he sets the standard for so many.
There are those who think of him as outdated, the "boy scout" whipped by his selflessness.
They do not, cannot, see him for what he is...
...a hero.

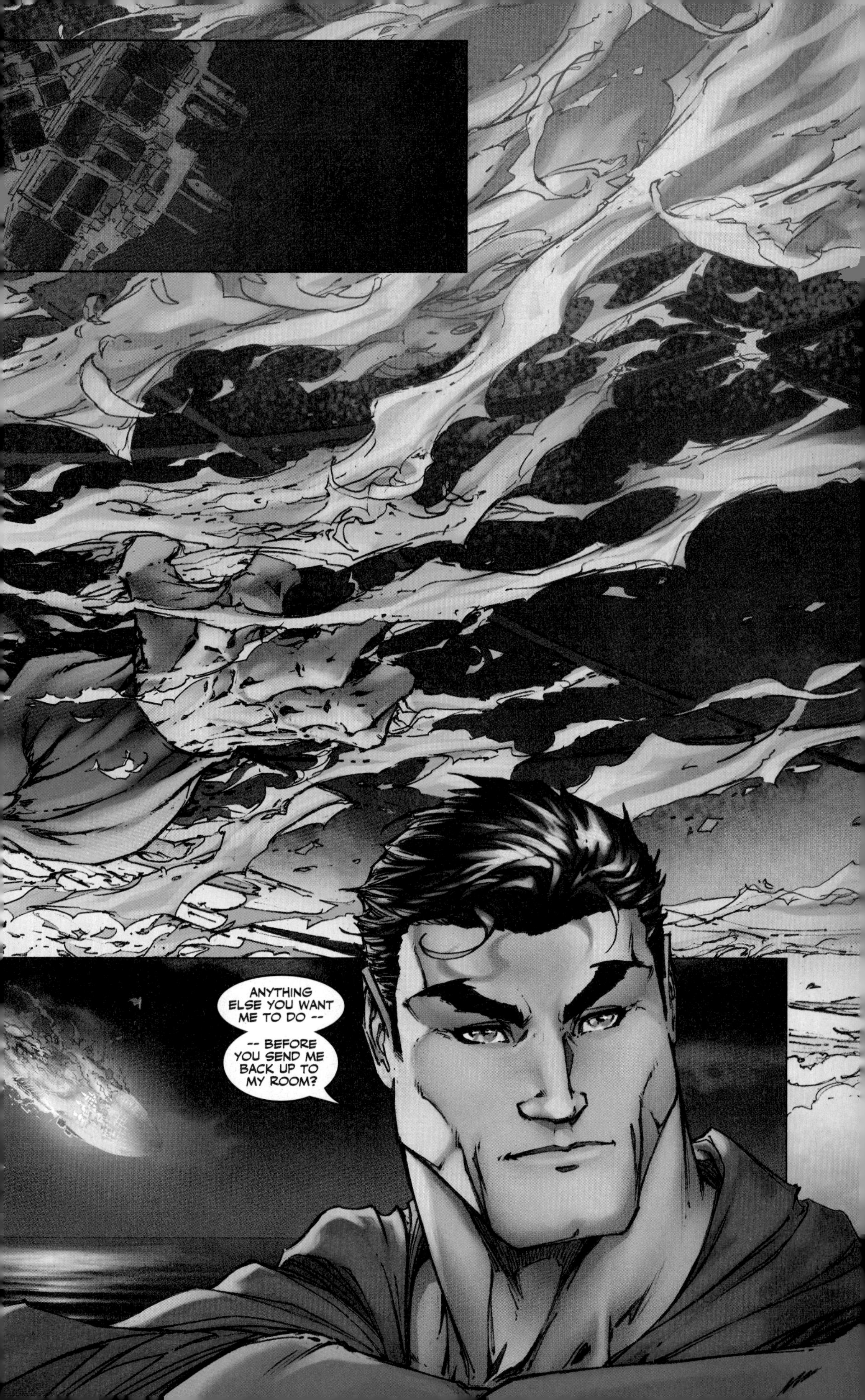
ANYTHING ELSE YOU WANT ME TO DO --
-- BEFORE YOU SEND ME BACK UP TO MY ROOM?

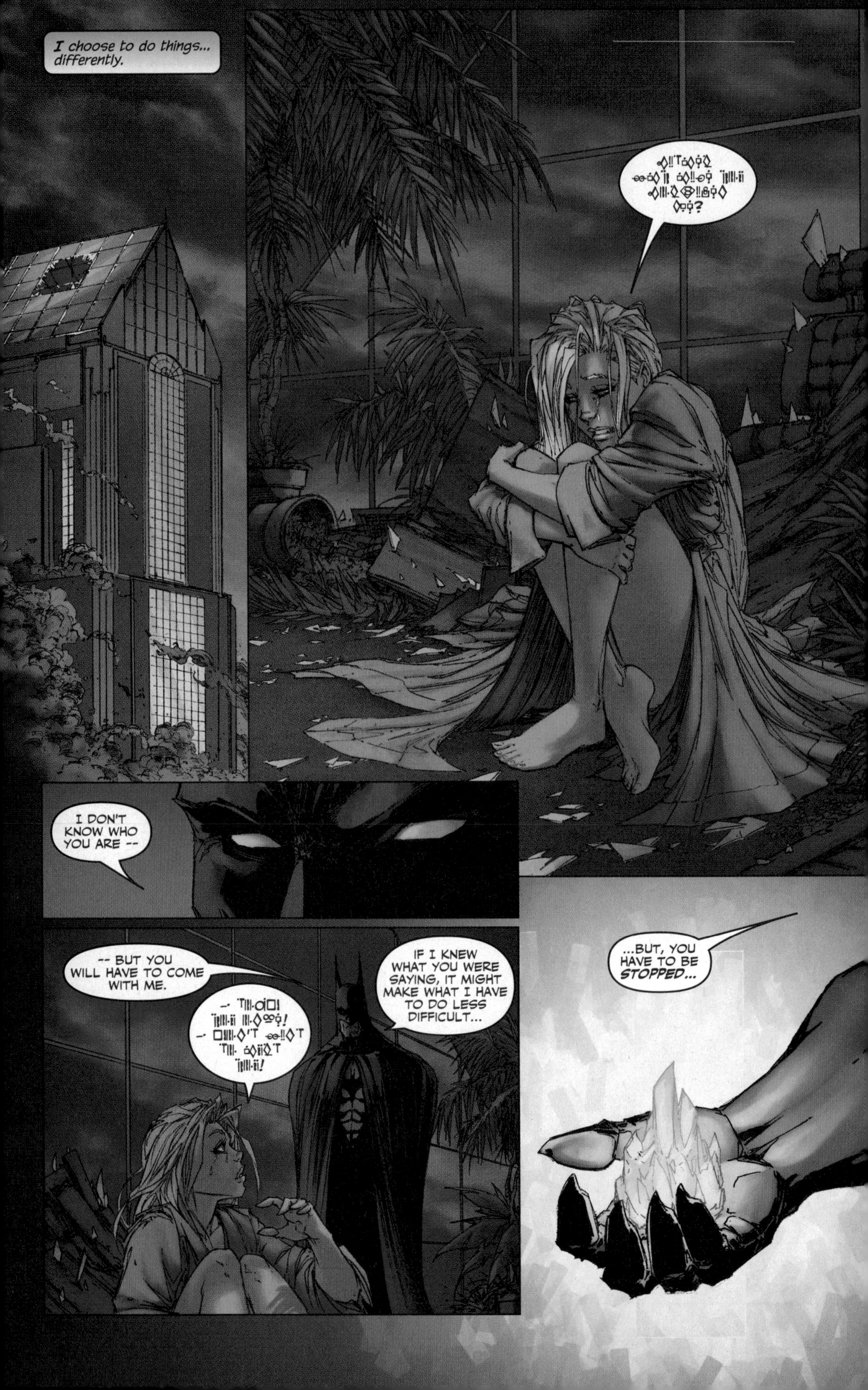
I choose to do things... differently.
I DON'T KNOW WHO YOU ARE --
-- BUT YOU WILL HAVE TO COME WITH ME.
IF I KNEW WHAT YOU WERE SAYING, IT MIGHT MAKE WHAT I HAVE TO DO LESS DIFFICULT...
...BUT, YOU HAVE TO BE *STOPPED*...

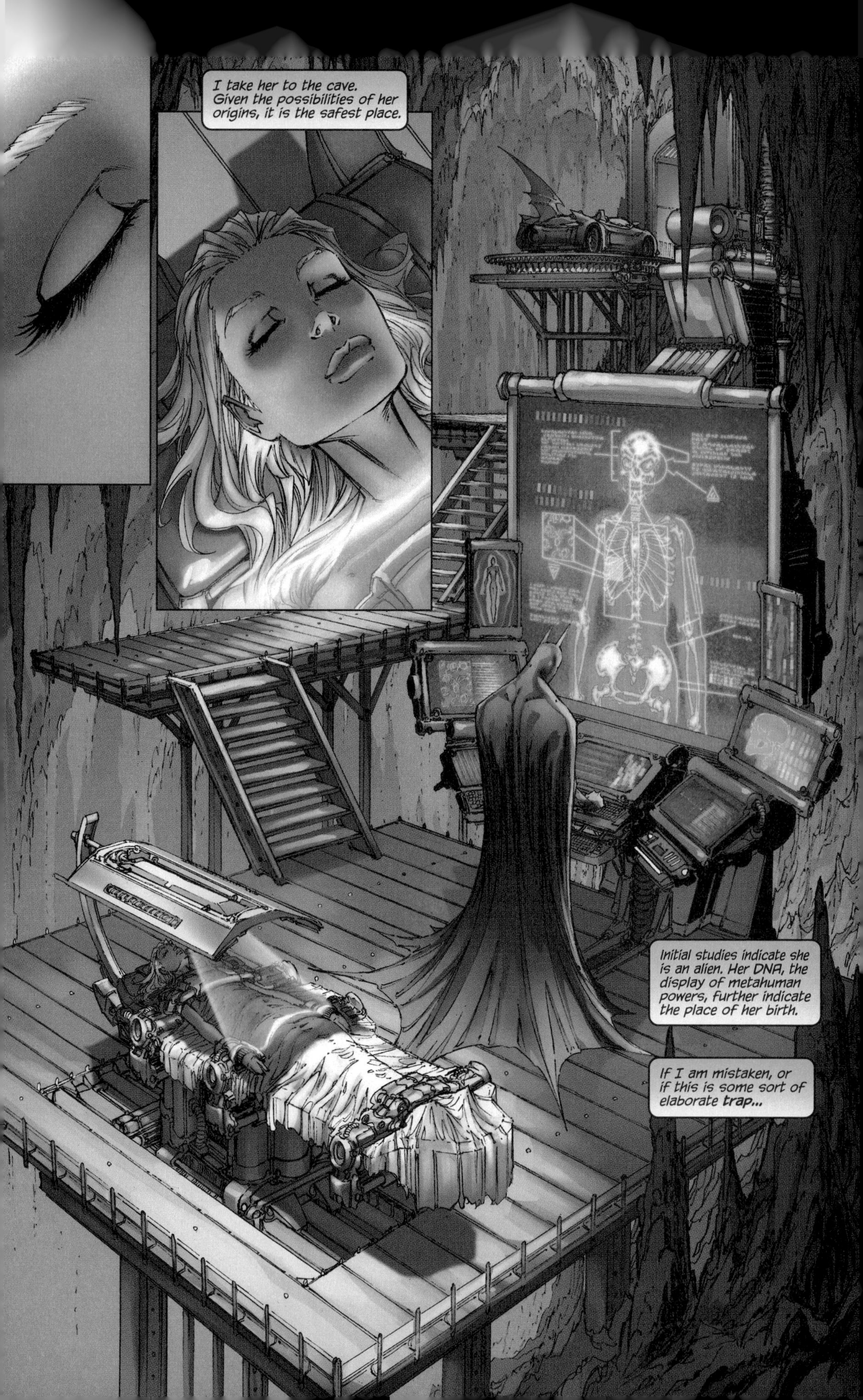
I take her to the cave. Given the possibilities of her origins, it is the safest place.
Initial studies indicate she is an alien. Her DNA, the display of metahuman powers, further indicate the place of her birth.
If I am mistaken, or if this is some sort of elaborate **trap...**

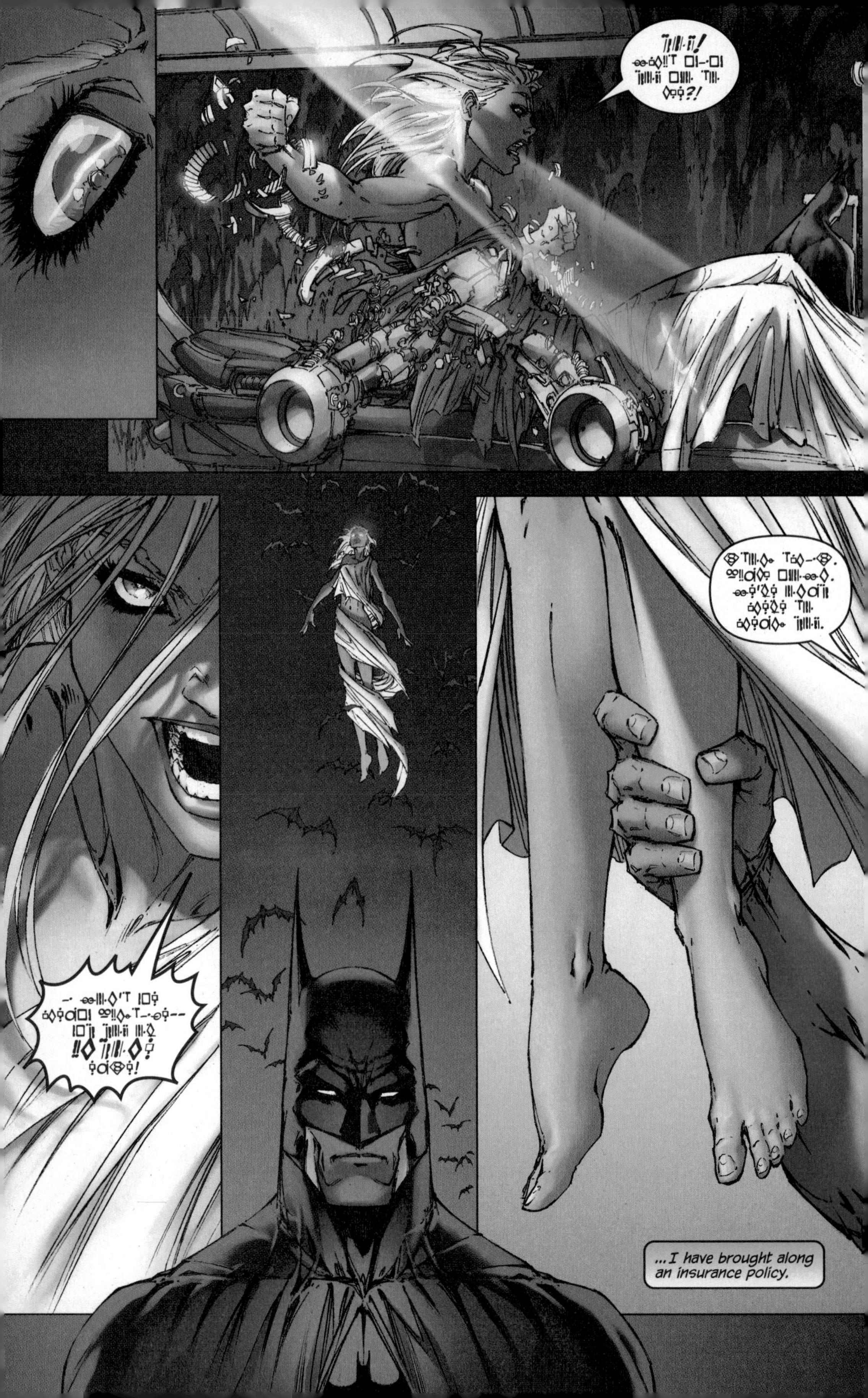
...I have brought along an insurance policy.

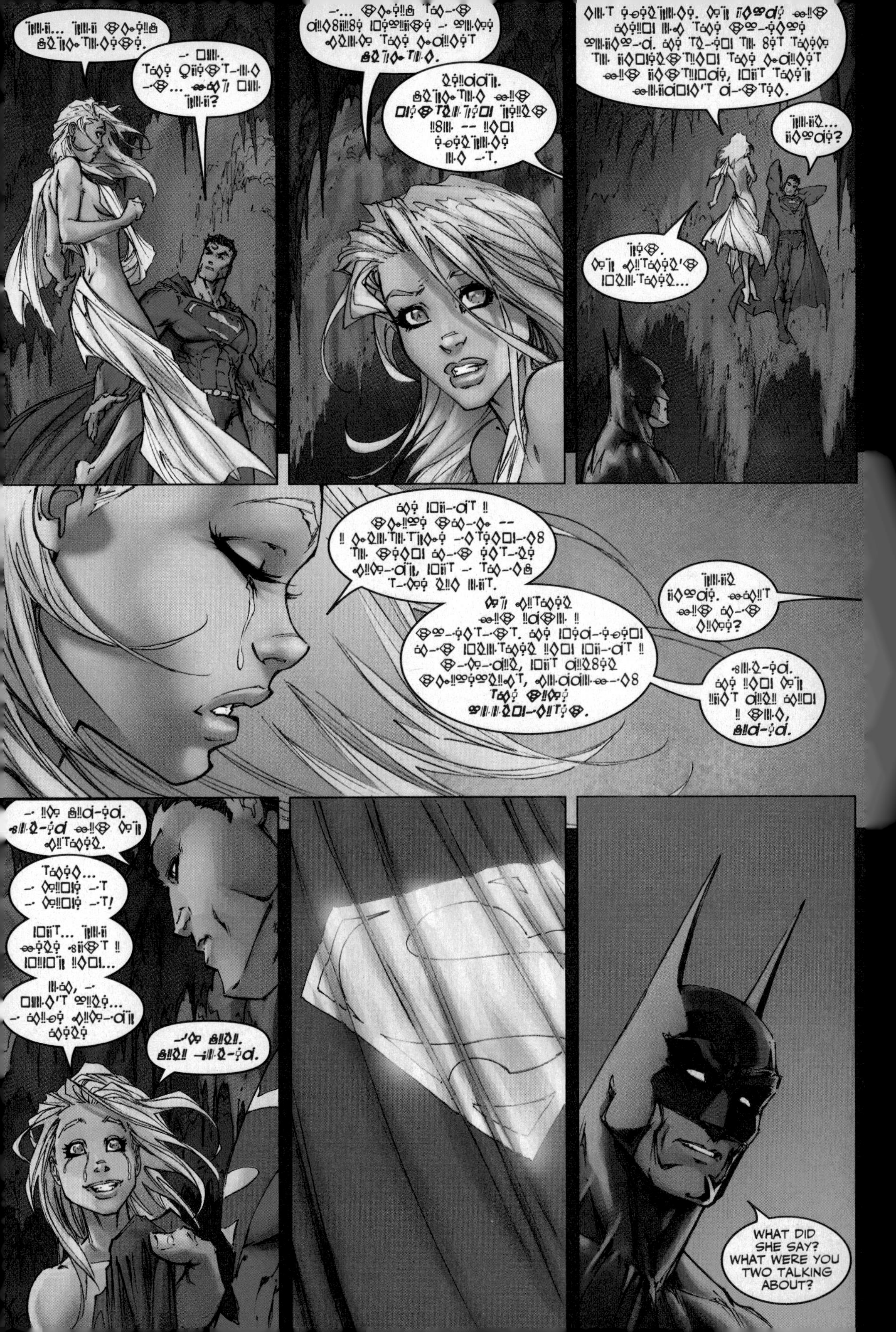
WHAT DID SHE SAY? WHAT WERE YOU TWO TALKING ABOUT?

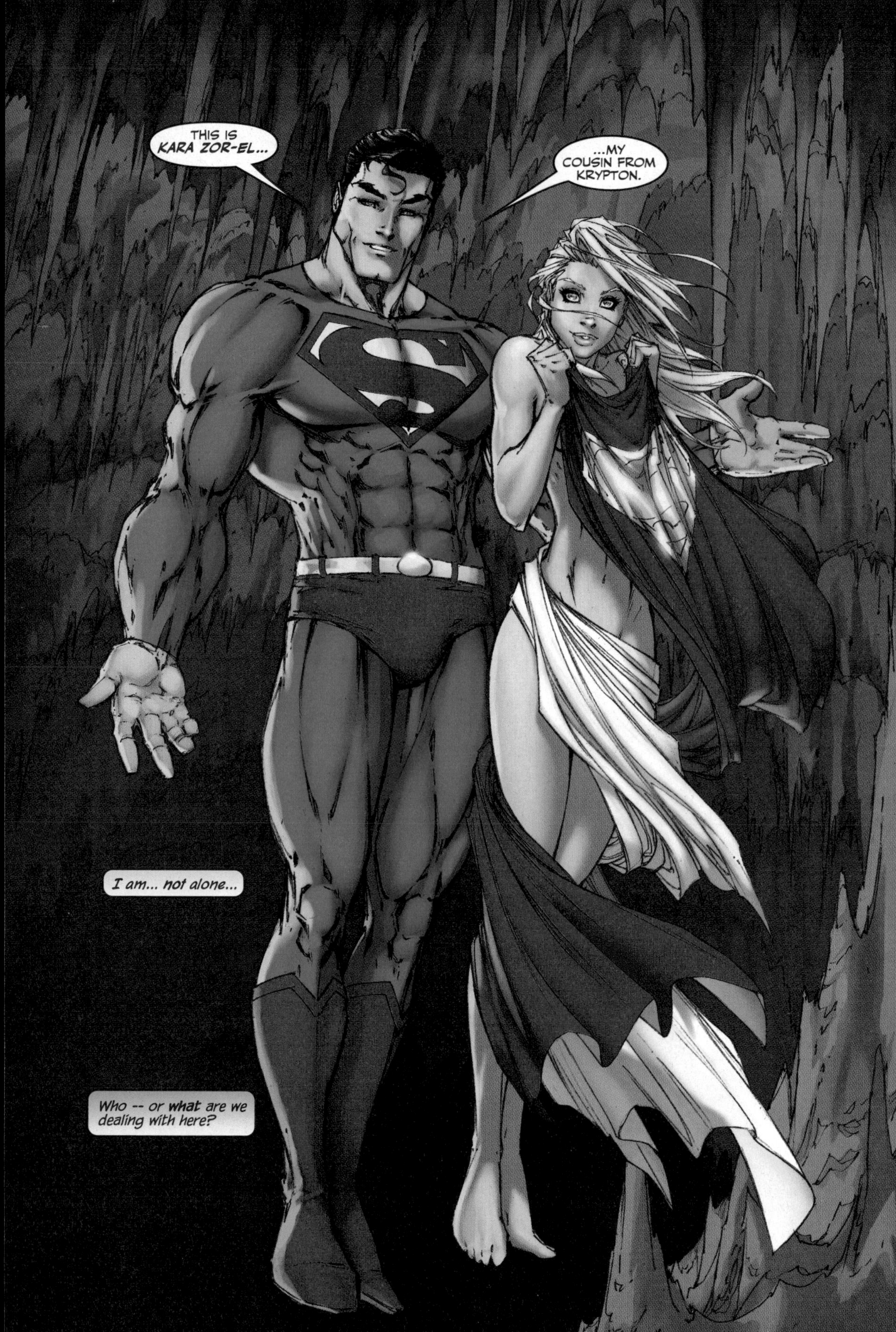
THIS IS KARA ZOR-EL...
...MY COUSIN FROM KRYPTON.
I am... not alone...
Who -- or what are we dealing with here?

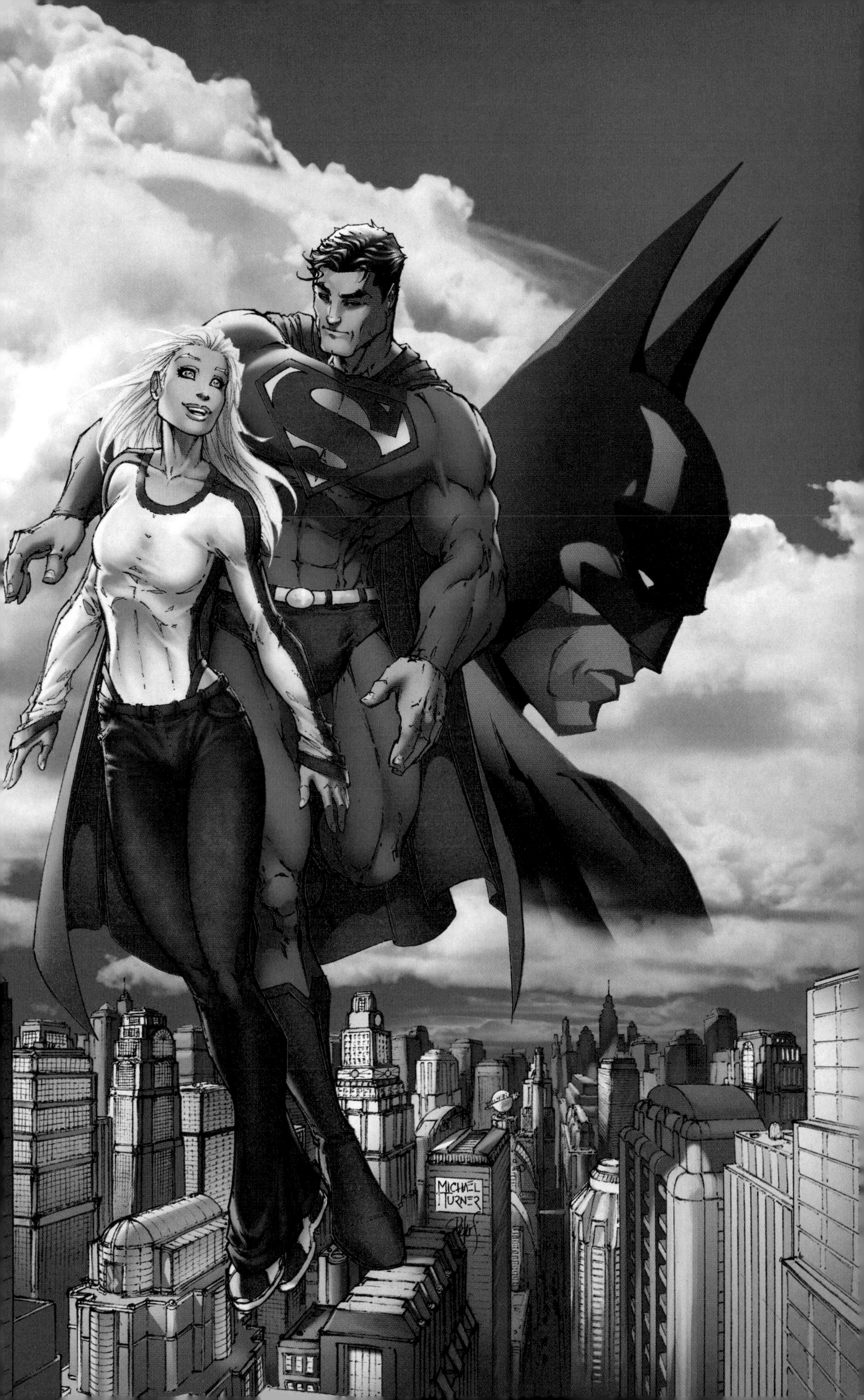
MICHAEL TURNER

VISITOR

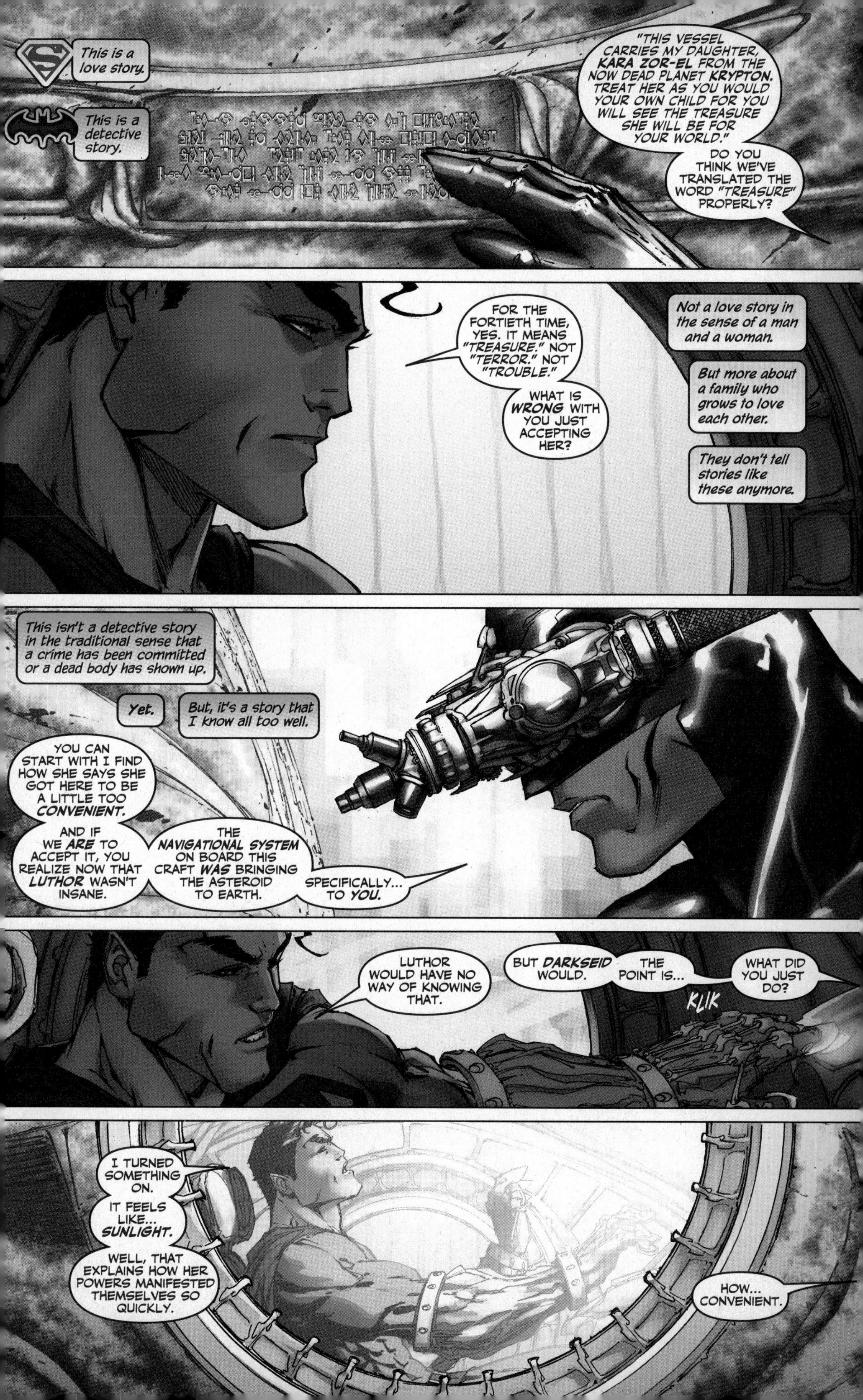
This is a love story.
This is a detective story.
"THIS VESSEL CARRIES MY DAUGHTER, KARA ZOR-EL FROM THE NOW DEAD PLANET KRYPTON. TREAT HER AS YOU WOULD YOUR OWN CHILD FOR YOU WILL SEE THE TREASURE SHE WILL BE FOR YOUR WORLD."
DO YOU THINK WE'VE TRANSLATED THE WORD "TREASURE" PROPERLY?
FOR THE FORTIETH TIME, YES. IT MEANS "TREASURE." NOT "TERROR." NOT "TROUBLE."
WHAT IS WRONG WITH YOU JUST ACCEPTING HER?
Not a love story in the sense of a man and a woman.
But more about a family who grows to love each other.
They don't tell stories like these anymore.
This isn't a detective story in the traditional sense that a crime has been committed or a dead body has shown up.
Yet.
But, it's a story that I know all too well.
YOU CAN START WITH I FIND HOW SHE SAYS SHE GOT HERE TO BE A LITTLE TOO CONVENIENT.
AND IF WE ARE TO ACCEPT IT, YOU REALIZE NOW THAT LUTHOR WASN'T INSANE.
THE NAVIGATIONAL SYSTEM ON BOARD THIS CRAFT WAS BRINGING THE ASTEROID TO EARTH.
SPECIFICALLY... TO YOU.
LUTHOR WOULD HAVE NO WAY OF KNOWING THAT.
BUT DARKSEID WOULD.
THE POINT IS...
KLIK
WHAT DID YOU JUST DO?
I TURNED SOMETHING ON.
IT FEELS LIKE... SUNLIGHT.
WELL, THAT EXPLAINS HOW HER POWERS MANIFESTED THEMSELVES SO QUICKLY.
HOW... CONVENIENT.

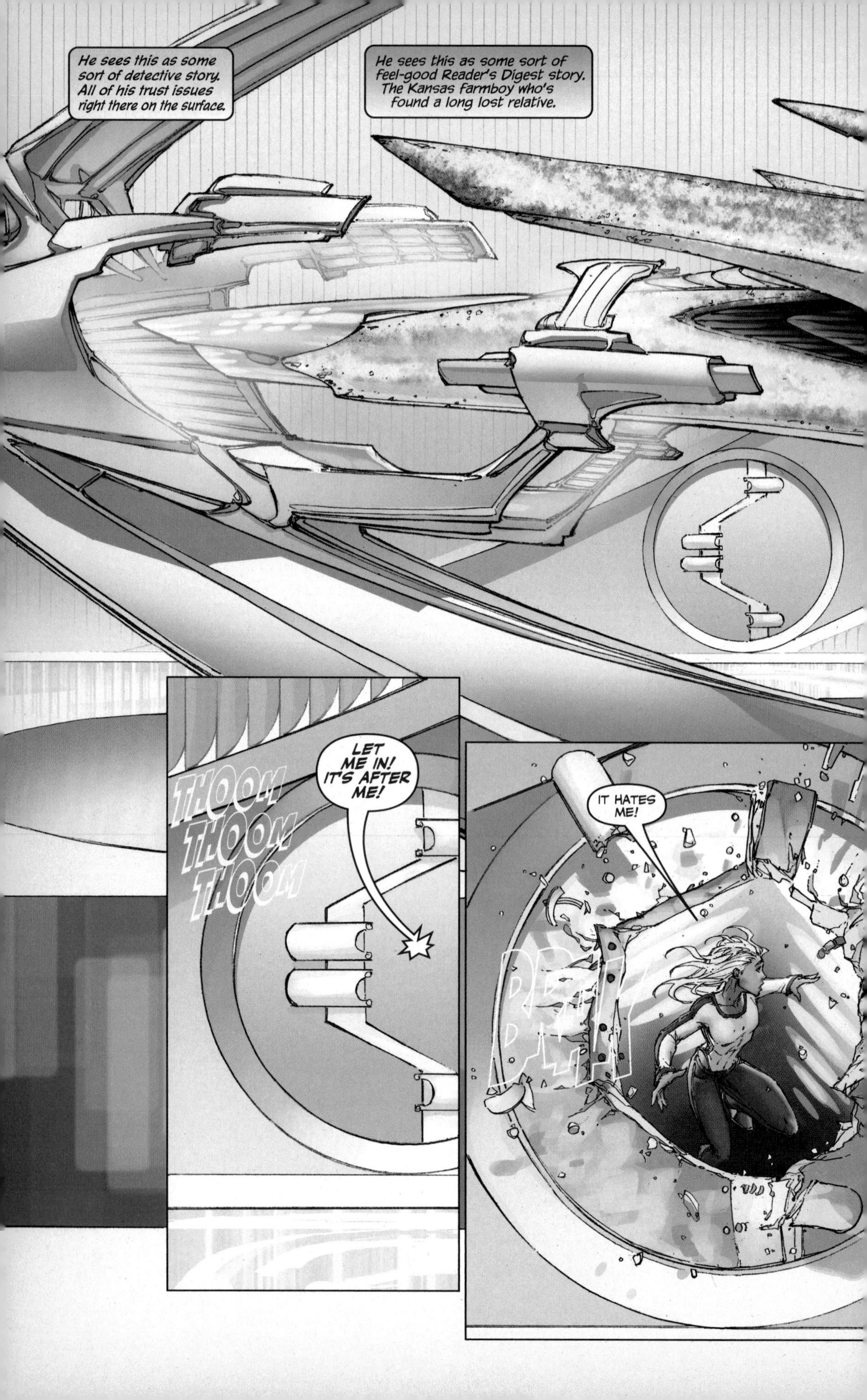
He sees this as some sort of detective story. All of his trust issues right there on the surface.
He sees this as some sort of feel-good Reader's Digest story. The Kansas farmboy who's found a long lost relative.
THOOM THOOM THOOM
LET ME IN! IT'S AFTER ME!
IT HATES ME!

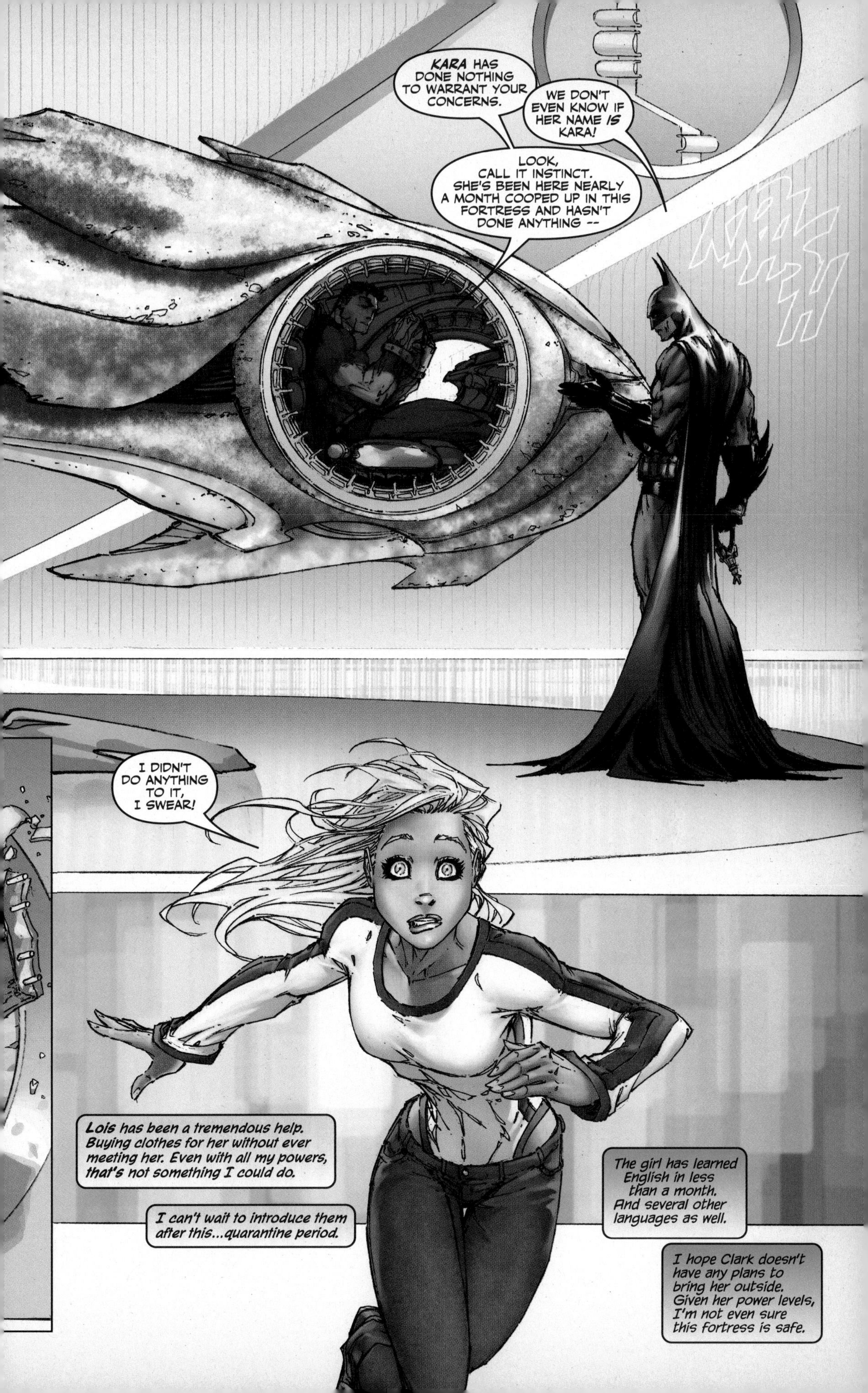
KARA HAS DONE NOTHING TO WARRANT YOUR CONCERNS.
WE DON'T EVEN KNOW IF HER NAME IS KARA!
LOOK, CALL IT INSTINCT. SHE'S BEEN HERE NEARLY A MONTH COOPED UP IN THIS FORTRESS AND HASN'T DONE ANYTHING --
I DIDN'T DO ANYTHING TO IT, I SWEAR!
Lois has been a tremendous help. Buying clothes for her without ever meeting her. Even with all my powers, that's not something I could do.
I can't wait to introduce them after this...quarantine period.
The girl has learned English in less than a month. And several other languages as well.
I hope Clark doesn't have any plans to bring her outside. Given her power levels, I'm not even sure this fortress is safe.

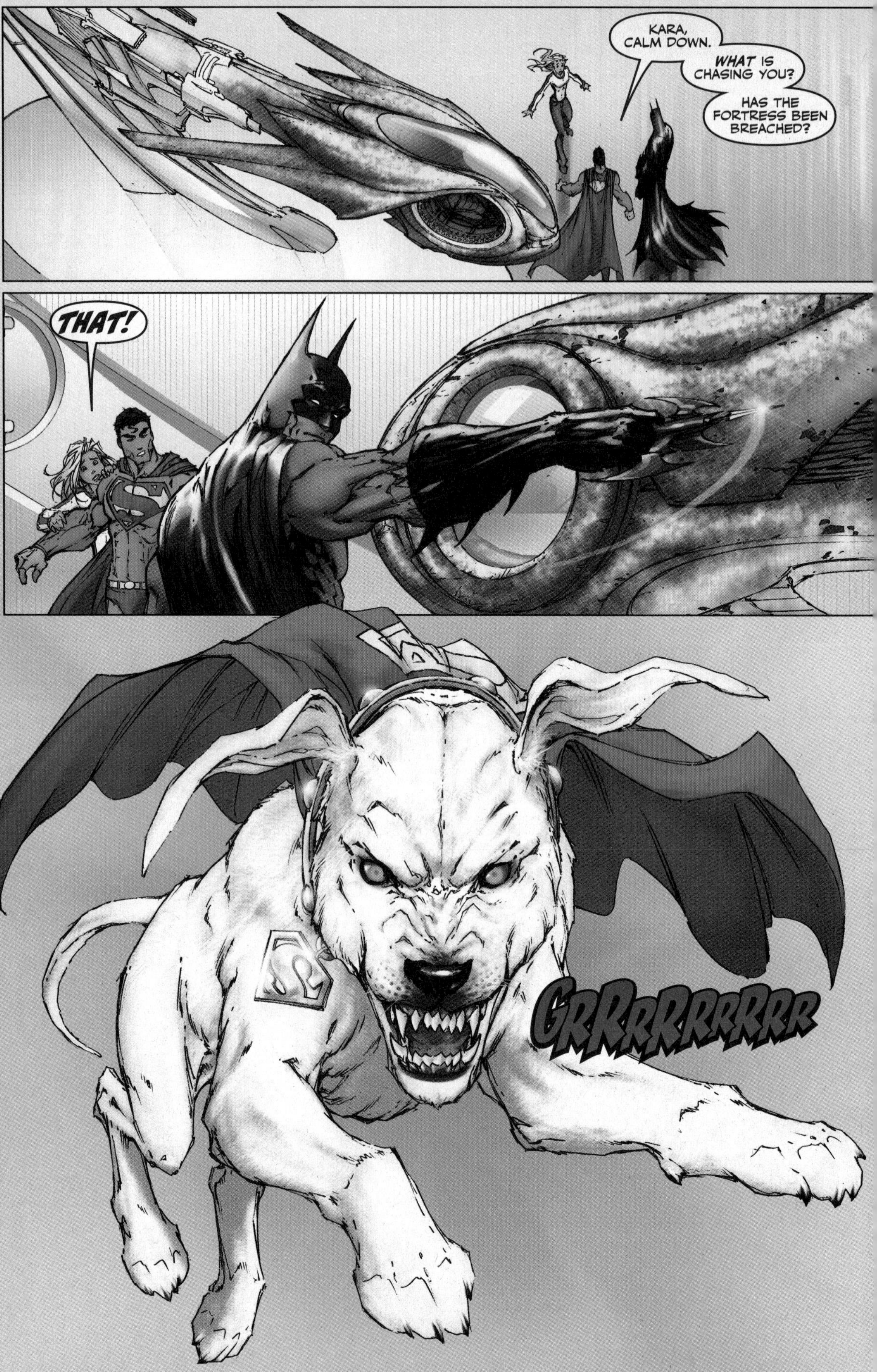
KARA, CALM DOWN.
WHAT IS CHASING YOU?
HAS THE FORTRESS BEEN BREACHED?
THAT!
GRRRRRRRRRR

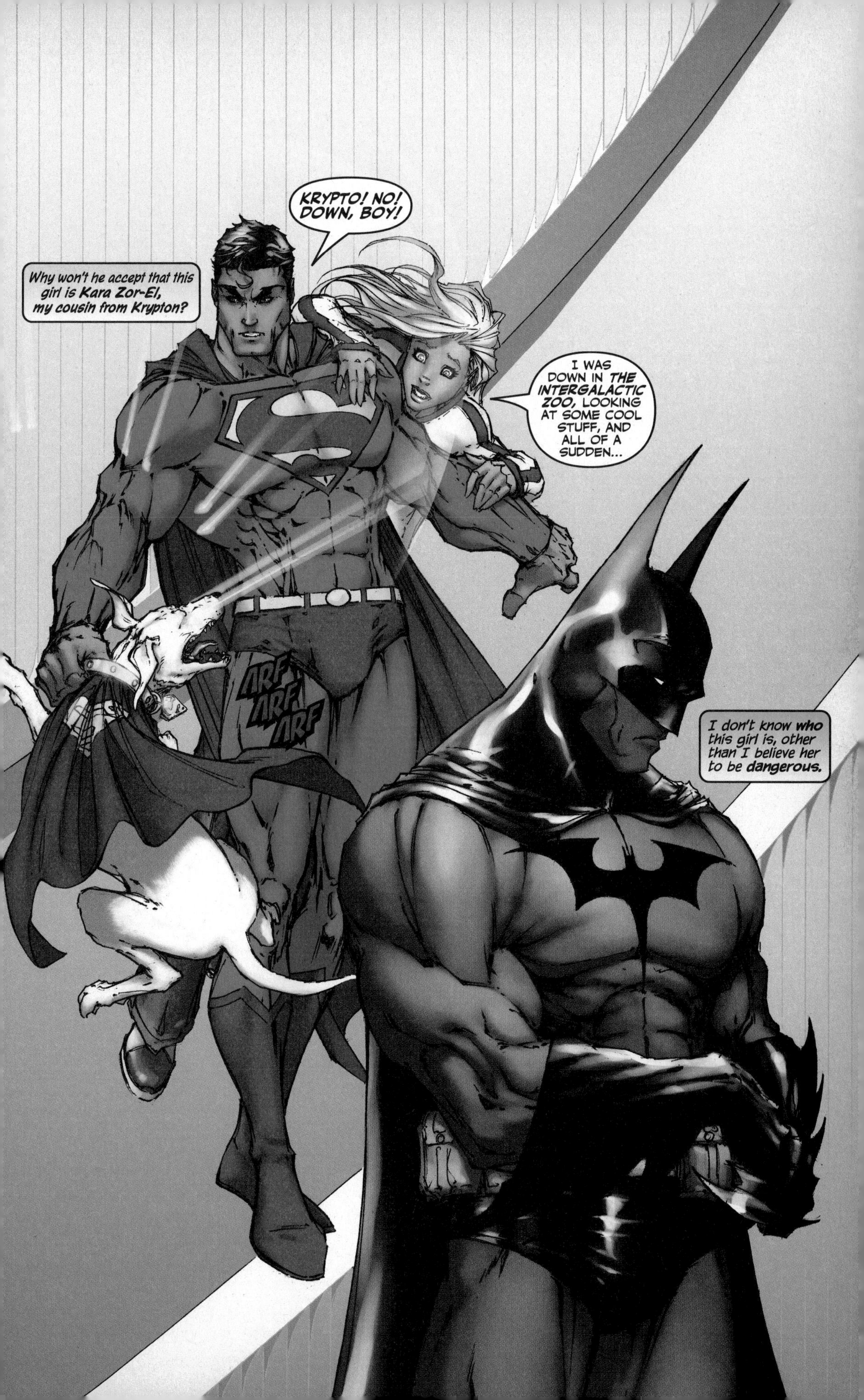
Why won't he accept that this girl is Kara Zor-El, my cousin from Krypton?
KRYPTO! NO! DOWN, BOY!
I WAS DOWN IN THE INTERGALACTIC ZOO, LOOKING AT SOME COOL STUFF, AND ALL OF A SUDDEN...
ARF ARF ARF
I don't know who this girl is, other than I believe her to be dangerous.

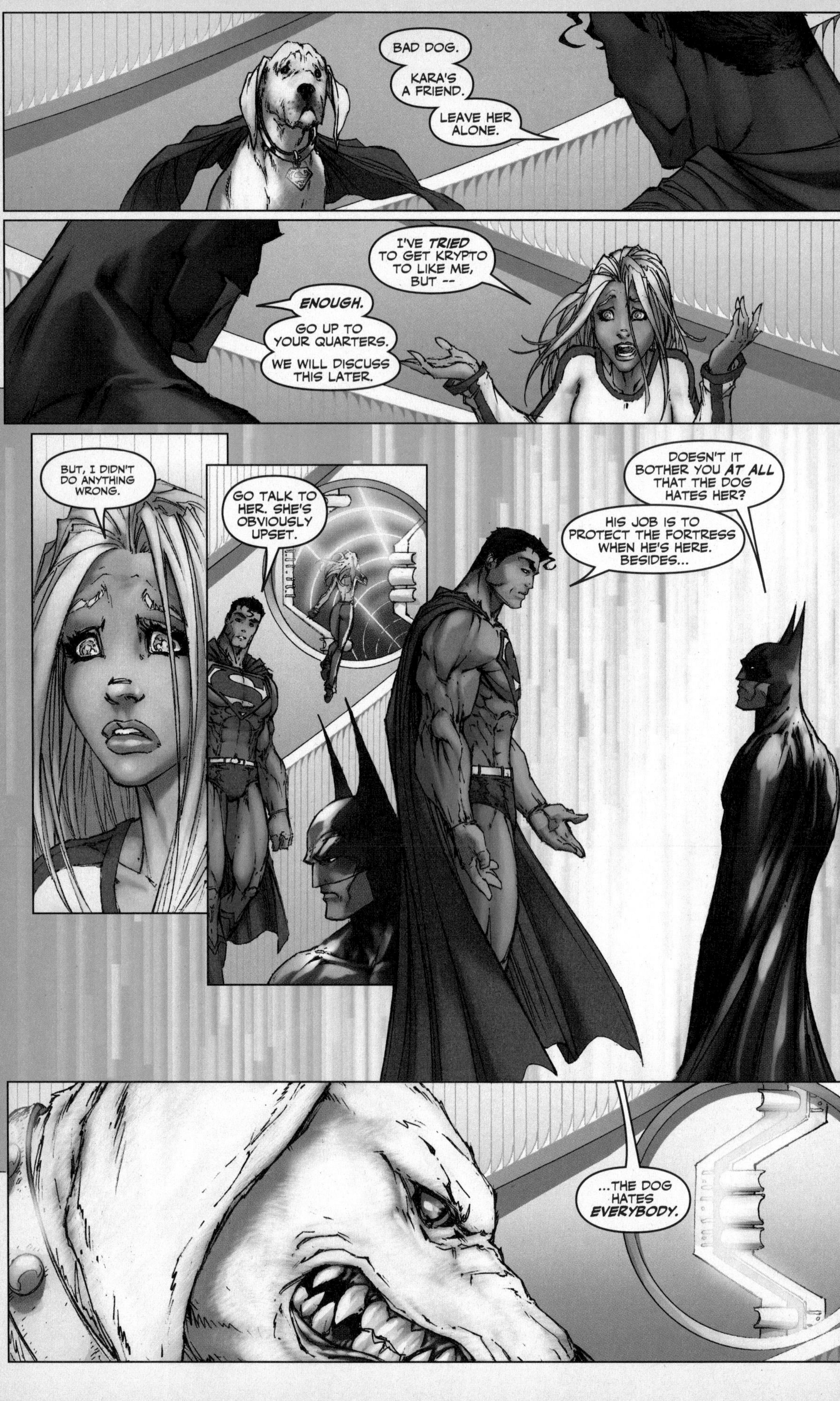

BAD DOG.
KARA'S A FRIEND.
LEAVE HER ALONE.
I'VE TRIED TO GET KRYPTO TO LIKE ME, BUT --
ENOUGH.
GO UP TO YOUR QUARTERS.
WE WILL DISCUSS THIS LATER.
BUT, I DIDN'T DO ANYTHING WRONG.
GO TALK TO HER. SHE'S OBVIOUSLY UPSET.
DOESN'T IT BOTHER YOU AT ALL THAT THE DOG HATES HER?
HIS JOB IS TO PROTECT THE FORTRESS WHEN HE'S HERE. BESIDES...
...THE DOG HATES EVERYBODY.

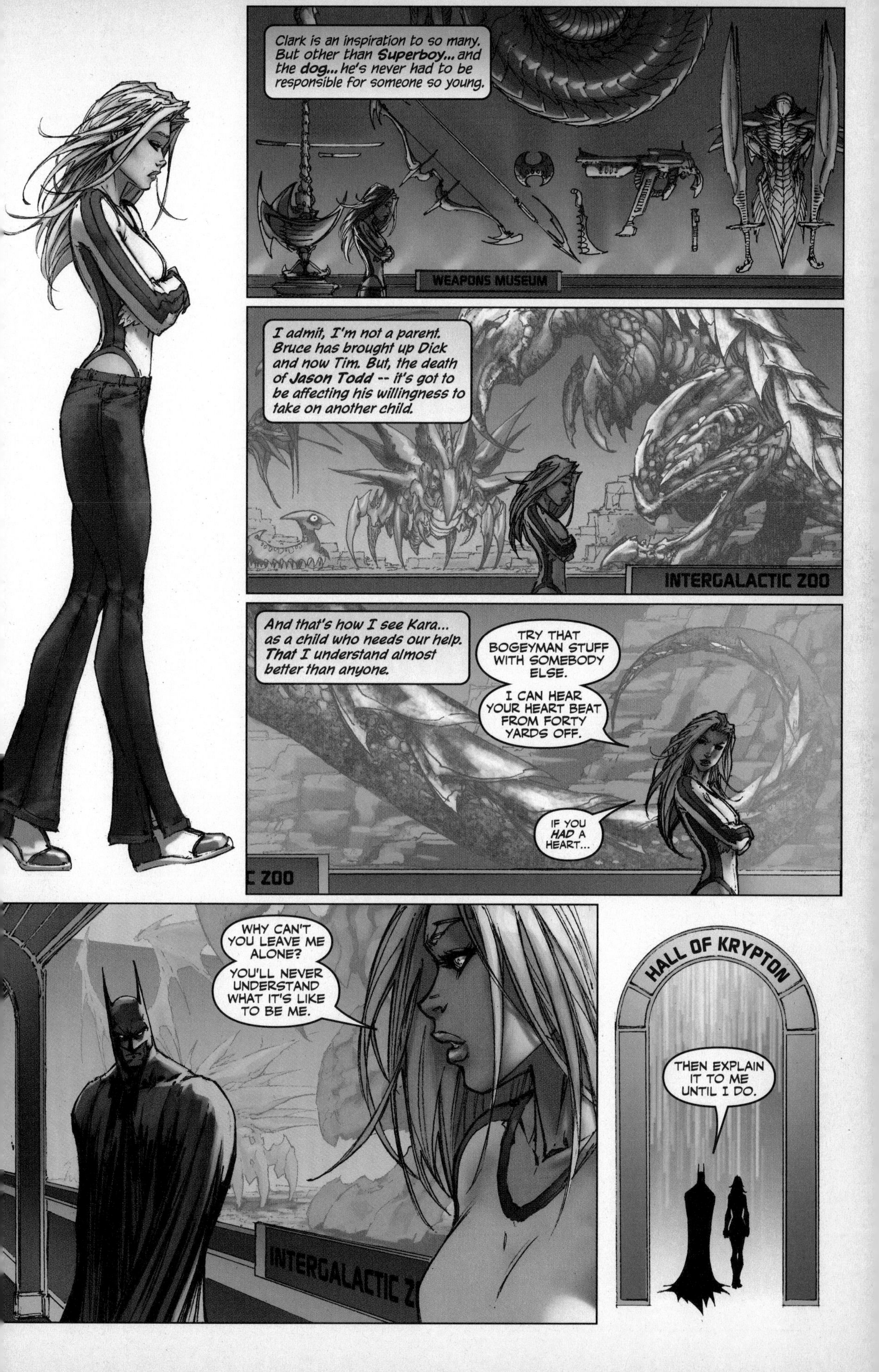
Clark is an inspiration to so many. But other than **Superboy...** and the **dog...** he's never had to be responsible for someone so young.
WEAPONS MUSEUM
I admit, I'm not a parent. Bruce has brought up Dick and now Tim. But, the death of **Jason Todd** -- it's got to be affecting his willingness to take on another child.
INTERGALACTIC ZOO
And that's how I see Kara... as a child who needs our help. That I understand almost better than anyone.
TRY THAT BOGEYMAN STUFF WITH SOMEBODY ELSE.
I CAN HEAR YOUR HEART BEAT FROM FORTY YARDS OFF.
IF YOU *HAD* A HEART...
C ZOO
WHY CAN'T YOU LEAVE ME ALONE?
YOU'LL NEVER UNDERSTAND WHAT IT'S LIKE TO BE ME.
INTERGALACTIC Z
HALL OF KRYPTON
THEN EXPLAIN IT TO ME UNTIL I DO.

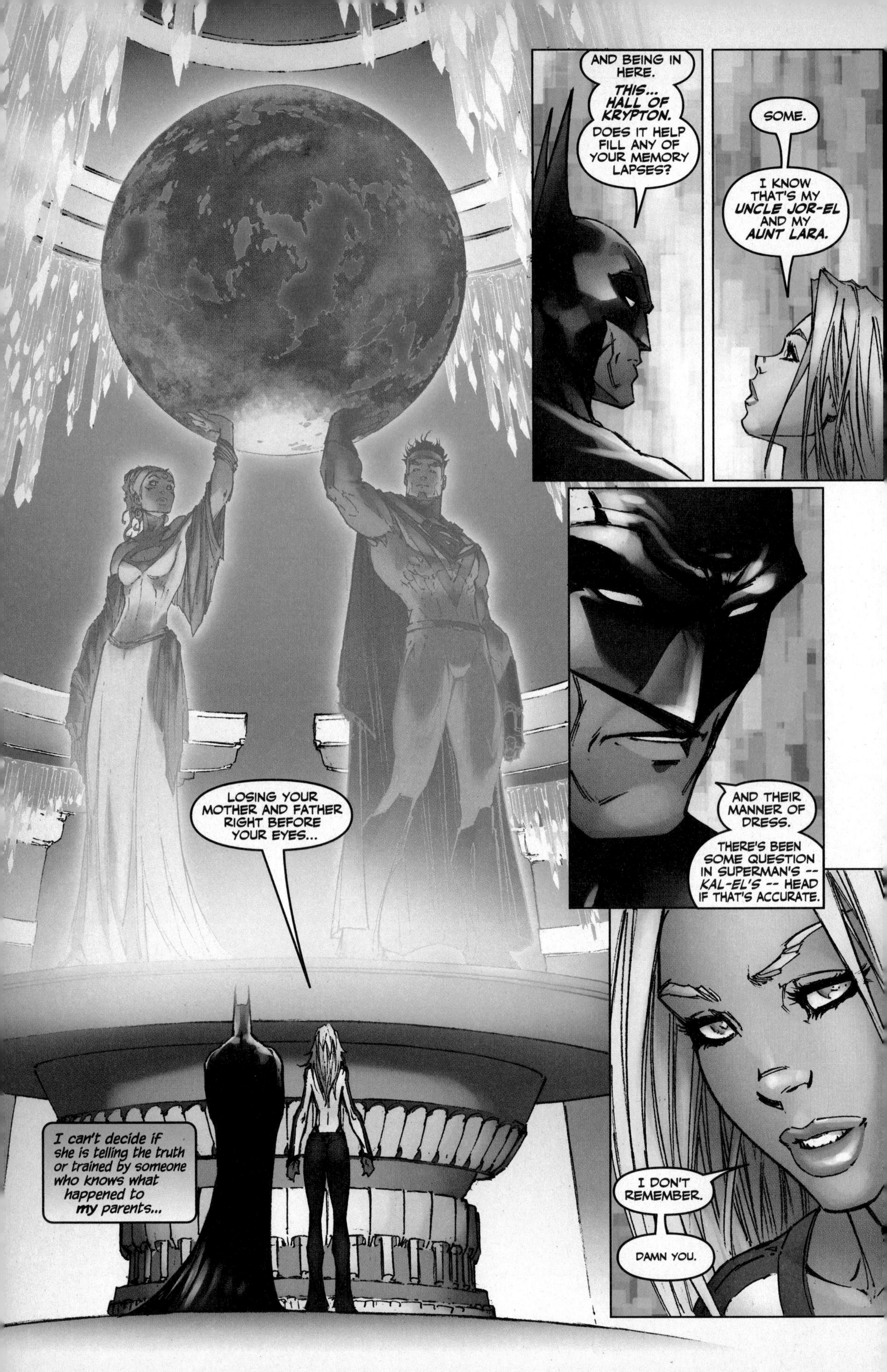
LOSING YOUR MOTHER AND FATHER RIGHT BEFORE YOUR EYES...
I can't decide if she is telling the truth or trained by someone who knows what happened to my parents...
AND BEING IN HERE.
THIS... HALL OF KRYPTON.
DOES IT HELP FILL ANY OF YOUR MEMORY LAPSES?
SOME.
I KNOW THAT'S MY UNCLE JOR-EL AND MY AUNT LARA.
AND THEIR MANNER OF DRESS.
THERE'S BEEN SOME QUESTION IN SUPERMAN'S -- KAL-EL'S -- HEAD IF THAT'S ACCURATE.
I DON'T REMEMBER.
DAMN YOU.

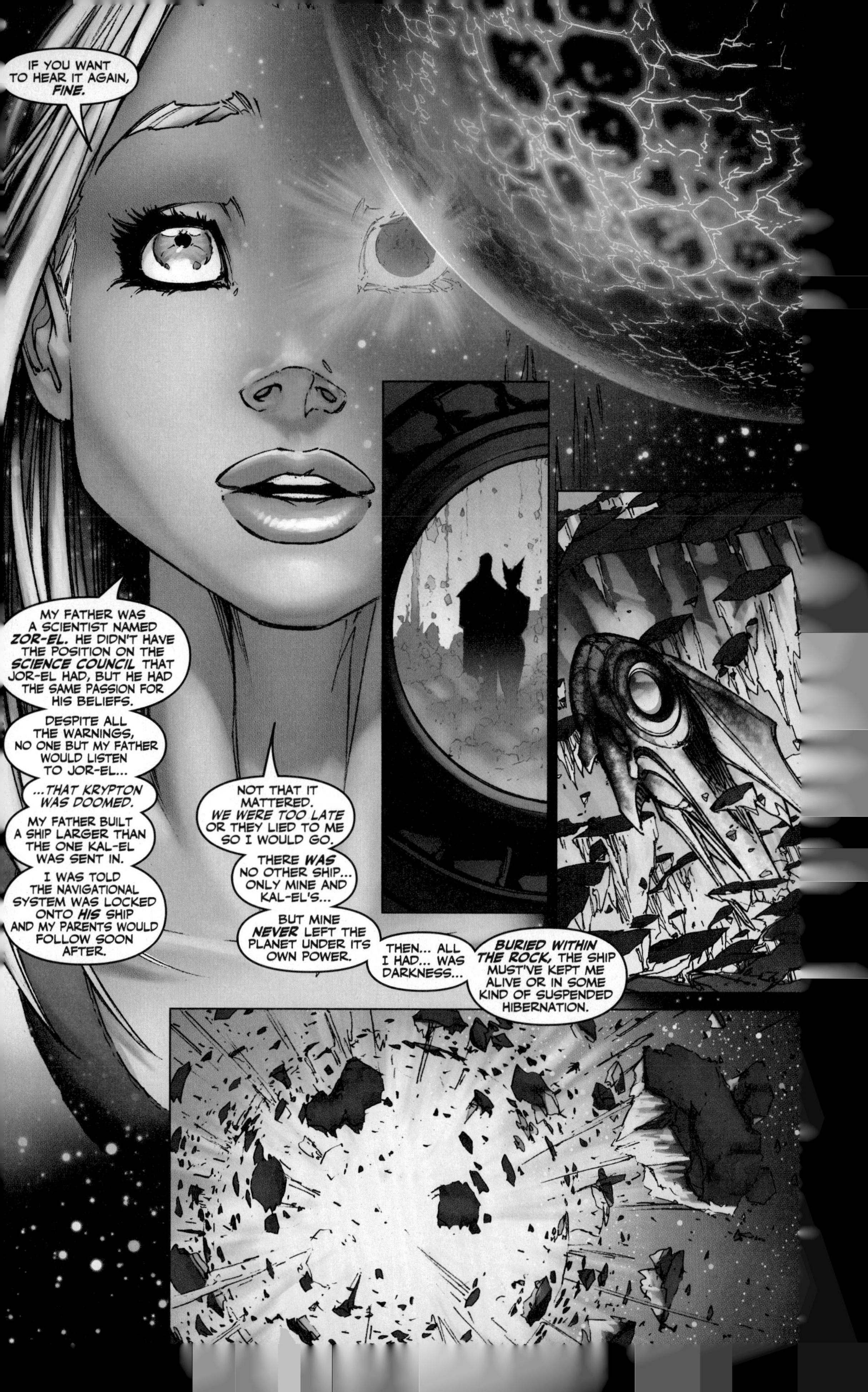
IF YOU WANT TO HEAR IT AGAIN, FINE.
MY FATHER WAS A SCIENTIST NAMED ZOR-EL. HE DIDN'T HAVE THE POSITION ON THE SCIENCE COUNCIL THAT JOR-EL HAD, BUT HE HAD THE SAME PASSION FOR HIS BELIEFS.
DESPITE ALL THE WARNINGS, NO ONE BUT MY FATHER WOULD LISTEN TO JOR-EL...
...THAT KRYPTON WAS DOOMED.
MY FATHER BUILT A SHIP LARGER THAN THE ONE KAL-EL WAS SENT IN.
I WAS TOLD THE NAVIGATIONAL SYSTEM WAS LOCKED ONTO HIS SHIP AND MY PARENTS WOULD FOLLOW SOON AFTER.
NOT THAT IT MATTERED. WE WERE TOO LATE OR THEY LIED TO ME SO I WOULD GO.
THERE WAS NO OTHER SHIP... ONLY MINE AND KAL-EL'S...
BUT MINE NEVER LEFT THE PLANET UNDER ITS OWN POWER.
THEN... ALL I HAD... WAS DARKNESS...
BURIED WITHIN THE ROCK, THE SHIP MUST'VE KEPT ME ALIVE OR IN SOME KIND OF SUSPENDED HIBERNATION.

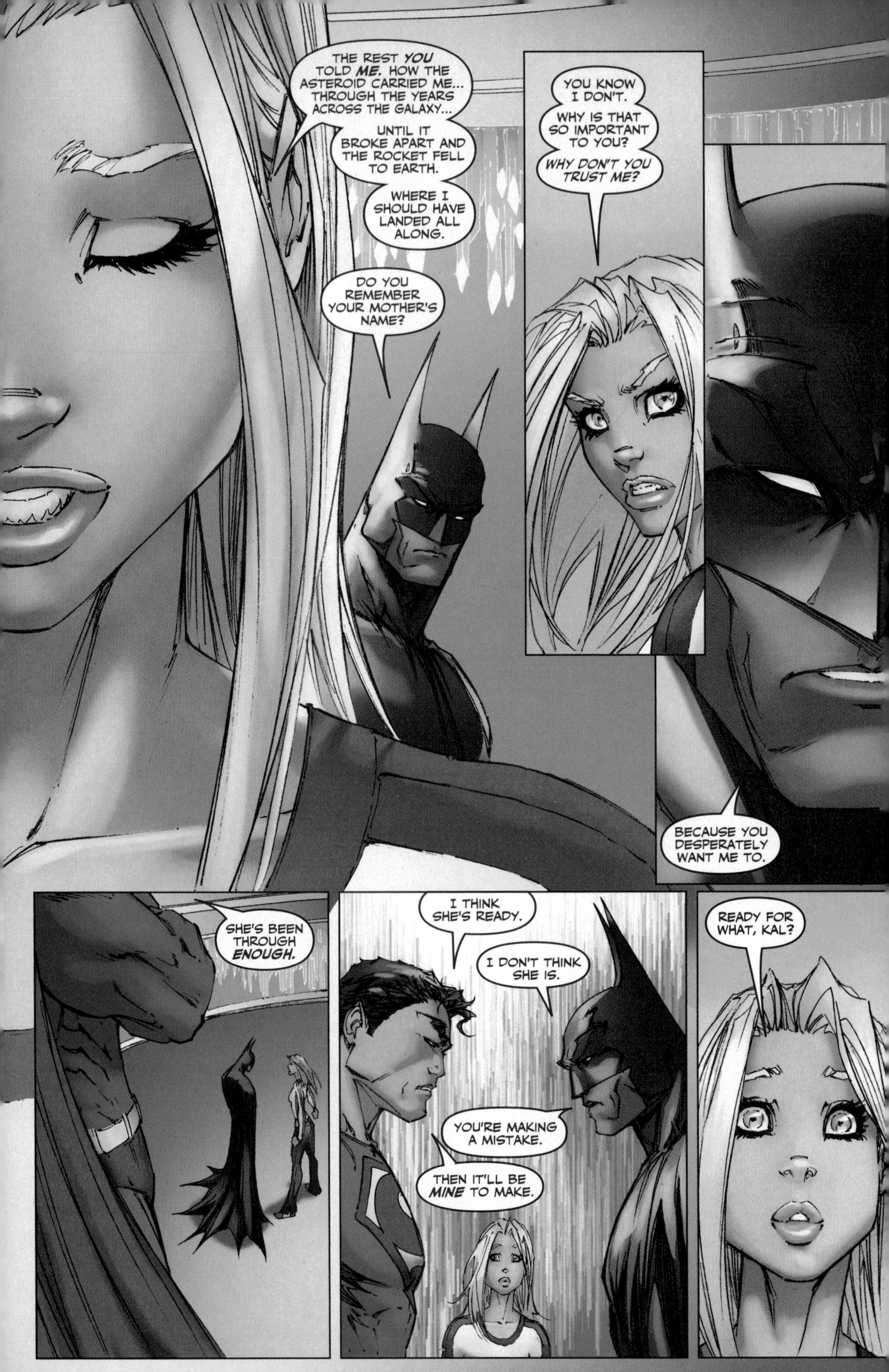
THE REST YOU TOLD ME. HOW THE ASTEROID CARRIED ME... THROUGH THE YEARS ACROSS THE GALAXY...
UNTIL IT BROKE APART AND THE ROCKET FELL TO EARTH.
WHERE I SHOULD HAVE LANDED ALL ALONG.
DO YOU REMEMBER YOUR MOTHER'S NAME?
YOU KNOW I DON'T.
WHY IS THAT SO IMPORTANT TO YOU?
WHY DON'T YOU TRUST ME?
BECAUSE YOU DESPERATELY WANT ME TO.
SHE'S BEEN THROUGH ENOUGH.
I THINK SHE'S READY.
I DON'T THINK SHE IS.
YOU'RE MAKING A MISTAKE.
THEN IT'LL BE MINE TO MAKE.
READY FOR WHAT, KAL?

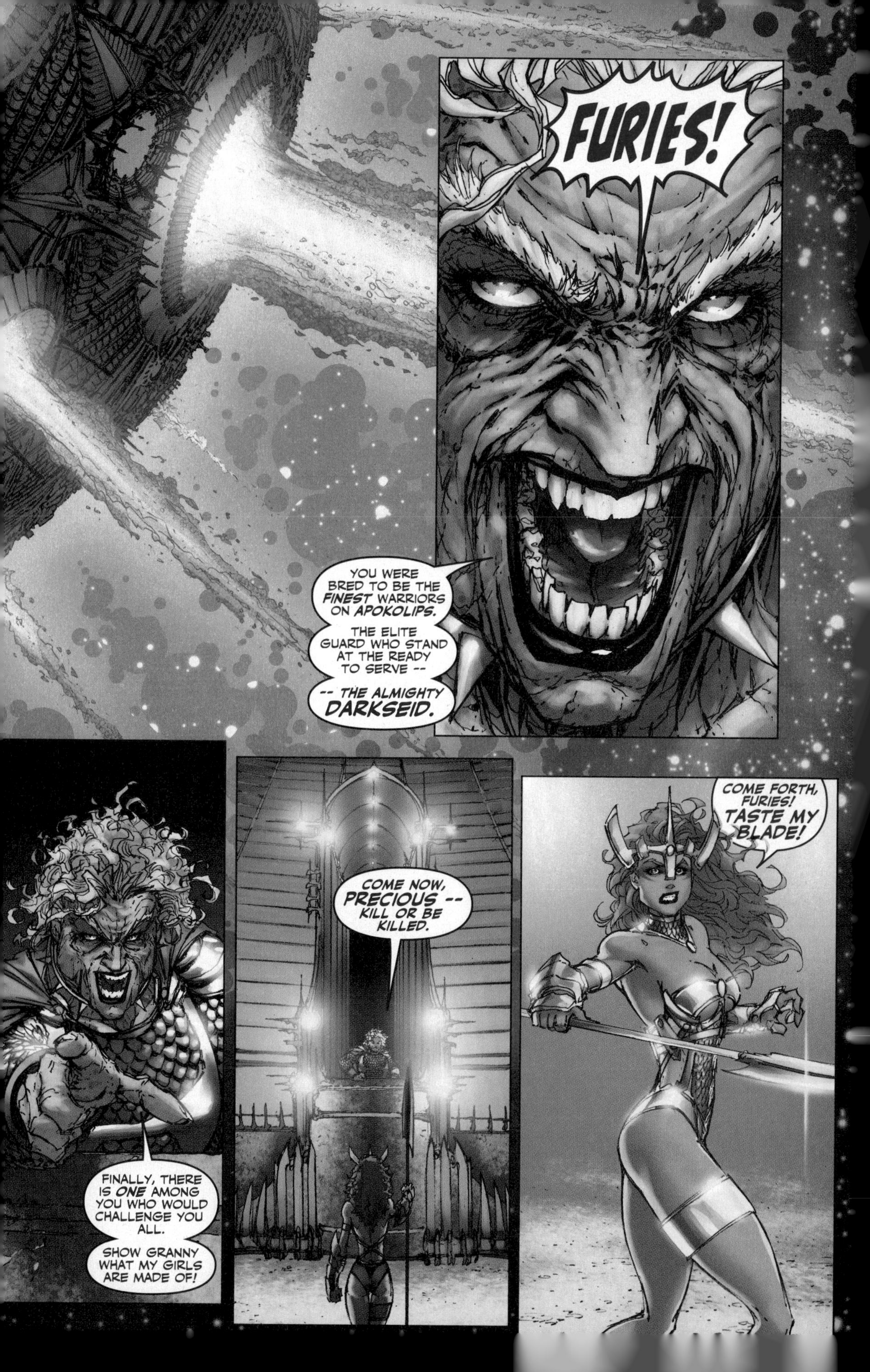
FURIES!
YOU WERE BRED TO BE THE FINEST WARRIORS ON APOKOLIPS.
THE ELITE GUARD WHO STAND AT THE READY TO SERVE --
-- THE ALMIGHTY DARKSEID.
FINALLY, THERE IS ONE AMONG YOU WHO WOULD CHALLENGE YOU ALL.
SHOW GRANNY WHAT MY GIRLS ARE MADE OF!
COME NOW, PRECIOUS -- KILL OR BE KILLED.
COME FORTH, FURIES! TASTE MY BLADE!

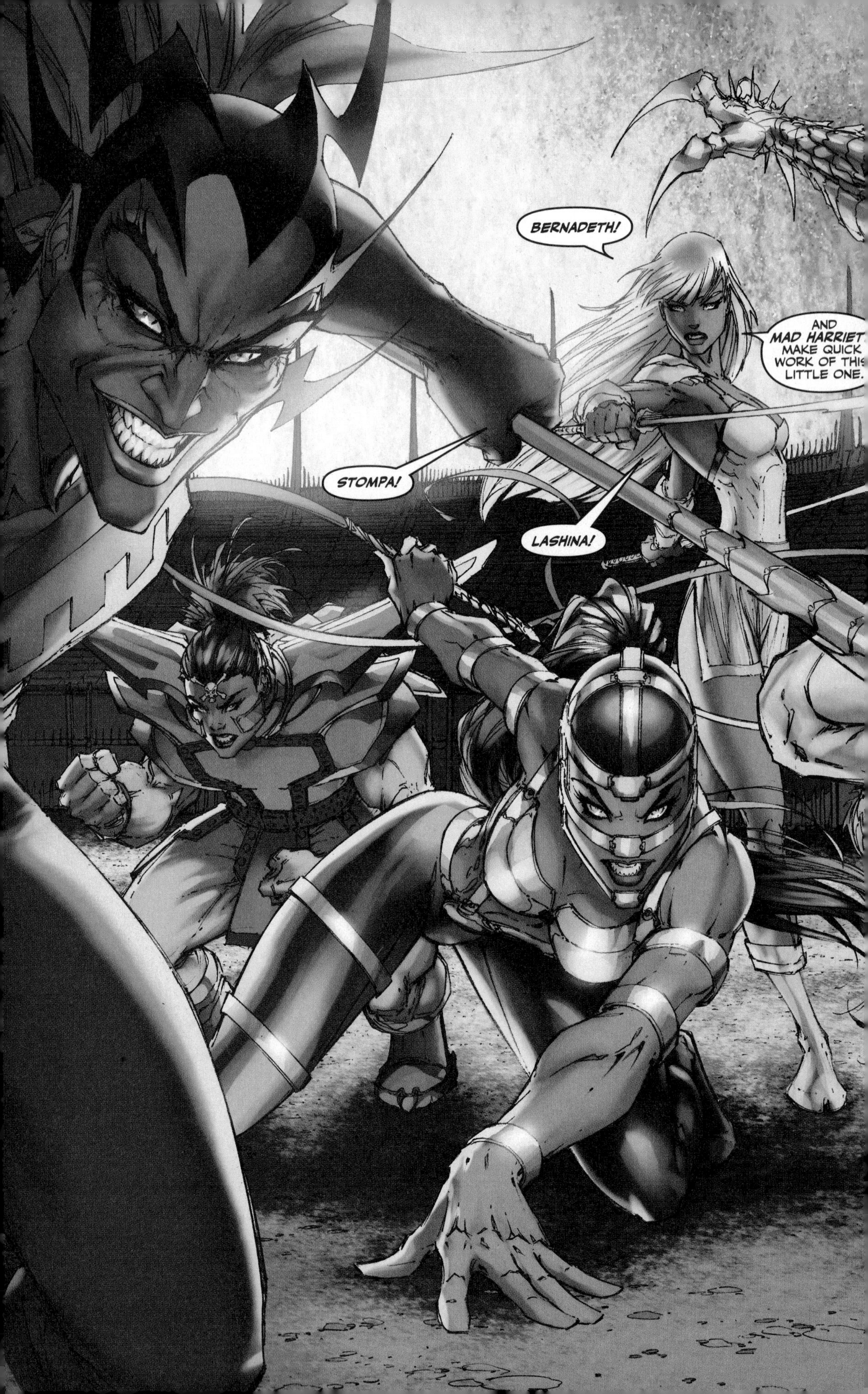
BERNADETH!
STOMPA!
LASHINA!
AND MAD HARRIET, MAKE QUICK WORK OF THIS LITTLE ONE.

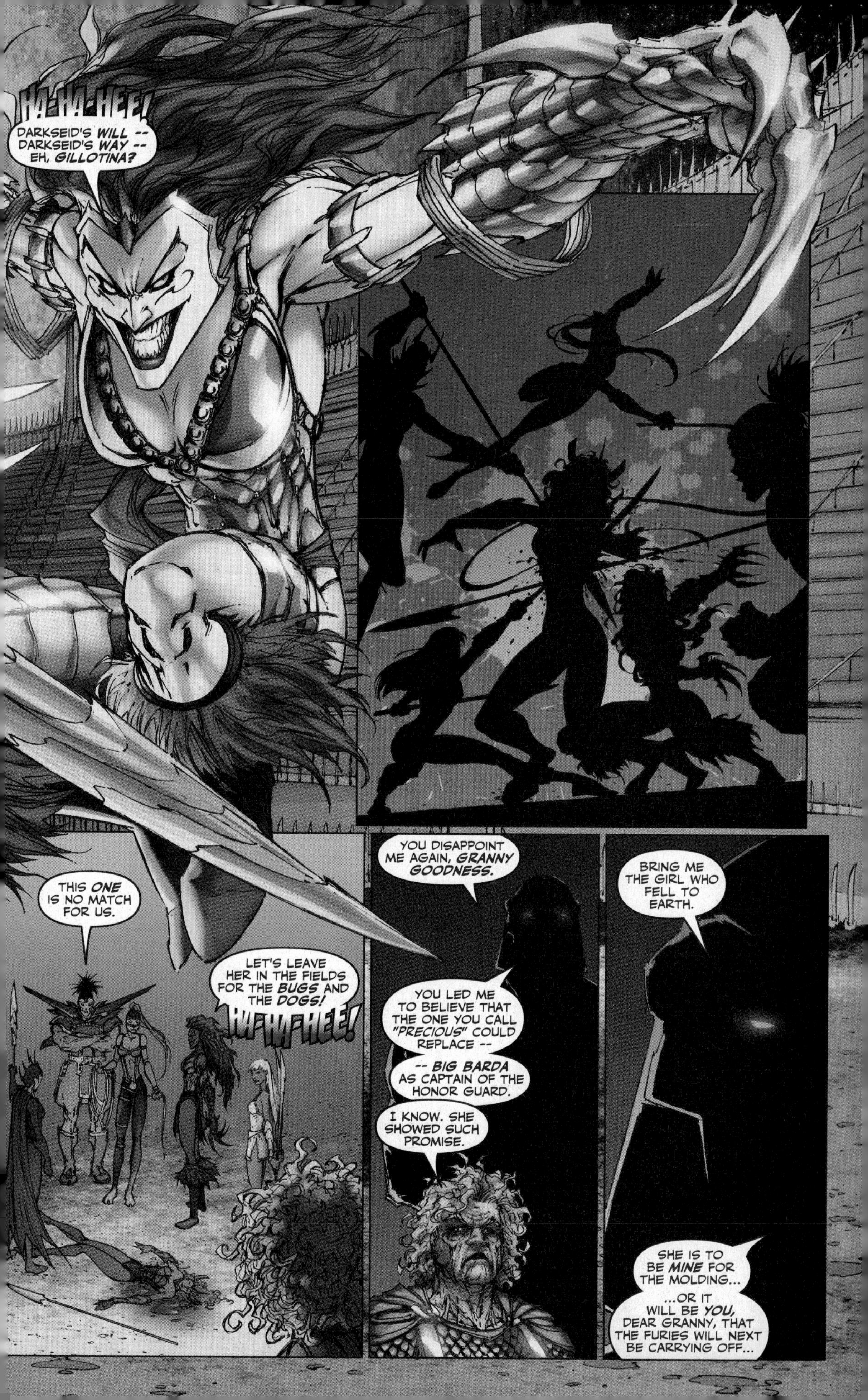
HA-HA-HEE!
DARKSEID'S WILL -- DARKSEID'S WAY -- EH, GILLOTINA?
THIS ONE IS NO MATCH FOR US.
LET'S LEAVE HER IN THE FIELDS FOR THE BUGS AND THE DOGS!
HA-HA-HEE!
YOU DISAPPOINT ME AGAIN, GRANNY GOODNESS.
YOU LED ME TO BELIEVE THAT THE ONE YOU CALL "PRECIOUS" COULD REPLACE --
-- BIG BARDA AS CAPTAIN OF THE HONOR GUARD.
I KNOW. SHE SHOWED SUCH PROMISE.
BRING ME THE GIRL WHO FELL TO EARTH.
SHE IS TO BE MINE FOR THE MOLDING...
...OR IT WILL BE YOU, DEAR GRANNY, THAT THE FURIES WILL NEXT BE CARRYING OFF...

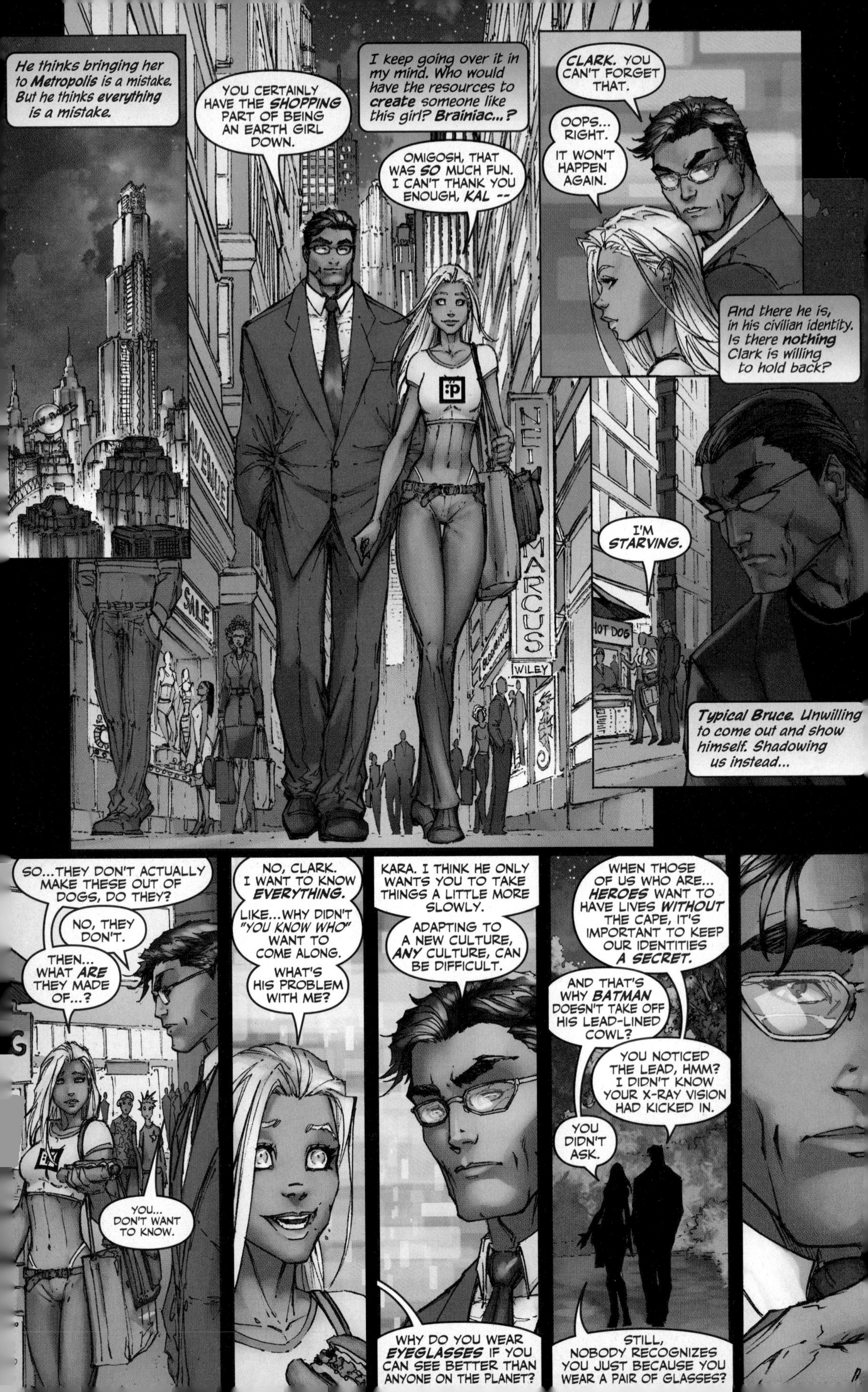

He thinks bringing her to Metropolis is a mistake. But he thinks everything is a mistake.
YOU CERTAINLY HAVE THE SHOPPING PART OF BEING AN EARTH GIRL DOWN.
I keep going over it in my mind. Who would have the resources to create someone like this girl? Brainiac...?
OMIGOSH, THAT WAS SO MUCH FUN. I CAN'T THANK YOU ENOUGH, KAL --
CLARK. YOU CAN'T FORGET THAT.
OOPS... RIGHT.
IT WON'T HAPPEN AGAIN.
And there he is, in his civilian identity. Is there nothing Clark is willing to hold back?
I'M STARVING.
Typical Bruce. Unwilling to come out and show himself. Shadowing us instead...
SALE
MARCUS
WILEY
HOT DOG
SO...THEY DON'T ACTUALLY MAKE THESE OUT OF DOGS, DO THEY?
NO, THEY DON'T.
THEN... WHAT ARE THEY MADE OF...?
YOU... DON'T WANT TO KNOW.
NO, CLARK. I WANT TO KNOW EVERYTHING.
LIKE...WHY DIDN'T "YOU KNOW WHO" WANT TO COME ALONG.
WHAT'S HIS PROBLEM WITH ME?
KARA. I THINK HE ONLY WANTS YOU TO TAKE THINGS A LITTLE MORE SLOWLY.
ADAPTING TO A NEW CULTURE, ANY CULTURE, CAN BE DIFFICULT.
WHY DO YOU WEAR EYEGLASSES IF YOU CAN SEE BETTER THAN ANYONE ON THE PLANET?
WHEN THOSE OF US WHO ARE... HEROES WANT TO HAVE LIVES WITHOUT THE CAPE, IT'S IMPORTANT TO KEEP OUR IDENTITIES A SECRET.
AND THAT'S WHY BATMAN DOESN'T TAKE OFF HIS LEAD-LINED COWL?
YOU NOTICED THE LEAD, HMM? I DIDN'T KNOW YOUR X-RAY VISION HAD KICKED IN.
YOU DIDN'T ASK.
STILL, NOBODY RECOGNIZES YOU JUST BECAUSE YOU WEAR A PAIR OF GLASSES?

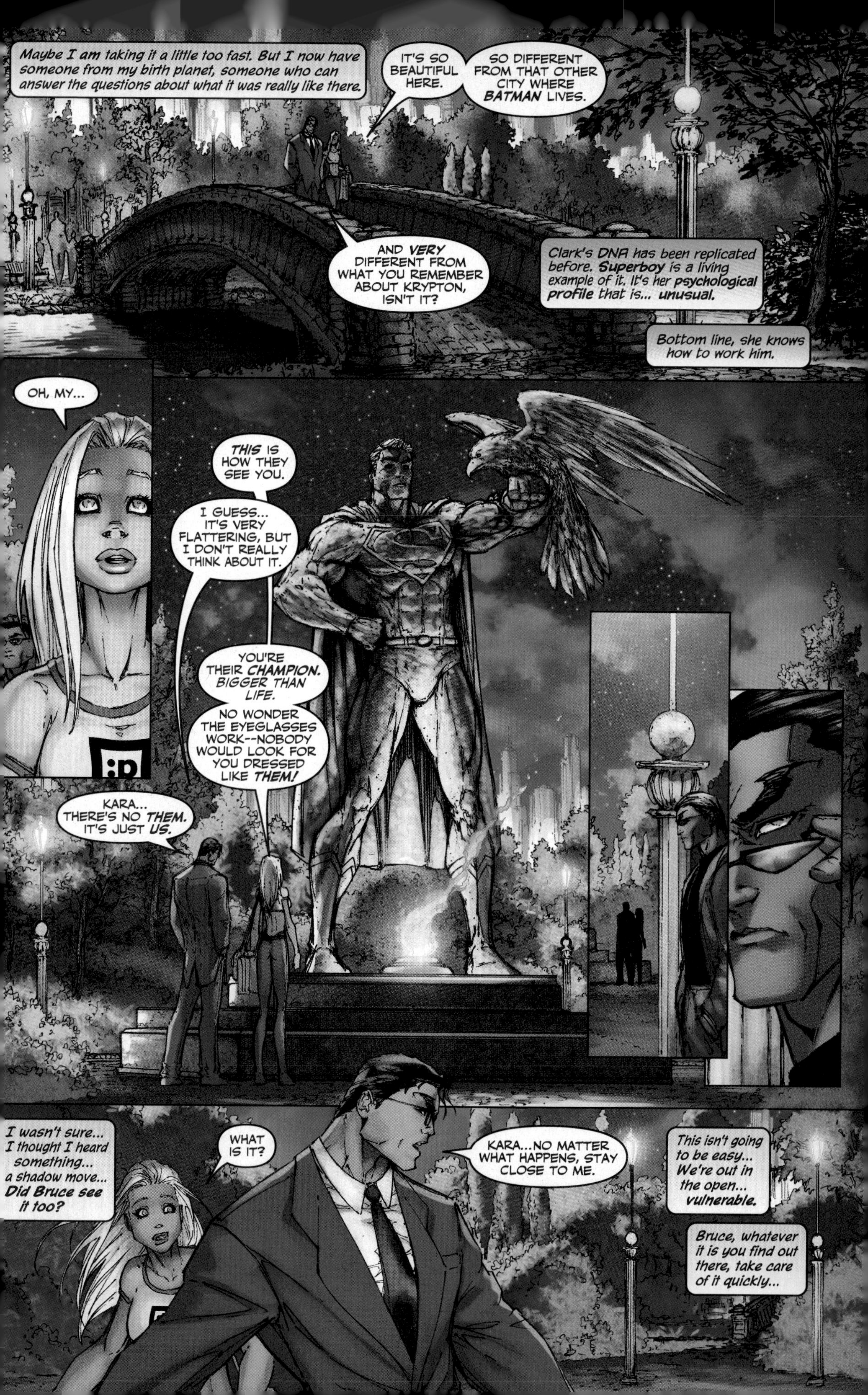

Maybe I am taking it a little too fast. But I now have someone from my birth planet, someone who can answer the questions about what it was really like there.
IT'S SO BEAUTIFUL HERE.
SO DIFFERENT FROM THAT OTHER CITY WHERE BATMAN LIVES.
AND VERY DIFFERENT FROM WHAT YOU REMEMBER ABOUT KRYPTON, ISN'T IT?
Clark's DNA has been replicated before. Superboy is a living example of it. It's her psychological profile that is... unusual.
Bottom line, she knows how to work him.
OH, MY...
THIS IS HOW THEY SEE YOU.
I GUESS... IT'S VERY FLATTERING, BUT I DON'T REALLY THINK ABOUT IT.
YOU'RE THEIR CHAMPION. BIGGER THAN LIFE.
NO WONDER THE EYEGLASSES WORK--NOBODY WOULD LOOK FOR YOU DRESSED LIKE THEM!
KARA... THERE'S NO THEM. IT'S JUST US.
I wasn't sure... I thought I heard something... a shadow move... Did Bruce see it too?
WHAT IS IT?
KARA...NO MATTER WHAT HAPPENS, STAY CLOSE TO ME.
This isn't going to be easy... We're out in the open... vulnerable.
Bruce, whatever it is you find out there, take care of it quickly...

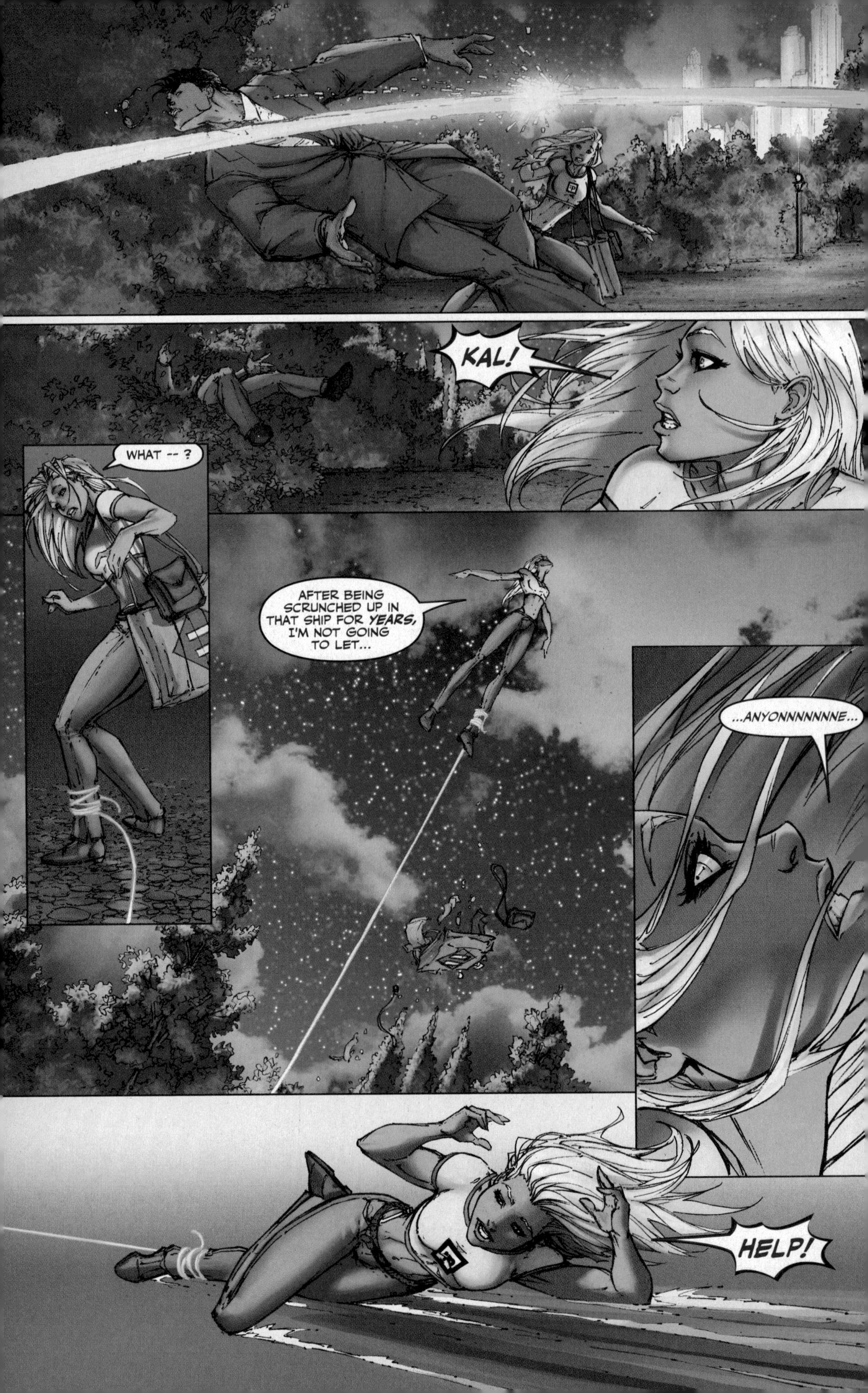
KAL!
WHAT -- ?
AFTER BEING SCRUNCHED UP IN THAT SHIP FOR YEARS, I'M NOT GOING TO LET...
...ANYONNNNNNE...
HELP!

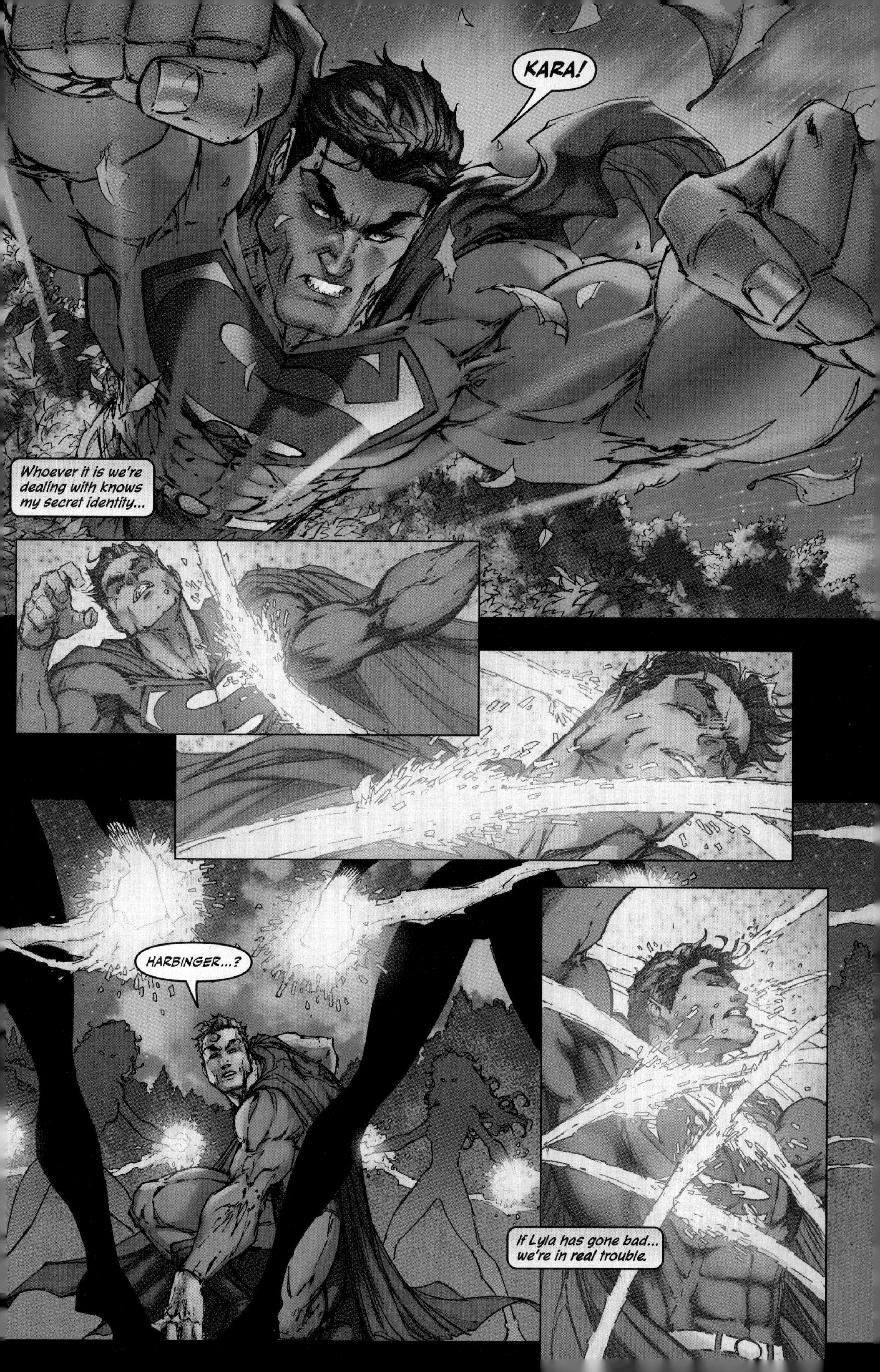
KARA!
Whoever it is we're dealing with knows my secret identity...
HARBINGER...?
If Lyla has gone bad... we're in real trouble.

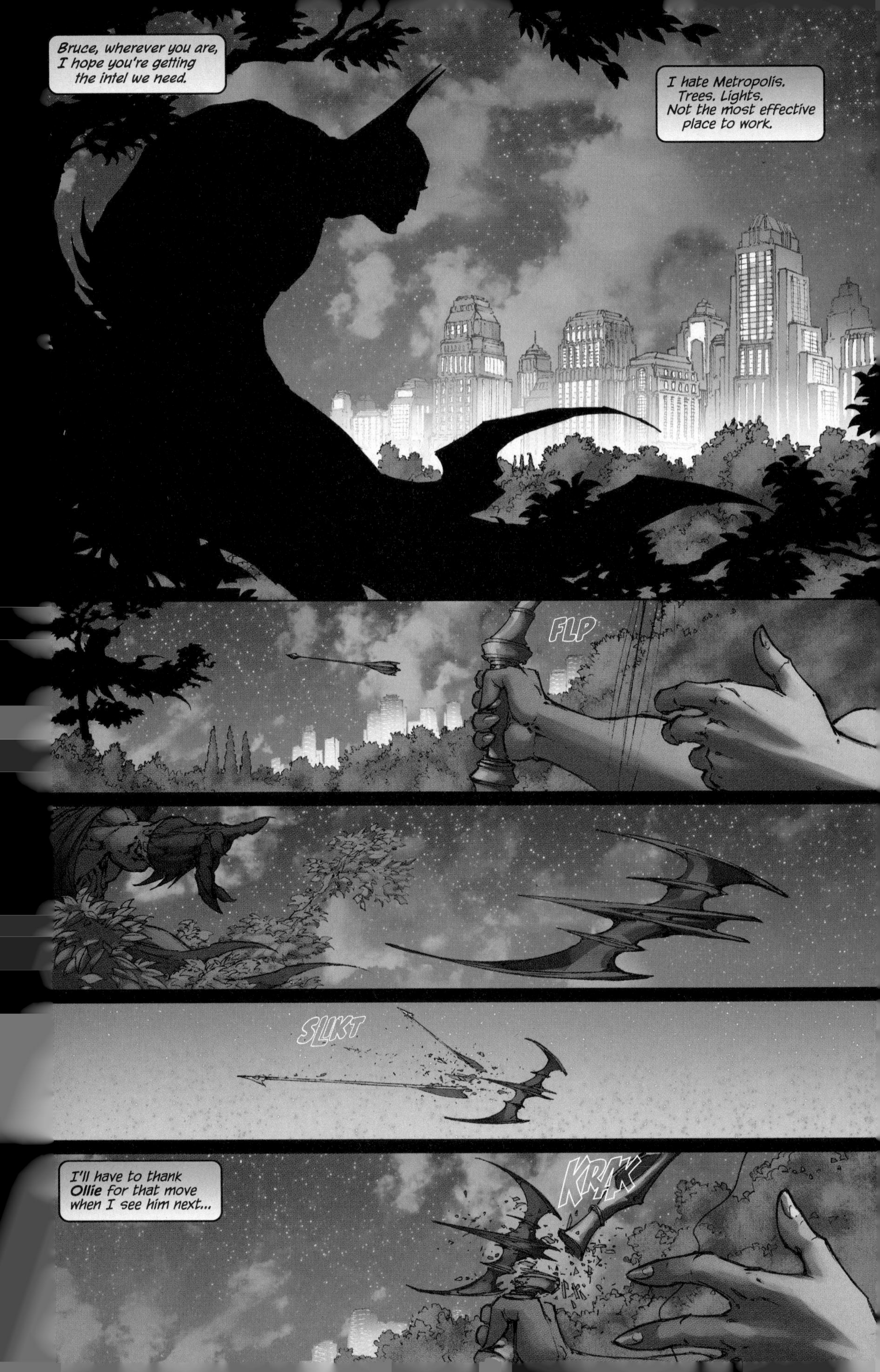
Bruce, wherever you are, I hope you're getting the intel we need.
I hate Metropolis. Trees. Lights. Not the most effective place to work.
FLP
SLIKT
I'll have to thank **Ollie** for that move when I see him next...
KRAK

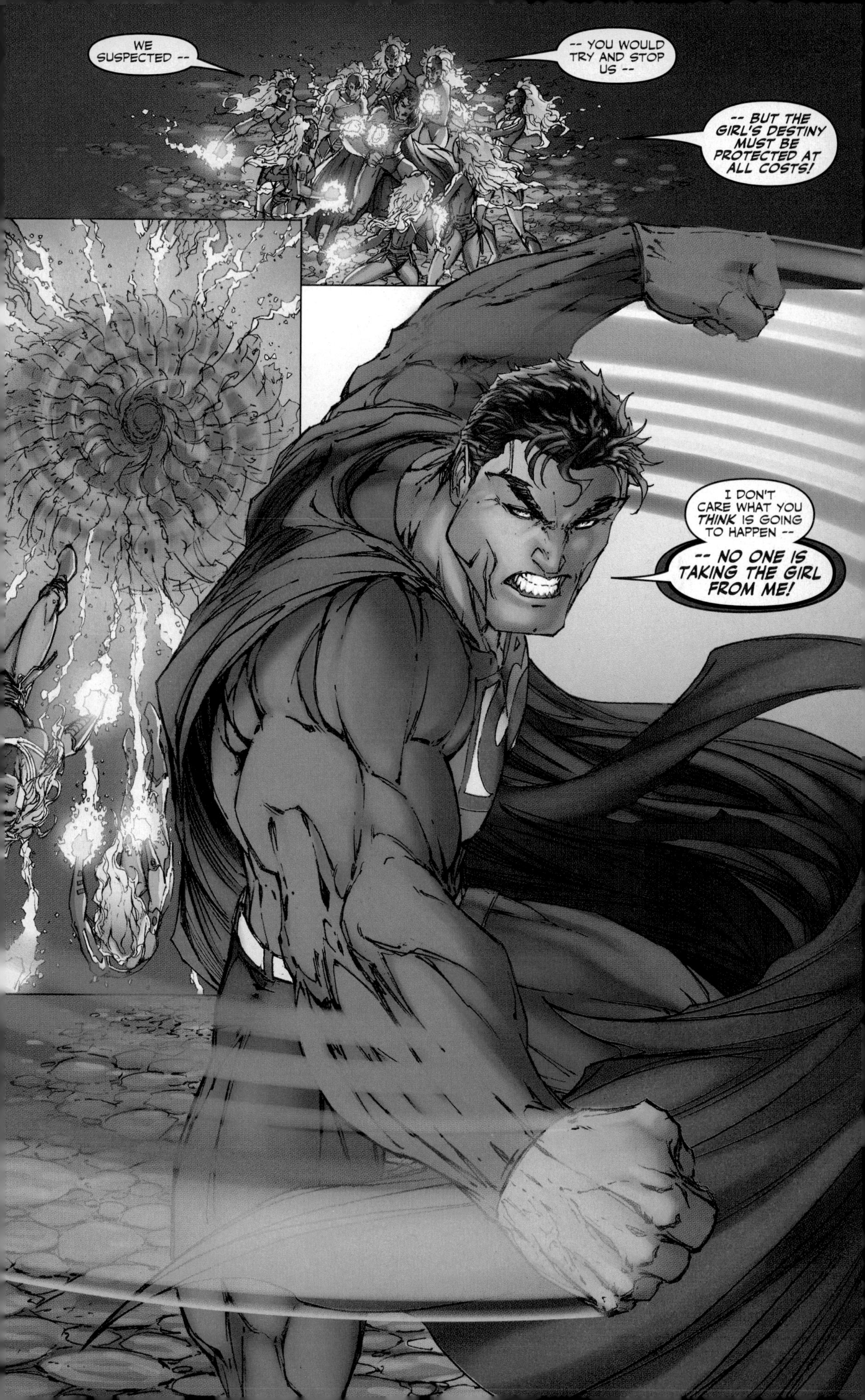
WE SUSPECTED --
-- YOU WOULD TRY AND STOP US --
-- BUT THE GIRL'S DESTINY MUST BE PROTECTED AT ALL COSTS!
I DON'T CARE WHAT YOU *THINK* IS GOING TO HAPPEN --
-- NO ONE IS TAKING THE GIRL FROM ME!

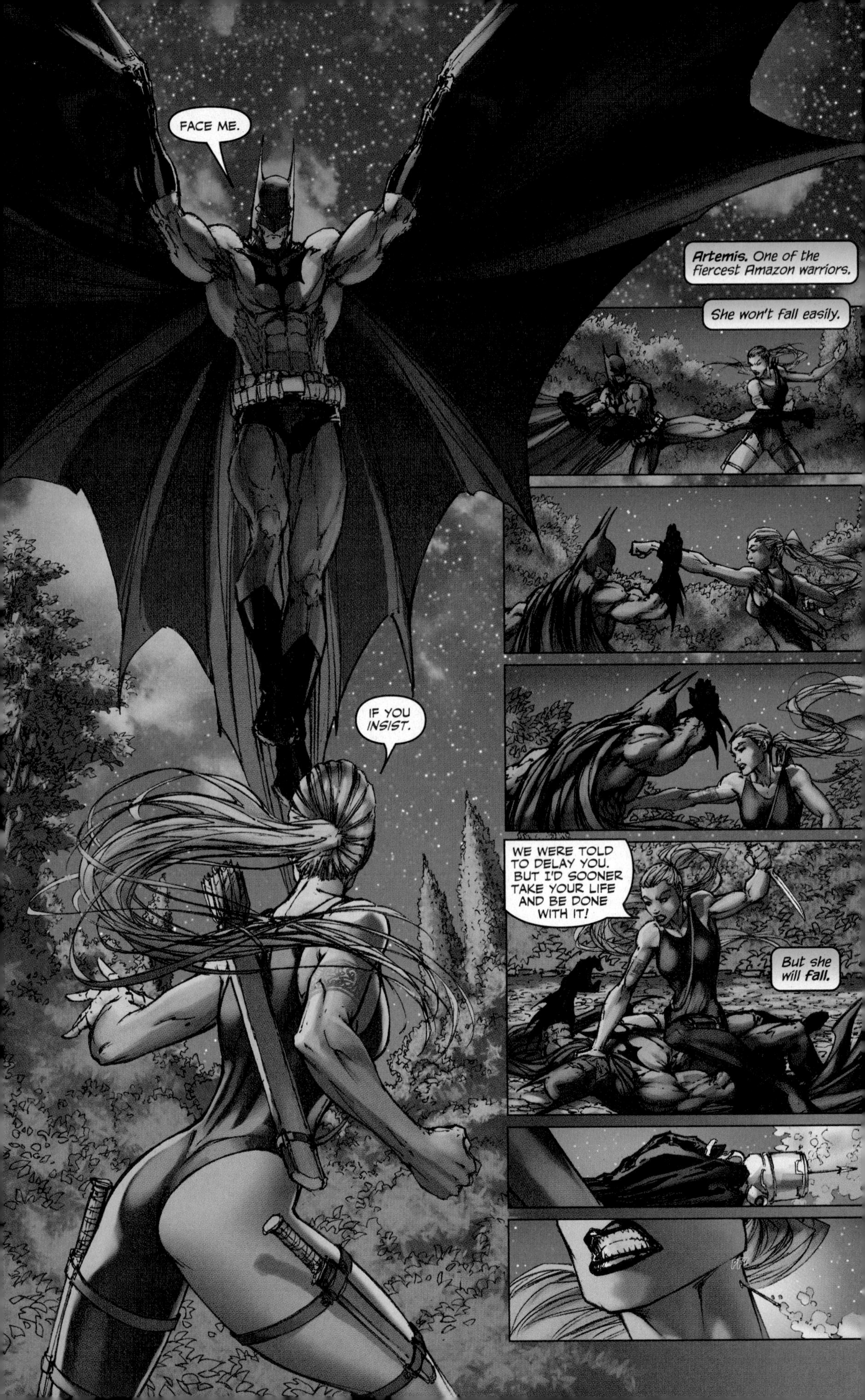
FACE ME.
IF YOU INSIST.
Artemis. One of the fiercest Amazon warriors.
She won't fall easily.
WE WERE TOLD TO DELAY YOU. BUT I'D SOONER TAKE YOUR LIFE AND BE DONE WITH IT!
But she will fall.

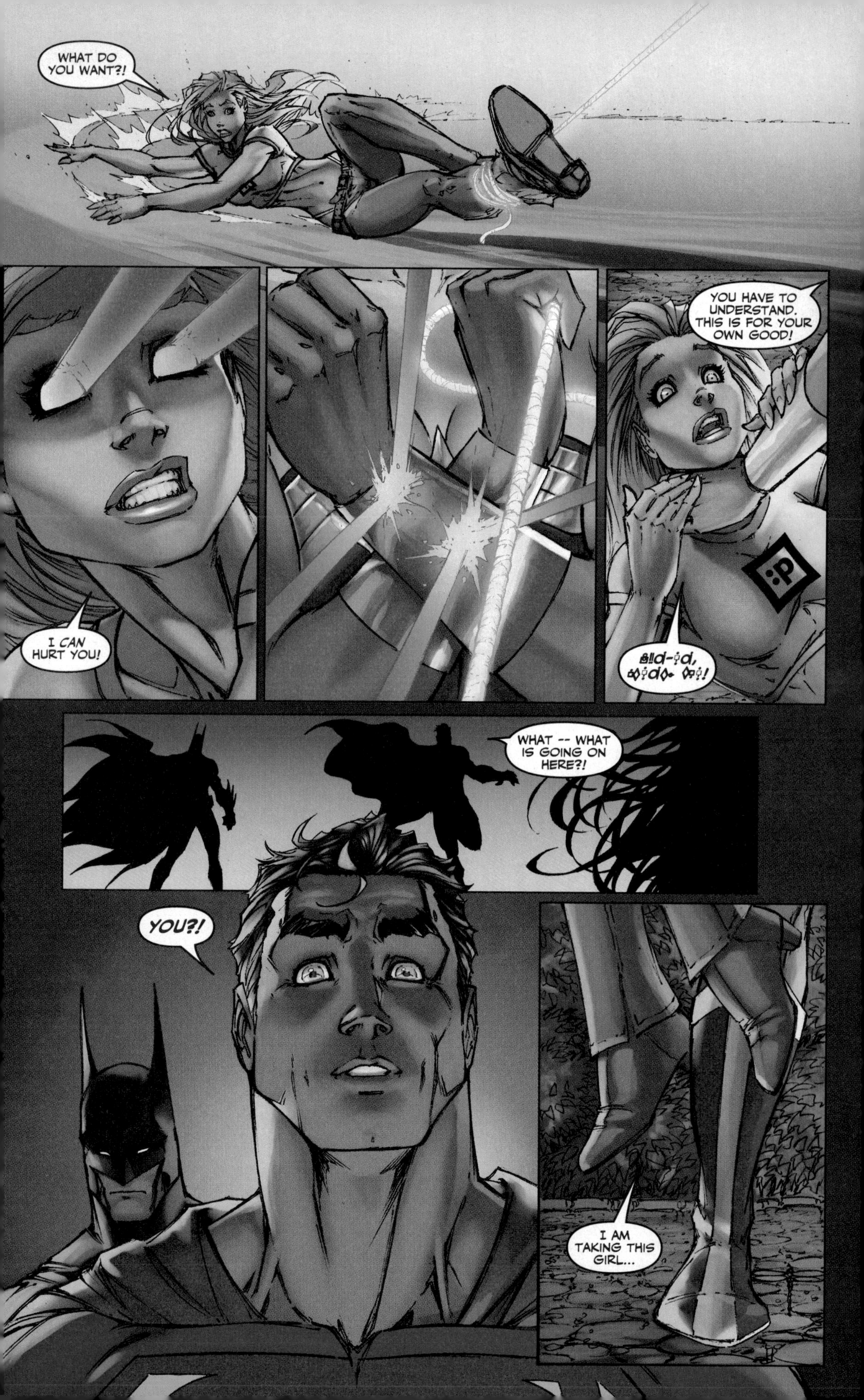
WHAT DO YOU WANT?!
I CAN HURT YOU!
YOU HAVE TO UNDERSTAND. THIS IS FOR YOUR OWN GOOD!
WHAT -- WHAT IS GOING ON HERE?!
YOU?!
I AM TAKING THIS GIRL...

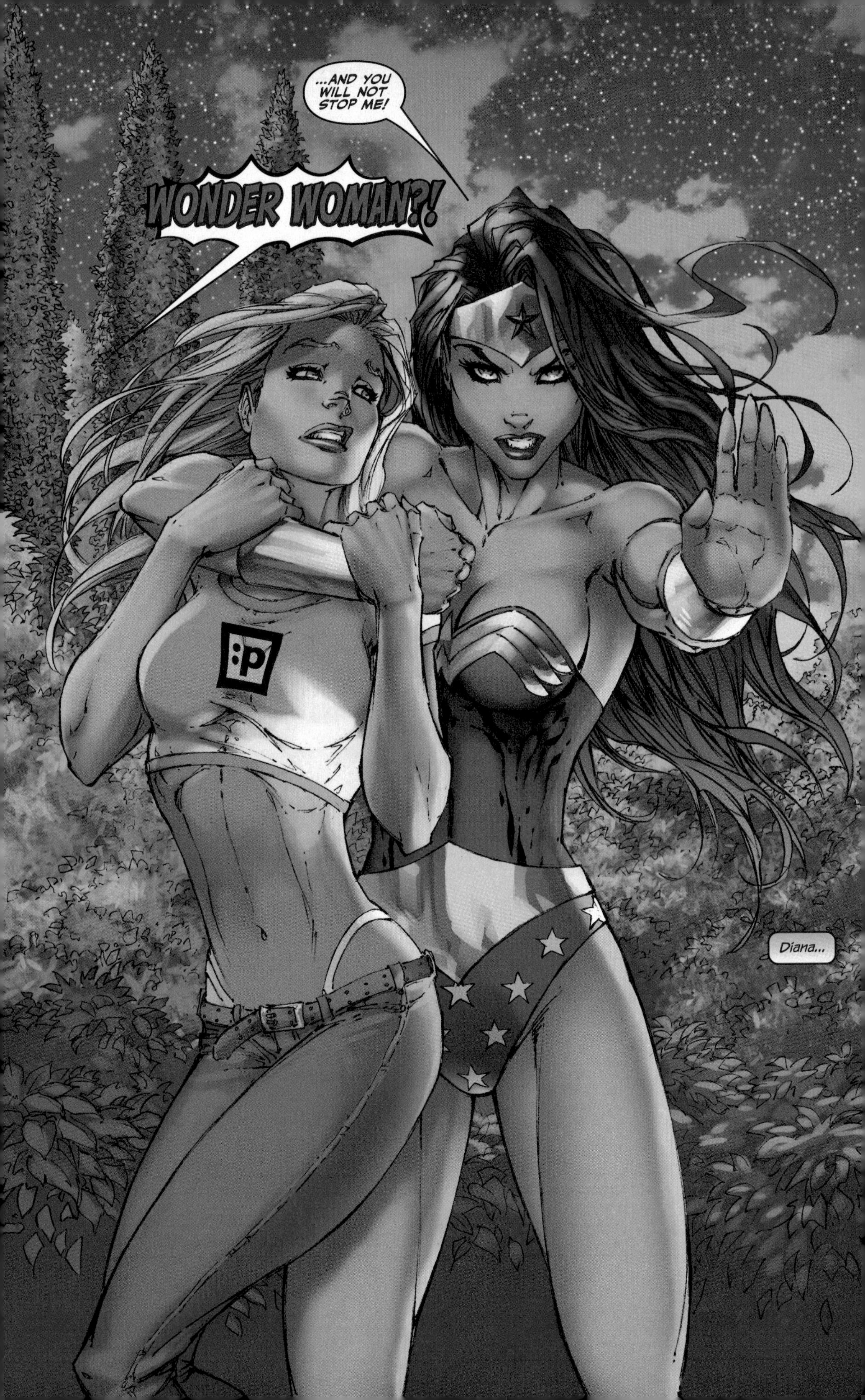
WONDER WOMAN?!
...AND YOU WILL NOT STOP ME!
Diana...

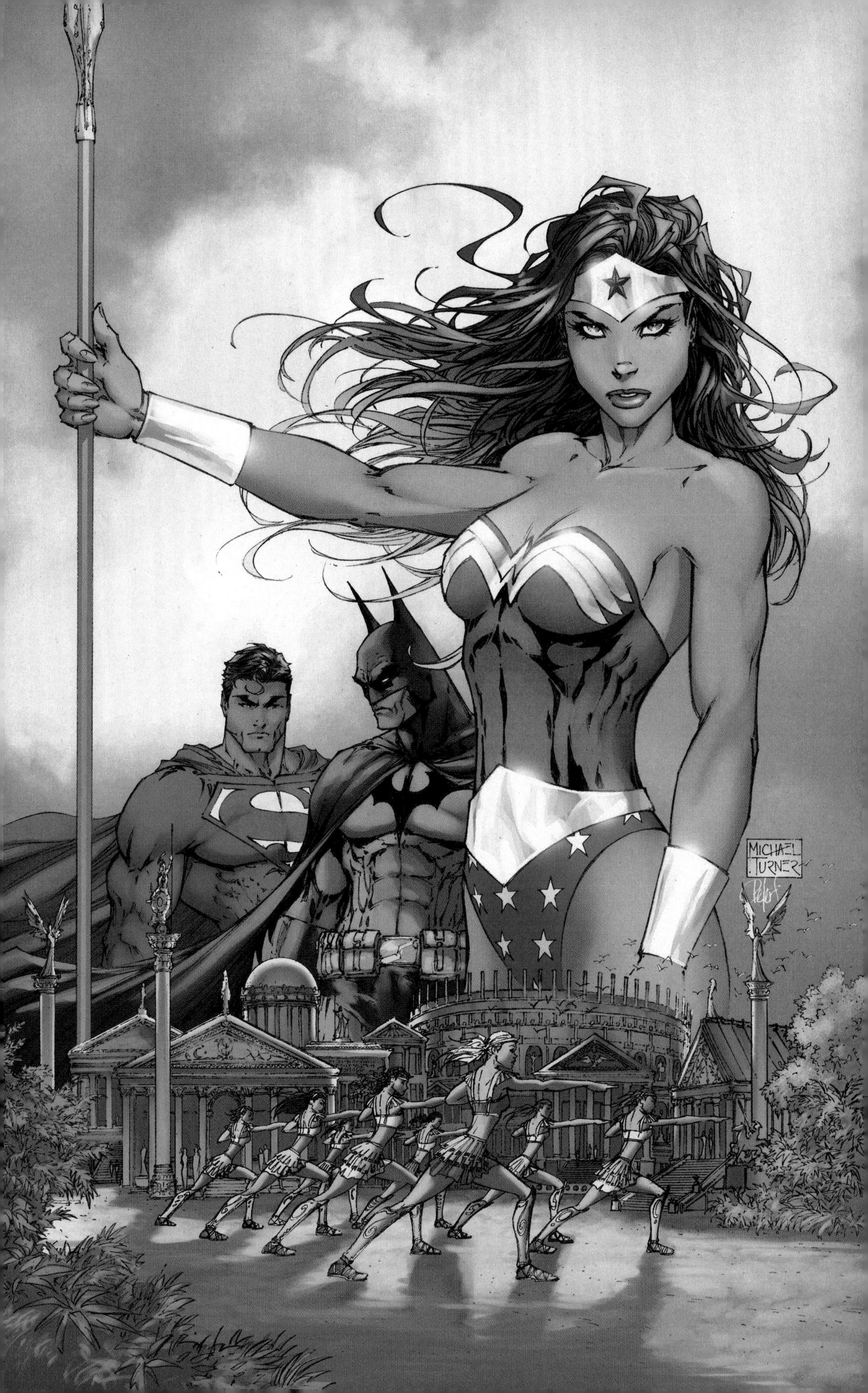
MICHAEL TURNER

WARRIOR

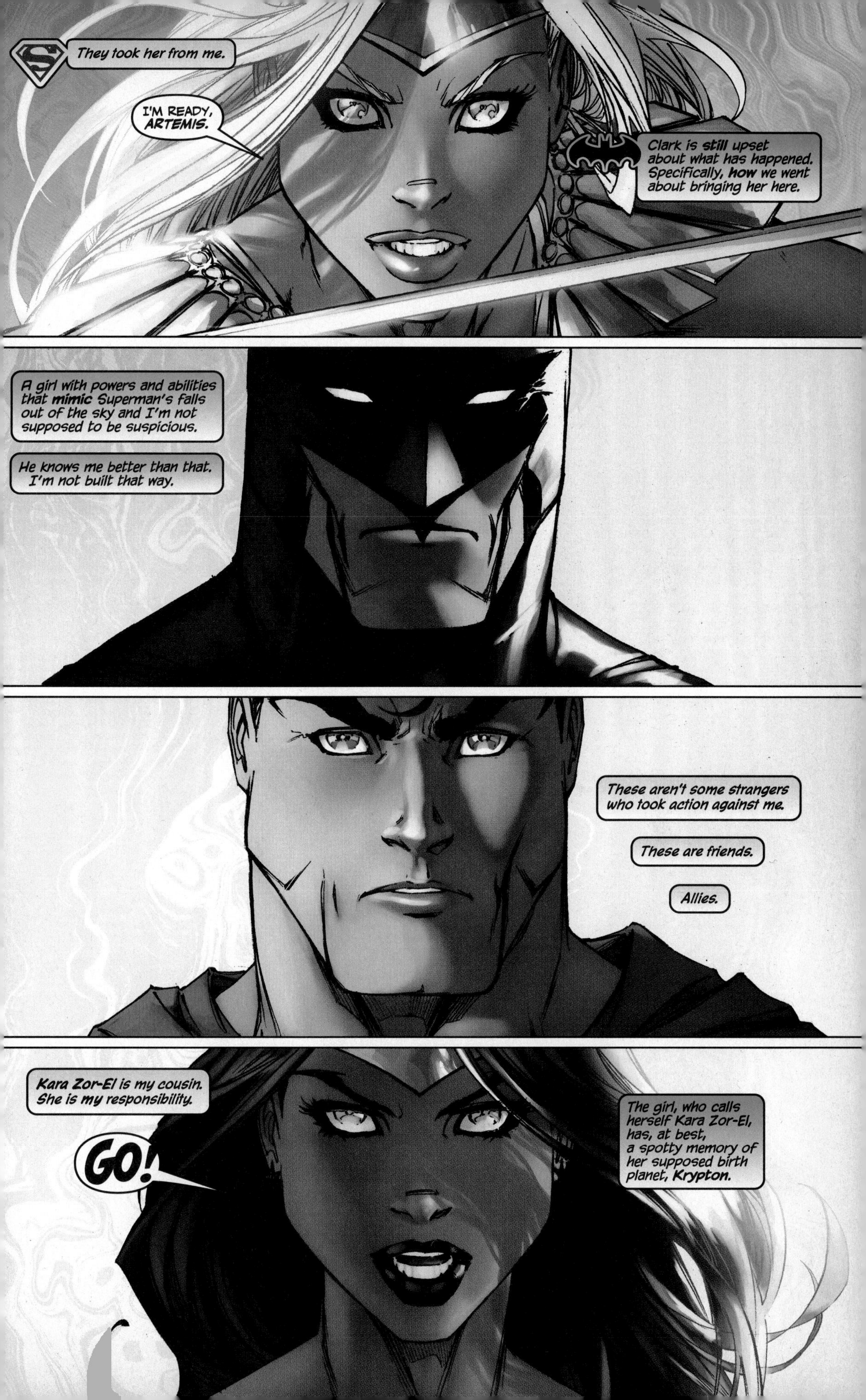

They took her from me.
I'M READY, ARTEMIS.
Clark is still upset about what has happened. Specifically, how we went about bringing her here.
A girl with powers and abilities that mimic Superman's falls out of the sky and I'm not supposed to be suspicious.
He knows me better than that. I'm not built that way.
These aren't some strangers who took action against me.
These are friends.
Allies.
Kara Zor-El is my cousin. She is my responsibility.
GO!
The girl, who calls herself Kara Zor-El, has, at best, a spotty memory of her supposed birth planet, Krypton.

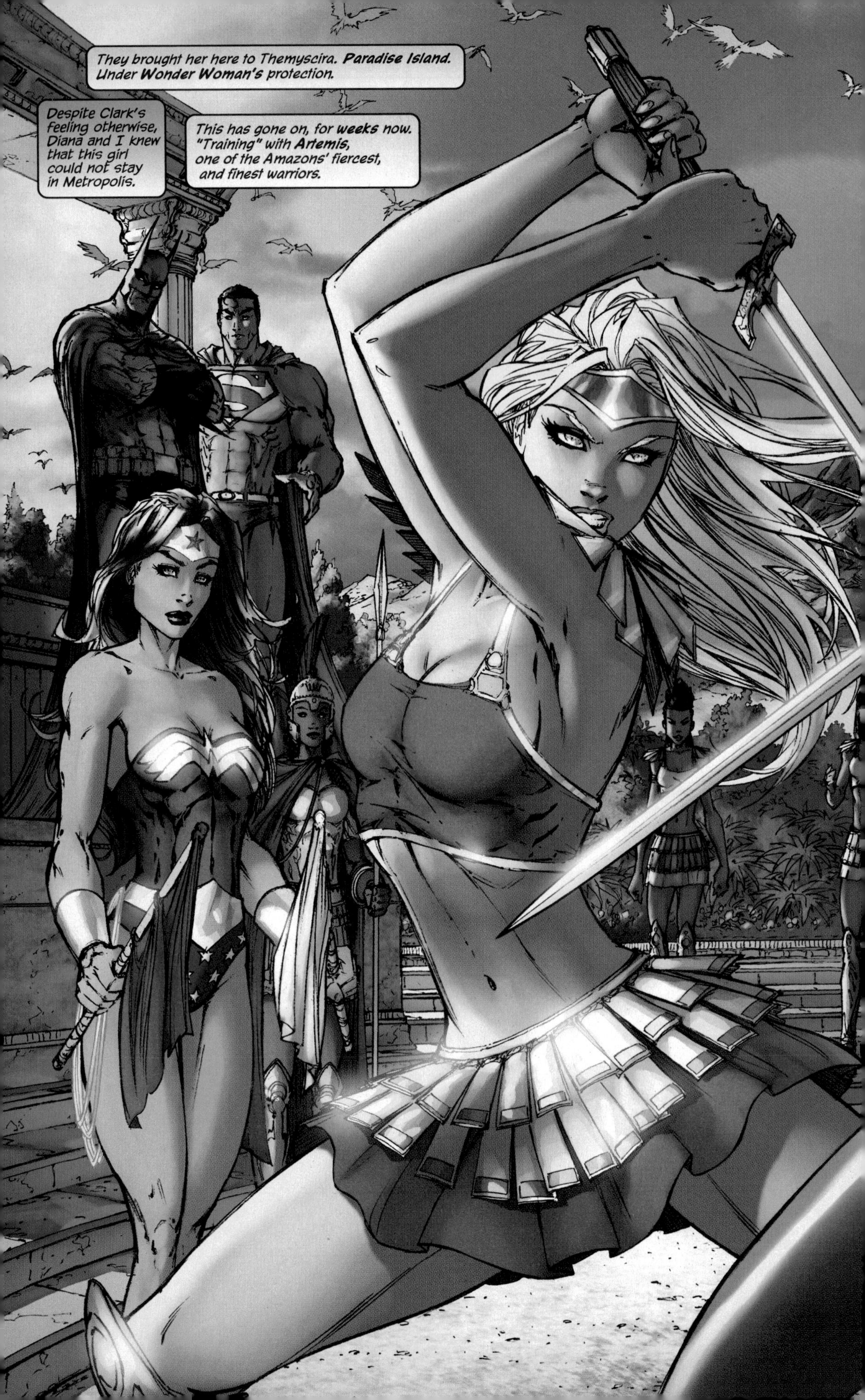
They brought her here to Themyscira. Paradise Island. Under Wonder Woman's protection.
Despite Clark's feeling otherwise, Diana and I knew that this girl could not stay in Metropolis.
This has gone on, for weeks now. "Training" with Artemis, one of the Amazons' fiercest, and finest warriors.

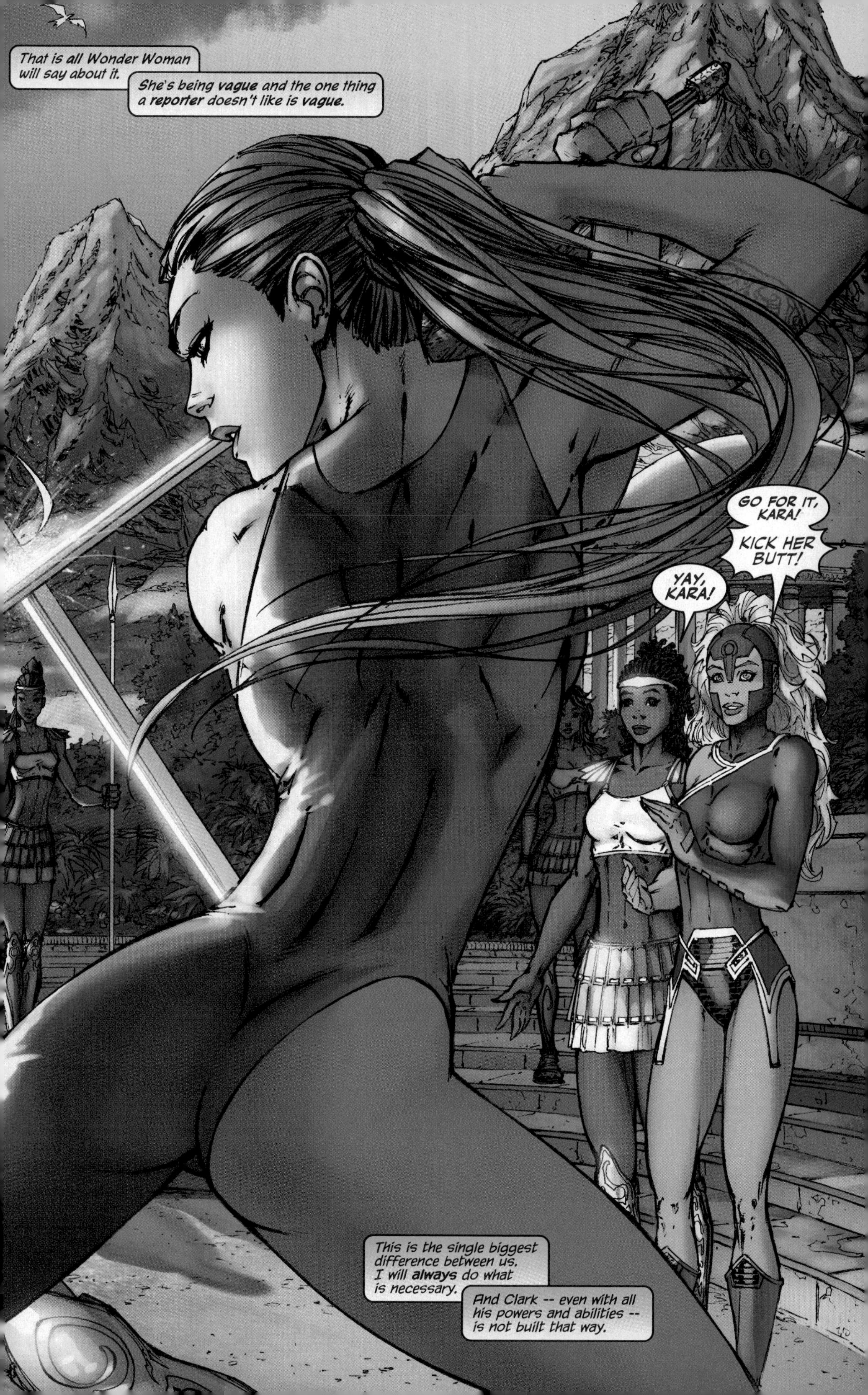
That is all Wonder Woman will say about it.
She's being **vague** and the one thing a **reporter** doesn't like is **vague.**
GO FOR IT, KARA!
KICK HER BUTT!
YAY, KARA!
This is the single biggest difference between us. I will **always** do what is necessary.
And Clark -- even with all his powers and abilities -- is not built that way.

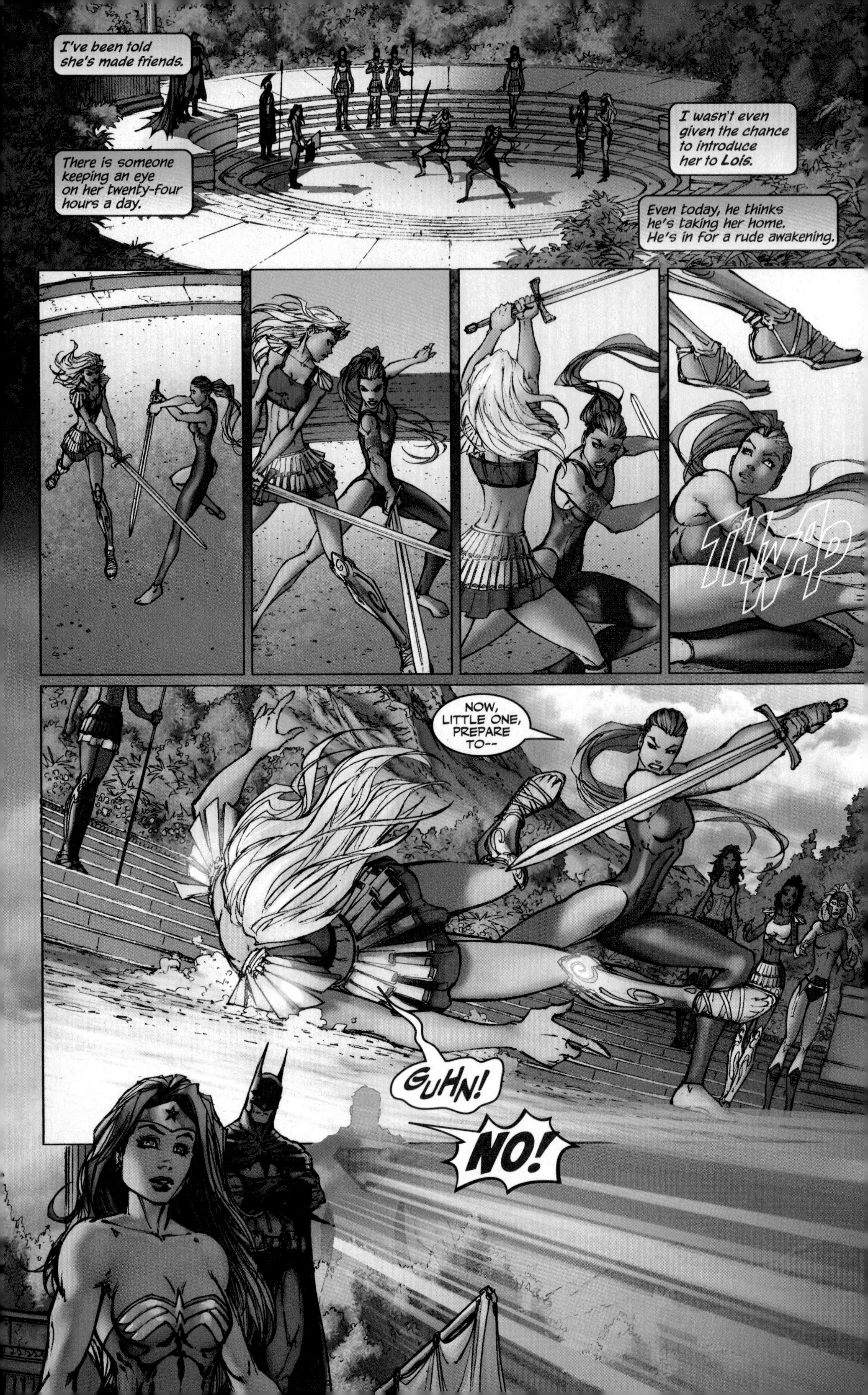
I've been told she's made friends.
There is someone keeping an eye on her twenty-four hours a day.
I wasn't even given the chance to introduce her to Lois.
Even today, he thinks he's taking her home. He's in for a rude awakening.
THWAP
NOW, LITTLE ONE, PREPARE TO--
GUHN!
NO!

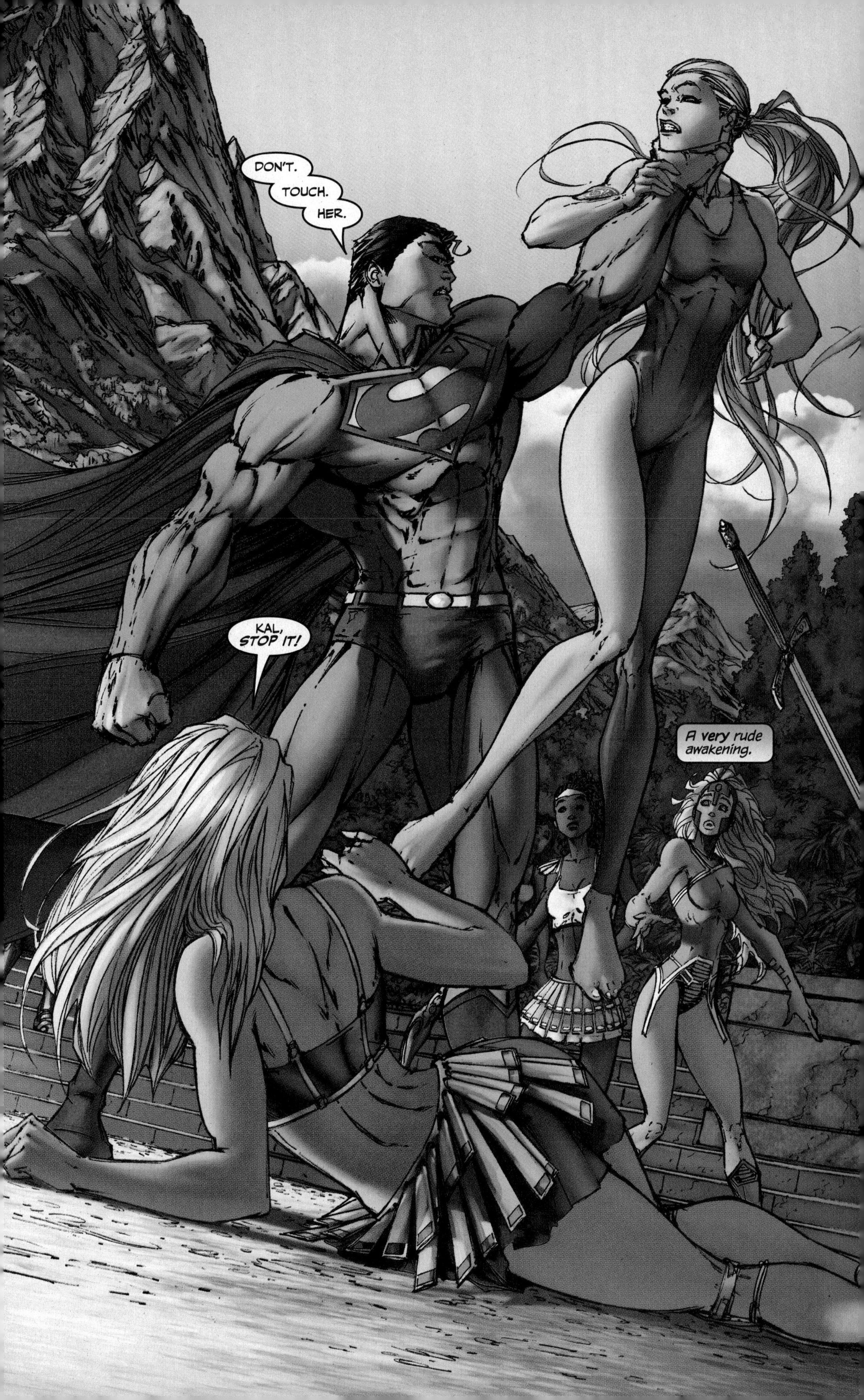
DON'T.
TOUCH.
HER.
KAL, STOP IT!
A very rude awakening.

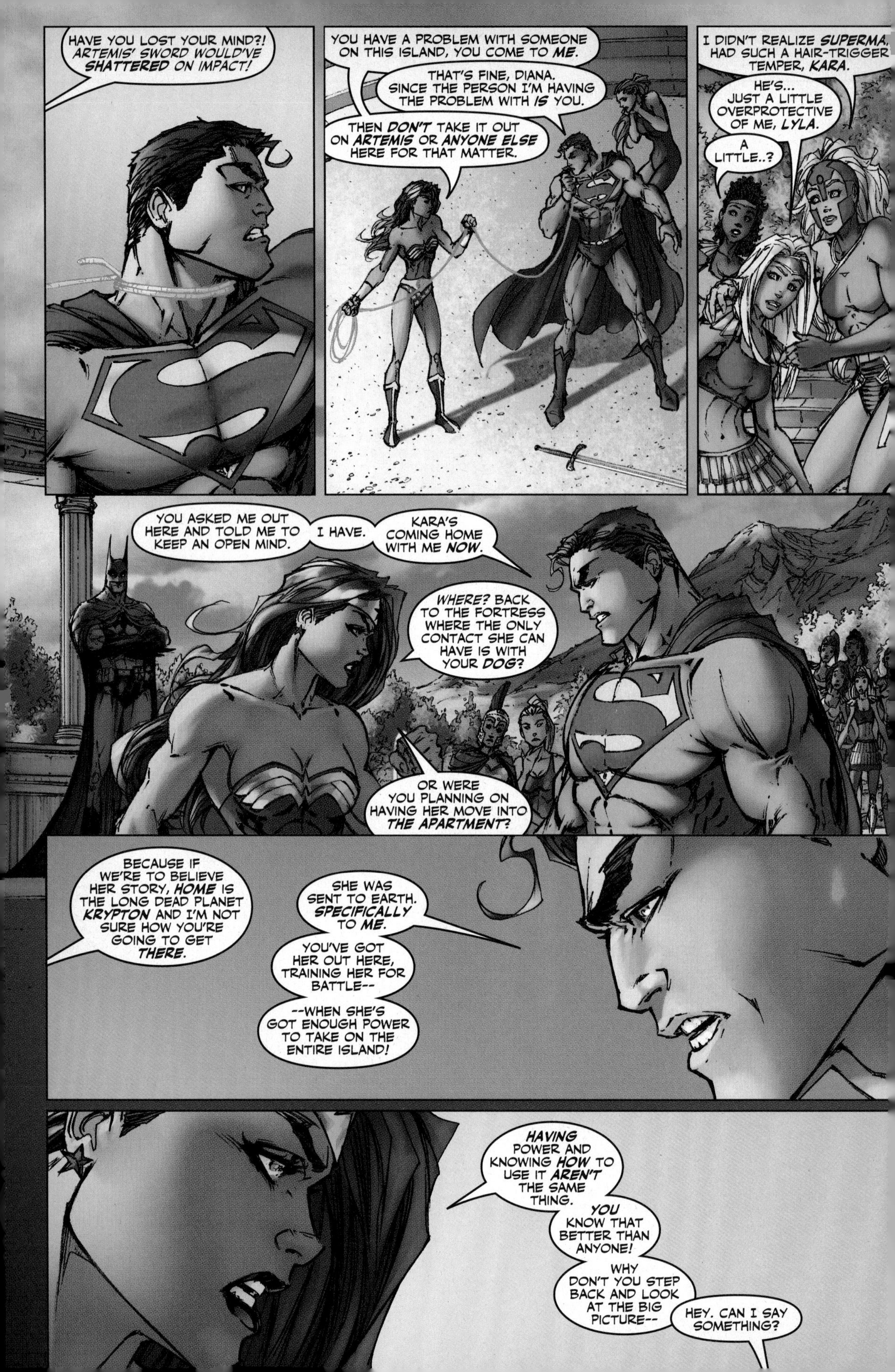

HAVE YOU LOST YOUR MIND?! ARTEMIS' SWORD WOULD'VE SHATTERED ON IMPACT!
YOU HAVE A PROBLEM WITH SOMEONE ON THIS ISLAND, YOU COME TO ME.
THAT'S FINE, DIANA. SINCE THE PERSON I'M HAVING THE PROBLEM WITH IS YOU.
THEN DON'T TAKE IT OUT ON ARTEMIS OR ANYONE ELSE HERE FOR THAT MATTER.
I DIDN'T REALIZE SUPERMA HAD SUCH A HAIR-TRIGGER TEMPER, KARA.
HE'S... JUST A LITTLE OVERPROTECTIVE OF ME, LYLA.
A LITTLE..?
YOU ASKED ME OUT HERE AND TOLD ME TO KEEP AN OPEN MIND.
I HAVE.
KARA'S COMING HOME WITH ME NOW.
WHERE? BACK TO THE FORTRESS WHERE THE ONLY CONTACT SHE CAN HAVE IS WITH YOUR DOG?
OR WERE YOU PLANNING ON HAVING HER MOVE INTO THE APARTMENT?
BECAUSE IF WE'RE TO BELIEVE HER STORY, HOME IS THE LONG DEAD PLANET KRYPTON AND I'M NOT SURE HOW YOU'RE GOING TO GET THERE.
SHE WAS SENT TO EARTH. SPECIFICALLY TO ME.
YOU'VE GOT HER OUT HERE, TRAINING HER FOR BATTLE--
--WHEN SHE'S GOT ENOUGH POWER TO TAKE ON THE ENTIRE ISLAND!
HAVING POWER AND KNOWING HOW TO USE IT AREN'T THE SAME THING.
YOU KNOW THAT BETTER THAN ANYONE!
WHY DON'T YOU STEP BACK AND LOOK AT THE BIG PICTURE--
HEY. CAN I SAY SOMETHING?

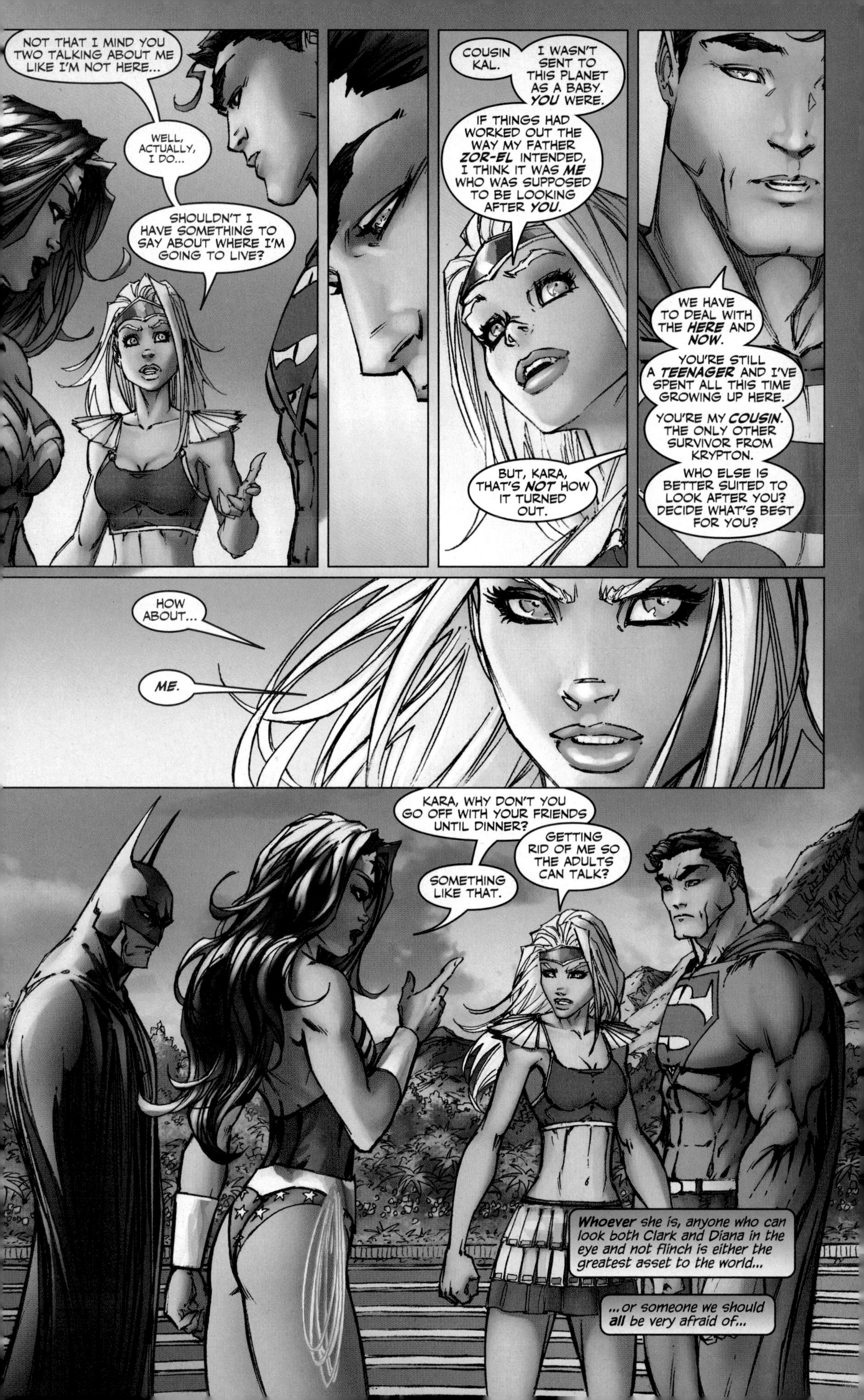
NOT THAT I MIND YOU TWO TALKING ABOUT ME LIKE I'M NOT HERE...
WELL, ACTUALLY, I DO...
SHOULDN'T I HAVE SOMETHING TO SAY ABOUT WHERE I'M GOING TO LIVE?
COUSIN KAL.
I WASN'T SENT TO THIS PLANET AS A BABY. YOU WERE.
IF THINGS HAD WORKED OUT THE WAY MY FATHER ZOR-EL INTENDED, I THINK IT WAS ME WHO WAS SUPPOSED TO BE LOOKING AFTER YOU.
BUT, KARA, THAT'S NOT HOW IT TURNED OUT.
WE HAVE TO DEAL WITH THE HERE AND NOW.
YOU'RE STILL A TEENAGER AND I'VE SPENT ALL THIS TIME GROWING UP HERE.
YOU'RE MY COUSIN. THE ONLY OTHER SURVIVOR FROM KRYPTON.
WHO ELSE IS BETTER SUITED TO LOOK AFTER YOU? DECIDE WHAT'S BEST FOR YOU?
HOW ABOUT...
ME.
KARA, WHY DON'T YOU GO OFF WITH YOUR FRIENDS UNTIL DINNER?
GETTING RID OF ME SO THE ADULTS CAN TALK?
SOMETHING LIKE THAT.
Whoever she is, anyone who can look both Clark and Diana in the eye and not flinch is either the greatest asset to the world...
...or someone we should all be very afraid of...

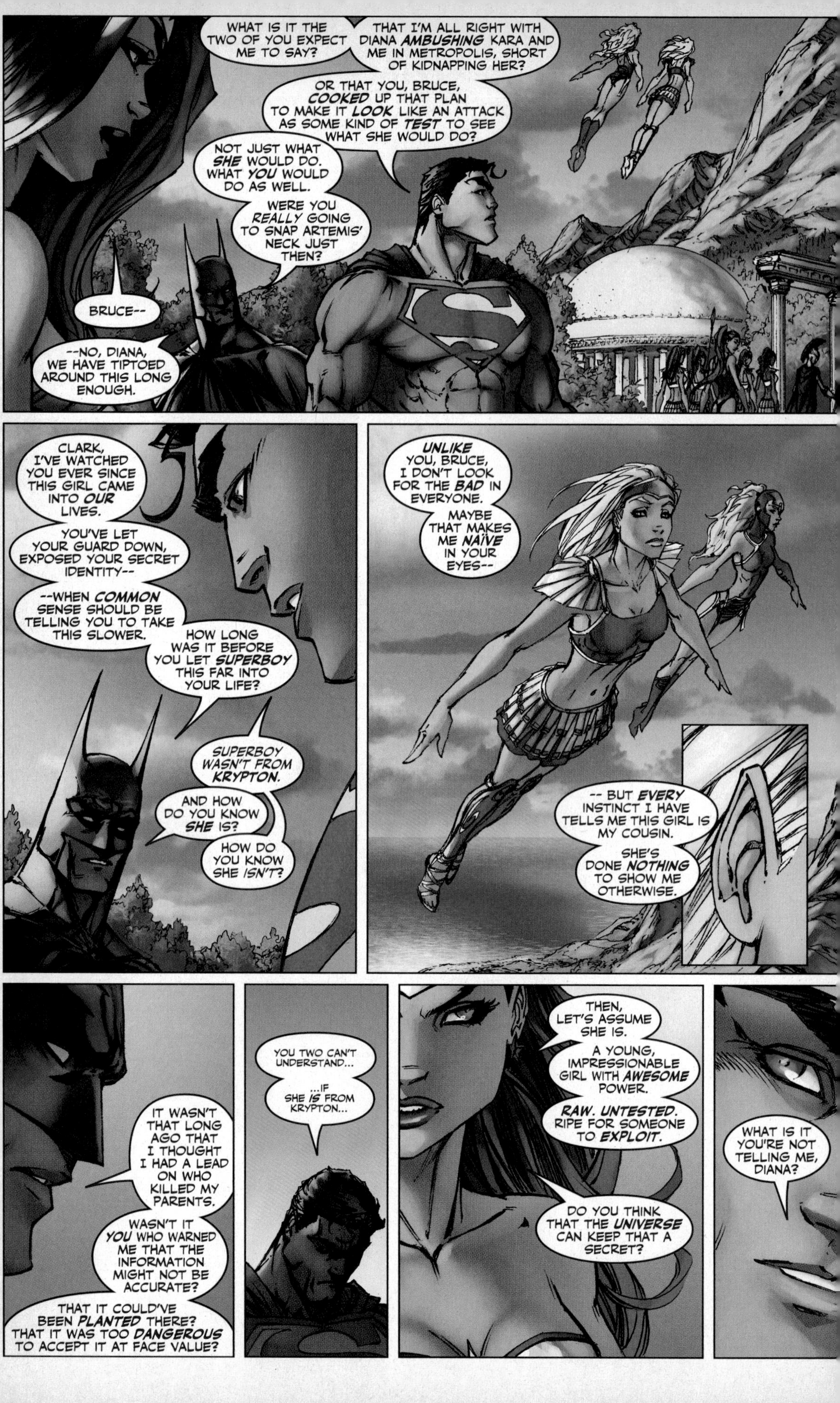

WHAT IS IT THE TWO OF YOU EXPECT ME TO SAY?
THAT I'M ALL RIGHT WITH DIANA AMBUSHING KARA AND ME IN METROPOLIS, SHORT OF KIDNAPPING HER?
OR THAT YOU, BRUCE, COOKED UP THAT PLAN TO MAKE IT LOOK LIKE AN ATTACK AS SOME KIND OF TEST TO SEE WHAT SHE WOULD DO?
NOT JUST WHAT SHE WOULD DO. WHAT YOU WOULD DO AS WELL.
WERE YOU REALLY GOING TO SNAP ARTEMIS' NECK JUST THEN?
BRUCE--
--NO, DIANA, WE HAVE TIPTOED AROUND THIS LONG ENOUGH.
CLARK, I'VE WATCHED YOU EVER SINCE THIS GIRL CAME INTO OUR LIVES.
YOU'VE LET YOUR GUARD DOWN, EXPOSED YOUR SECRET IDENTITY--
--WHEN COMMON SENSE SHOULD BE TELLING YOU TO TAKE THIS SLOWER.
HOW LONG WAS IT BEFORE YOU LET SUPERBOY THIS FAR INTO YOUR LIFE?
SUPERBOY WASN'T FROM KRYPTON.
AND HOW DO YOU KNOW SHE IS?
HOW DO YOU KNOW SHE ISN'T?
UNLIKE YOU, BRUCE, I DON'T LOOK FOR THE BAD IN EVERYONE.
MAYBE THAT MAKES ME NAÏVE IN YOUR EYES--
-- BUT EVERY INSTINCT I HAVE TELLS ME THIS GIRL IS MY COUSIN.
SHE'S DONE NOTHING TO SHOW ME OTHERWISE.
IT WASN'T THAT LONG AGO THAT I THOUGHT I HAD A LEAD ON WHO KILLED MY PARENTS.
WASN'T IT YOU WHO WARNED ME THAT THE INFORMATION MIGHT NOT BE ACCURATE?
THAT IT COULD'VE BEEN PLANTED THERE? THAT IT WAS TOO DANGEROUS TO ACCEPT IT AT FACE VALUE?
YOU TWO CAN'T UNDERSTAND...
...IF SHE IS FROM KRYPTON...
THEN, LET'S ASSUME SHE IS.
A YOUNG, IMPRESSIONABLE GIRL WITH AWESOME POWER.
RAW. UNTESTED. RIPE FOR SOMEONE TO EXPLOIT.
DO YOU THINK THAT THE UNIVERSE CAN KEEP THAT A SECRET?
WHAT IS IT YOU'RE NOT TELLING ME, DIANA?

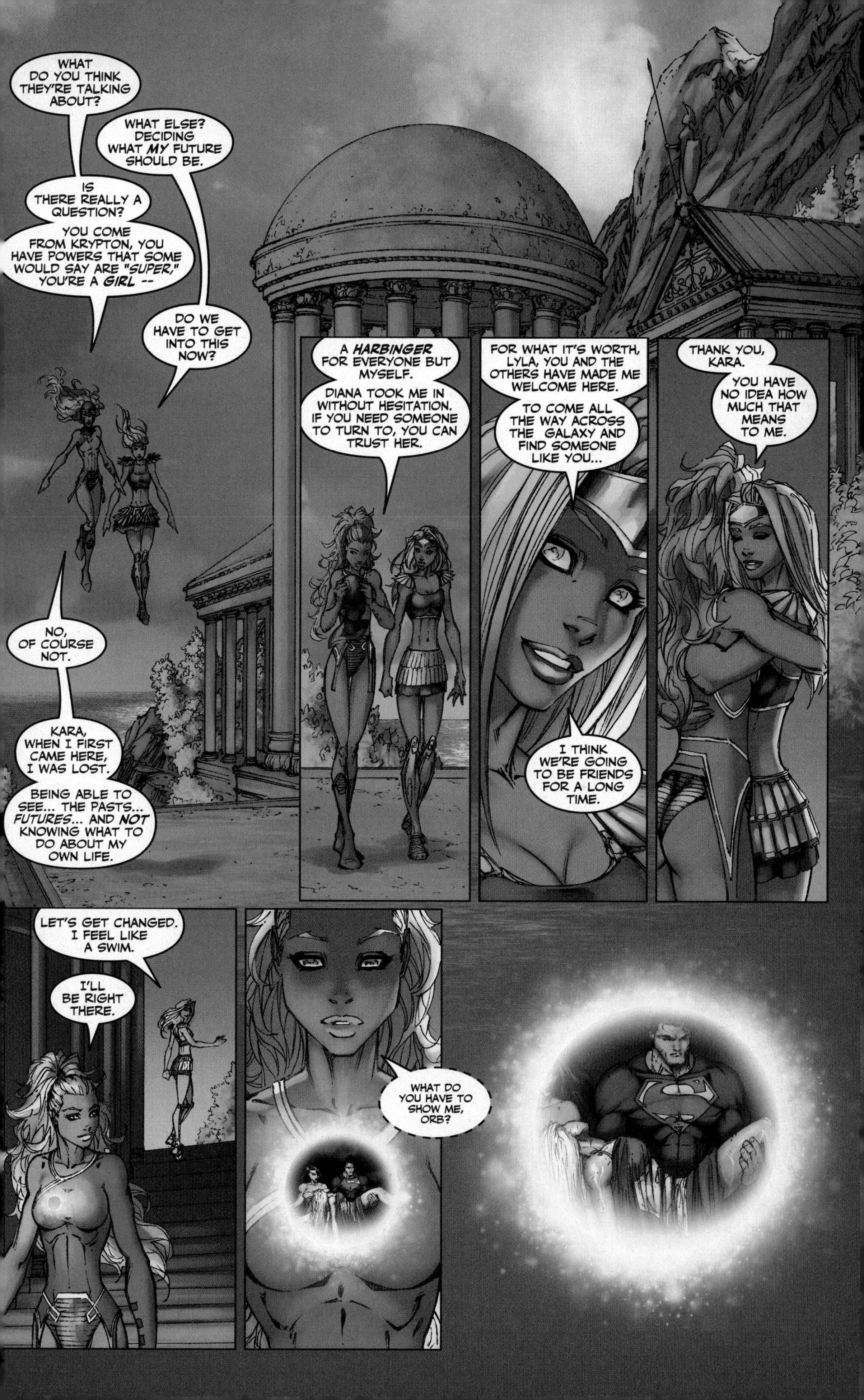
WHAT DO YOU THINK THEY'RE TALKING ABOUT?
WHAT ELSE? DECIDING WHAT *MY* FUTURE SHOULD BE.
IS THERE REALLY A QUESTION?
YOU COME FROM KRYPTON, YOU HAVE POWERS THAT SOME WOULD SAY ARE "*SUPER*," YOU'RE A *GIRL* --
DO WE HAVE TO GET INTO THIS NOW?
NO, OF COURSE NOT.
KARA, WHEN I FIRST CAME HERE, I WAS LOST.
BEING ABLE TO SEE... THE PASTS... *FUTURES*... AND *NOT* KNOWING WHAT TO DO ABOUT MY OWN LIFE.
A *HARBINGER* FOR EVERYONE BUT MYSELF.
DIANA TOOK ME IN WITHOUT HESITATION. IF YOU NEED SOMEONE TO TURN TO, YOU CAN TRUST HER.
FOR WHAT IT'S WORTH, LYLA, YOU AND THE OTHERS HAVE MADE ME WELCOME HERE.
TO COME ALL THE WAY ACROSS THE GALAXY AND FIND SOMEONE LIKE YOU...
I THINK WE'RE GOING TO BE FRIENDS FOR A LONG TIME.
THANK YOU, KARA.
YOU HAVE NO IDEA HOW MUCH THAT MEANS TO ME.
LET'S GET CHANGED. I FEEL LIKE A SWIM.
I'LL BE RIGHT THERE.
WHAT DO YOU HAVE TO SHOW ME, ORB?

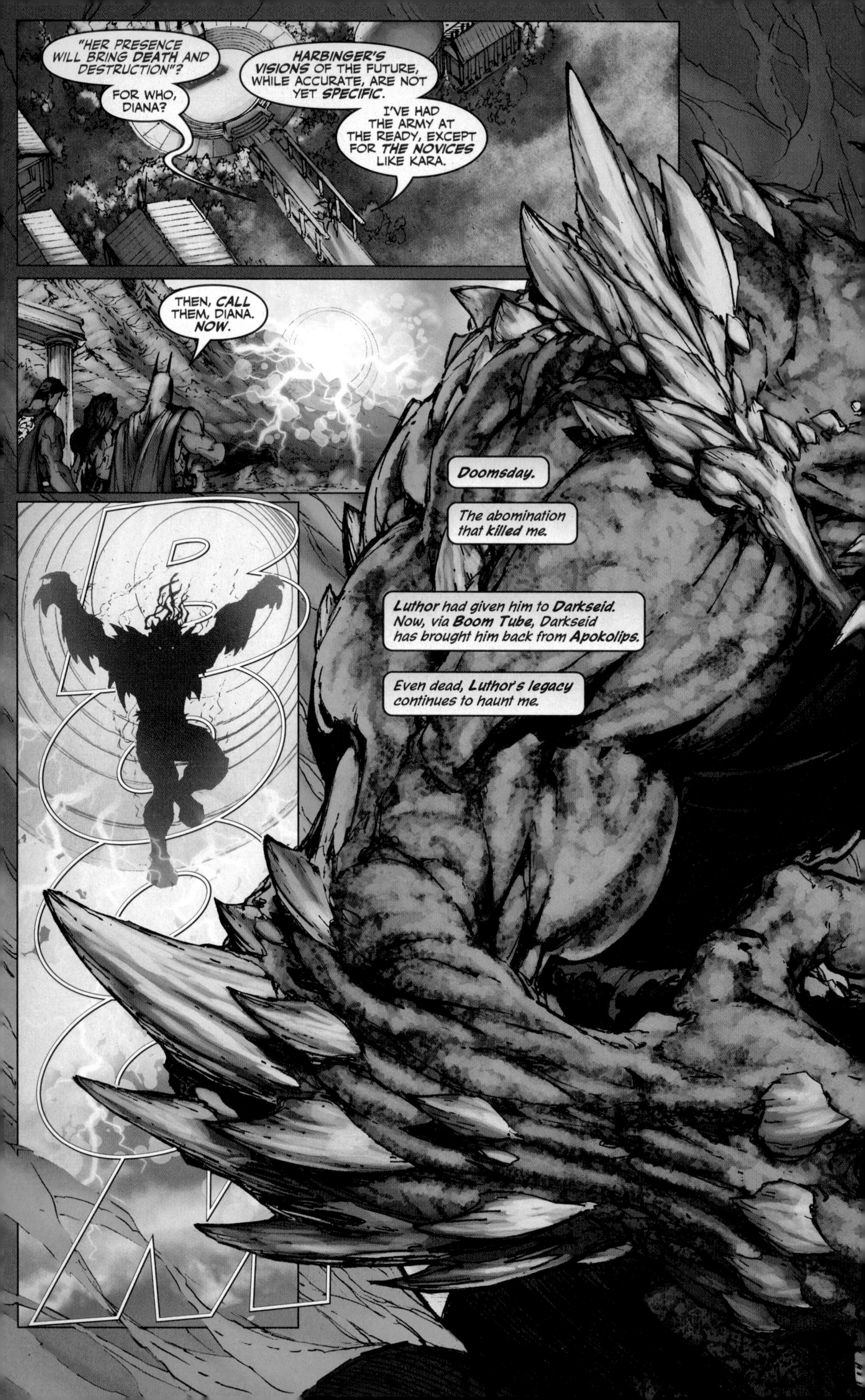
"HER PRESENCE WILL BRING DEATH AND DESTRUCTION"?
FOR WHO, DIANA?
HARBINGER'S VISIONS OF THE FUTURE, WHILE ACCURATE, ARE NOT YET SPECIFIC.
I'VE HAD THE ARMY AT THE READY, EXCEPT FOR THE NOVICES LIKE KARA.
THEN, CALL THEM, DIANA. NOW.
Doomsday.
The abomination that killed me.
Luthor had given him to Darkseid. Now, via Boom Tube, Darkseid has brought him back from Apokolips.
Even dead, Luthor's legacy continues to haunt me.

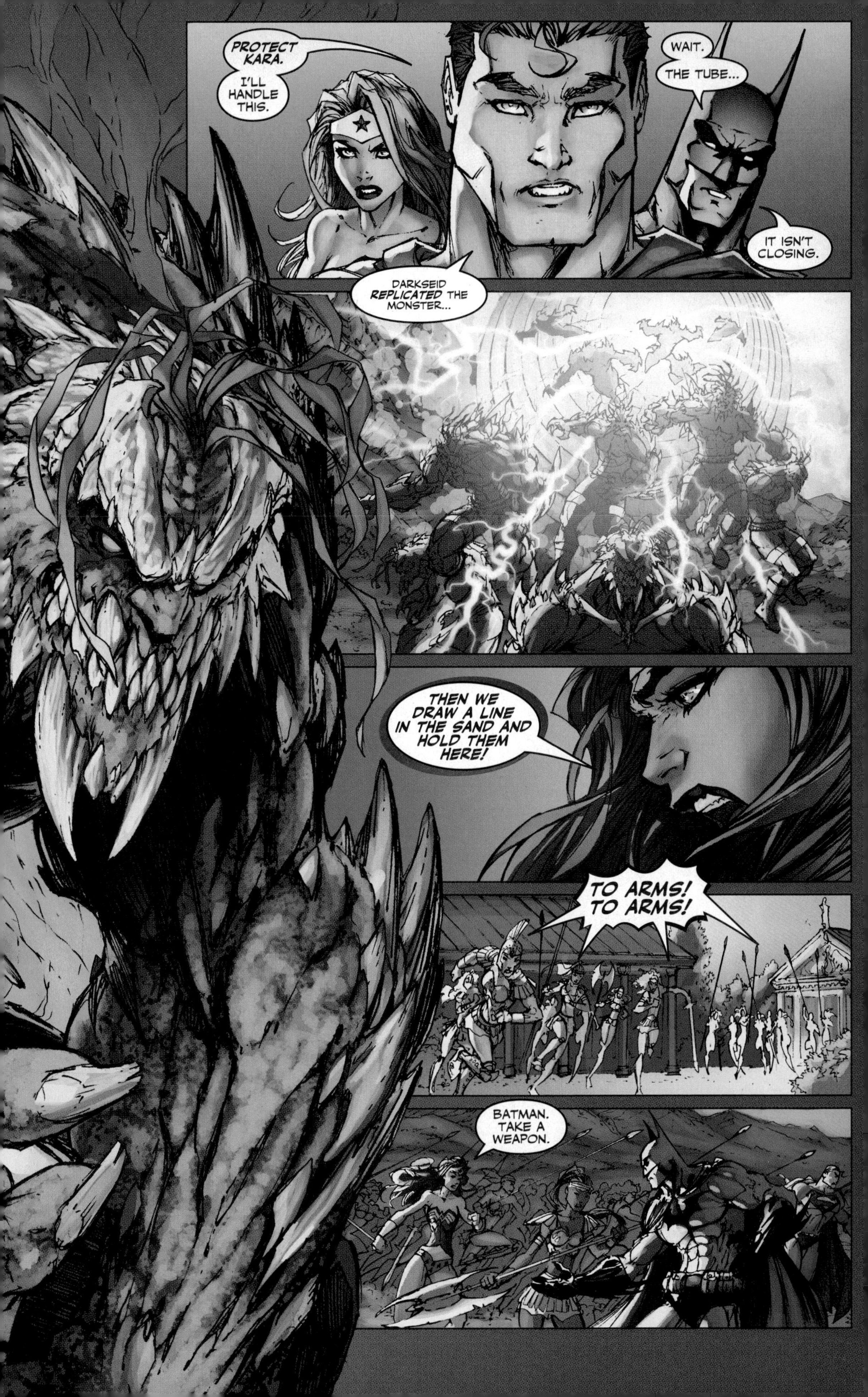
PROTECT KARA.
I'LL HANDLE THIS.
WAIT.
THE TUBE...
IT ISN'T CLOSING.
DARKSEID REPLICATED THE MONSTER...
THEN WE DRAW A LINE IN THE SAND AND HOLD THEM HERE!
TO ARMS! TO ARMS!
BATMAN. TAKE A WEAPON.

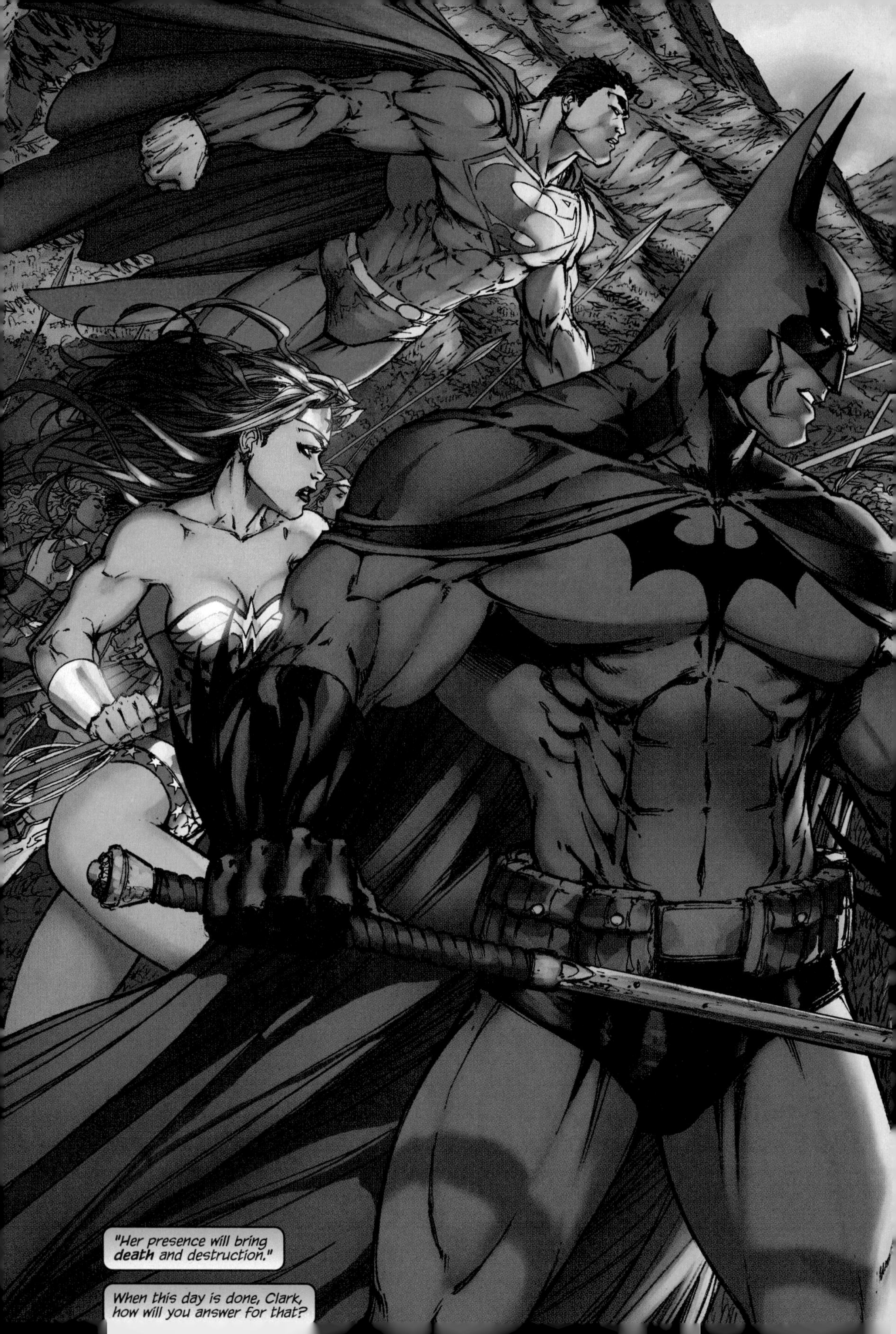
"Her presence will bring **death** and destruction."
When this day is done, Clark, how will you answer for that?

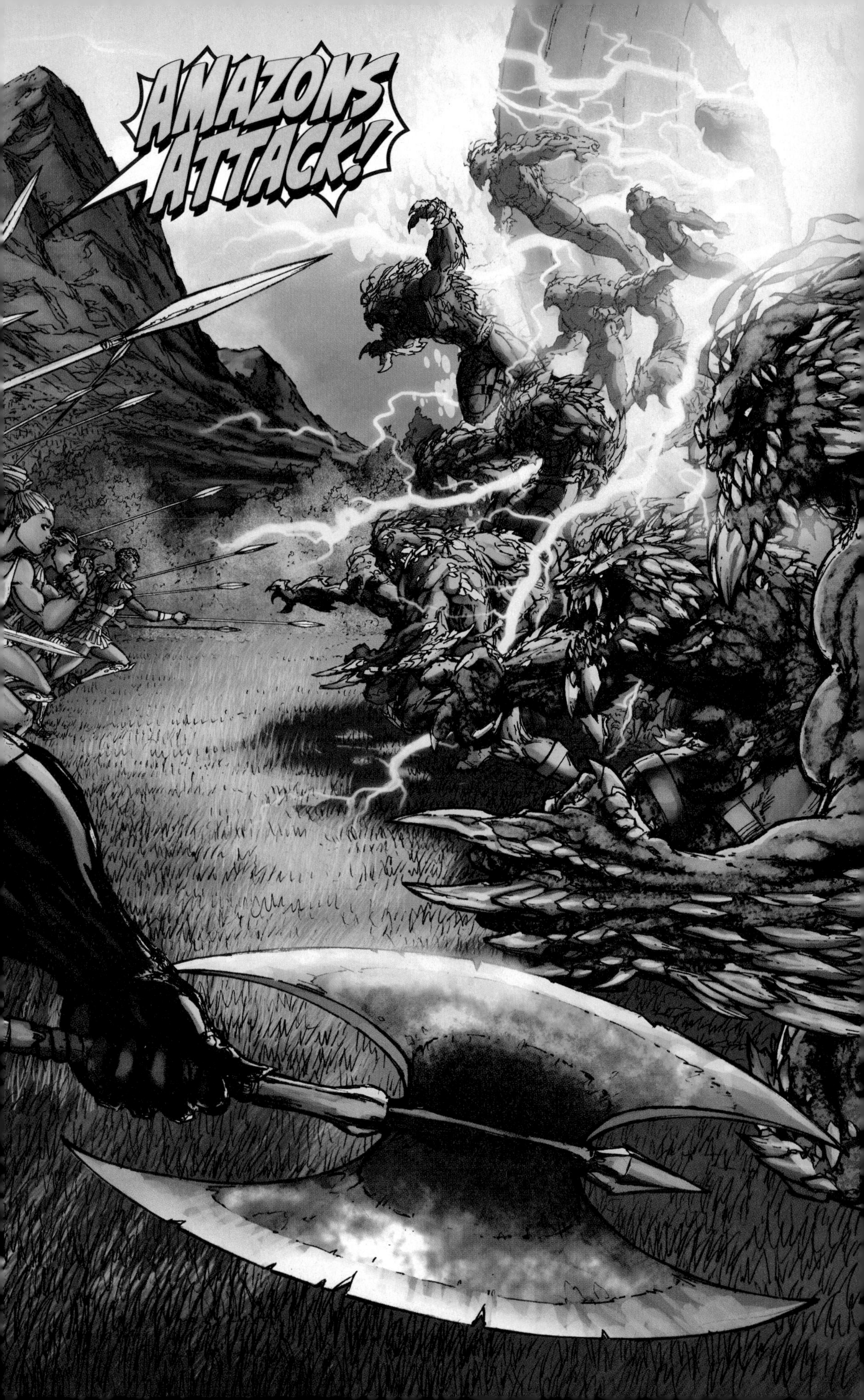
AMAZONS ATTACK!

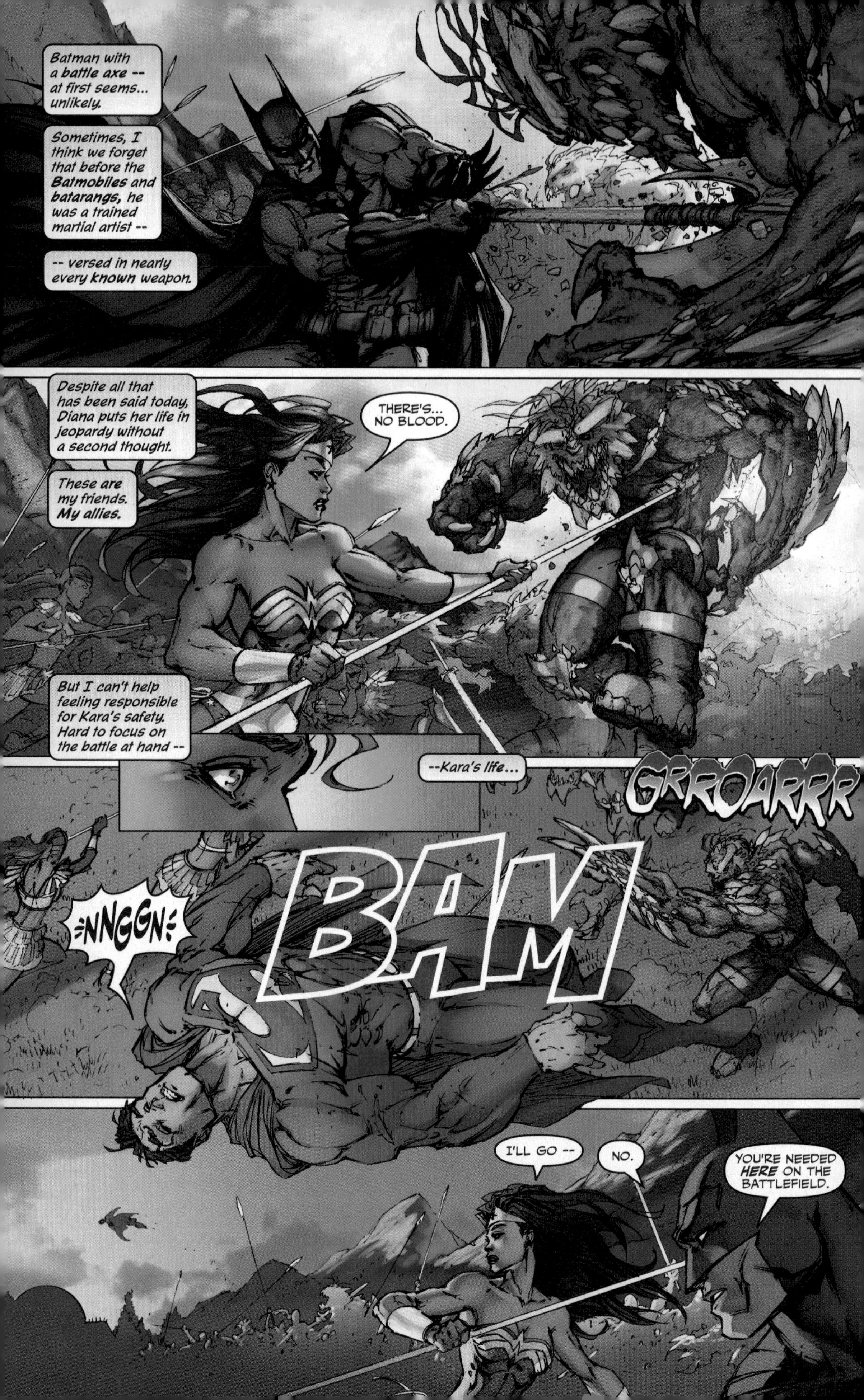

Batman with a battle axe -- at first seems... unlikely.
Sometimes, I think we forget that before the Batmobiles and batarangs, he was a trained martial artist --
-- versed in nearly every known weapon.
Despite all that has been said today, Diana puts her life in jeopardy without a second thought.
THERE'S... NO BLOOD.
These are my friends. My allies.
But I can't help feeling responsible for Kara's safety. Hard to focus on the battle at hand --
--Kara's life...
GRROARRR
BAM
NNGGN
I'LL GO --
NO.
YOU'RE NEEDED HERE ON THE BATTLEFIELD.

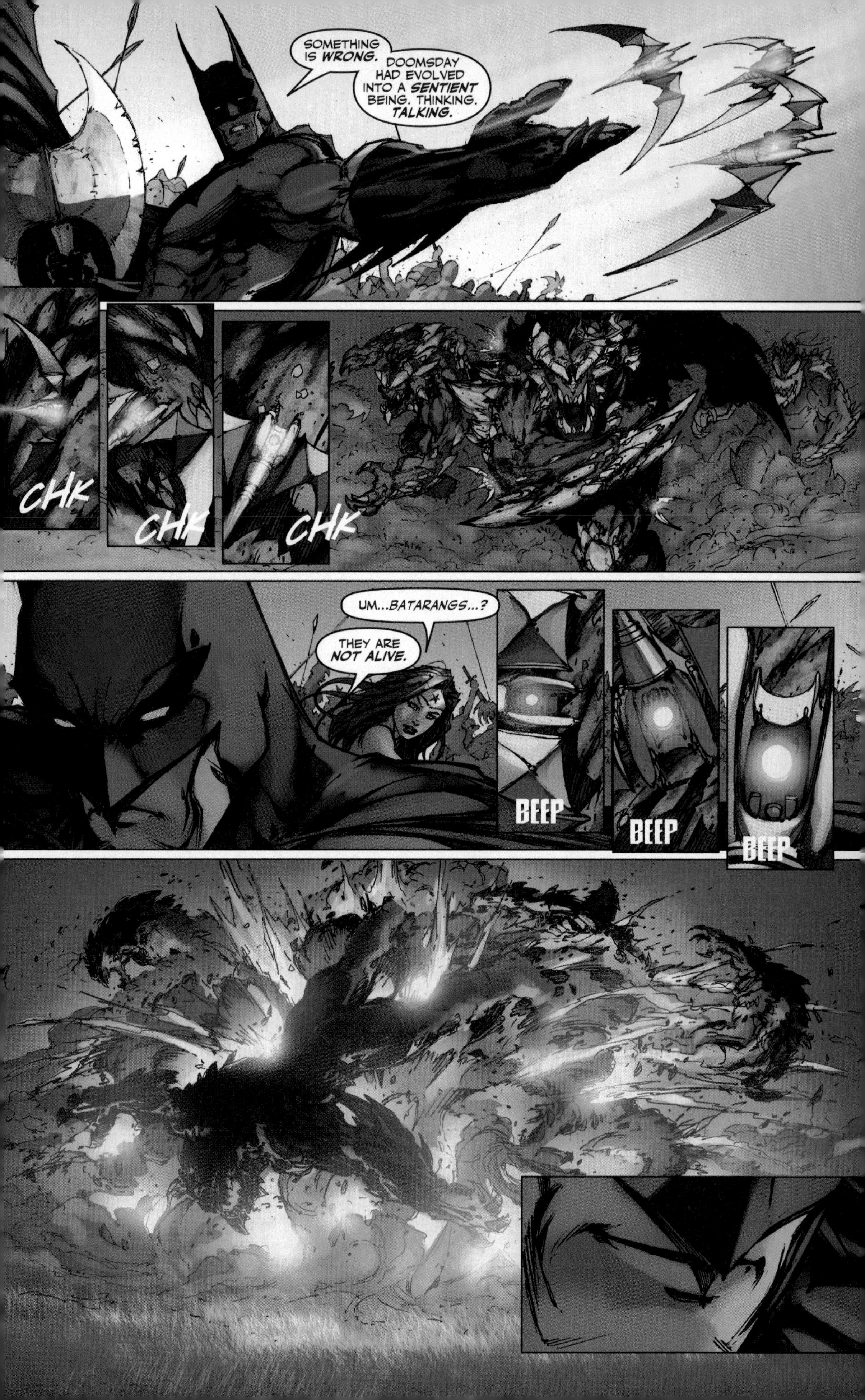
SOMETHING IS WRONG. DOOMSDAY HAD EVOLVED INTO A SENTIENT BEING. THINKING. TALKING.
CHK
CHK
CHK
UM...BATARANGS...?
THEY ARE NOT ALIVE.
BEEP
BEEP
BEEP

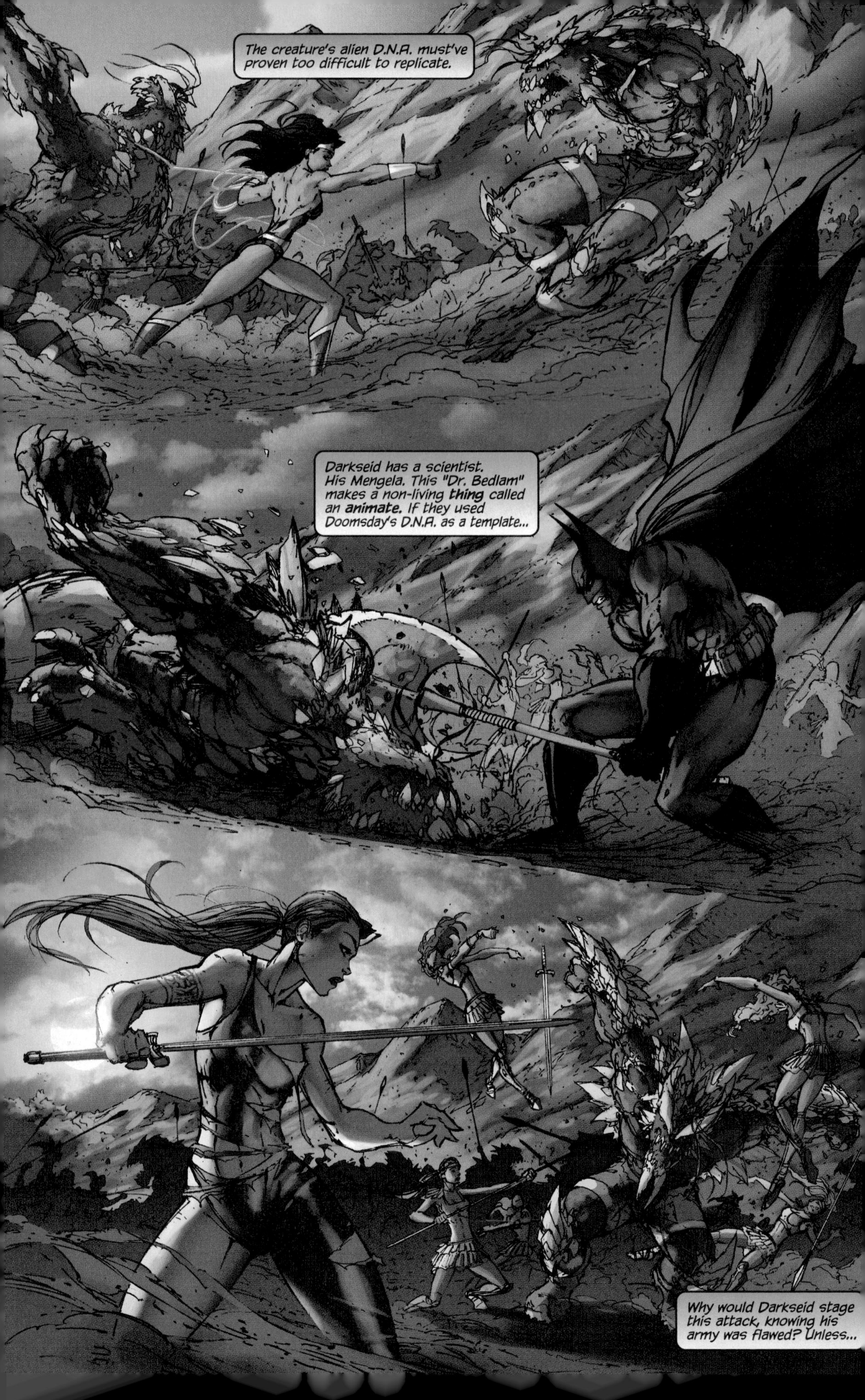
The creature's alien D.N.A. must've proven too difficult to replicate.
Darkseid has a scientist. His Mengela. This "Dr. Bedlam" makes a non-living thing called an animate. If they used Doomsday's D.N.A. as a template...
Why would Darkseid stage this attack, knowing his army was flawed? Unless...

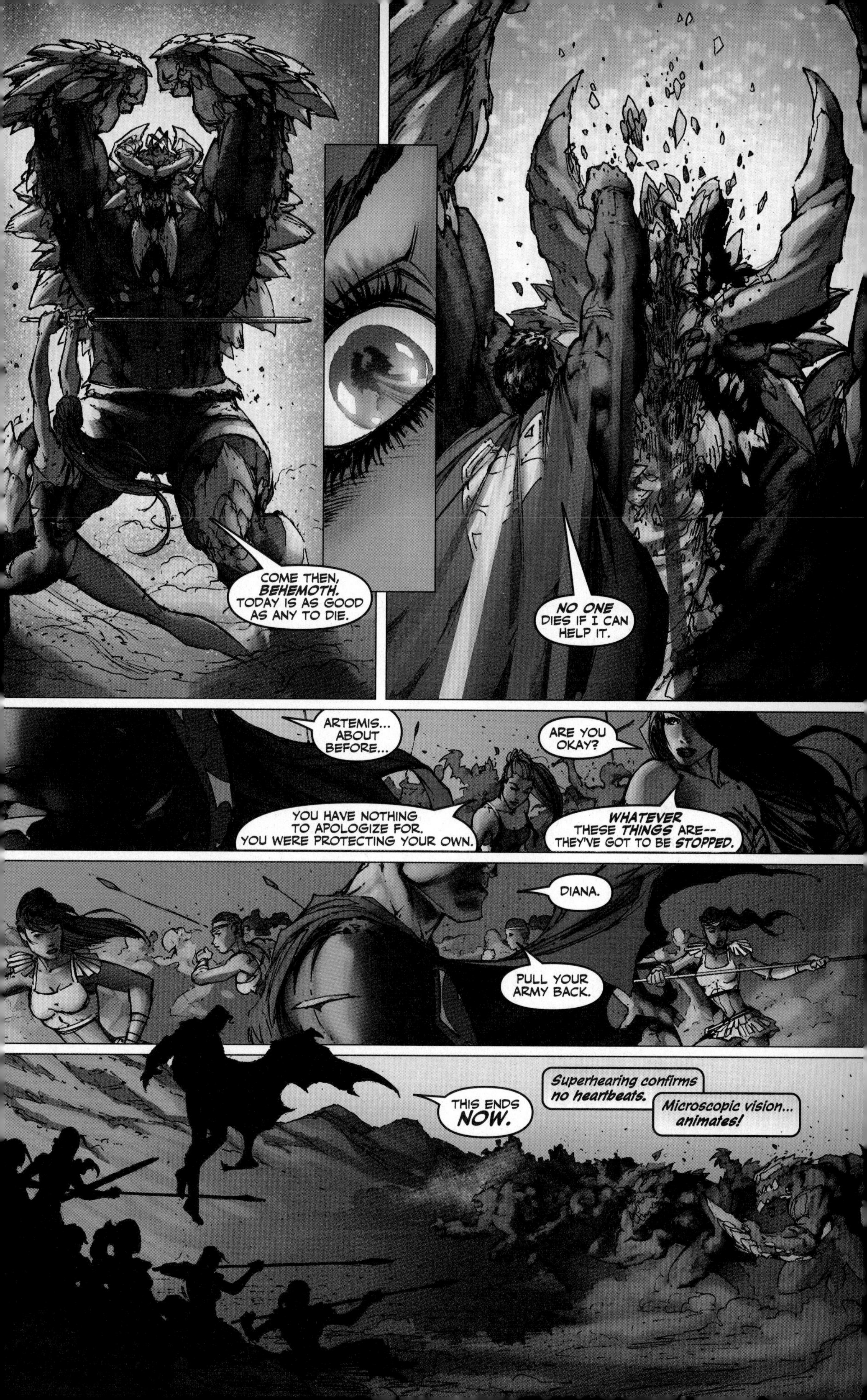
COME THEN, BEHEMOTH. TODAY IS AS GOOD AS ANY TO DIE.
NO ONE DIES IF I CAN HELP IT.
ARTEMIS... ABOUT BEFORE...
YOU HAVE NOTHING TO APOLOGIZE FOR. YOU WERE PROTECTING YOUR OWN.
ARE YOU OKAY?
WHATEVER THESE THINGS ARE-- THEY'VE GOT TO BE STOPPED.
DIANA.
PULL YOUR ARMY BACK.
THIS ENDS NOW.
Superhearing confirms no heartbeats.
Microscopic vision... animates!

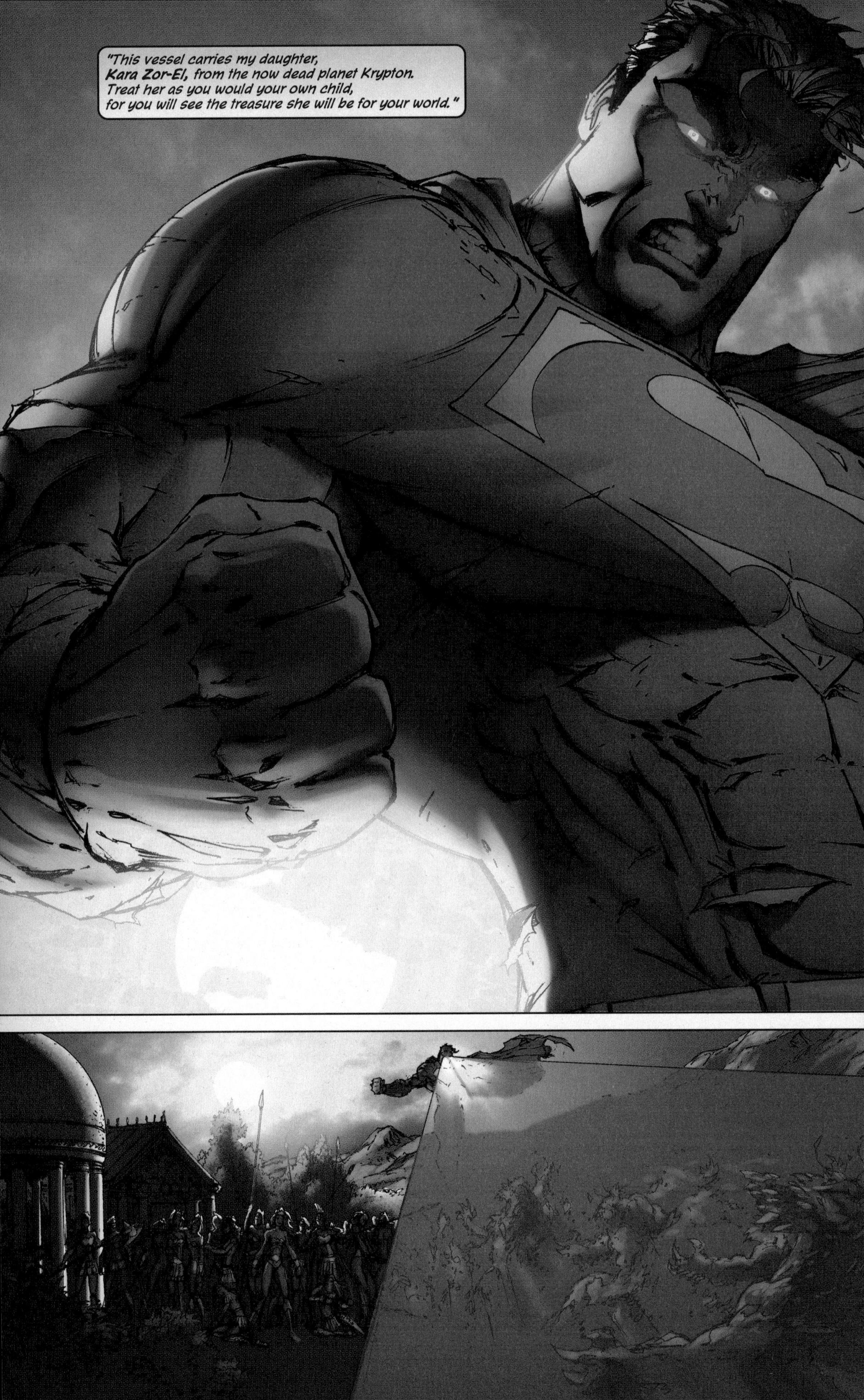
"This vessel carries my daughter, Kara Zor-El, from the now dead planet Krypton. Treat her as you would your own child, for you will see the treasure she will be for your world."

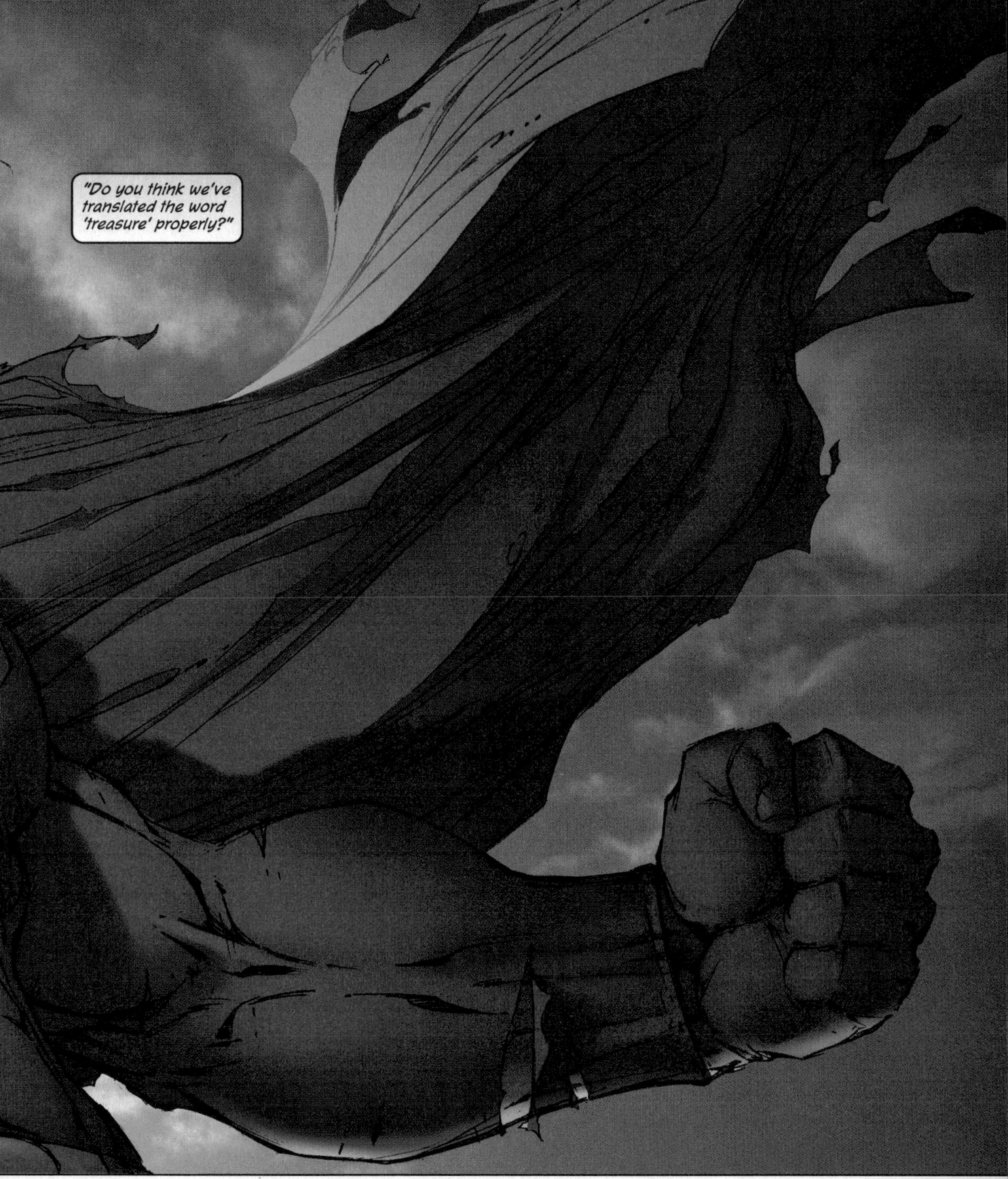
"Do you think we've translated the word 'treasure' properly?"

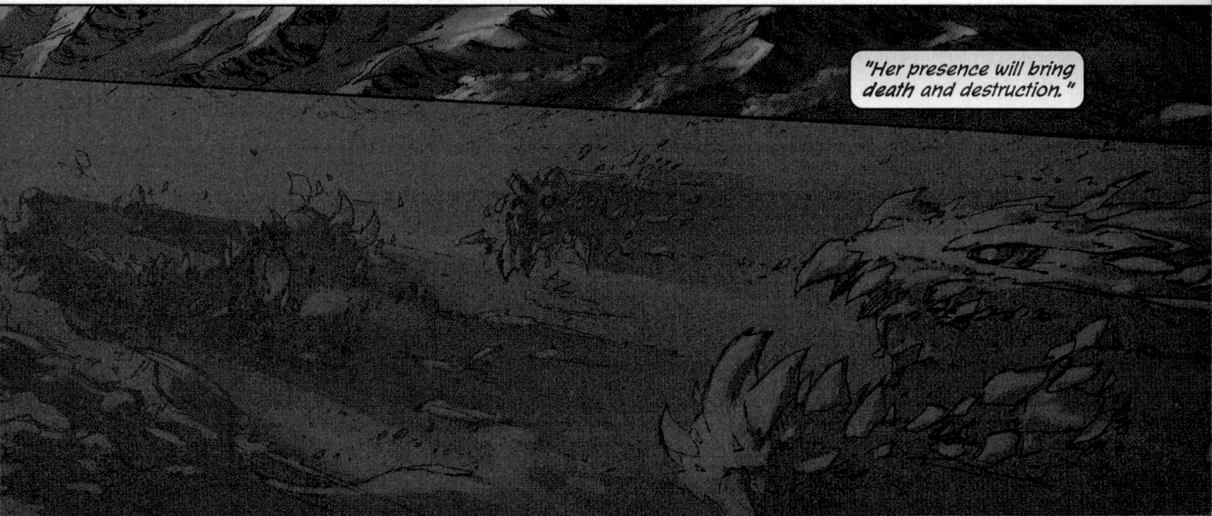
"Her presence will bring death and destruction."

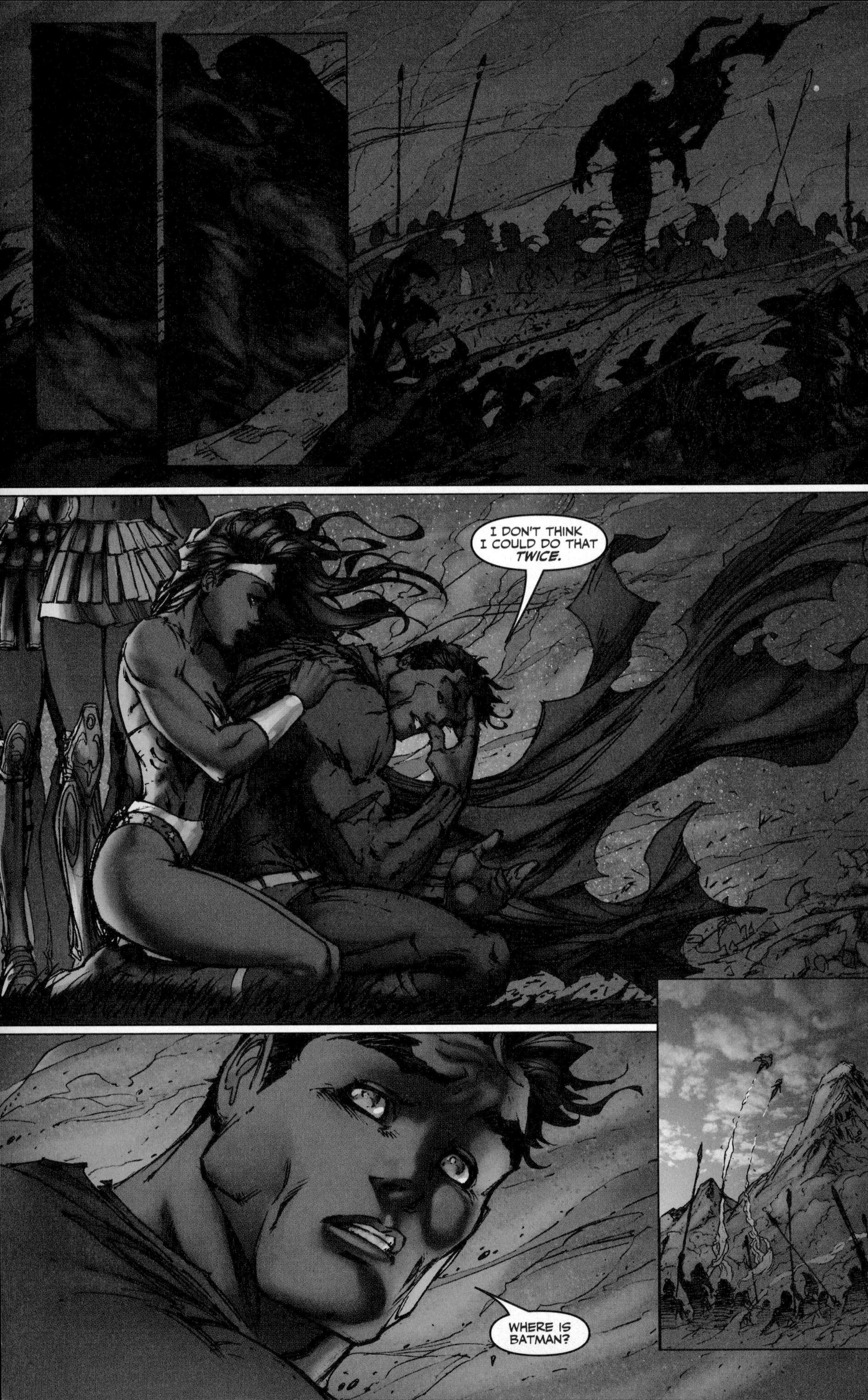
I DON'T THINK I COULD DO THAT *TWICE.*
WHERE IS BATMAN?

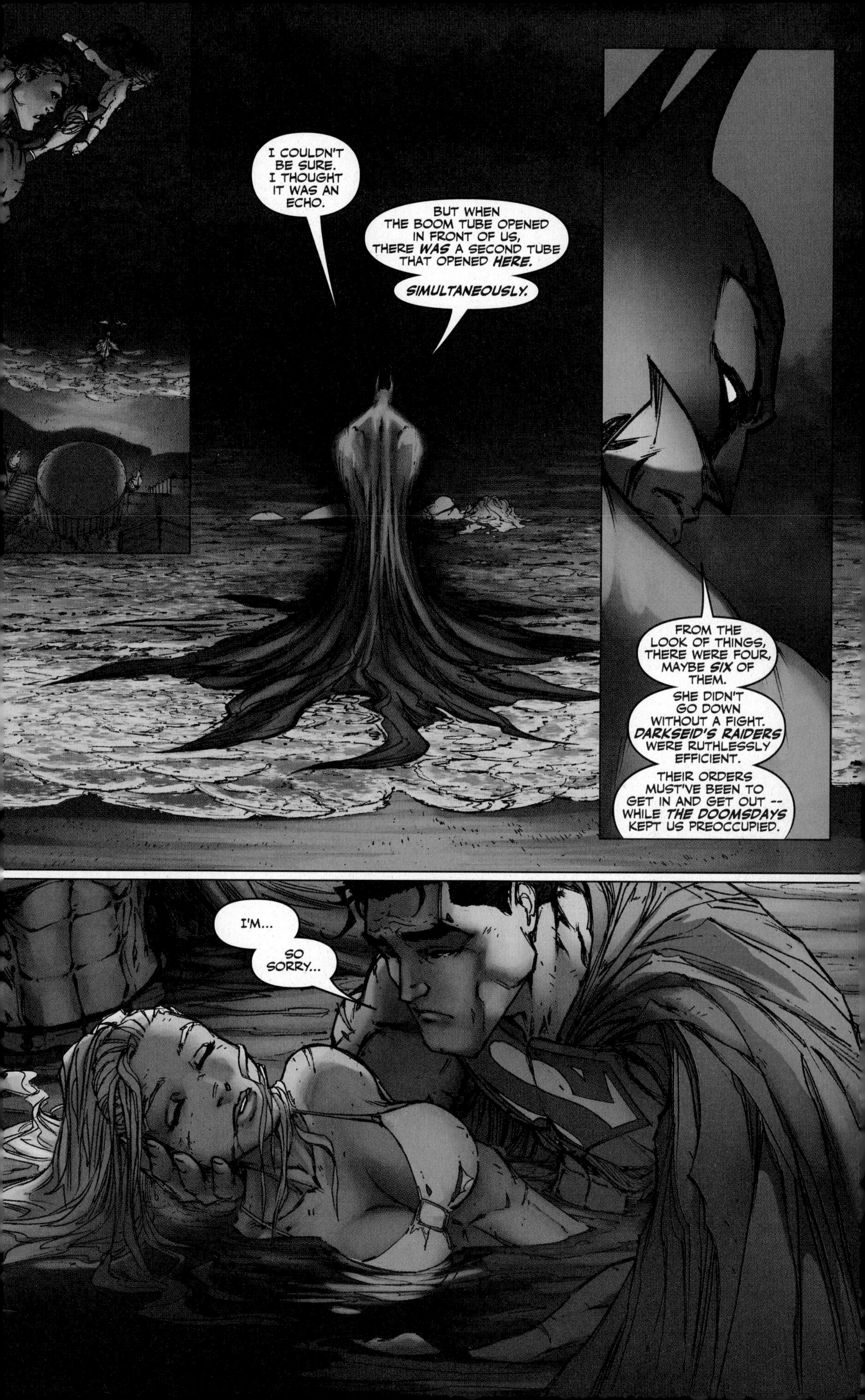

I COULDN'T BE SURE. I THOUGHT IT WAS AN ECHO.
BUT WHEN THE BOOM TUBE OPENED IN FRONT OF US, THERE *WAS* A SECOND TUBE THAT OPENED *HERE.*
SIMULTANEOUSLY.
FROM THE LOOK OF THINGS, THERE WERE FOUR, MAYBE *SIX* OF THEM.
SHE DIDN'T GO DOWN WITHOUT A FIGHT. *DARKSEID'S RAIDERS* WERE RUTHLESSLY EFFICIENT.
THEIR ORDERS MUST'VE BEEN TO GET IN AND GET OUT -- WHILE *THE DOOMSDAYS* KEPT US PREOCCUPIED.
I'M...
SO SORRY...

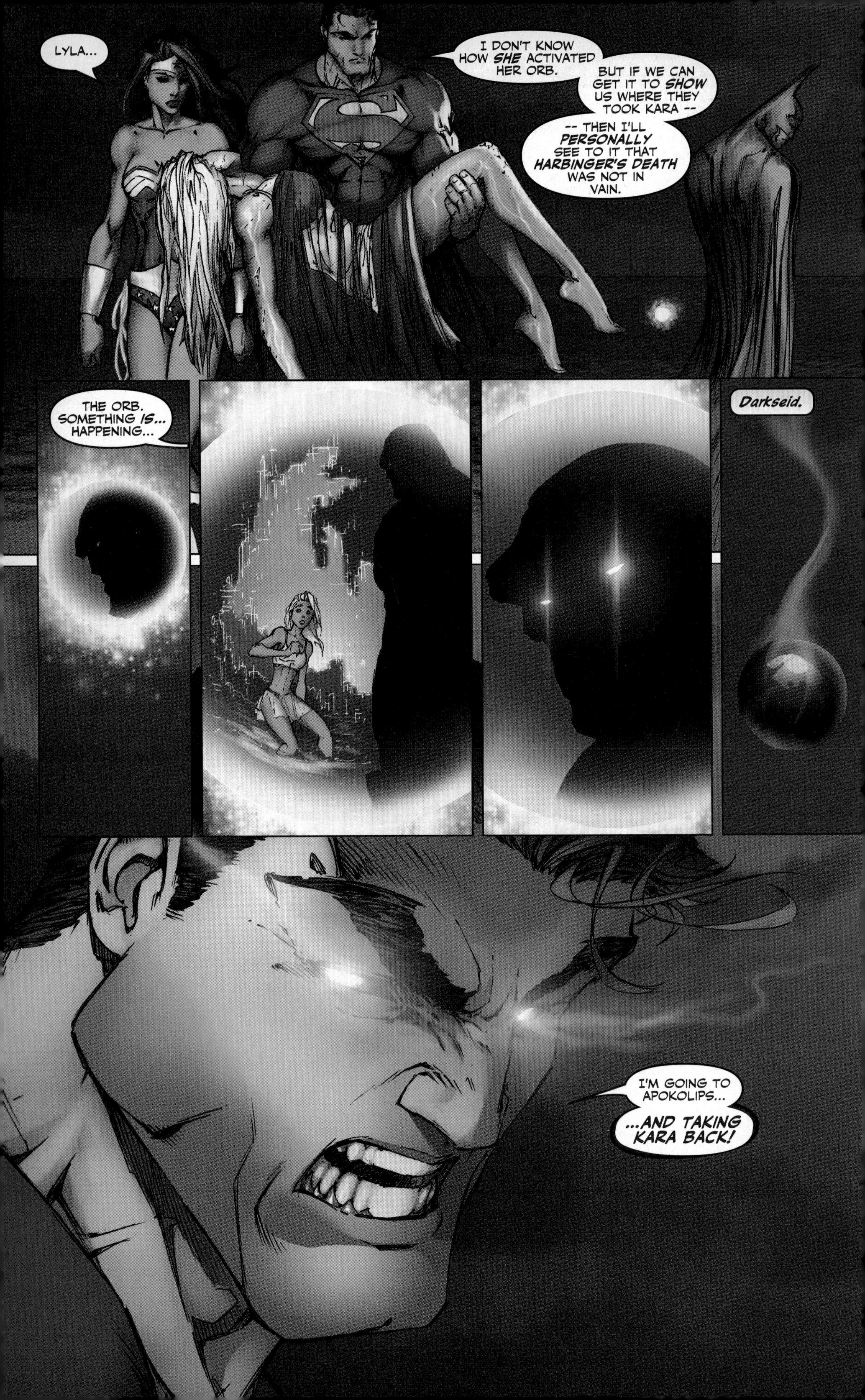
LYLA...
I DON'T KNOW HOW SHE ACTIVATED HER ORB.
BUT IF WE CAN GET IT TO SHOW US WHERE THEY TOOK KARA --
-- THEN I'LL PERSONALLY SEE TO IT THAT HARBINGER'S DEATH WAS NOT IN VAIN.
THE ORB. SOMETHING IS... HAPPENING...
Darkseid.
I'M GOING TO APOKOLIPS...
...AND TAKING KARA BACK!

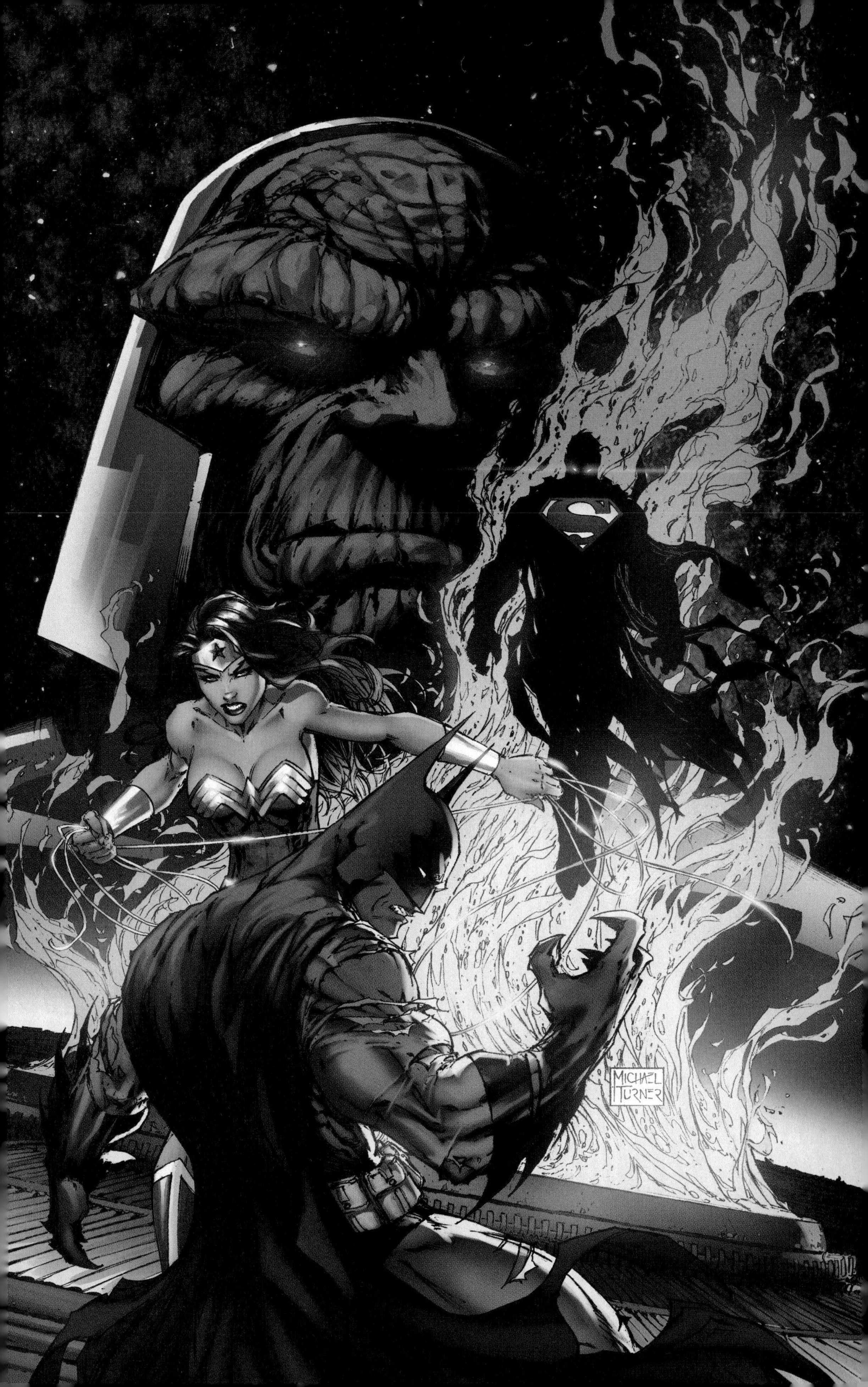
MICHAEL TURNER

PRISONER

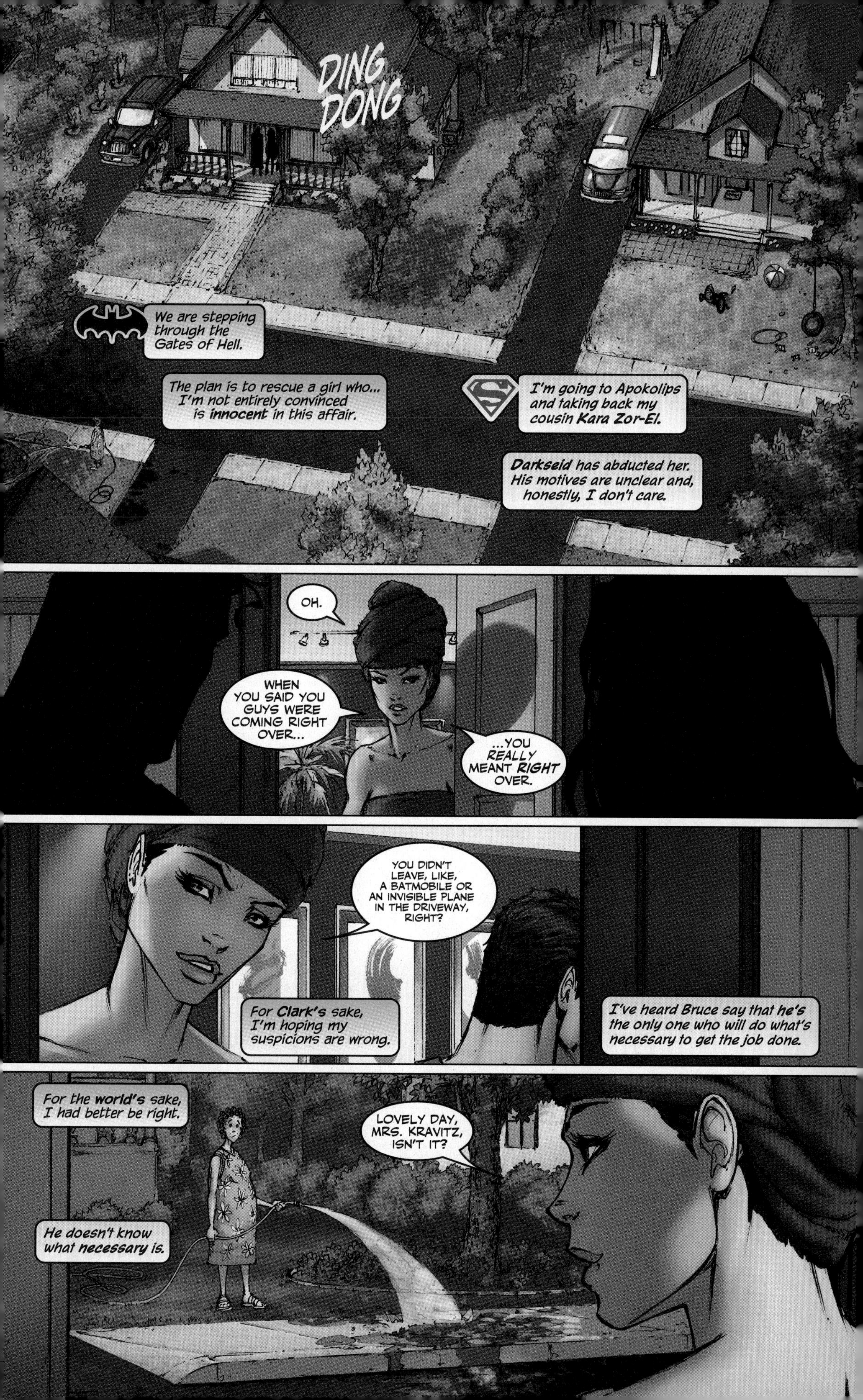
DING DONG
We are stepping through the Gates of Hell.
The plan is to rescue a girl who... I'm not entirely convinced is innocent in this affair.
I'm going to Apokolips and taking back my cousin Kara Zor-El.
Darkseid has abducted her. His motives are unclear and, honestly, I don't care.
OH.
WHEN YOU SAID YOU GUYS WERE COMING RIGHT OVER...
...YOU REALLY MEANT RIGHT OVER.
YOU DIDN'T LEAVE, LIKE, A BATMOBILE OR AN INVISIBLE PLANE IN THE DRIVEWAY, RIGHT?
For Clark's sake, I'm hoping my suspicions are wrong.
I've heard Bruce say that he's the only one who will do what's necessary to get the job done.
For the world's sake, I had better be right.
LOVELY DAY, MRS. KRAVITZ, ISN'T IT?
He doesn't know what necessary is.

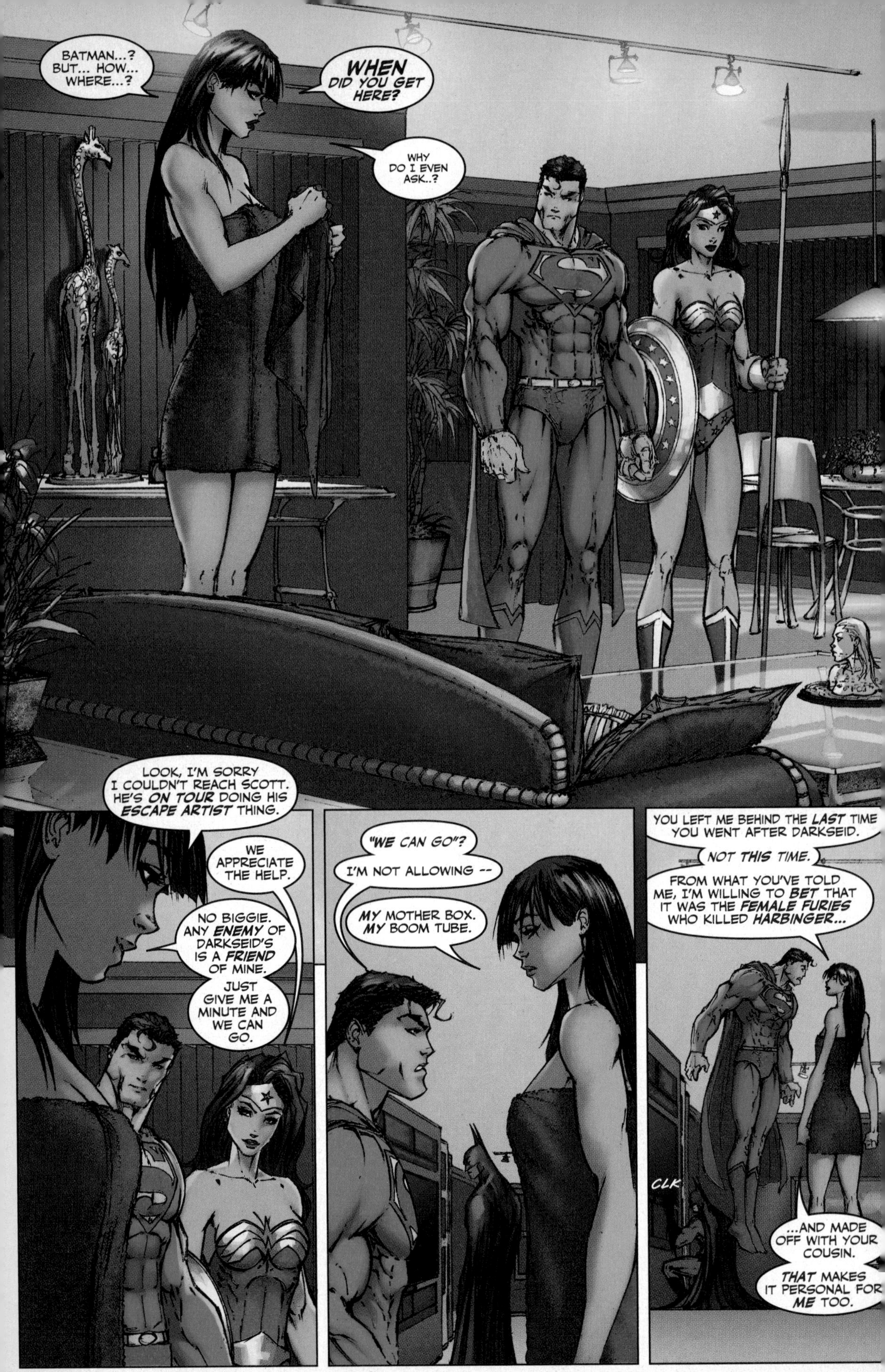
BATMAN...? BUT... HOW... WHERE...?
WHEN DID YOU GET HERE?
WHY DO I EVEN ASK..?
LOOK, I'M SORRY I COULDN'T REACH SCOTT. HE'S ON TOUR DOING HIS ESCAPE ARTIST THING.
WE APPRECIATE THE HELP.
NO BIGGIE. ANY ENEMY OF DARKSEID'S IS A FRIEND OF MINE.
JUST GIVE ME A MINUTE AND WE CAN GO.
"WE CAN GO"?
I'M NOT ALLOWING --
MY MOTHER BOX. MY BOOM TUBE.
YOU LEFT ME BEHIND THE LAST TIME YOU WENT AFTER DARKSEID.
NOT THIS TIME.
FROM WHAT YOU'VE TOLD ME, I'M WILLING TO BET THAT IT WAS THE FEMALE FURIES WHO KILLED HARBINGER...
...AND MADE OFF WITH YOUR COUSIN.
THAT MAKES IT PERSONAL FOR ME TOO.
CLK

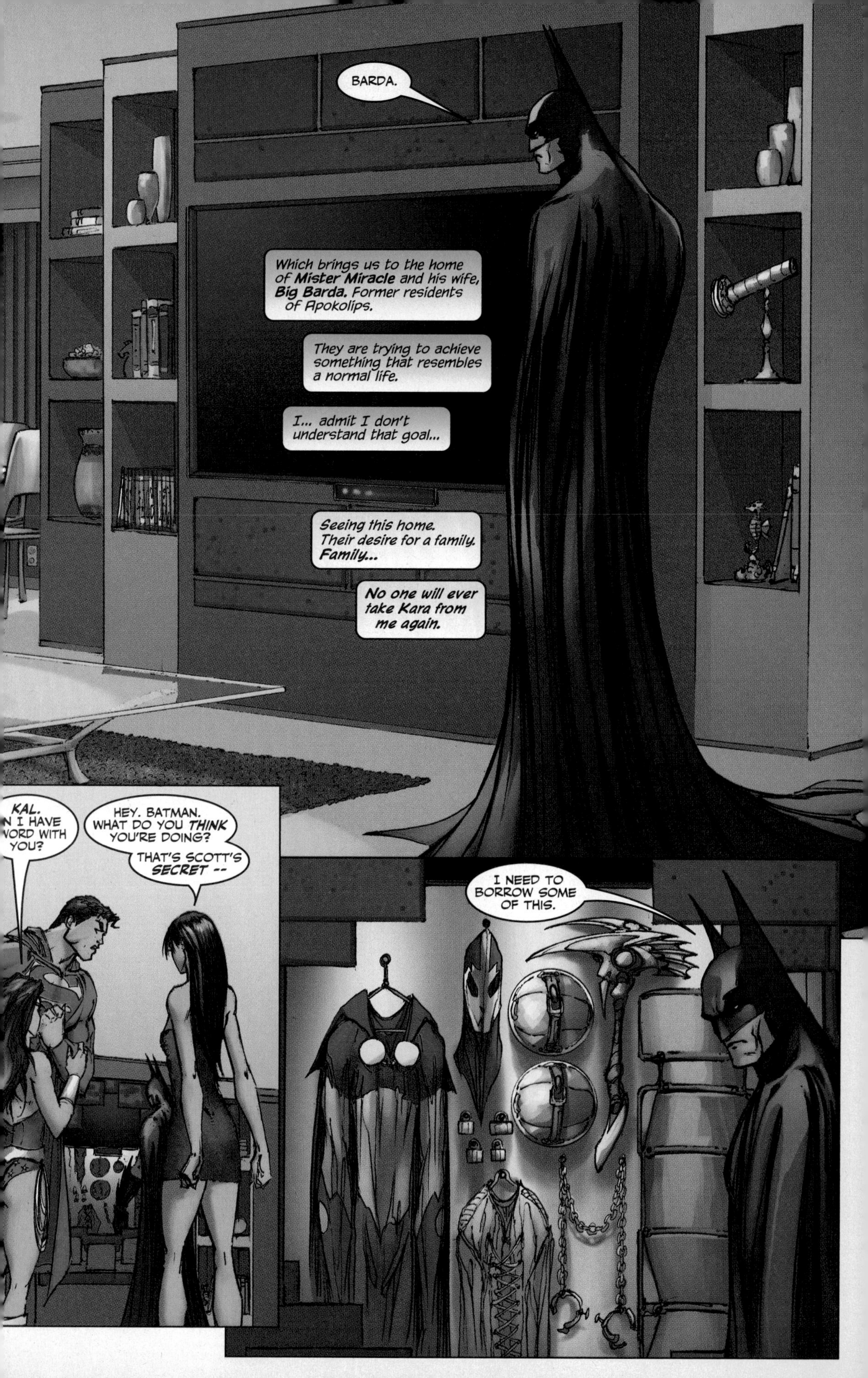

BARDA.
Which brings us to the home of Mister Miracle and his wife, Big Barda. Former residents of Apokolips.
They are trying to achieve something that resembles a normal life.
I... admit I don't understand that goal...
Seeing this home. Their desire for a family. Family...
No one will ever take Kara from me again.
KAL. N I HAVE VORD WITH YOU?
HEY. BATMAN. WHAT DO YOU THINK YOU'RE DOING?
THAT'S SCOTT'S SECRET --
I NEED TO BORROW SOME OF THIS.

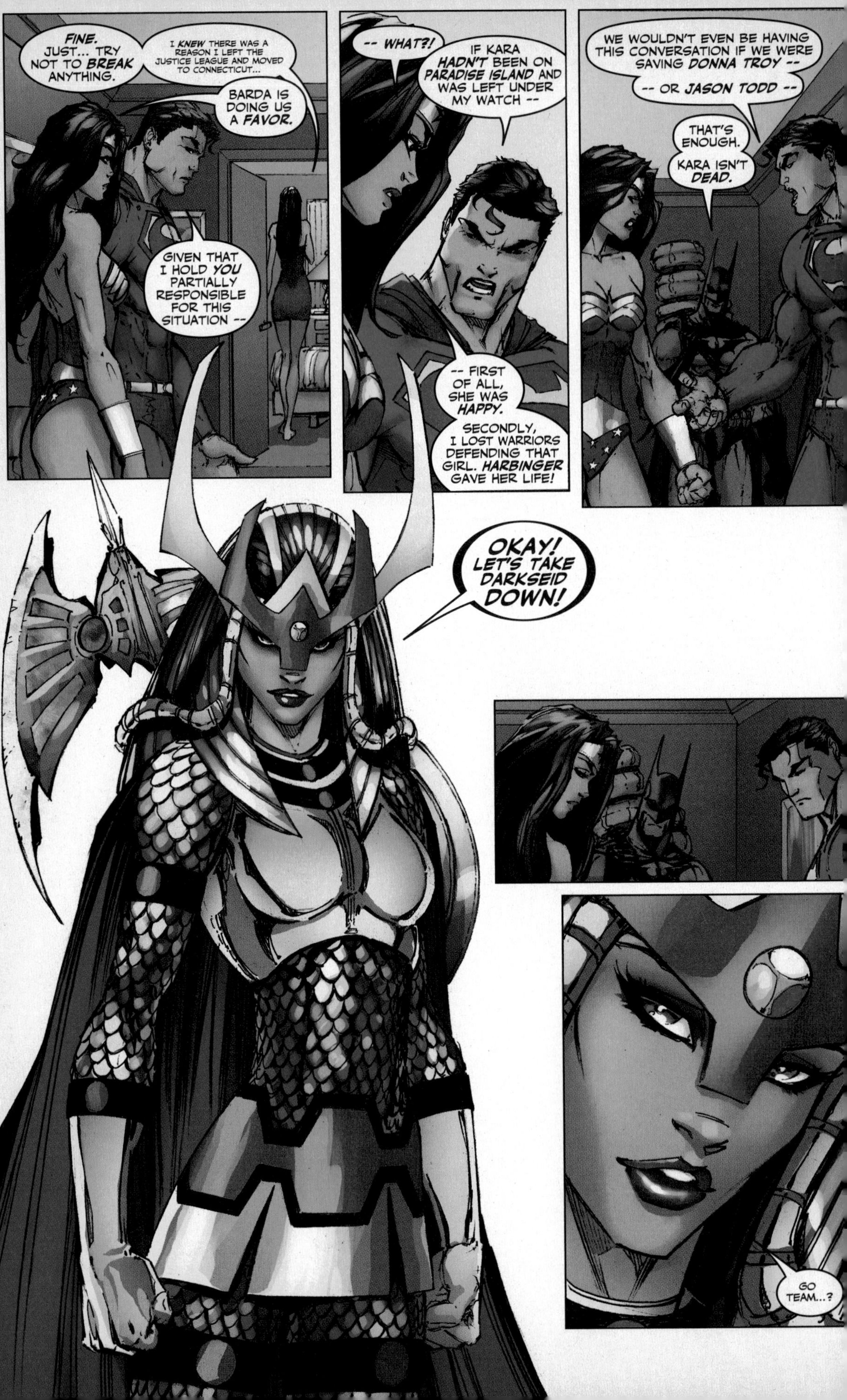
FINE. JUST... TRY NOT TO BREAK ANYTHING.
I KNEW THERE WAS A REASON I LEFT THE JUSTICE LEAGUE AND MOVED TO CONNECTICUT...
BARDA IS DOING US A FAVOR.
GIVEN THAT I HOLD YOU PARTIALLY RESPONSIBLE FOR THIS SITUATION --
-- WHAT?!
IF KARA HADN'T BEEN ON PARADISE ISLAND AND WAS LEFT UNDER MY WATCH --
-- FIRST OF ALL, SHE WAS HAPPY.
SECONDLY, I LOST WARRIORS DEFENDING THAT GIRL. HARBINGER GAVE HER LIFE!
WE WOULDN'T EVEN BE HAVING THIS CONVERSATION IF WE WERE SAVING DONNA TROY --
-- OR JASON TODD --
THAT'S ENOUGH.
KARA ISN'T DEAD.
OKAY! LET'S TAKE DARKSEID DOWN!
GO TEAM...?

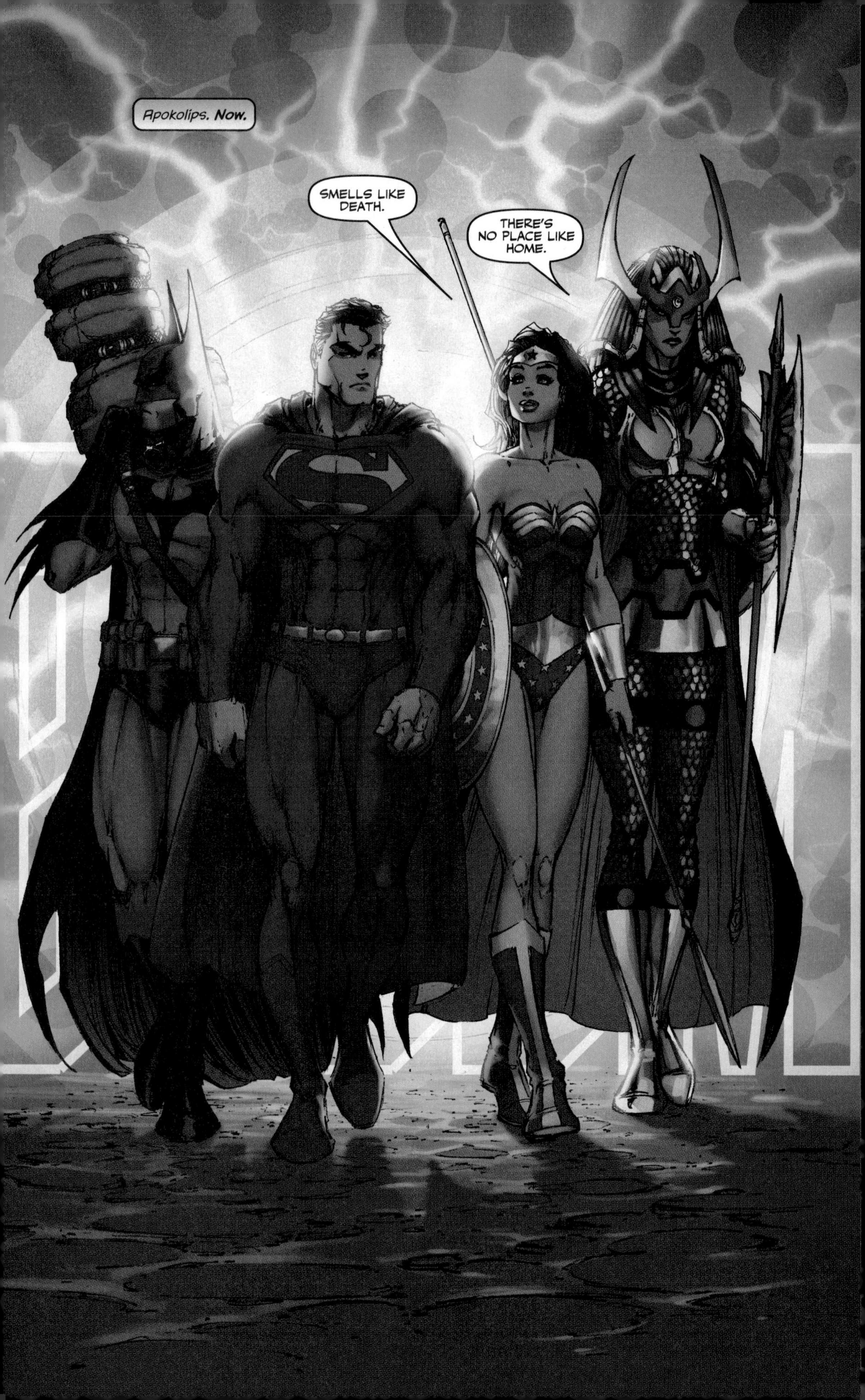

Apokolips. Now.
SMELLS LIKE DEATH.
THERE'S NO PLACE LIKE HOME.

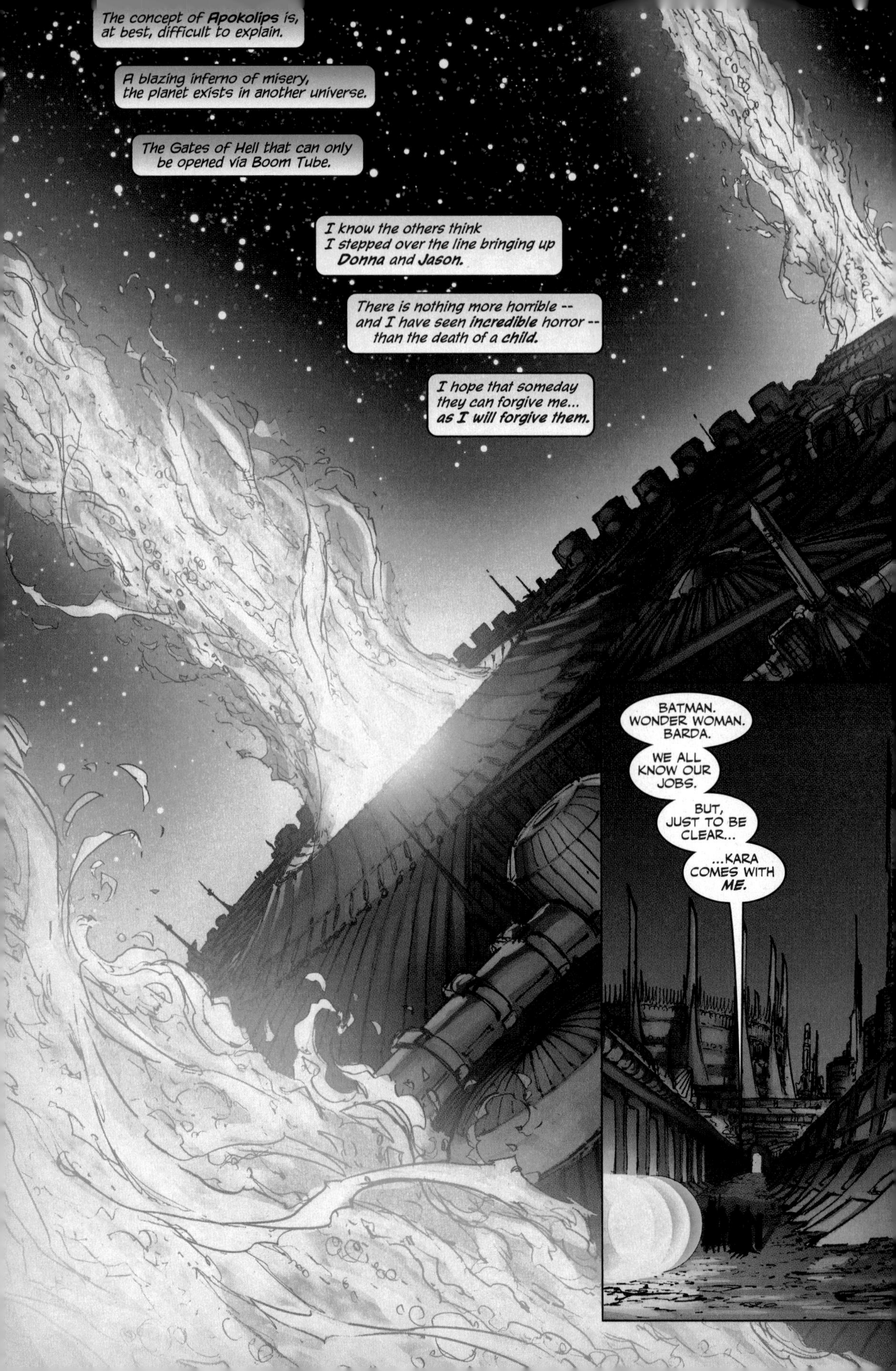
The concept of Apokolips is, at best, difficult to explain.
A blazing inferno of misery, the planet exists in another universe.
The Gates of Hell that can only be opened via Boom Tube.
I know the others think I stepped over the line bringing up Donna and Jason.
There is nothing more horrible -- and I have seen incredible horror -- than the death of a child.
I hope that someday they can forgive me... as I will forgive them.
BATMAN. WONDER WOMAN. BARDA.
WE ALL KNOW OUR JOBS.
BUT, JUST TO BE CLEAR...
...KARA COMES WITH ME.

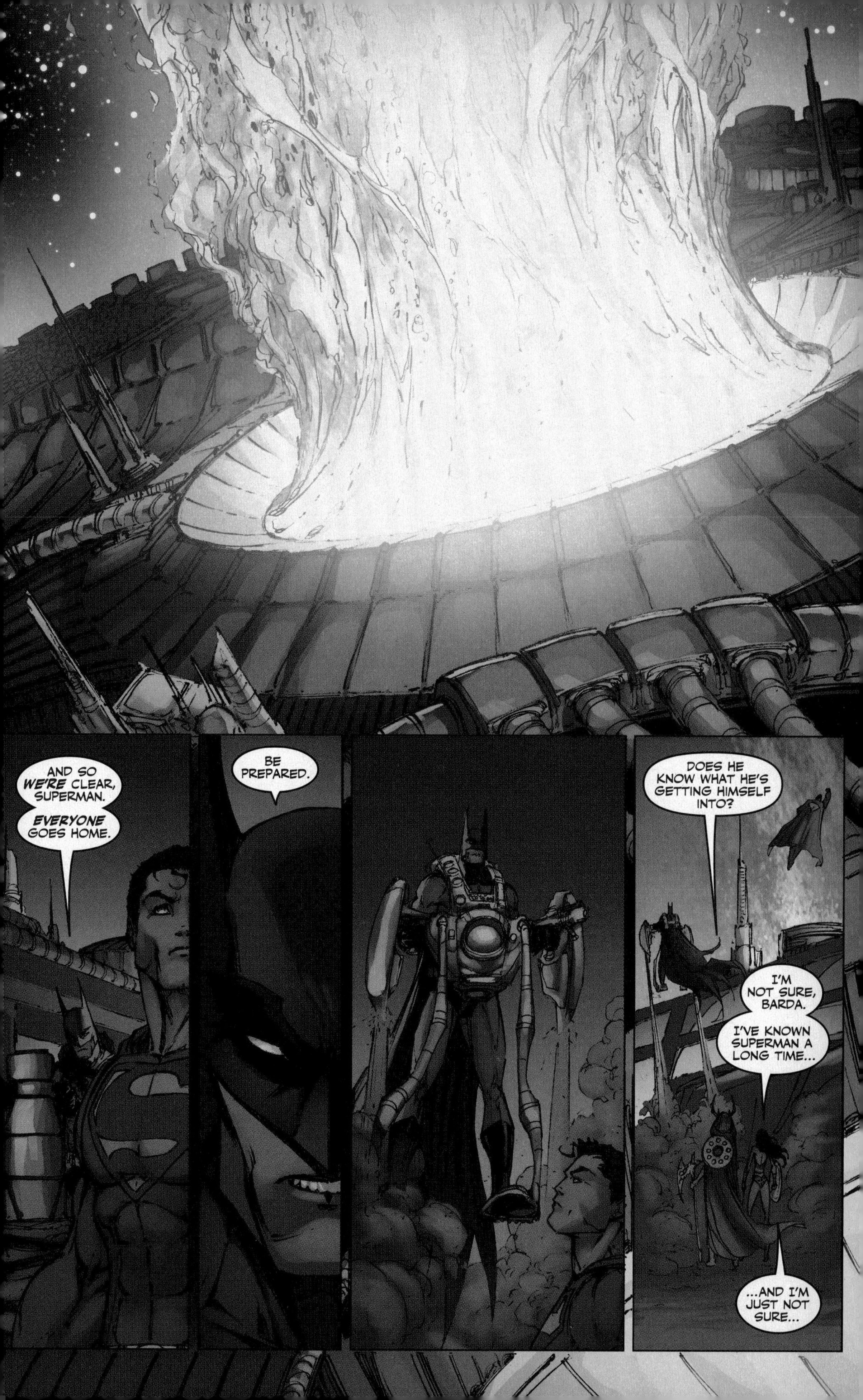
AND SO *WE'RE* CLEAR, SUPERMAN.
EVERYONE GOES HOME.
BE PREPARED.
DOES HE KNOW WHAT HE'S GETTING HIMSELF INTO?
I'M NOT SURE, BARDA.
I'VE KNOWN SUPERMAN A LONG TIME...
...AND I'M JUST NOT SURE...

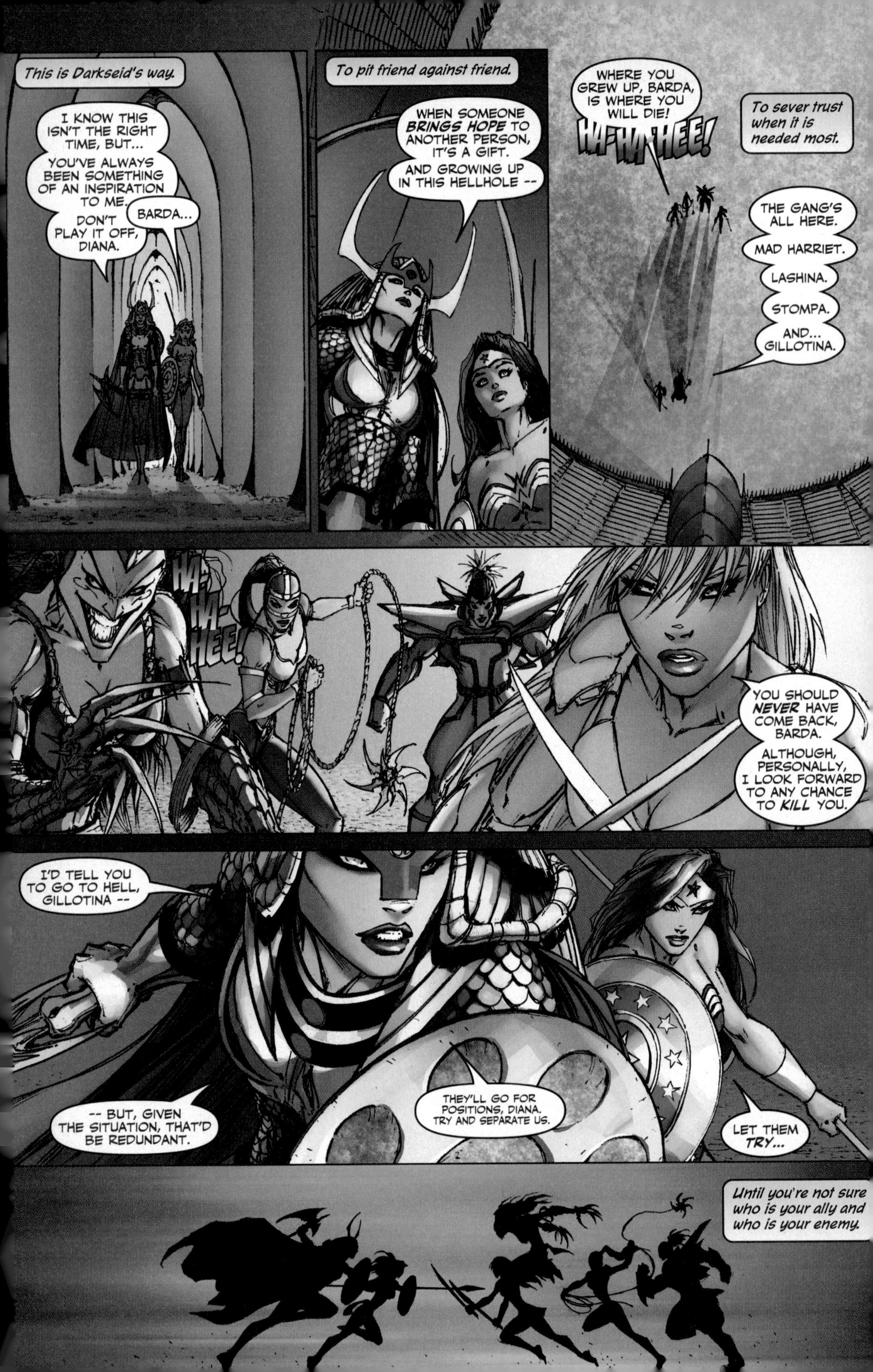

This is Darkseid's way.
I KNOW THIS ISN'T THE RIGHT TIME, BUT... YOU'VE ALWAYS BEEN SOMETHING OF AN INSPIRATION TO ME.
BARDA...
DON'T PLAY IT OFF, DIANA.
To pit friend against friend.
WHEN SOMEONE BRINGS HOPE TO ANOTHER PERSON, IT'S A GIFT. AND GROWING UP IN THIS HELLHOLE --
WHERE YOU GREW UP, BARDA, IS WHERE YOU WILL DIE!
HA-HA-HEE!
To sever trust when it is needed most.
THE GANG'S ALL HERE.
MAD HARRIET.
LASHINA.
STOMPA.
AND... GILLOTINA.
HA-HA-HEE!
YOU SHOULD NEVER HAVE COME BACK, BARDA.
ALTHOUGH, PERSONALLY, I LOOK FORWARD TO ANY CHANCE TO KILL YOU.
I'D TELL YOU TO GO TO HELL, GILLOTINA --
-- BUT, GIVEN THE SITUATION, THAT'D BE REDUNDANT.
THEY'LL GO FOR POSITIONS, DIANA. TRY AND SEPARATE US.
LET THEM TRY...
Until you're not sure who is your ally and who is your enemy.

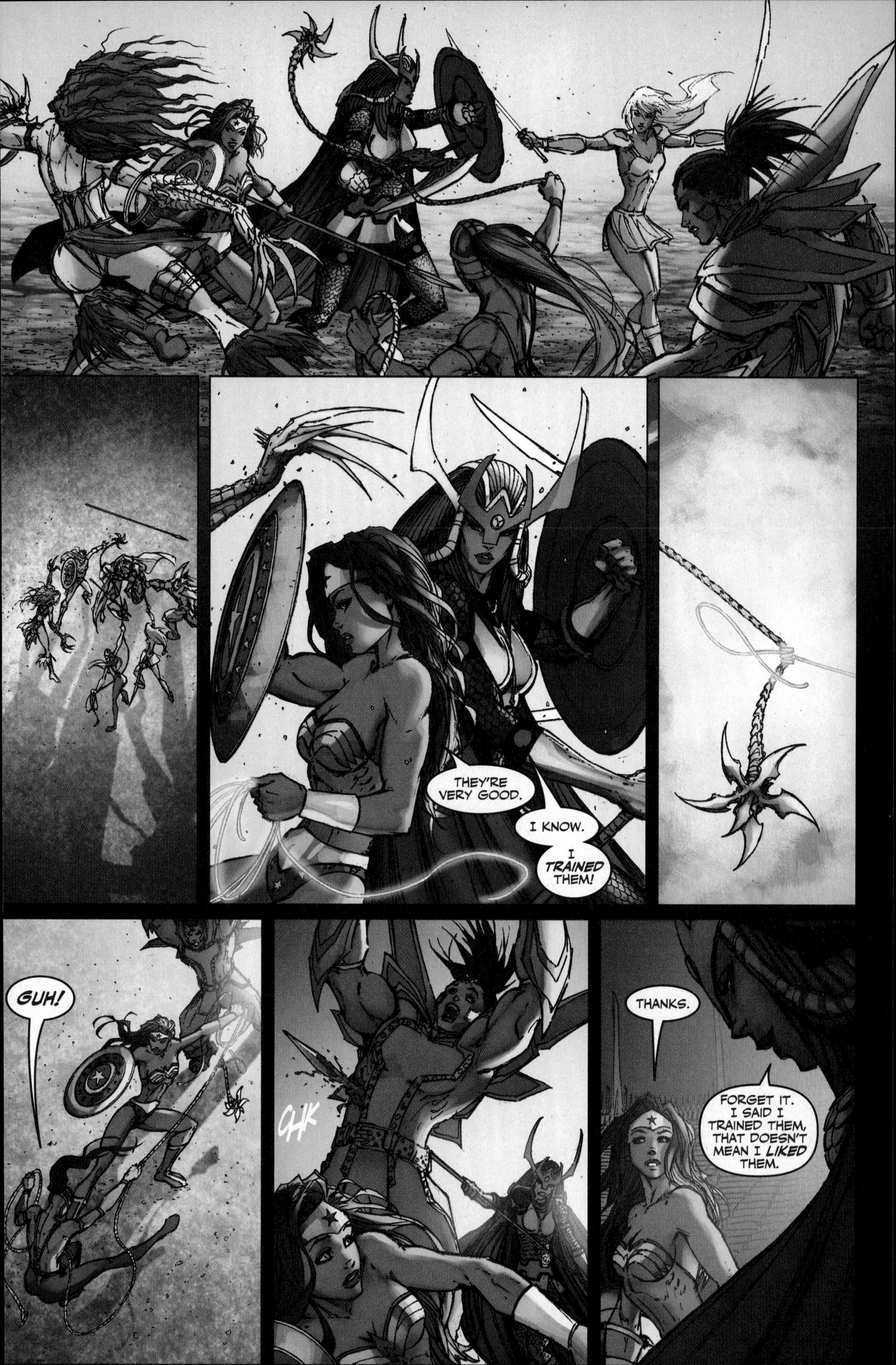
THEY'RE VERY GOOD.
I KNOW.
I *TRAINED* THEM!
GUH!
CHK
THANKS.
FORGET IT. I SAID I TRAINED THEM, THAT DOESN'T MEAN I *LIKED* THEM.

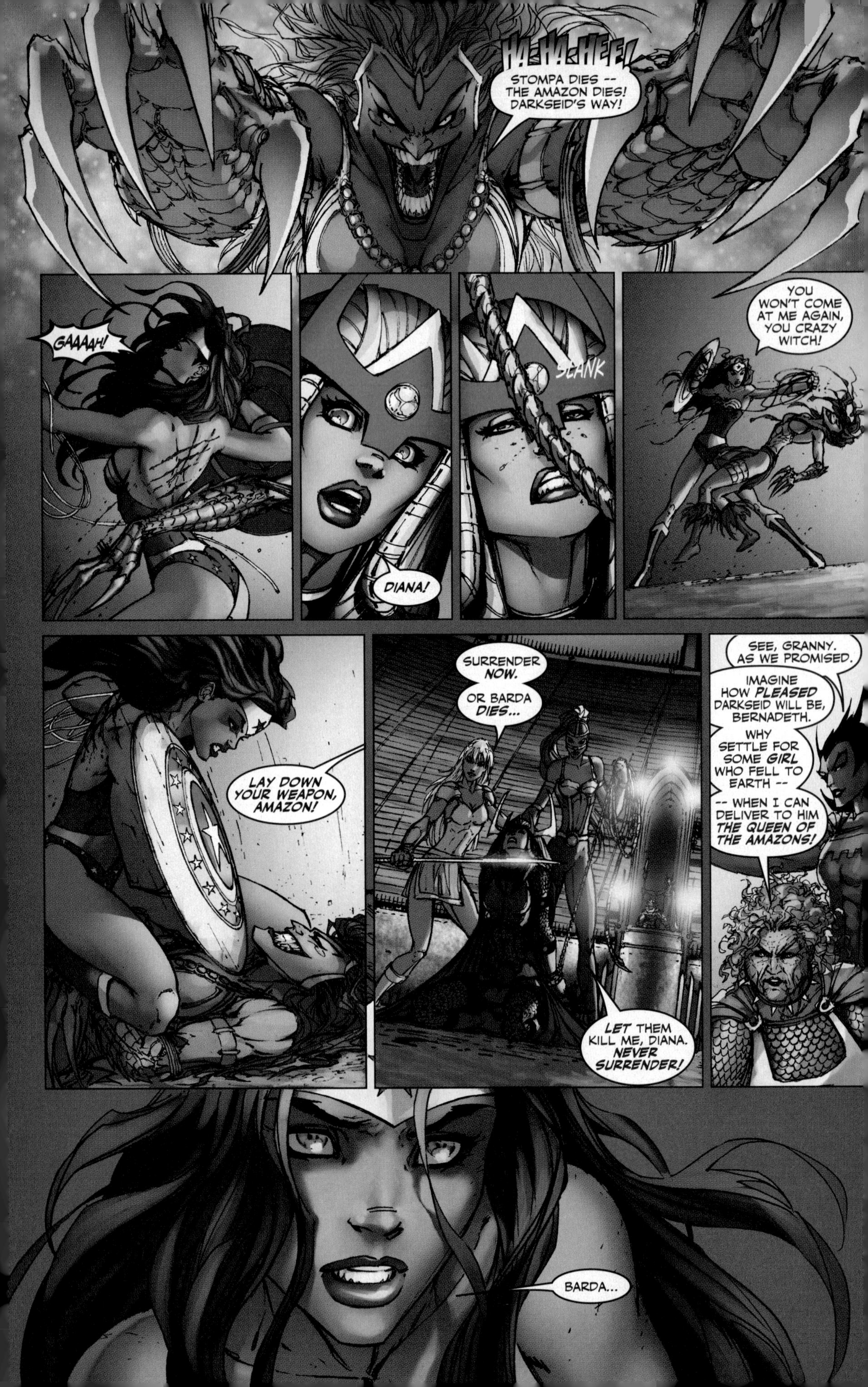
HA-HA-HEE!
STOMPA DIES -- THE AMAZON DIES! DARKSEID'S WAY!
GAAAAH!
DIANA!
SLANK
YOU WON'T COME AT ME AGAIN, YOU CRAZY WITCH!
LAY DOWN YOUR WEAPON, AMAZON!
SURRENDER NOW.
OR BARDA DIES...
LET THEM KILL ME, DIANA. NEVER SURRENDER!
SEE, GRANNY. AS WE PROMISED.
IMAGINE HOW PLEASED DARKSEID WILL BE, BERNADETH.
WHY SETTLE FOR SOME GIRL WHO FELL TO EARTH --
-- WHEN I CAN DELIVER TO HIM THE QUEEN OF THE AMAZONS!
BARDA...

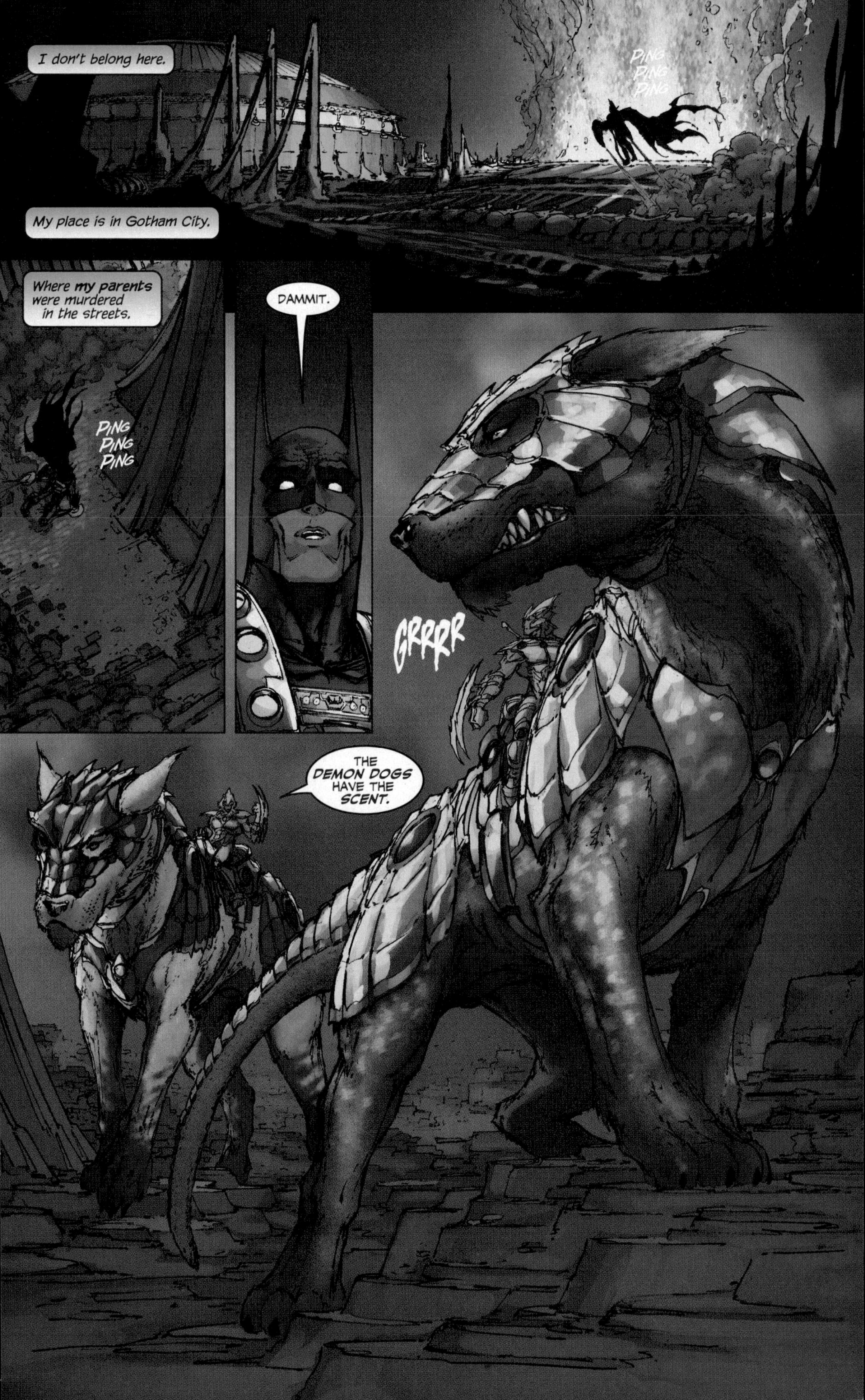

I don't belong here.
PING PING PING
My place is in Gotham City.
Where my parents were murdered in the streets.
PING PING PING
DAMMIT.
GRRRR
THE DEMON DOGS HAVE THE SCENT.

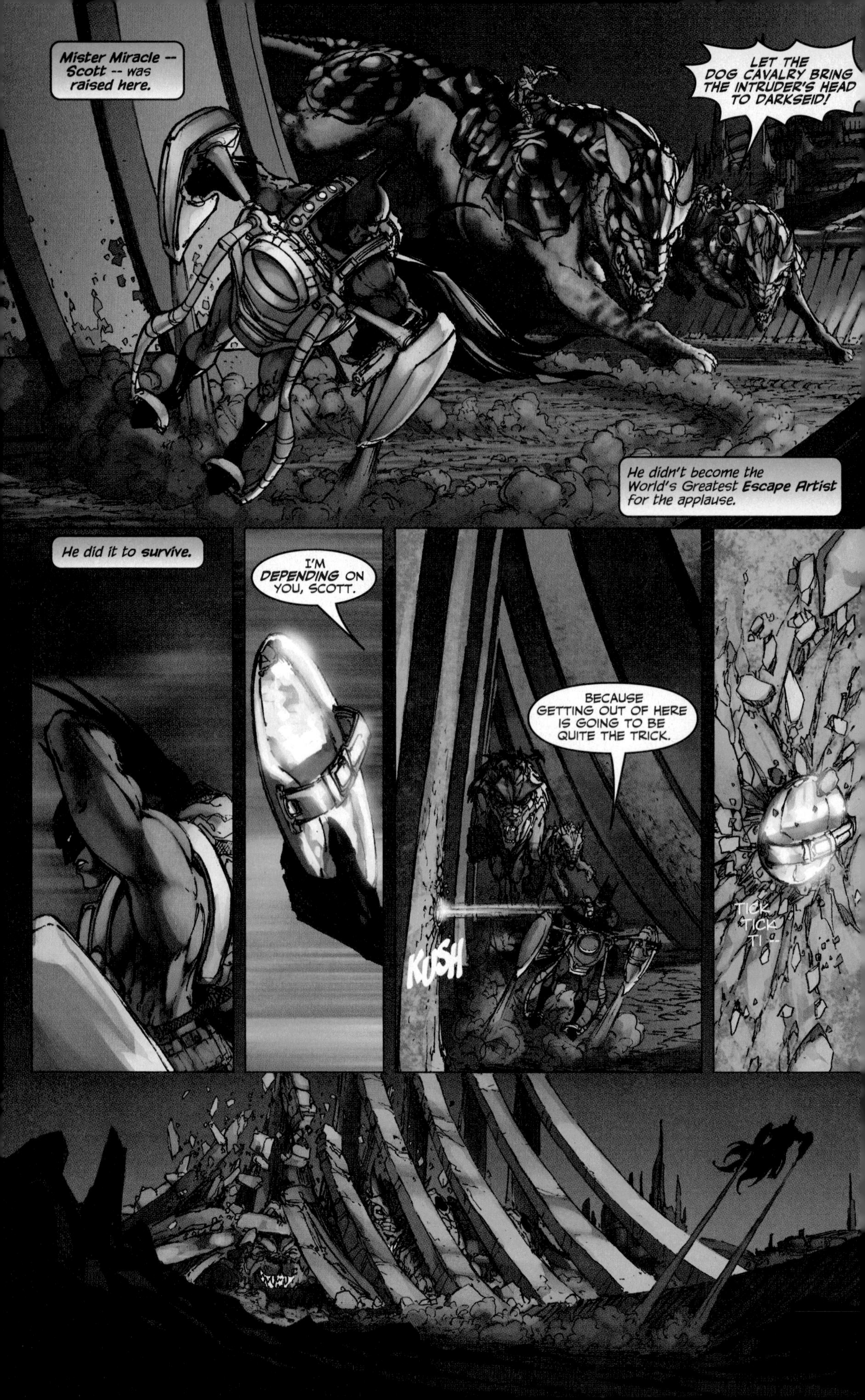

Mister Miracle -- Scott -- was raised here.
LET THE DOG CAVALRY BRING THE INTRUDER'S HEAD TO DARKSEID!
He didn't become the World's Greatest Escape Artist for the applause.
He did it to survive.
I'M DEPENDING ON YOU, SCOTT.
BECAUSE GETTING OUT OF HERE IS GOING TO BE QUITE THE TRICK.
KUSH
TICK TICK TI--

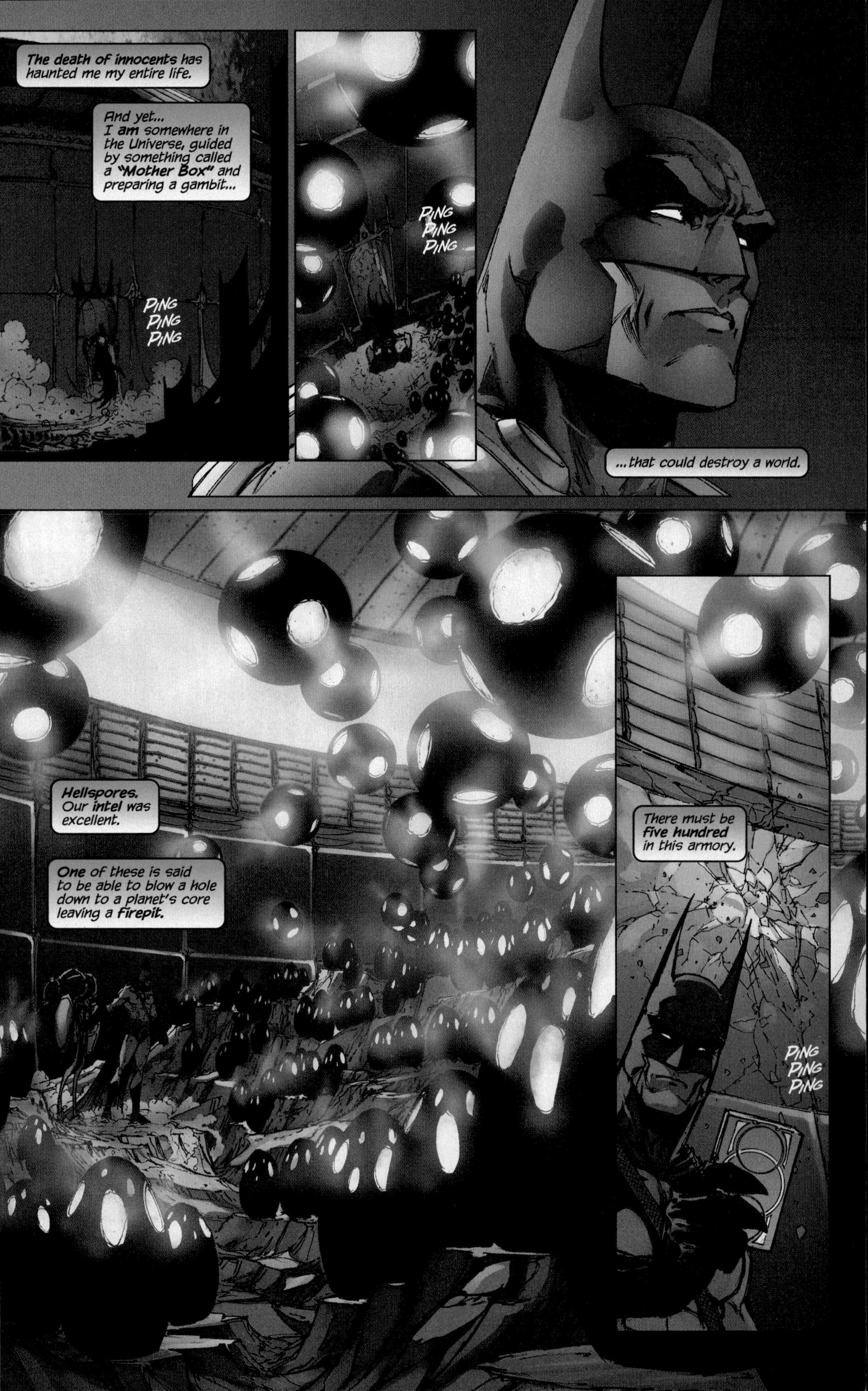

The death of innocents has haunted me my entire life.
And yet... I am somewhere in the Universe, guided by something called a "Mother Box" and preparing a gambit...
PING PING PING
PING PING PING
...that could destroy a world.
Hellspores. Our intel was excellent.
One of these is said to be able to blow a hole down to a planet's core leaving a firepit.
There must be five hundred in this armory.
PING PING PING

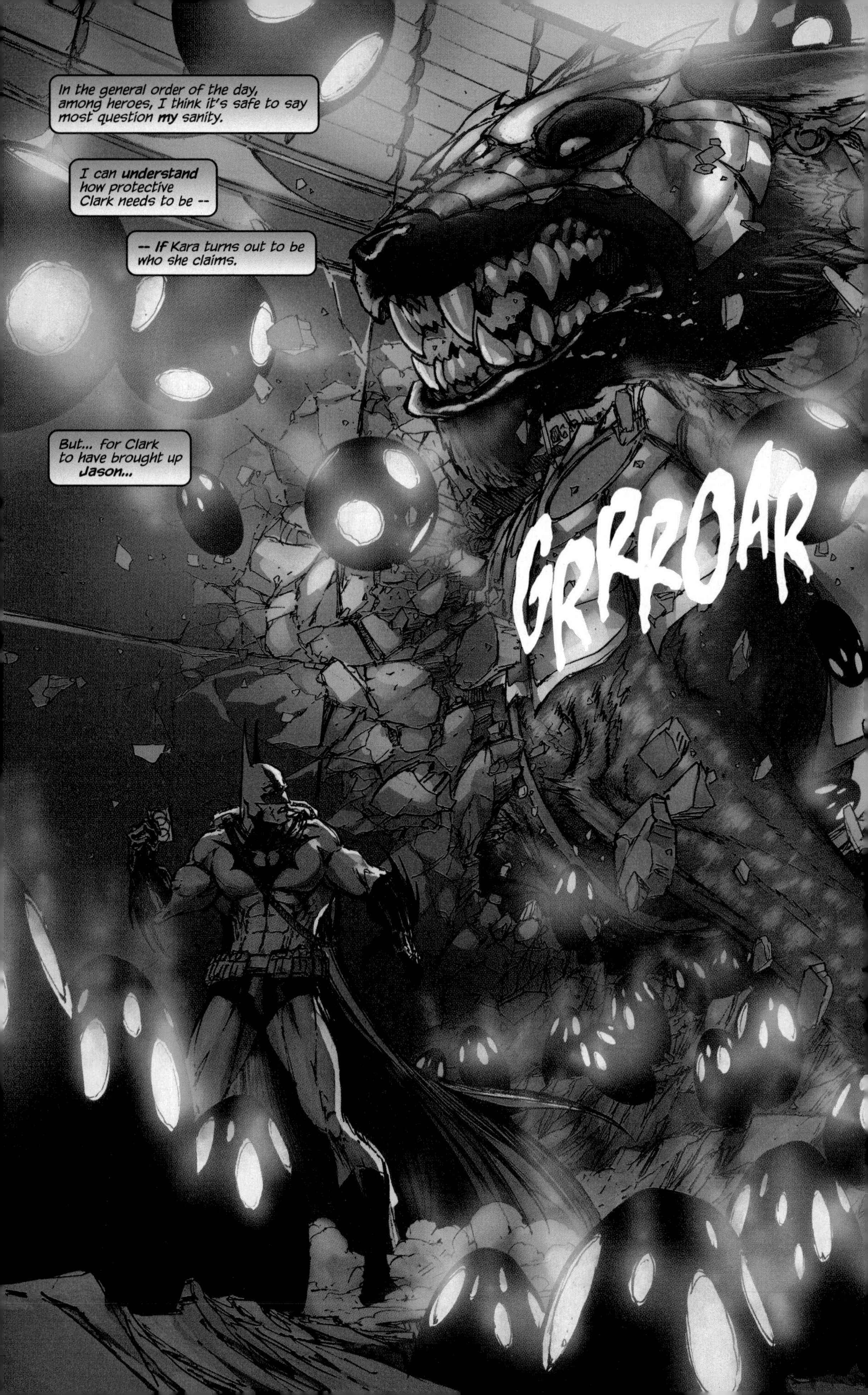
In the general order of the day, among heroes, I think it's safe to say most question **my** sanity.
I can **understand** how protective Clark needs to be --
-- **If** Kara turns out to be who she claims.
But... for Clark to have brought up **Jason...**
GRRROAR

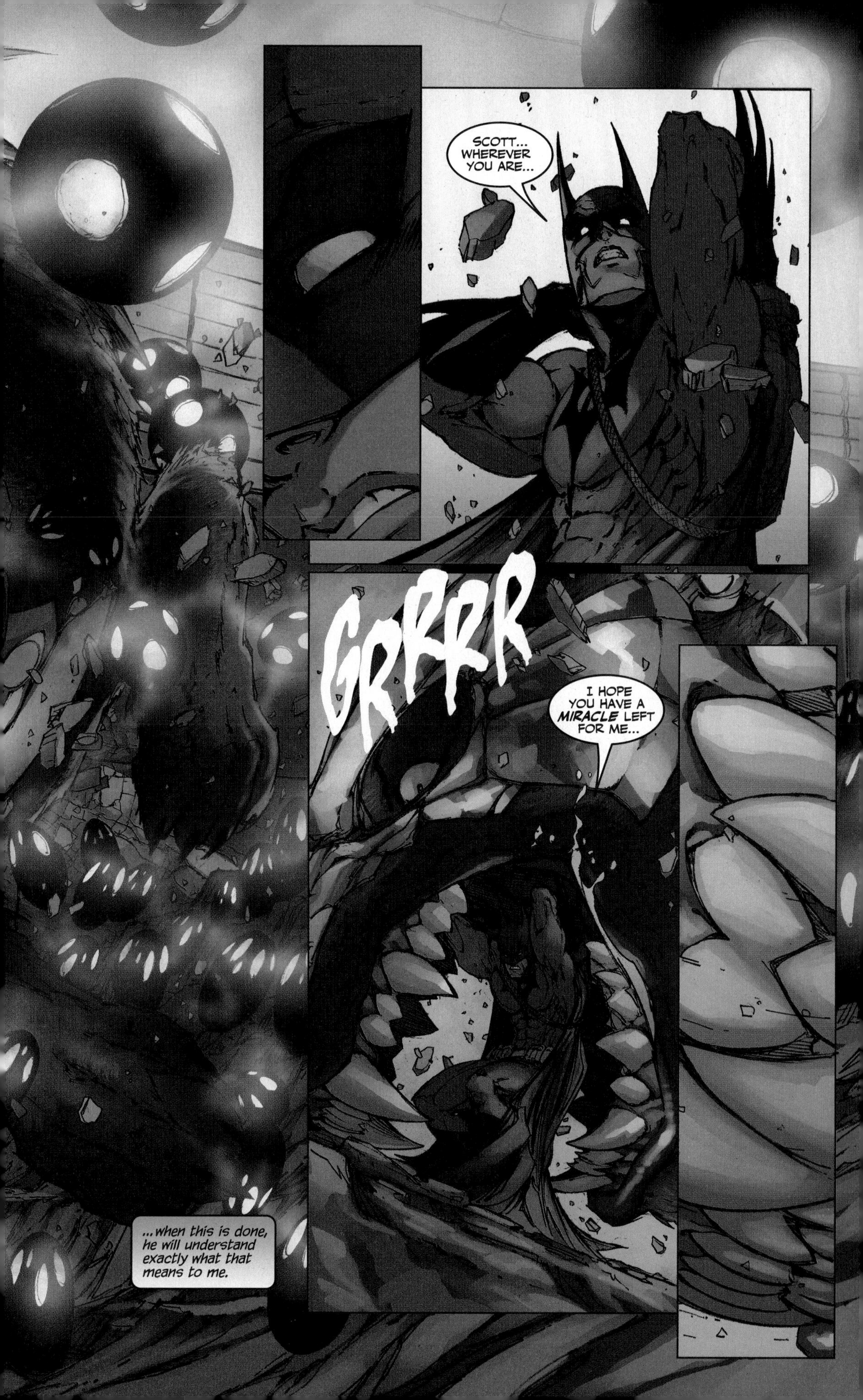
SCOTT... WHEREVER YOU ARE...
GRRRR
I HOPE YOU HAVE A MIRACLE LEFT FOR ME...
...when this is done, he will understand exactly what that means to me.

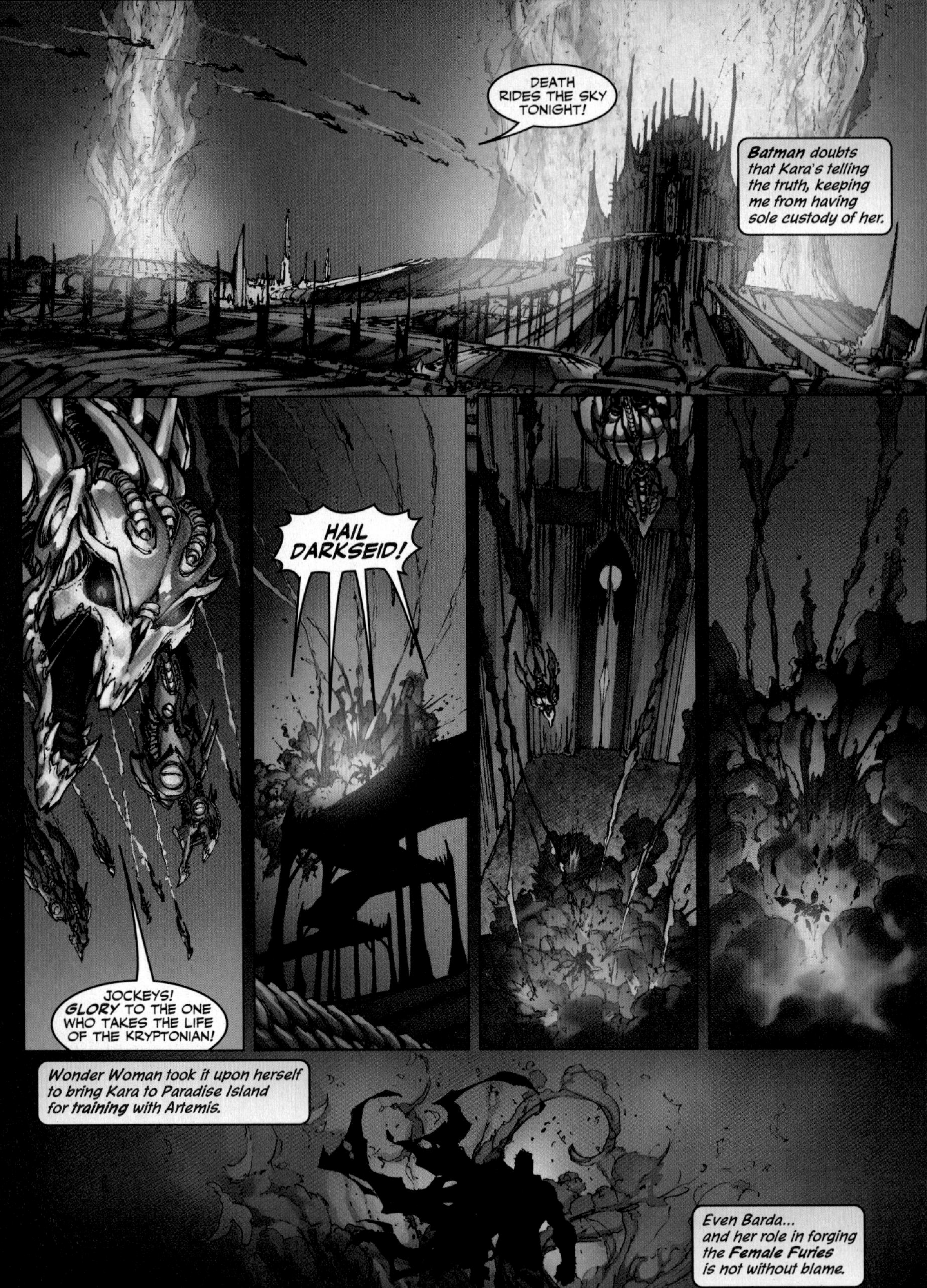
DEATH RIDES THE SKY TONIGHT!
Batman doubts that Kara's telling the truth, keeping me from having sole custody of her.
JOCKEYS! GLORY TO THE ONE WHO TAKES THE LIFE OF THE KRYPTONIAN!
HAIL DARKSEID!
Wonder Woman took it upon herself to bring Kara to Paradise Island for training with Artemis.
Even Barda... and her role in forging the Female Furies is not without blame.

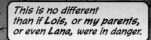 This is no different than if *Lois*, or my parents, or even *Lana*, were in danger.

Kara Zor-El is family.

 DARKSEID!

Any action I take is justified.

 KARA LEAVES WITH ME!

KARA...?

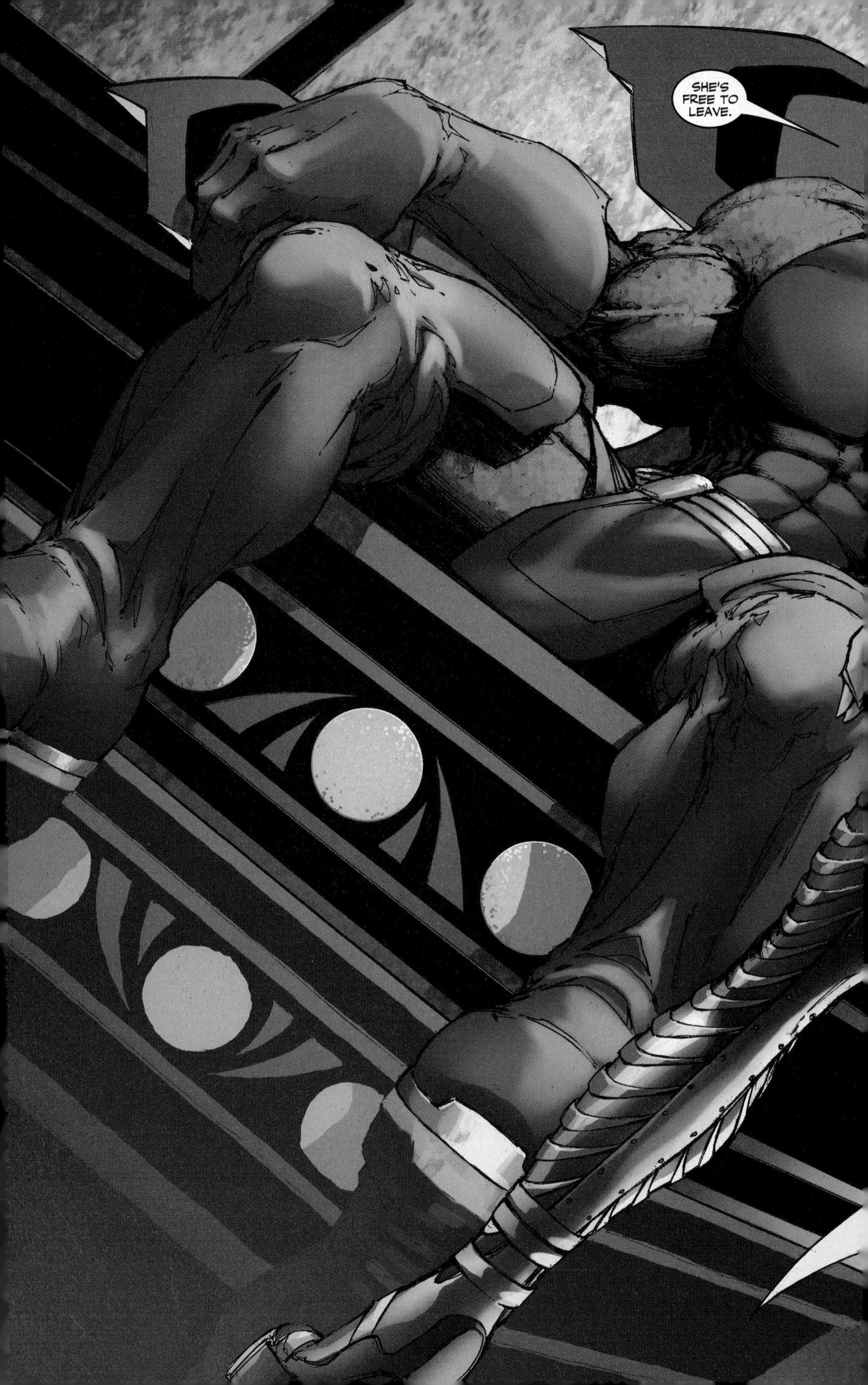
SHE'S FREE TO LEAVE.

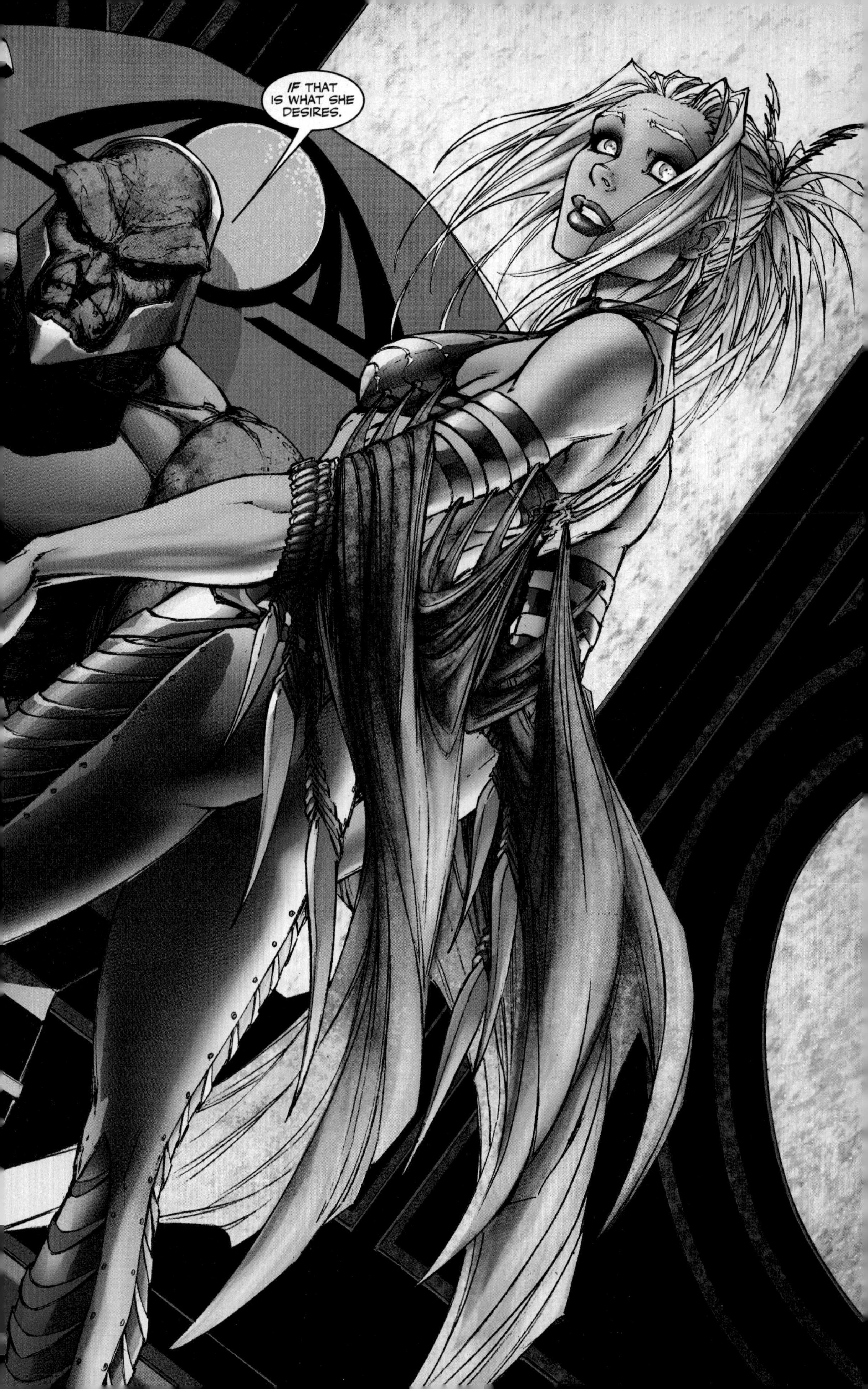
IF THAT IS WHAT SHE DESIRES.

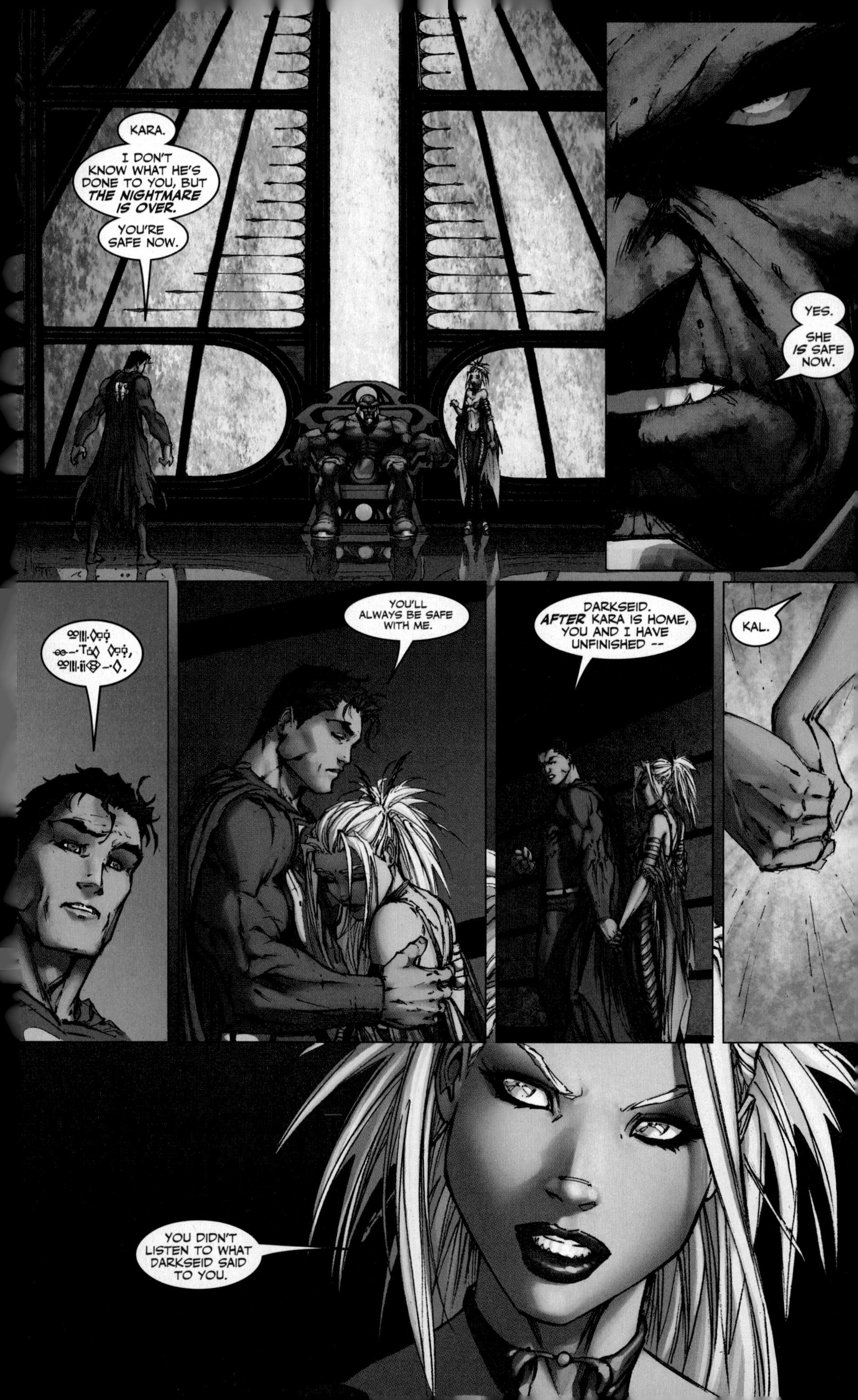
KARA.
I DON'T KNOW WHAT HE'S DONE TO YOU, BUT ***THE NIGHTMARE IS OVER.***
YOU'RE SAFE NOW.
YES.
SHE ***IS*** SAFE NOW.
YOU'LL ALWAYS BE SAFE WITH ME.
DARKSEID. ***AFTER*** KARA IS HOME, YOU AND I HAVE UNFINISHED --
KAL.
YOU DIDN'T LISTEN TO WHAT DARKSEID SAID TO YOU.

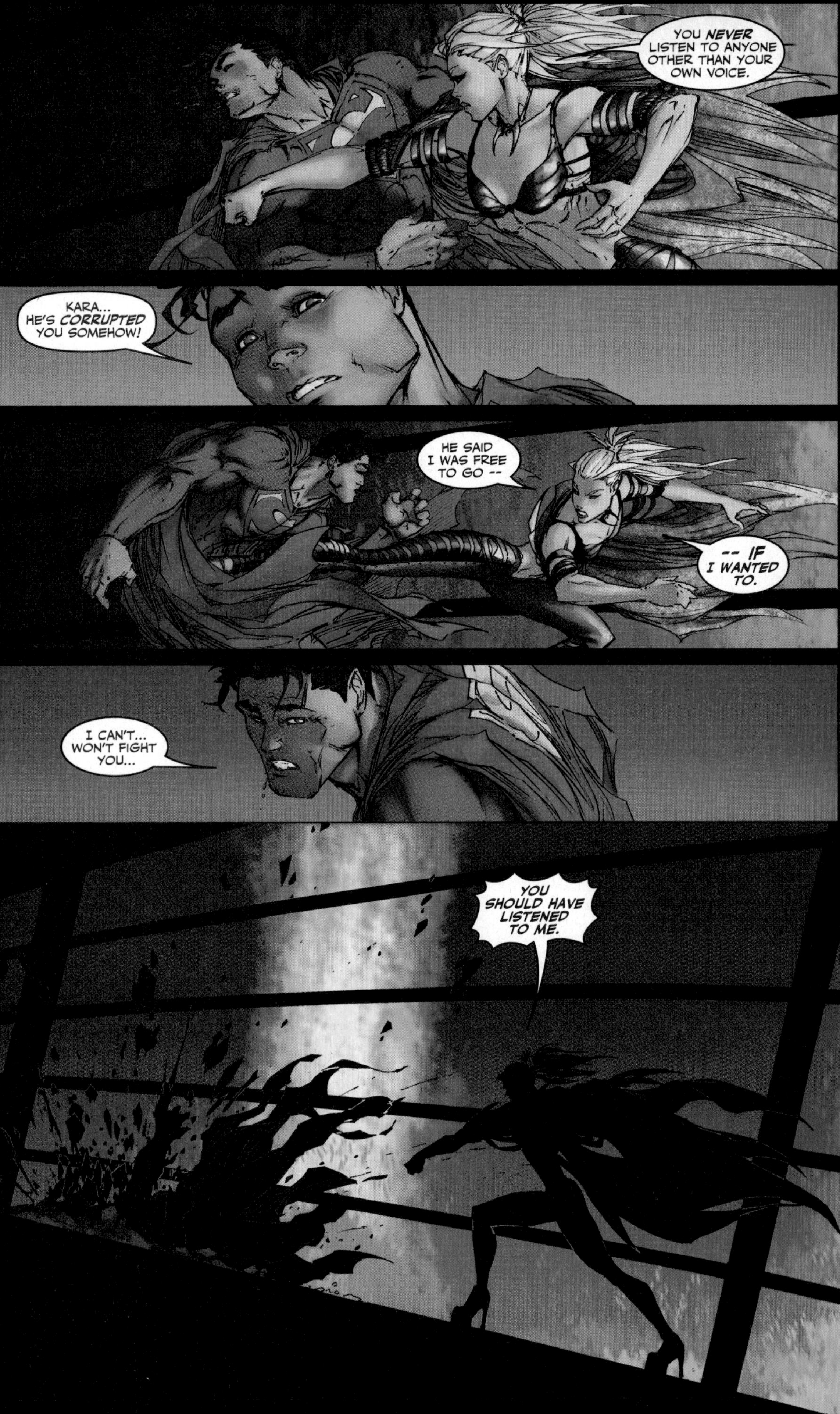
YOU NEVER LISTEN TO ANYONE OTHER THAN YOUR OWN VOICE.
KARA... HE'S CORRUPTED YOU SOMEHOW!
HE SAID I WAS FREE TO GO --
-- IF I WANTED TO.
I CAN'T... WON'T FIGHT YOU...
YOU SHOULD HAVE LISTENED TO ME.

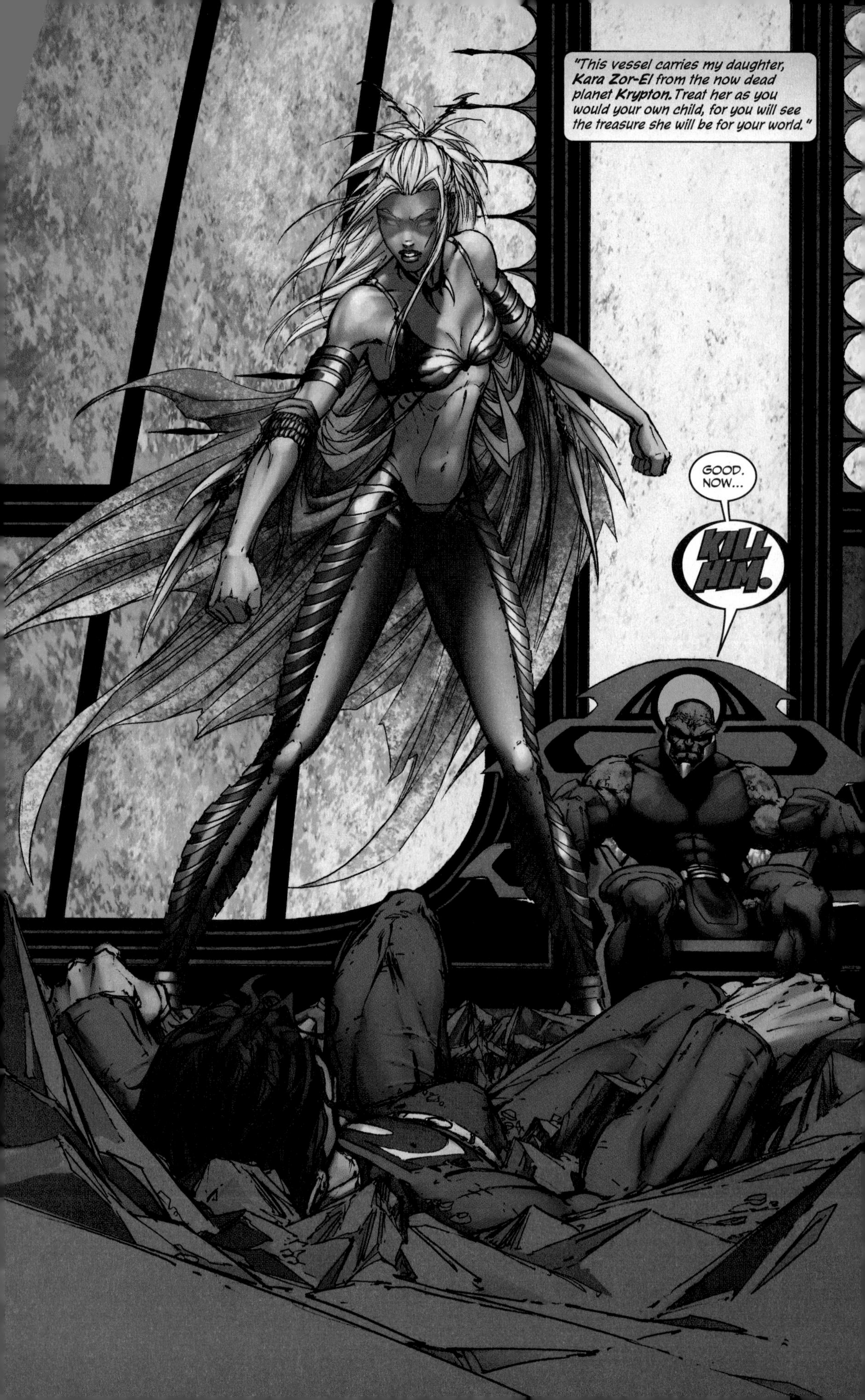
"This vessel carries my daughter, Kara Zor-El from the now dead planet Krypton. Treat her as you would your own child, for you will see the treasure she will be for your world."
GOOD. NOW...
KILL HIM.

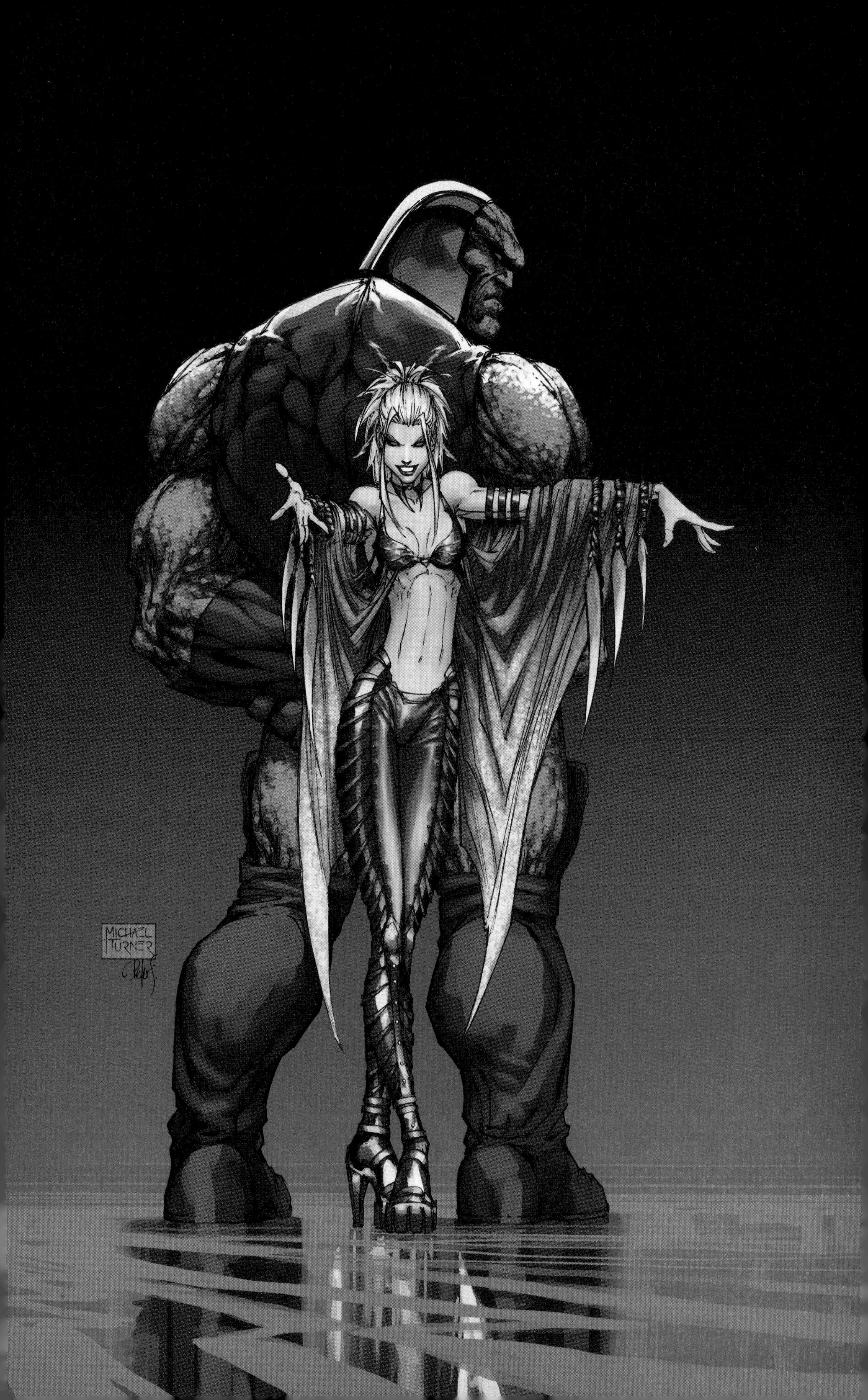
MICHAEL TURNER

TRAITOR

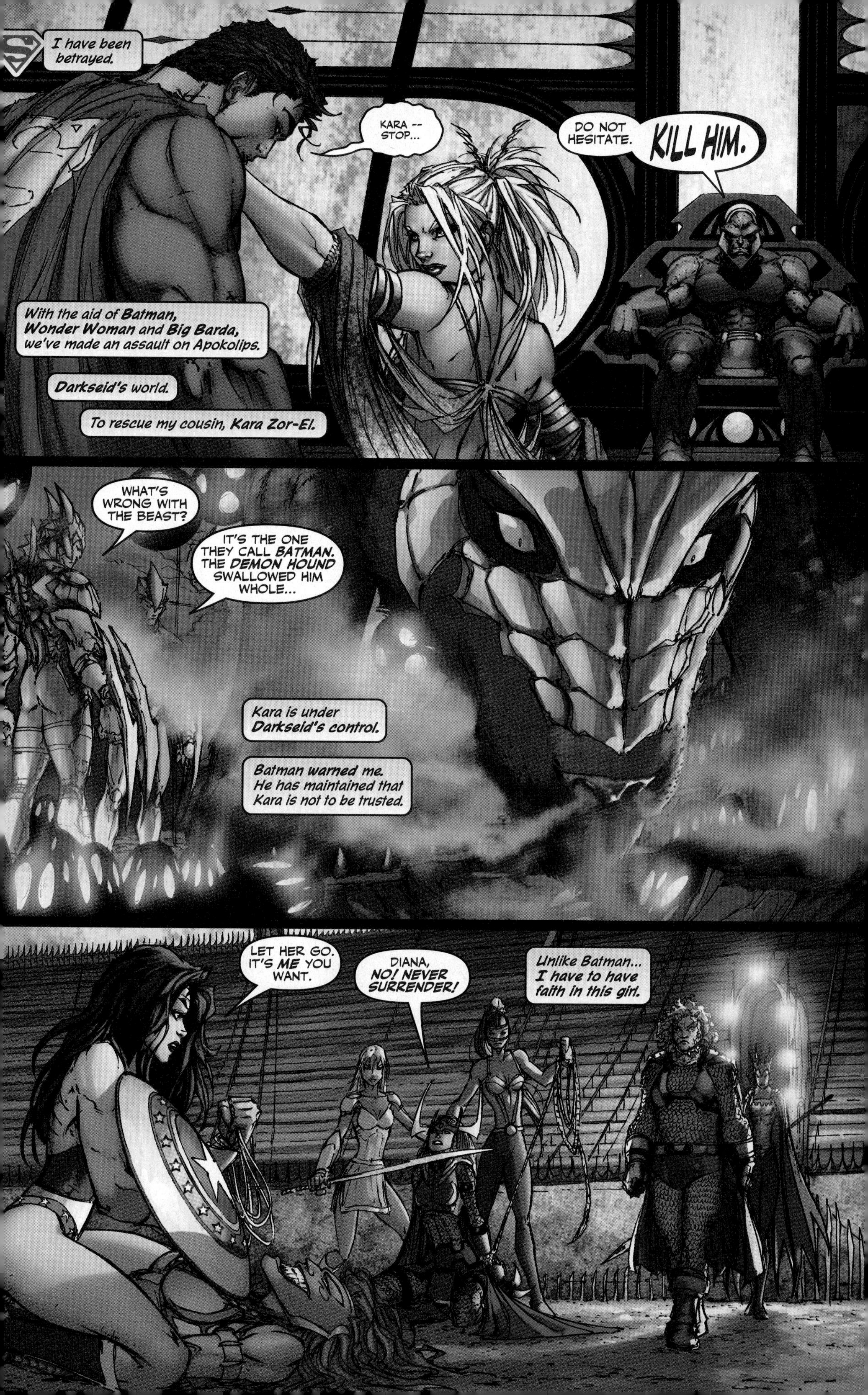

I have been betrayed.
KARA -- STOP...
DO NOT HESITATE.
KILL HIM.
With the aid of Batman, Wonder Woman and Big Barda, we've made an assault on Apokolips.
Darkseid's world.
To rescue my cousin, Kara Zor-El.
WHAT'S WRONG WITH THE BEAST?
IT'S THE ONE THEY CALL BATMAN. THE DEMON HOUND SWALLOWED HIM WHOLE...
Kara is under Darkseid's control.
Batman warned me. He has maintained that Kara is not to be trusted.
LET HER GO. IT'S ME YOU WANT.
DIANA, NO! NEVER SURRENDER!
Unlike Batman... I have to have faith in this girl.

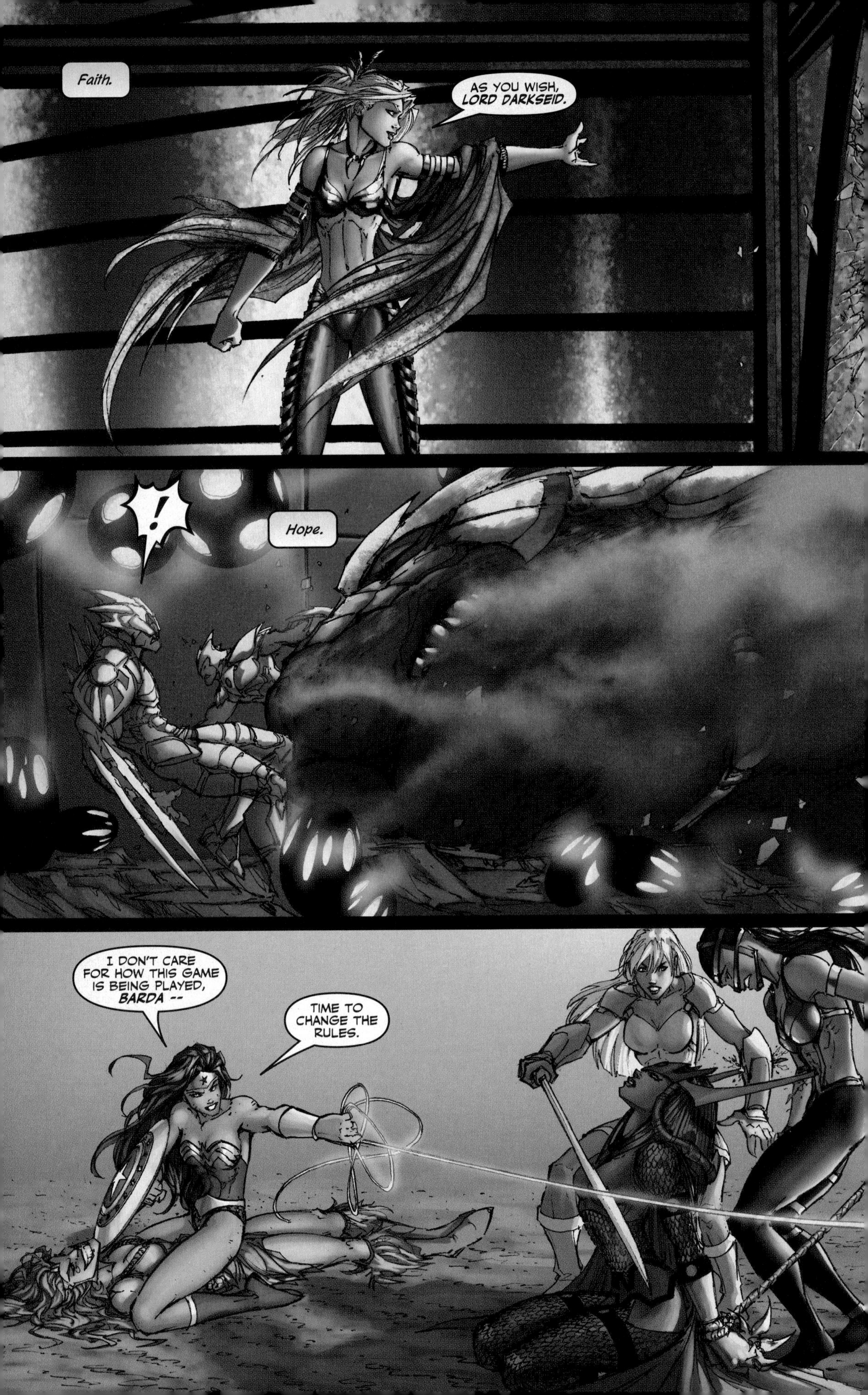
Faith.
AS YOU WISH, LORD DARKSEID.
!
Hope.
I DON'T CARE FOR HOW THIS GAME IS BEING PLAYED, BARDA --
TIME TO CHANGE THE RULES.

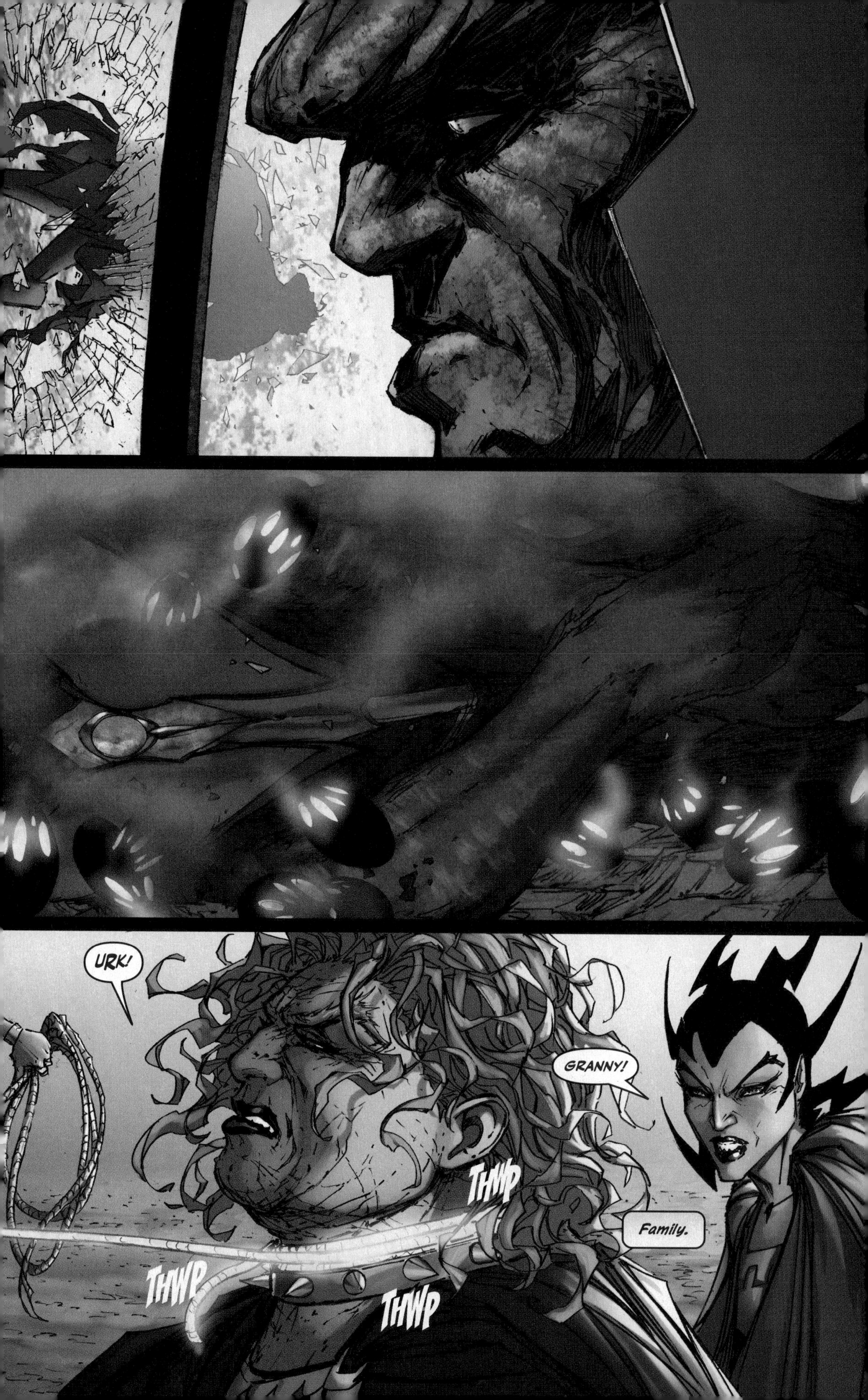
URK!
GRANNY!
THWP
Family.
THWP
THWP

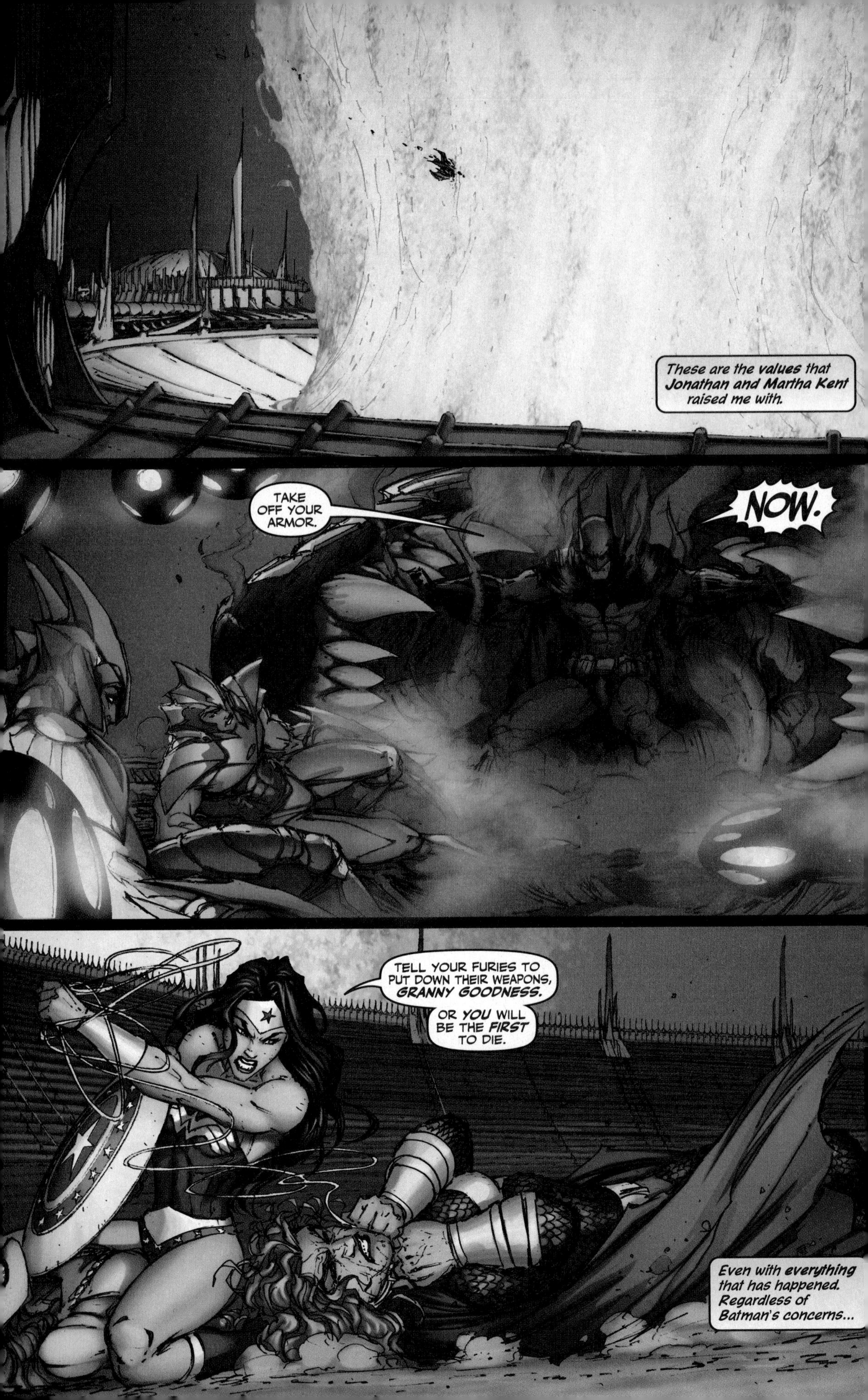
These are the values that Jonathan and Martha Kent raised me with.
TAKE OFF YOUR ARMOR.
NOW.
TELL YOUR FURIES TO PUT DOWN THEIR WEAPONS, GRANNY GOODNESS.
OR YOU WILL BE THE FIRST TO DIE.
Even with everything that has happened. Regardless of Batman's concerns...

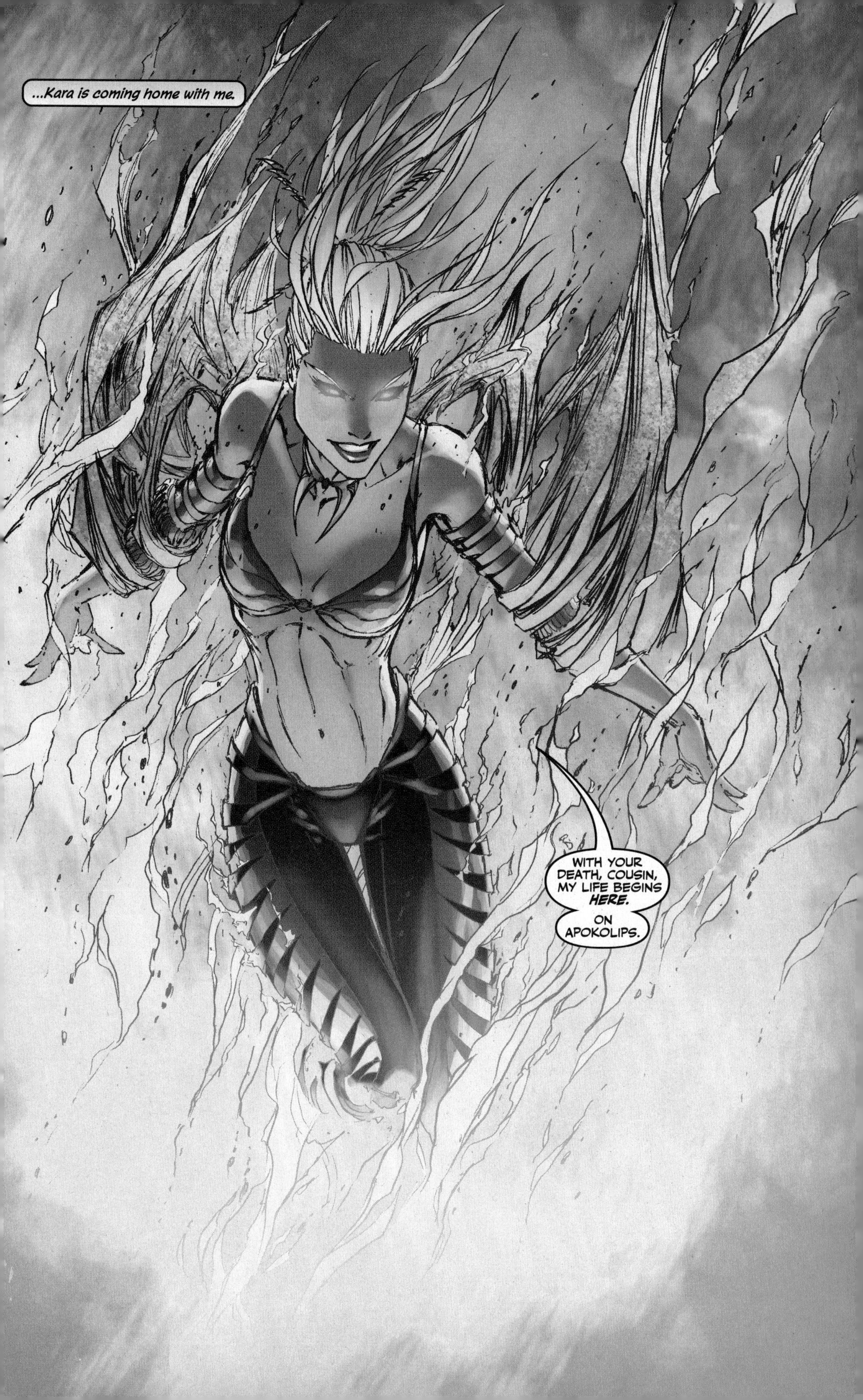
...Kara is coming home with me.
WITH YOUR DEATH, COUSIN, MY LIFE BEGINS *HERE.*
ON APOKOLIPS.

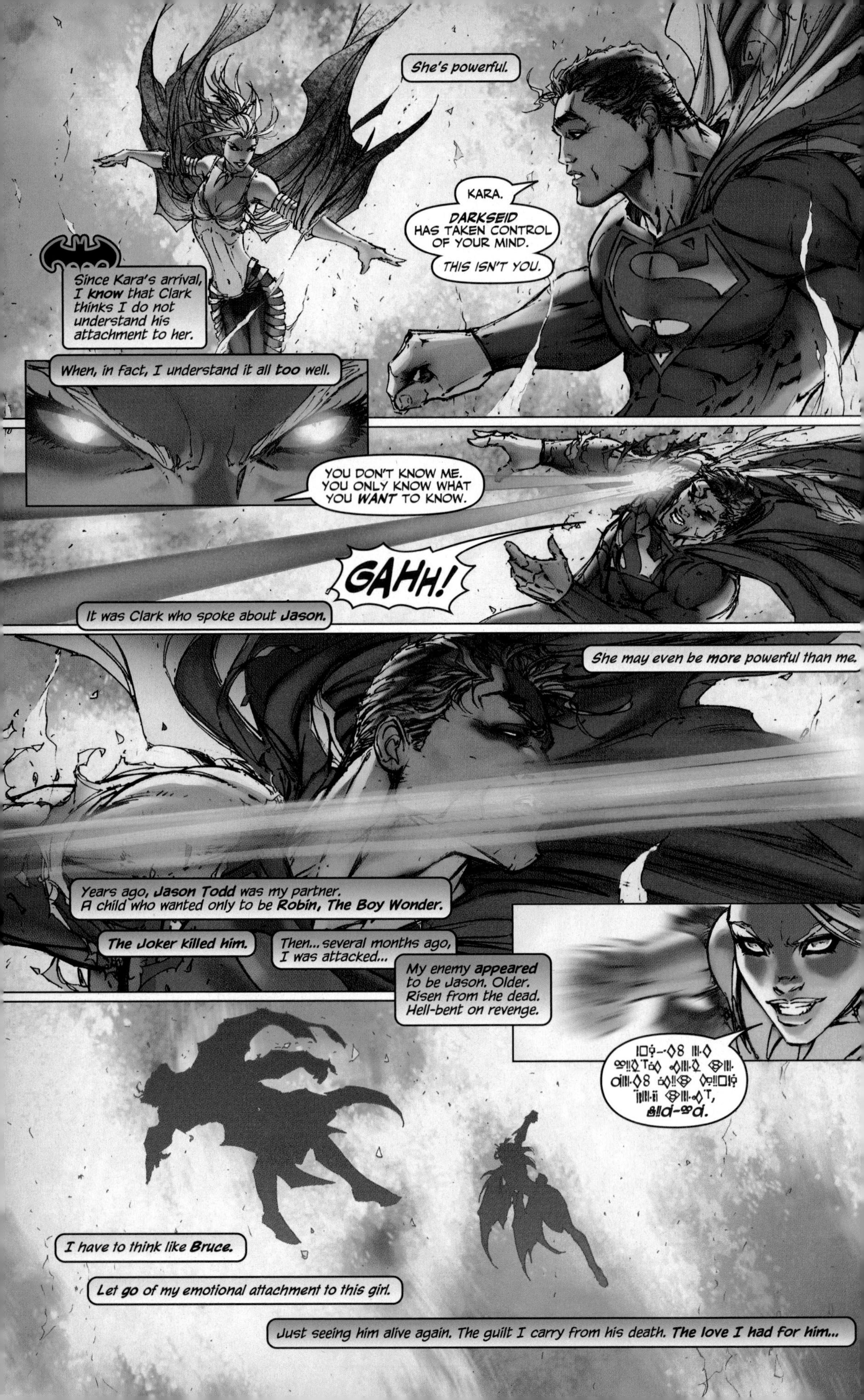
She's powerful.
KARA.
DARKSEID HAS TAKEN CONTROL OF YOUR MIND.
THIS ISN'T YOU.
Since Kara's arrival, I know that Clark thinks I do not understand his attachment to her.
When, in fact, I understand it all too well.
YOU DON'T KNOW ME. YOU ONLY KNOW WHAT YOU WANT TO KNOW.
GAHH!
It was Clark who spoke about Jason.
She may even be more powerful than me.
Years ago, Jason Todd was my partner. A child who wanted only to be Robin, The Boy Wonder.
The Joker killed him.
Then... several months ago, I was attacked...
My enemy appeared to be Jason. Older. Risen from the dead. Hell-bent on revenge.
I have to think like Bruce.
Let go of my emotional attachment to this girl.
Just seeing him alive again. The guilt I carry from his death. The love I had for him...

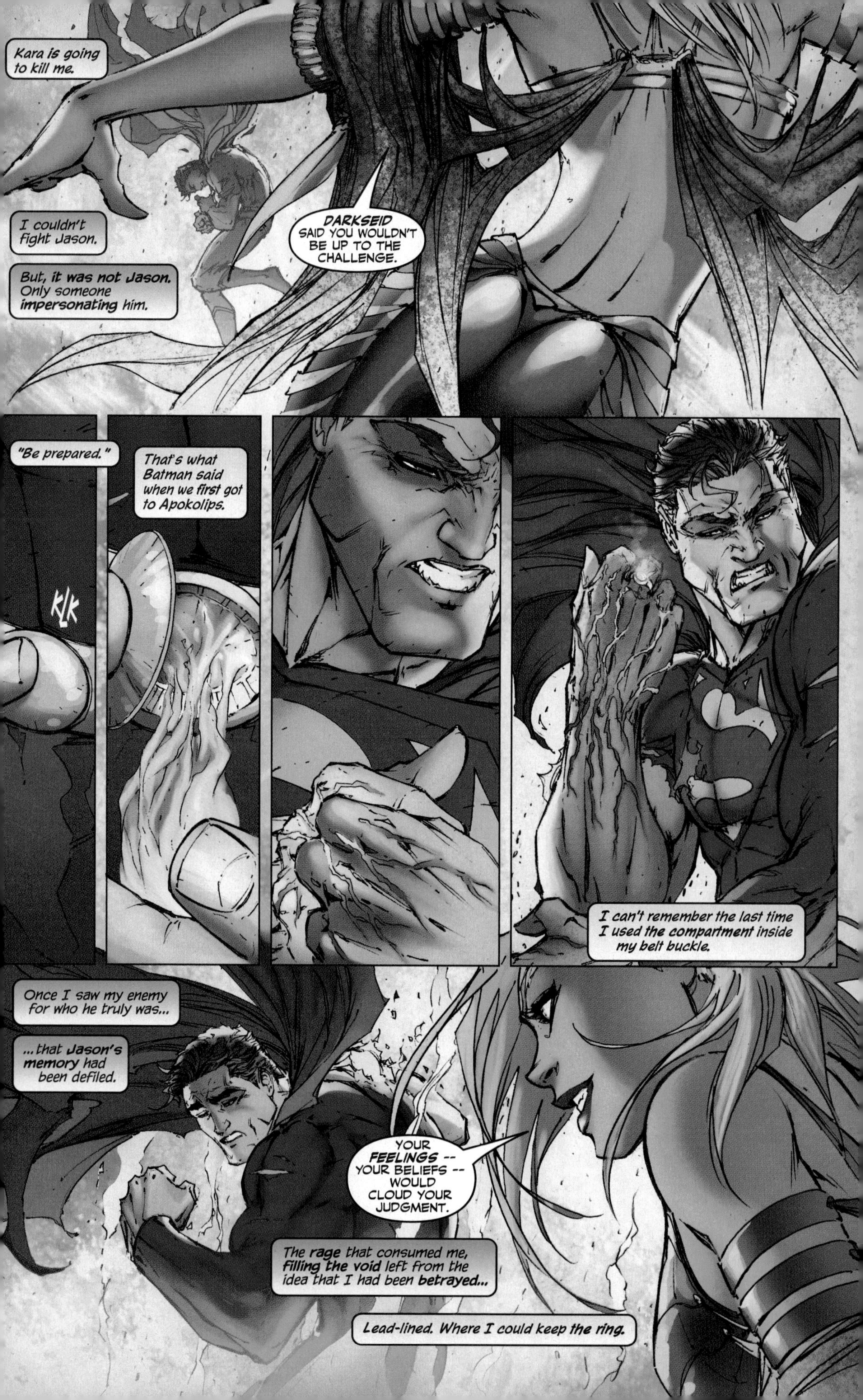
Kara is going to kill me.
I couldn't fight Jason.
But, it was not Jason. Only someone impersonating him.
DARKSEID SAID YOU WOULDN'T BE UP TO THE CHALLENGE.
"Be prepared."
That's what Batman said when we first got to Apokolips.
KLIK
I can't remember the last time I used the compartment inside my belt buckle.
Once I saw my enemy for who he truly was...
...that Jason's memory had been defiled.
YOUR FEELINGS -- YOUR BELIEFS -- WOULD CLOUD YOUR JUDGMENT.
The rage that consumed me, filling the void left from the idea that I had been betrayed...
Lead-lined. Where I could keep the ring.

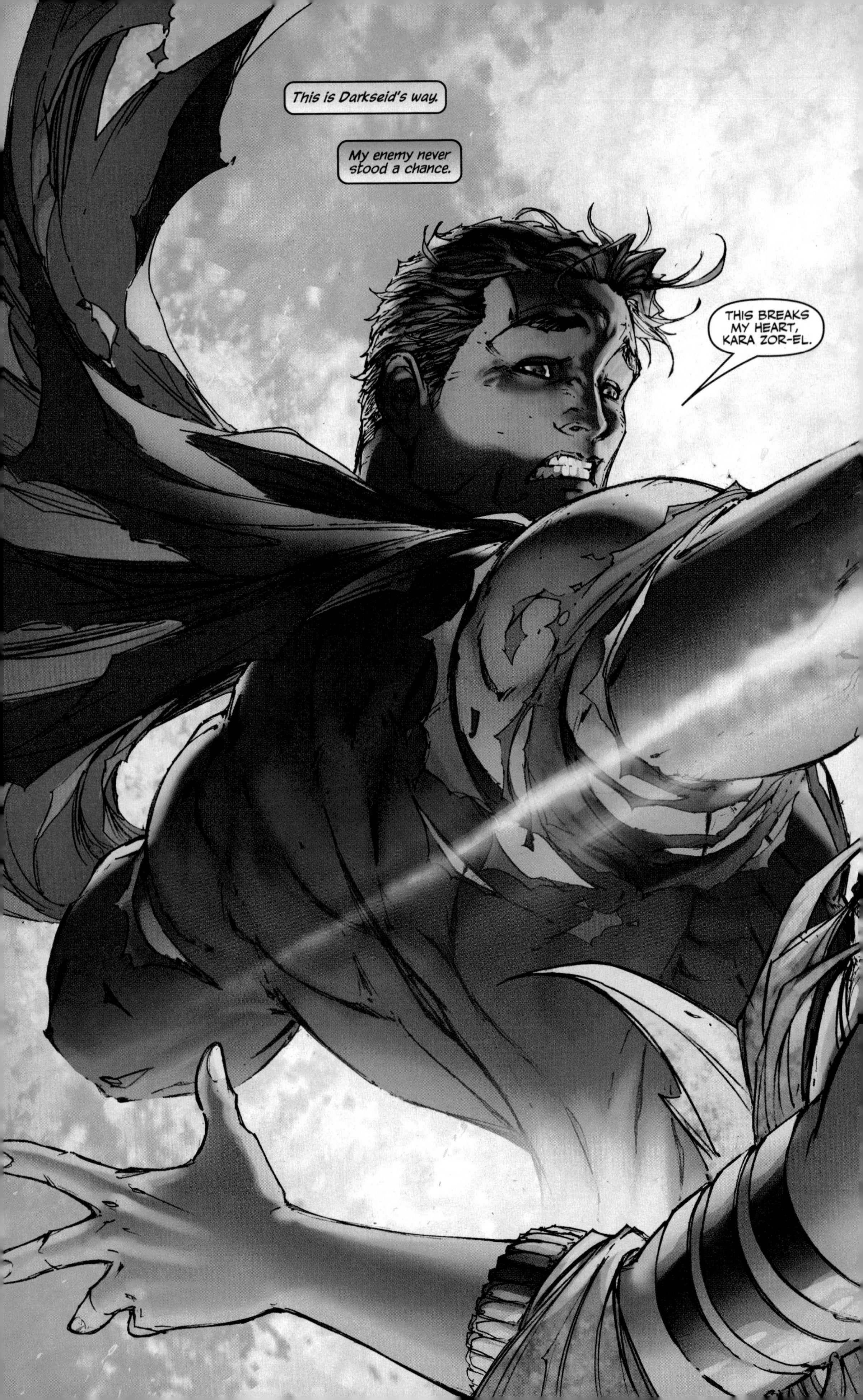
This is Darkseid's way.
My enemy never stood a chance.
THIS BREAKS MY HEART, KARA ZOR-EL.

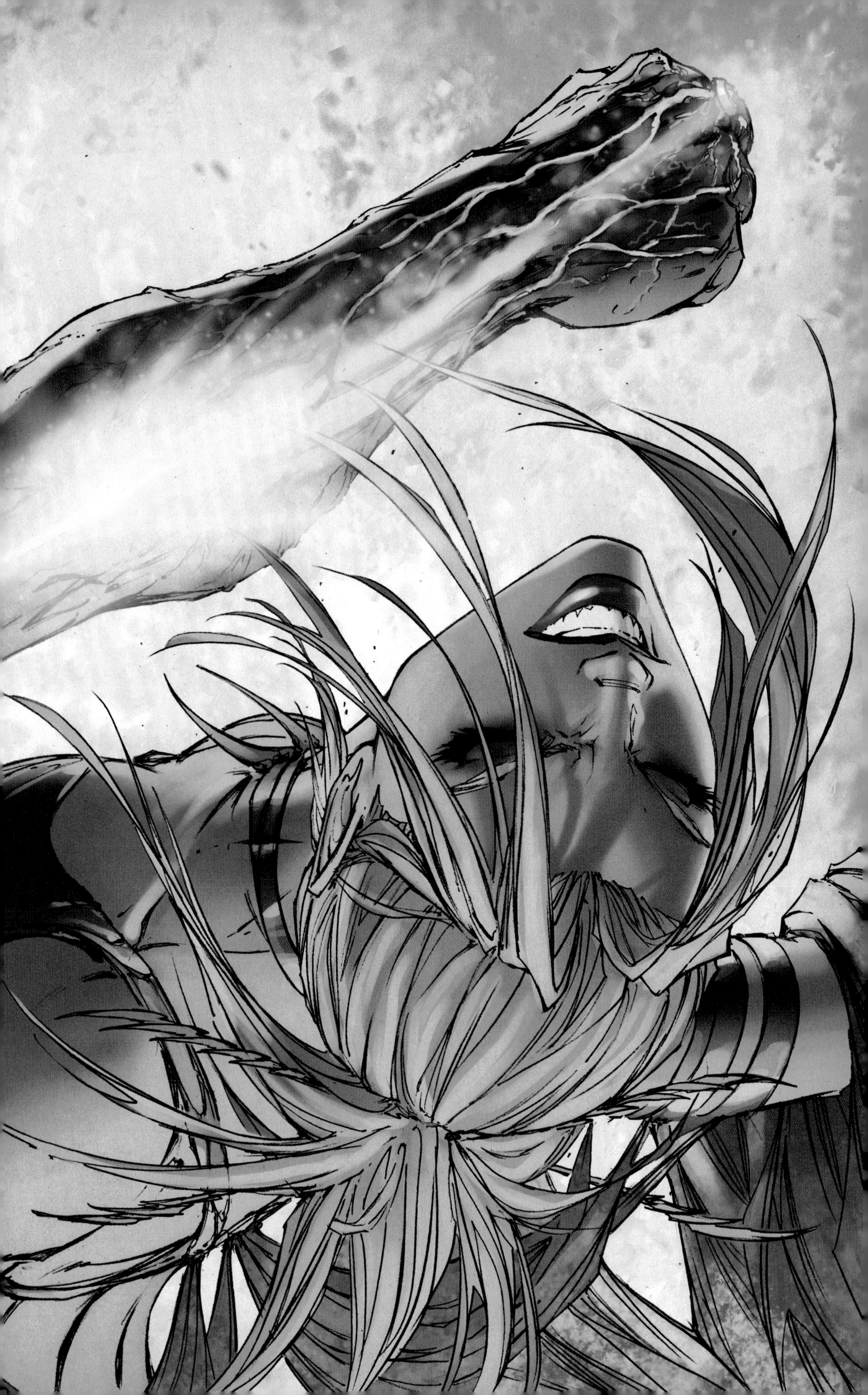

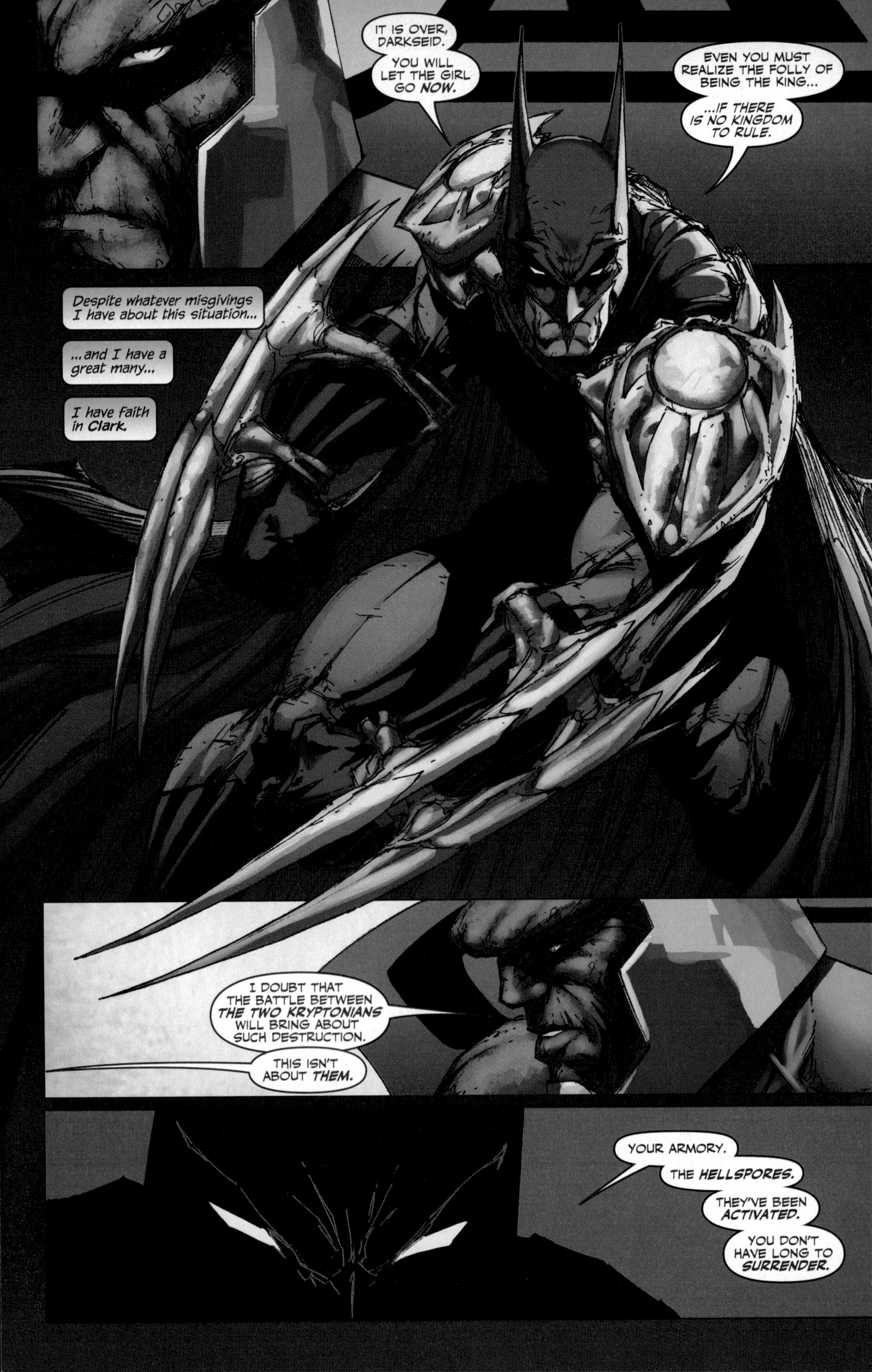
IT IS OVER, DARKSEID.
YOU WILL LET THE GIRL GO NOW.
EVEN YOU MUST REALIZE THE FOLLY OF BEING THE KING...
...IF THERE IS NO KINGDOM TO RULE.
Despite whatever misgivings I have about this situation...
...and I have a great many...
I have faith in Clark.
I DOUBT THAT THE BATTLE BETWEEN THE TWO KRYPTONIANS WILL BRING ABOUT SUCH DESTRUCTION.
THIS ISN'T ABOUT THEM.
YOUR ARMORY.
THE HELLSPORES.
THEY'VE BEEN ACTIVATED.
YOU DON'T HAVE LONG TO SURRENDER.

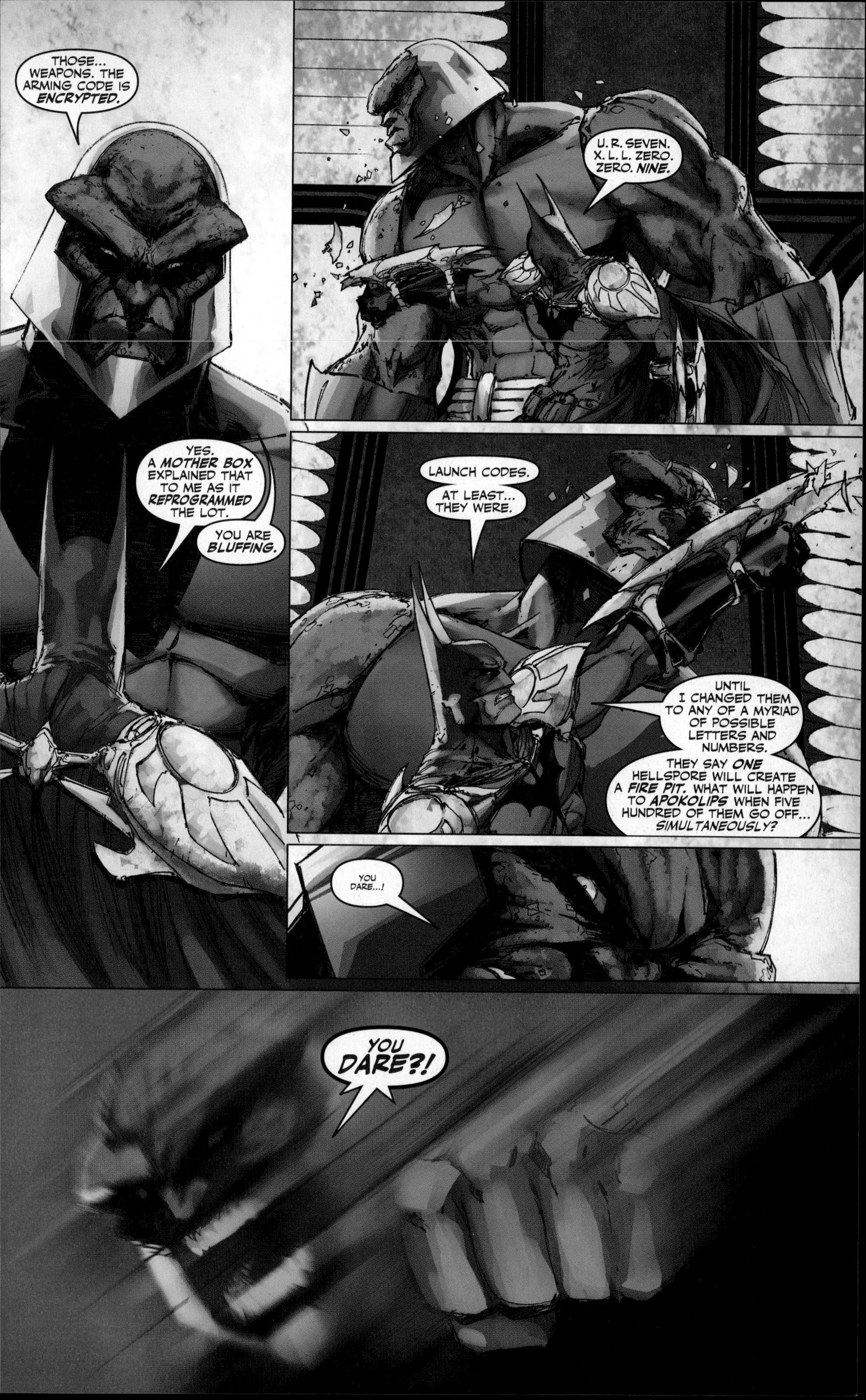
THOSE... WEAPONS. THE ARMING CODE IS *ENCRYPTED.*
U. R. SEVEN. X. L. L. ZERO. ZERO. *NINE.*
YES. A *MOTHER BOX* EXPLAINED THAT TO ME AS IT *REPROGRAMMED* THE LOT.
YOU ARE *BLUFFING.*
LAUNCH CODES.
AT LEAST... THEY WERE.
UNTIL I CHANGED THEM TO ANY OF A MYRIAD OF POSSIBLE LETTERS AND NUMBERS.
THEY SAY *ONE* HELLSPORE WILL CREATE A *FIRE PIT.* WHAT WILL HAPPEN TO *APOKOLIPS* WHEN FIVE HUNDRED OF THEM GO OFF... *SIMULTANEOUSLY?*
YOU DARE...!
YOU *DARE?!*

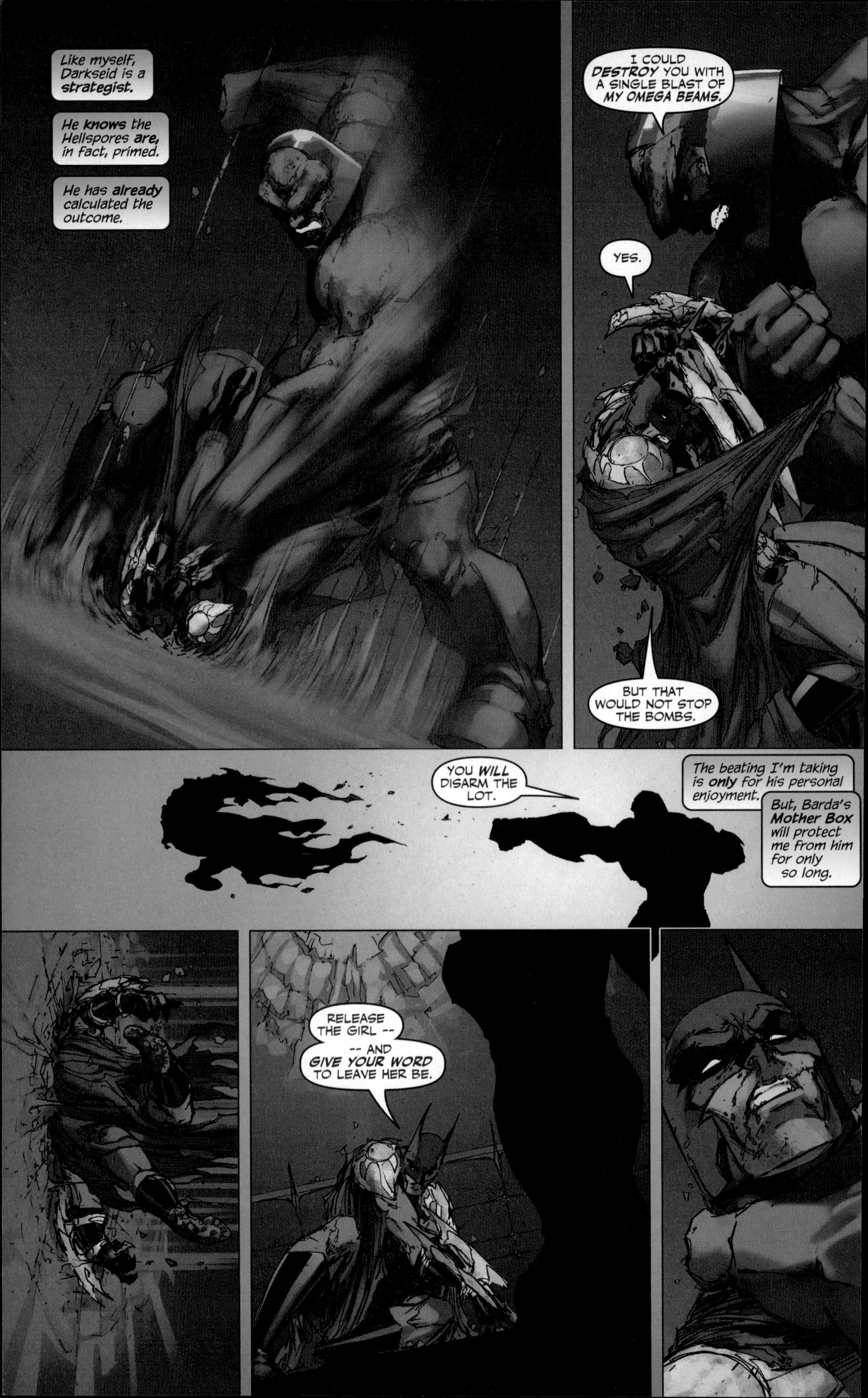
Like myself, Darkseid is a **strategist.**
He **knows** the Hellspores **are,** in fact, primed.
He has **already** calculated the outcome.
I COULD **DESTROY** YOU WITH A SINGLE BLAST OF **MY OMEGA BEAMS.**
YES.
BUT THAT WOULD NOT STOP THE BOMBS.
YOU **WILL** DISARM THE LOT.
The beating I'm taking is **only** for his personal enjoyment.
But, Barda's **Mother Box** will protect me from him for only so long.
RELEASE THE GIRL --
-- AND **GIVE YOUR WORD** TO LEAVE HER BE.

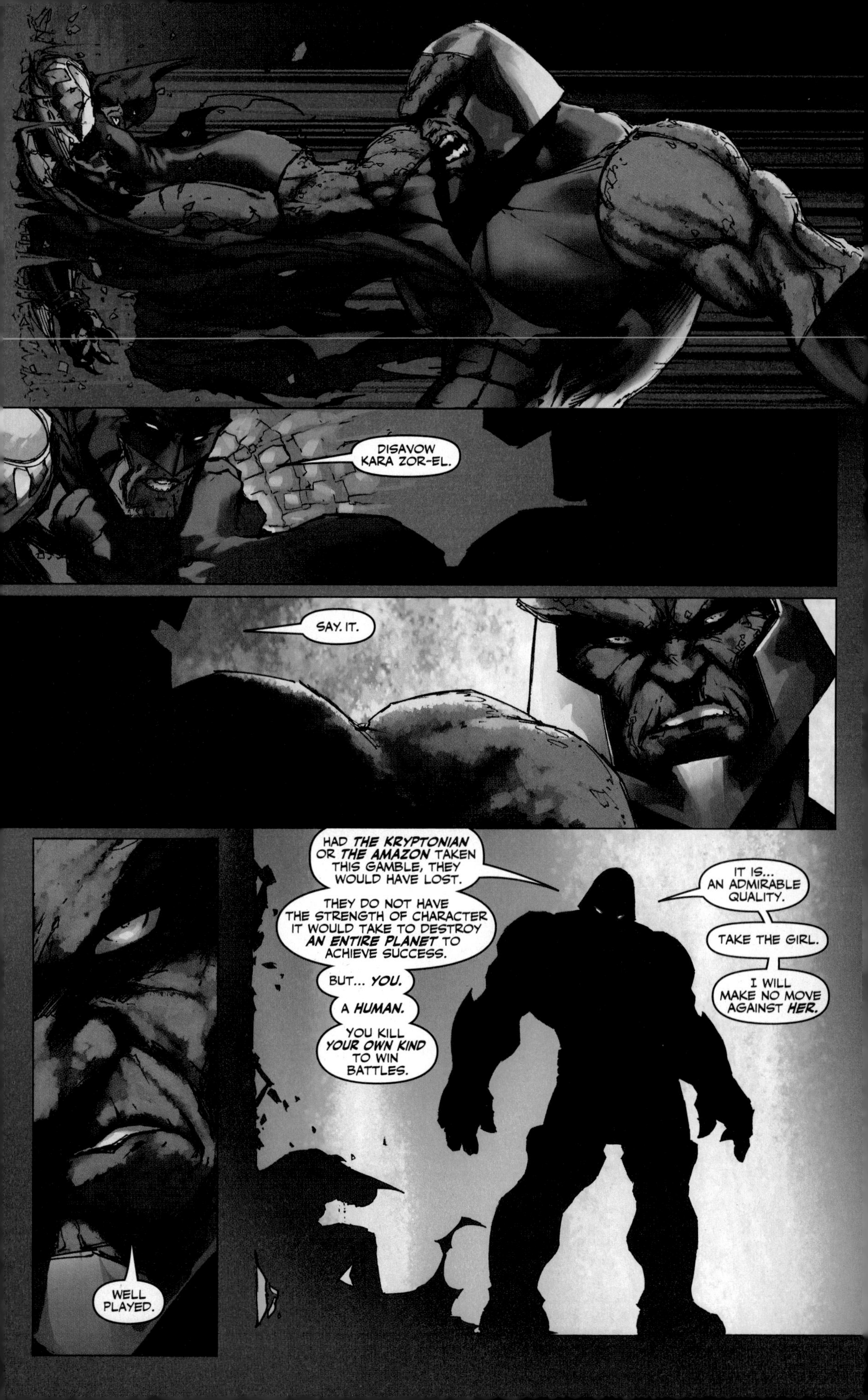
DISAVOW KARA ZOR-EL.
SAY. IT.
HAD *THE KRYPTONIAN* OR *THE AMAZON* TAKEN THIS GAMBLE, THEY WOULD HAVE LOST.
THEY DO NOT HAVE THE STRENGTH OF CHARACTER IT WOULD TAKE TO DESTROY *AN ENTIRE PLANET* TO ACHIEVE SUCCESS.
BUT... *YOU.*
A *HUMAN.*
YOU KILL *YOUR OWN KIND* TO WIN BATTLES.
IT IS... AN ADMIRABLE QUALITY.
TAKE THE GIRL.
I WILL MAKE NO MOVE AGAINST *HER.*
WELL PLAYED.

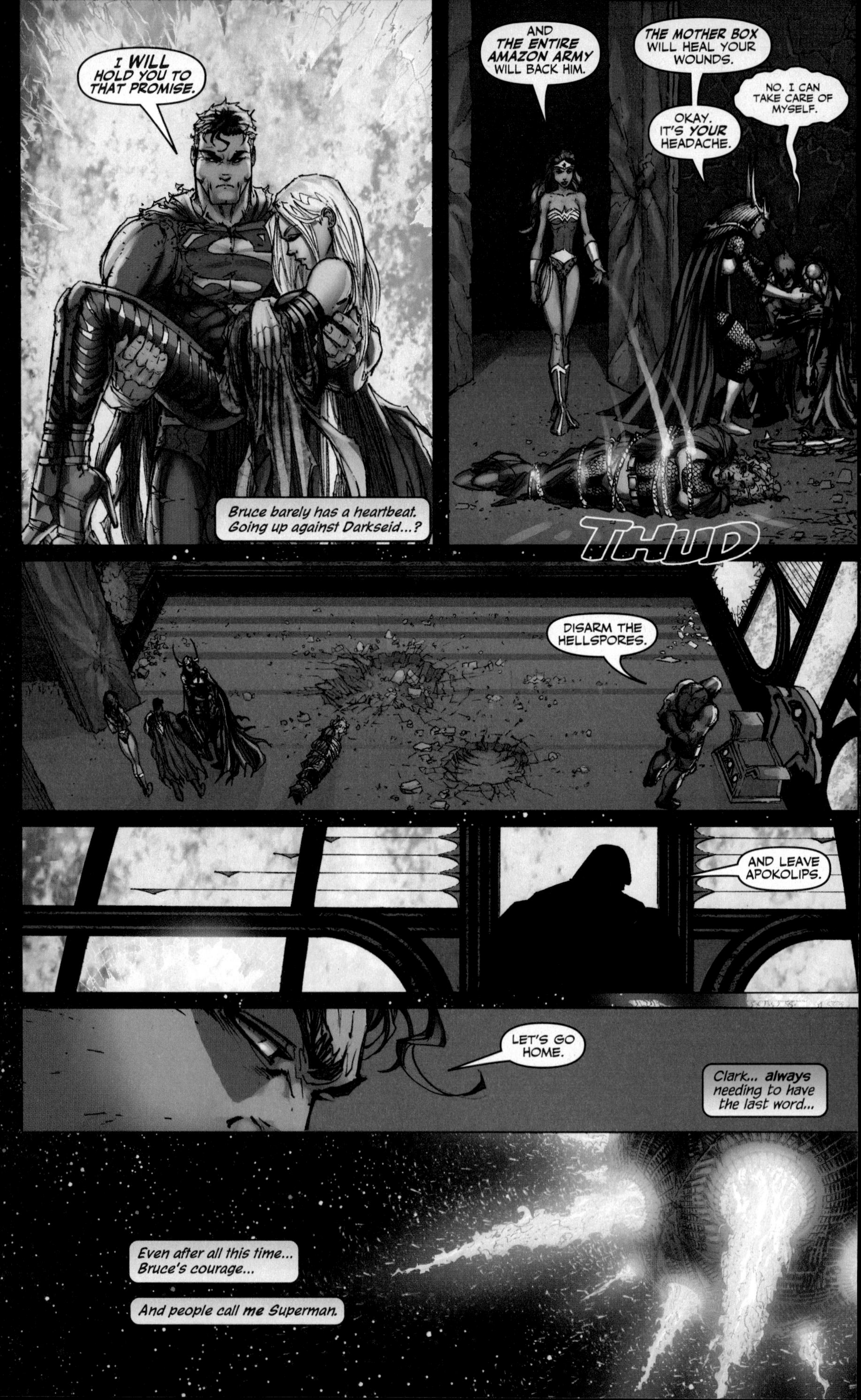

I WILL HOLD YOU TO THAT PROMISE.
Bruce barely has a heartbeat. Going up against Darkseid...?
AND THE ENTIRE AMAZON ARMY WILL BACK HIM.
THE MOTHER BOX WILL HEAL YOUR WOUNDS.
NO. I CAN TAKE CARE OF MYSELF.
OKAY. IT'S YOUR HEADACHE.
THUD
DISARM THE HELLSPORES.
AND LEAVE APOKOLIPS.
LET'S GO HOME.
Clark... always needing to have the last word...
Even after all this time... Bruce's courage...
And people call me Superman.

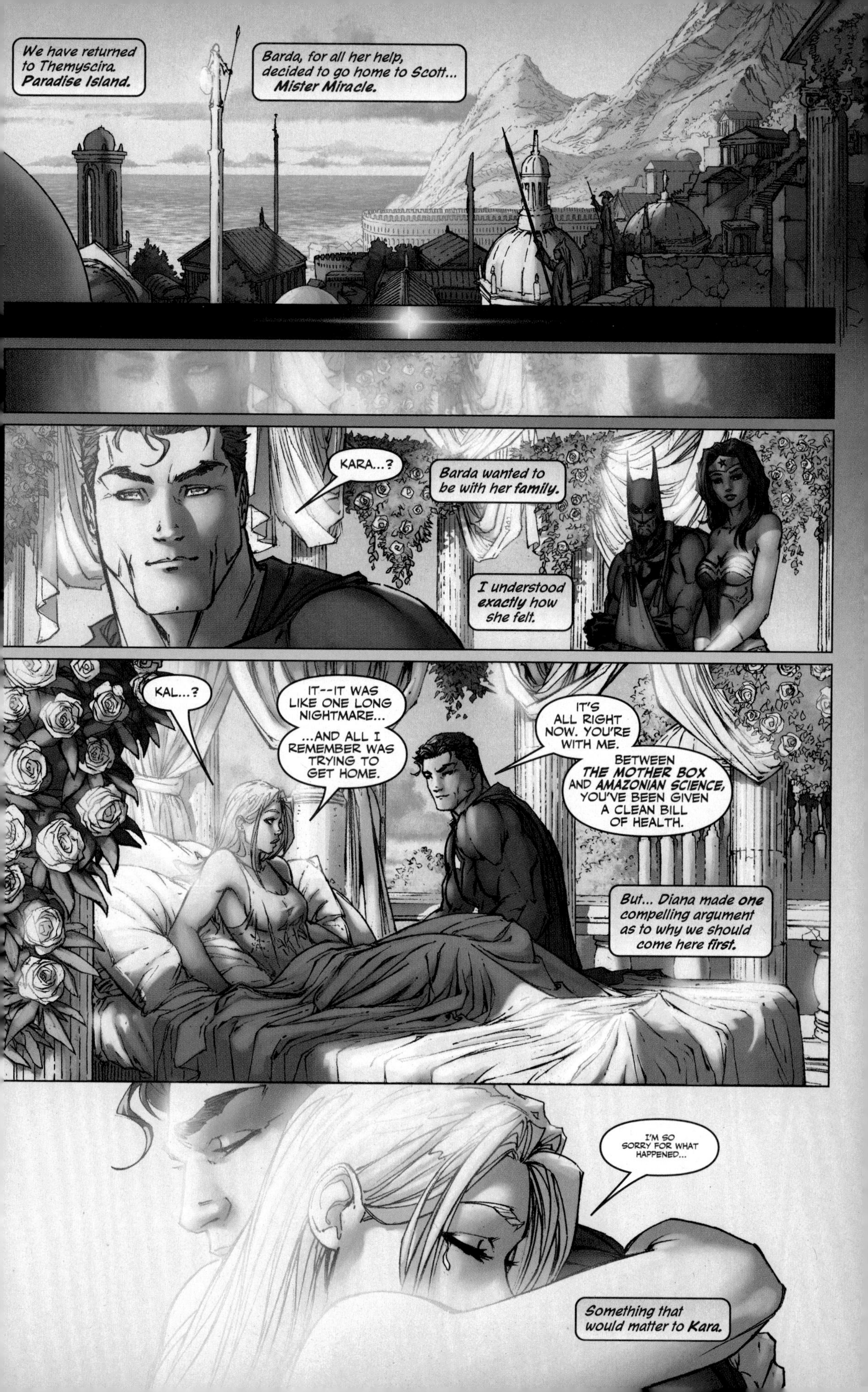
We have returned to Themyscira. Paradise Island.
Barda, for all her help, decided to go home to Scott... Mister Miracle.
KARA...?
Barda wanted to be with her family.
I understood exactly how she felt.
KAL...?
IT--IT WAS LIKE ONE LONG NIGHTMARE...
...AND ALL I REMEMBER WAS TRYING TO GET HOME.
IT'S ALL RIGHT NOW. YOU'RE WITH ME.
BETWEEN THE MOTHER BOX AND AMAZONIAN SCIENCE, YOU'VE BEEN GIVEN A CLEAN BILL OF HEALTH.
But... Diana made one compelling argument as to why we should come here first.
I'M SO SORRY FOR WHAT HAPPENED...
Something that would matter to Kara.

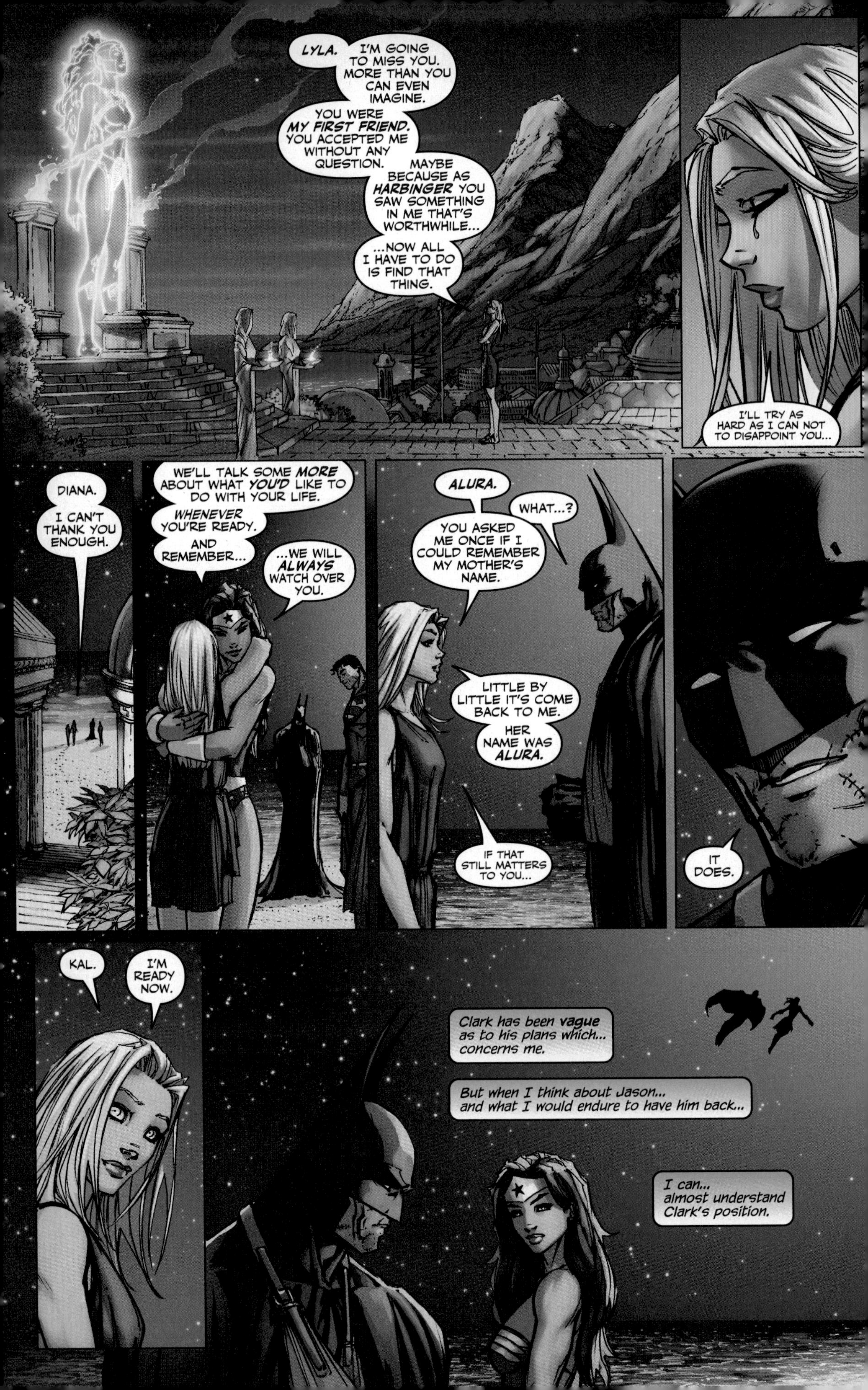
LYLA.
I'M GOING TO MISS YOU. MORE THAN YOU CAN EVEN IMAGINE.
YOU WERE MY FIRST FRIEND. YOU ACCEPTED ME WITHOUT ANY QUESTION.
MAYBE BECAUSE AS HARBINGER YOU SAW SOMETHING IN ME THAT'S WORTHWHILE...
...NOW ALL I HAVE TO DO IS FIND THAT THING.
I'LL TRY AS HARD AS I CAN NOT TO DISAPPOINT YOU...
DIANA.
I CAN'T THANK YOU ENOUGH.
WE'LL TALK SOME MORE ABOUT WHAT YOU'D LIKE TO DO WITH YOUR LIFE.
WHENEVER YOU'RE READY.
AND REMEMBER...
...WE WILL ALWAYS WATCH OVER YOU.
ALURA.
WHAT...?
YOU ASKED ME ONCE IF I COULD REMEMBER MY MOTHER'S NAME.
LITTLE BY LITTLE IT'S COME BACK TO ME.
HER NAME WAS ALURA.
IF THAT STILL MATTERS TO YOU...
IT DOES.
KAL.
I'M READY NOW.
Clark has been vague as to his plans which... concerns me.
But when I think about Jason... and what I would endure to have him back...
I can... almost understand Clark's position.

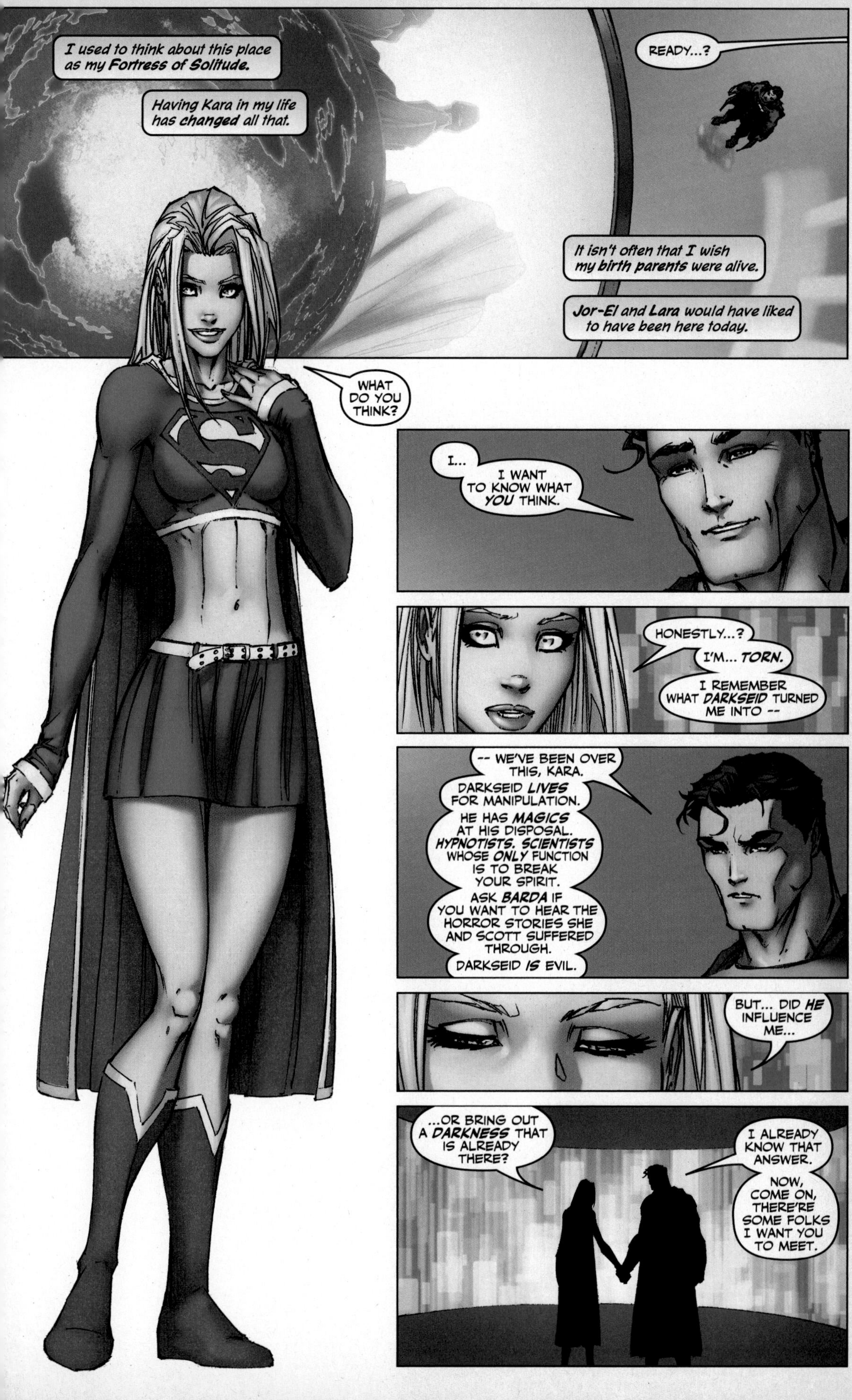

I used to think about this place as my Fortress of Solitude.
Having Kara in my life has changed all that.
READY...?
It isn't often that I wish my birth parents were alive.
Jor-El and Lara would have liked to have been here today.
WHAT DO YOU THINK?
I...
I WANT TO KNOW WHAT YOU THINK.
HONESTLY...?
I'M... TORN.
I REMEMBER WHAT DARKSEID TURNED ME INTO --
-- WE'VE BEEN OVER THIS, KARA.
DARKSEID LIVES FOR MANIPULATION.
HE HAS MAGICS AT HIS DISPOSAL.
HYPNOTISTS. SCIENTISTS WHOSE ONLY FUNCTION IS TO BREAK YOUR SPIRIT.
ASK BARDA IF YOU WANT TO HEAR THE HORROR STORIES SHE AND SCOTT SUFFERED THROUGH.
DARKSEID IS EVIL.
BUT... DID HE INFLUENCE ME...
...OR BRING OUT A DARKNESS THAT IS ALREADY THERE?
I ALREADY KNOW THAT ANSWER.
NOW, COME ON, THERE'RE SOME FOLKS I WANT YOU TO MEET.

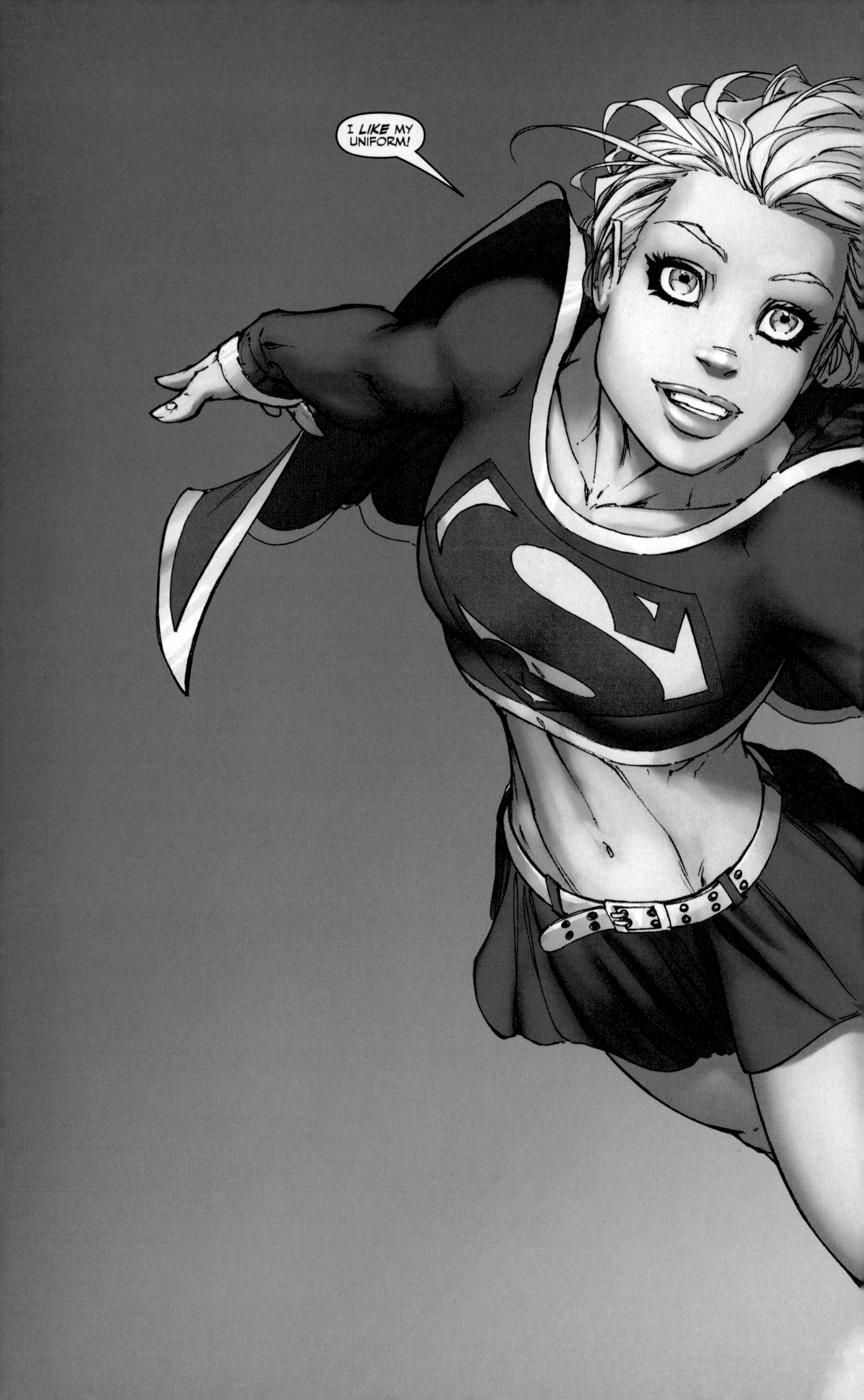
I LIKE MY UNIFORM!

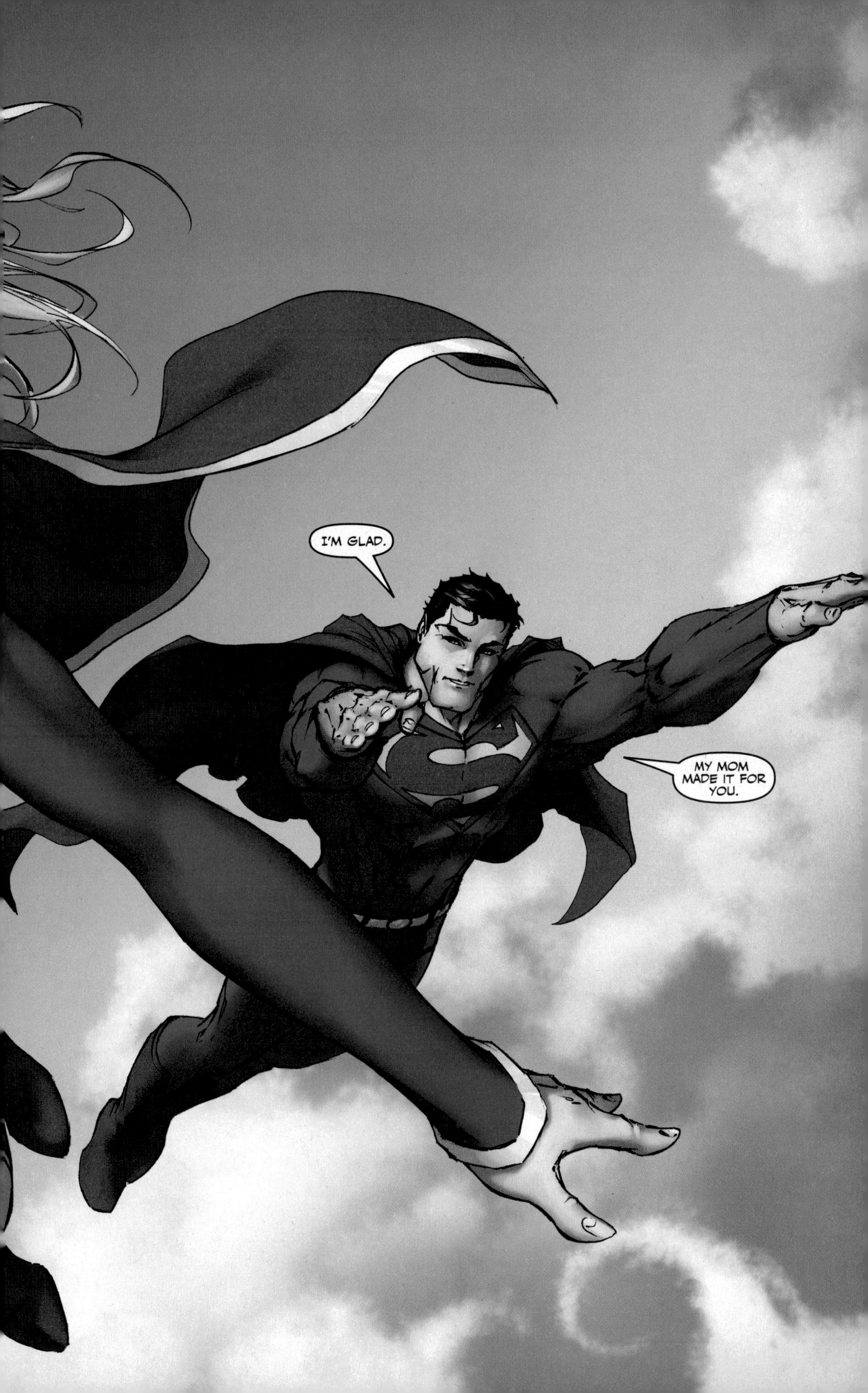
I'M GLAD.
MY MOM MADE IT FOR YOU.

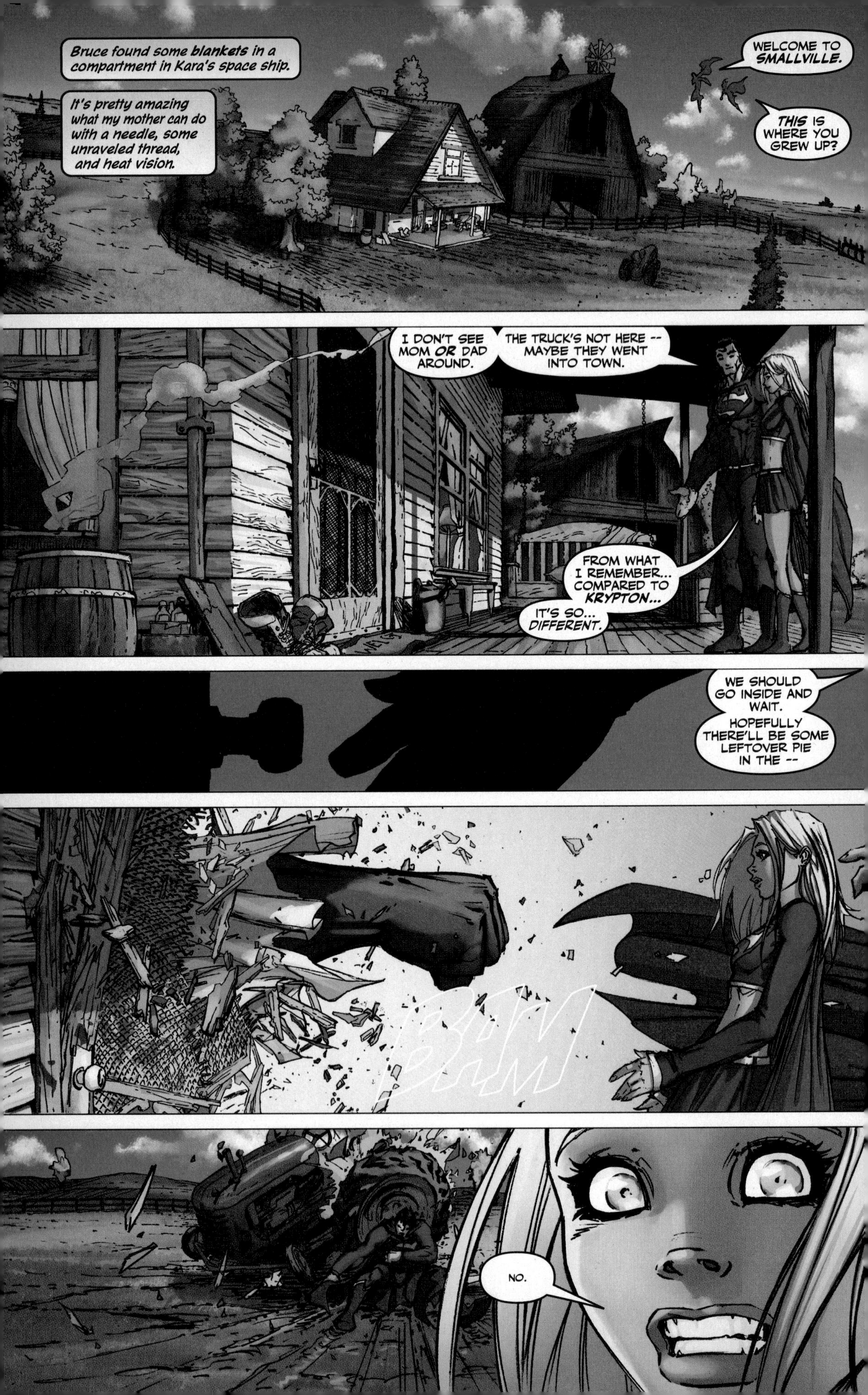

Bruce found some **blankets** in a compartment in Kara's space ship.
It's pretty amazing what my mother can do with a needle, some unraveled thread, and heat vision.
WELCOME TO **SMALLVILLE.**
THIS IS WHERE YOU GREW UP?
I DON'T SEE MOM ***OR*** DAD AROUND.
THE TRUCK'S NOT HERE -- MAYBE THEY WENT INTO TOWN.
FROM WHAT I REMEMBER... COMPARED TO ***KRYPTON...***
IT'S SO... ***DIFFERENT.***
WE SHOULD GO INSIDE AND WAIT.
HOPEFULLY THERE'LL BE SOME LEFTOVER PIE IN THE --
BAM
NO.

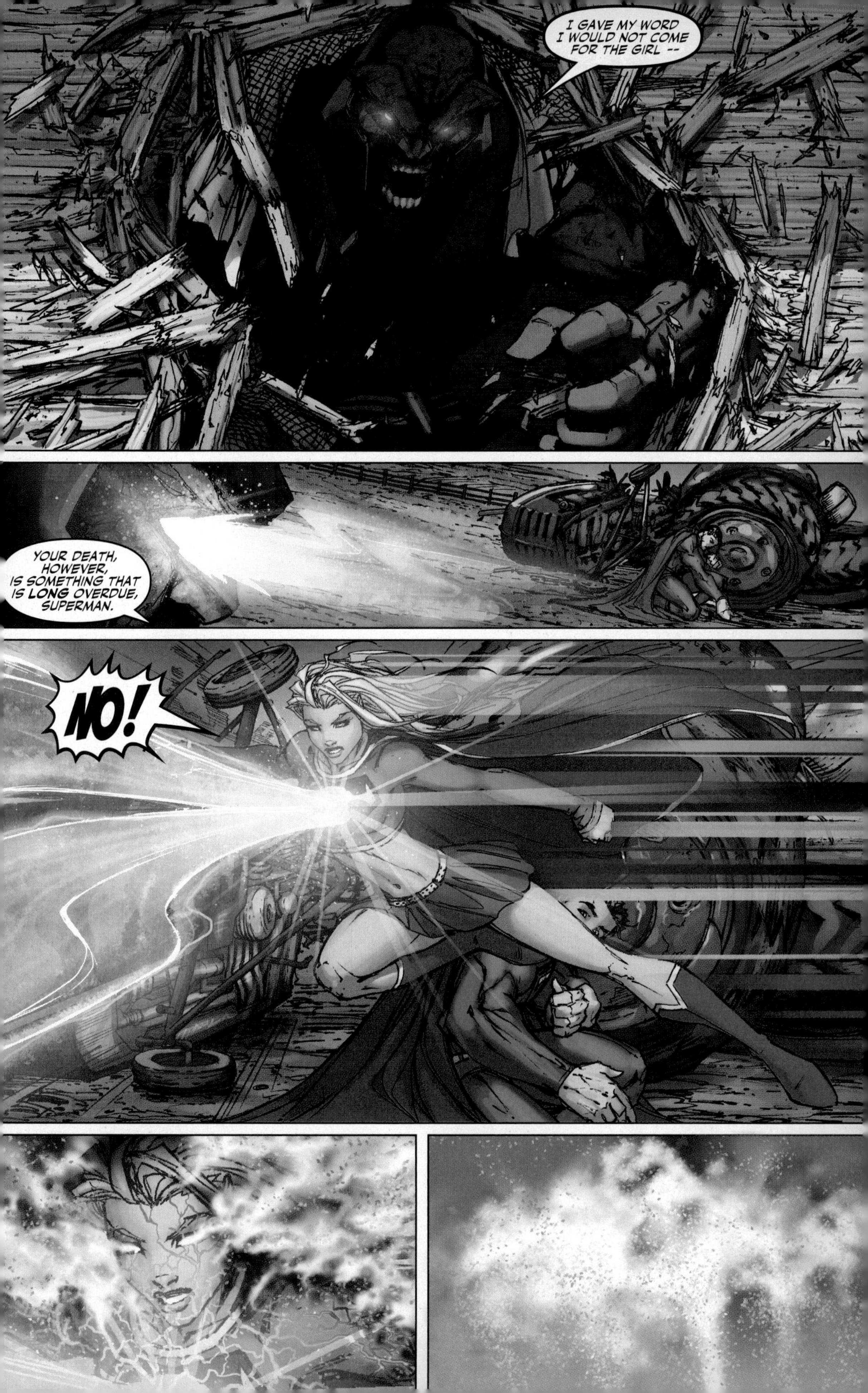
I GAVE MY WORD I WOULD NOT COME FOR THE GIRL --
YOUR DEATH, HOWEVER, IS SOMETHING THAT IS **LONG** OVERDUE, SUPERMAN.
NO!

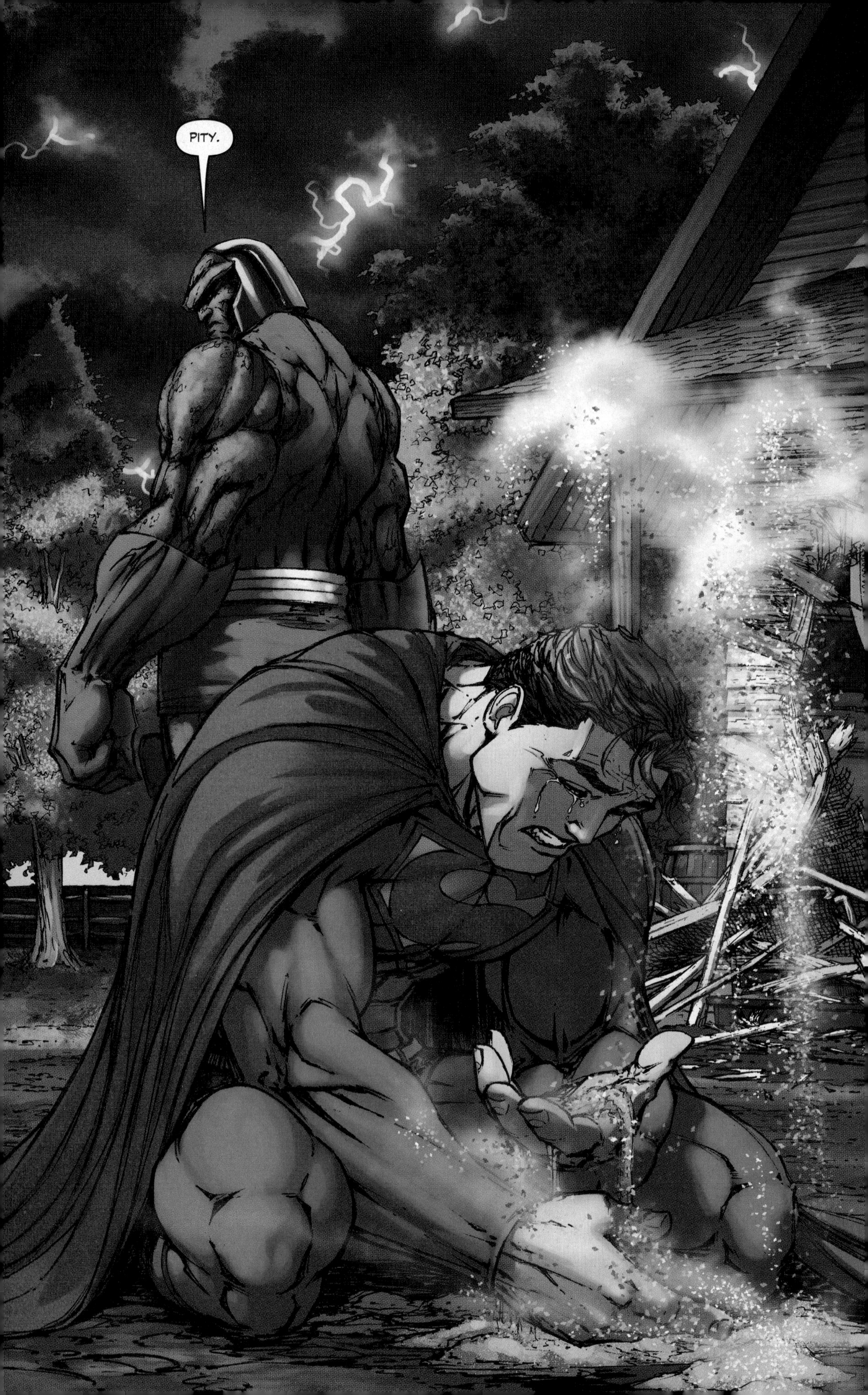
PITY.

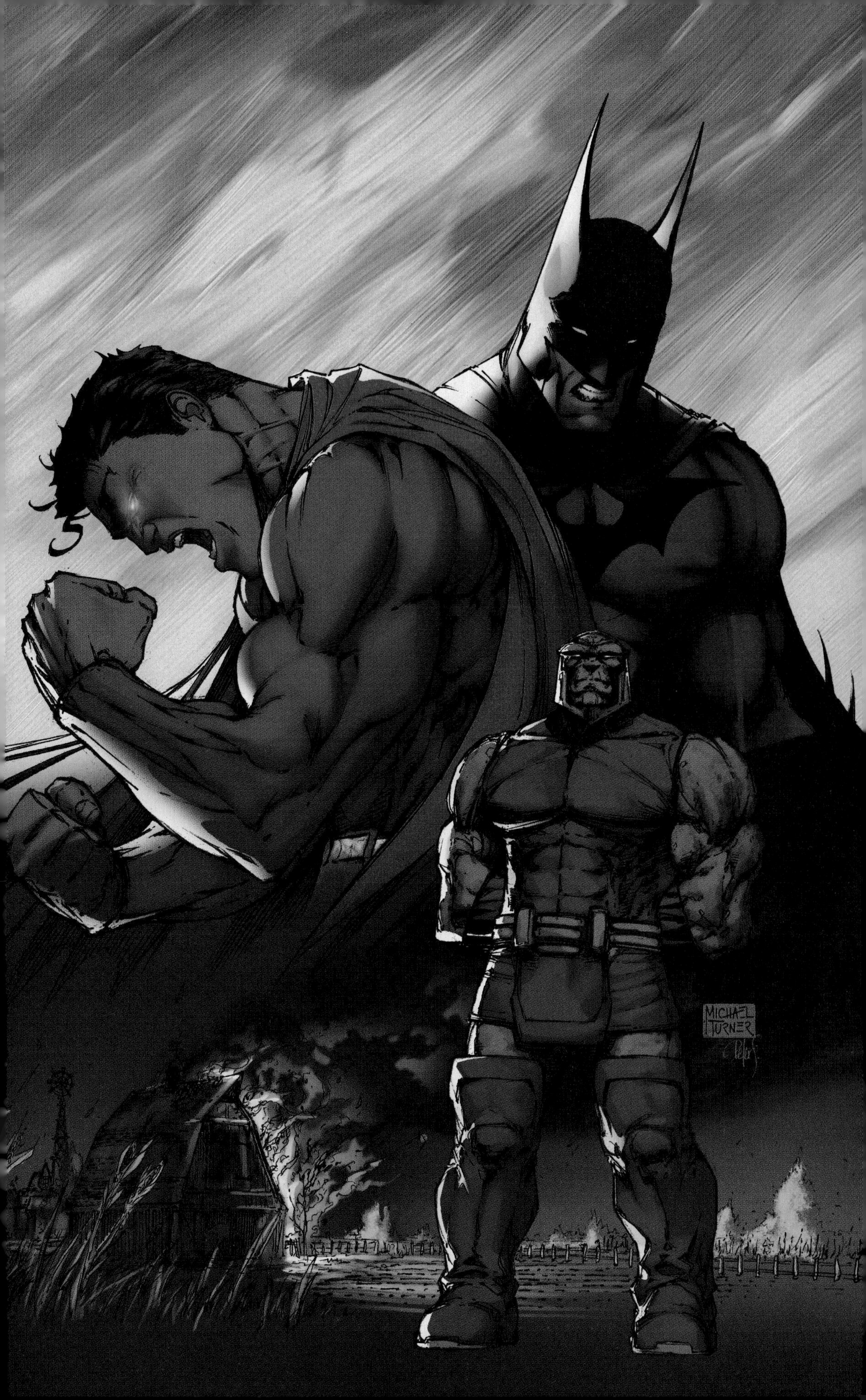
MICHAEL TURNER

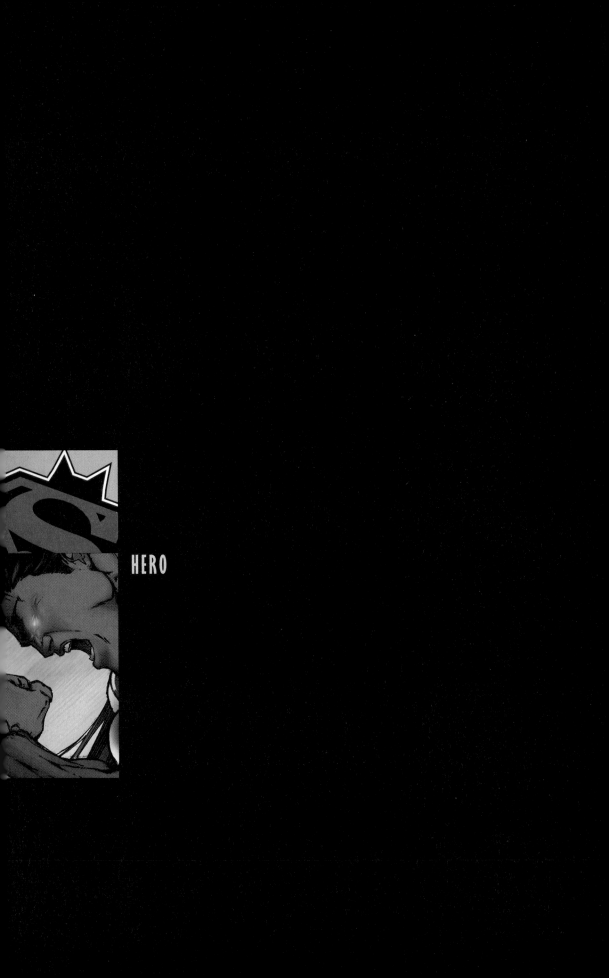

HERO

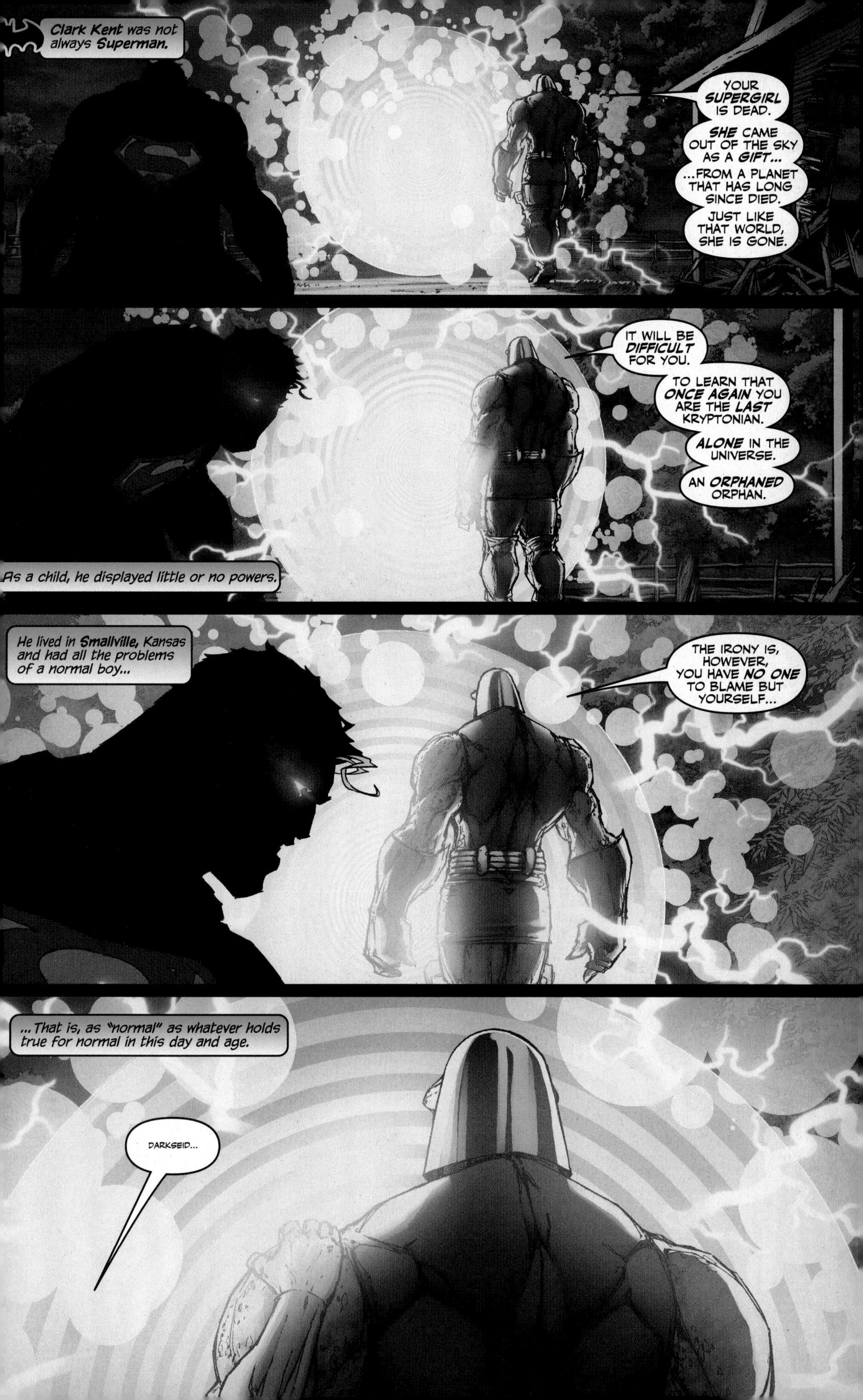
Clark Kent was not always Superman.
YOUR SUPERGIRL IS DEAD.
SHE CAME OUT OF THE SKY AS A GIFT...
...FROM A PLANET THAT HAS LONG SINCE DIED.
JUST LIKE THAT WORLD, SHE IS GONE.
IT WILL BE DIFFICULT FOR YOU.
TO LEARN THAT ONCE AGAIN YOU ARE THE LAST KRYPTONIAN.
ALONE IN THE UNIVERSE.
AN ORPHANED ORPHAN.
As a child, he displayed little or no powers.
He lived in Smallville, Kansas and had all the problems of a normal boy...
THE IRONY IS, HOWEVER, YOU HAVE NO ONE TO BLAME BUT YOURSELF...
...That is, as "normal" as whatever holds true for normal in this day and age.
DARKSEID...

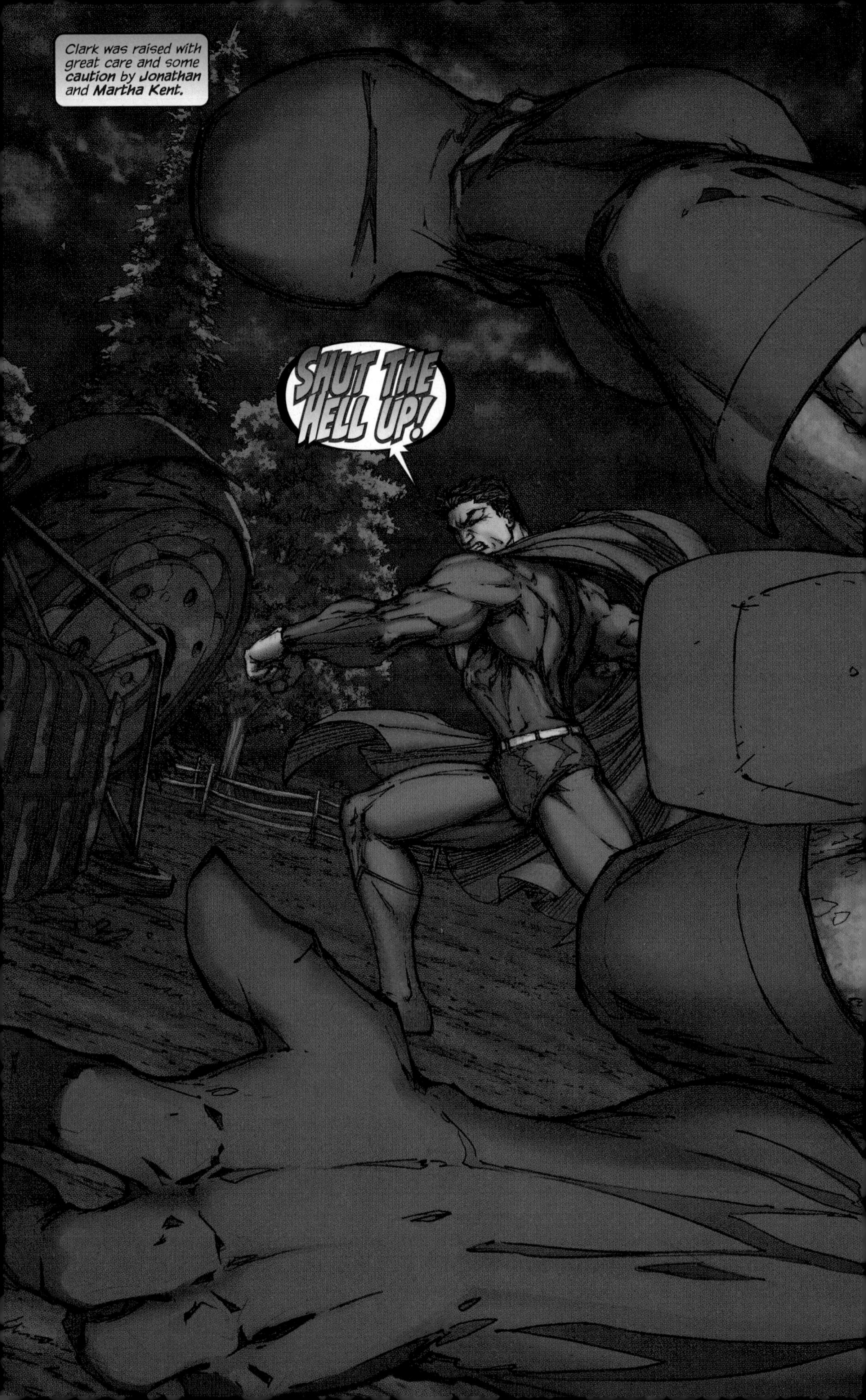
Clark was raised with great care and some caution by Jonathan and Martha Kent.
SHUT THE HELL UP!

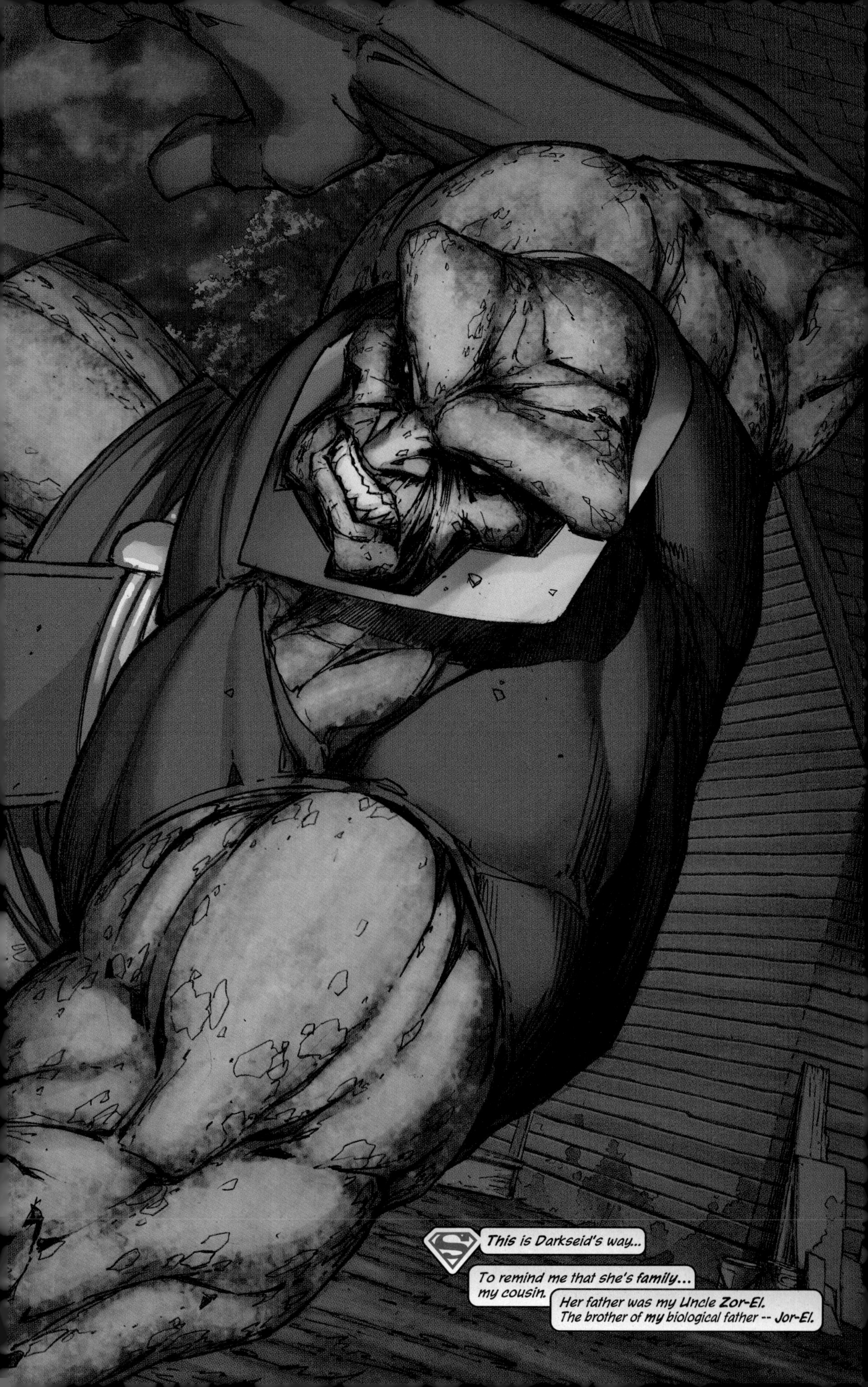
This is Darkseid's way...
To remind me that she's family... my cousin.
Her father was my Uncle Zor-El. The brother of my biological father -- Jor-El.

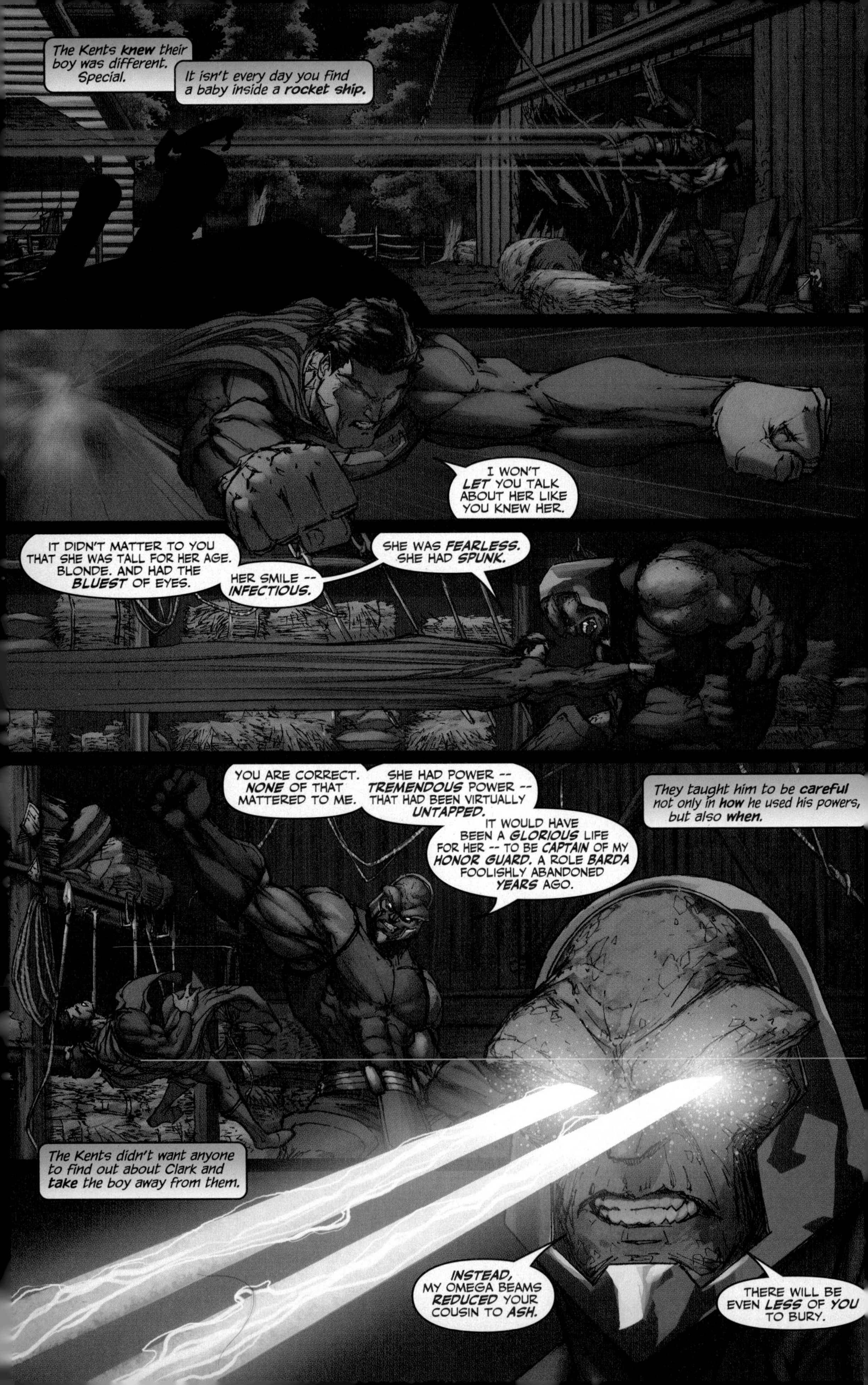
The Kents knew their boy was different. Special.
It isn't every day you find a baby inside a rocket ship.
I WON'T LET YOU TALK ABOUT HER LIKE YOU KNEW HER.
IT DIDN'T MATTER TO YOU THAT SHE WAS TALL FOR HER AGE. BLONDE. AND HAD THE BLUEST OF EYES.
HER SMILE -- INFECTIOUS.
SHE WAS FEARLESS. SHE HAD SPUNK.
YOU ARE CORRECT. NONE OF THAT MATTERED TO ME.
SHE HAD POWER -- TREMENDOUS POWER -- THAT HAD BEEN VIRTUALLY UNTAPPED.
IT WOULD HAVE BEEN A GLORIOUS LIFE FOR HER -- TO BE CAPTAIN OF MY HONOR GUARD. A ROLE BARDA FOOLISHLY ABANDONED YEARS AGO.
They taught him to be careful not only in how he used his powers, but also when.
The Kents didn't want anyone to find out about Clark and take the boy away from them.
INSTEAD, MY OMEGA BEAMS REDUCED YOUR COUSIN TO ASH.
THERE WILL BE EVEN LESS OF YOU TO BURY.

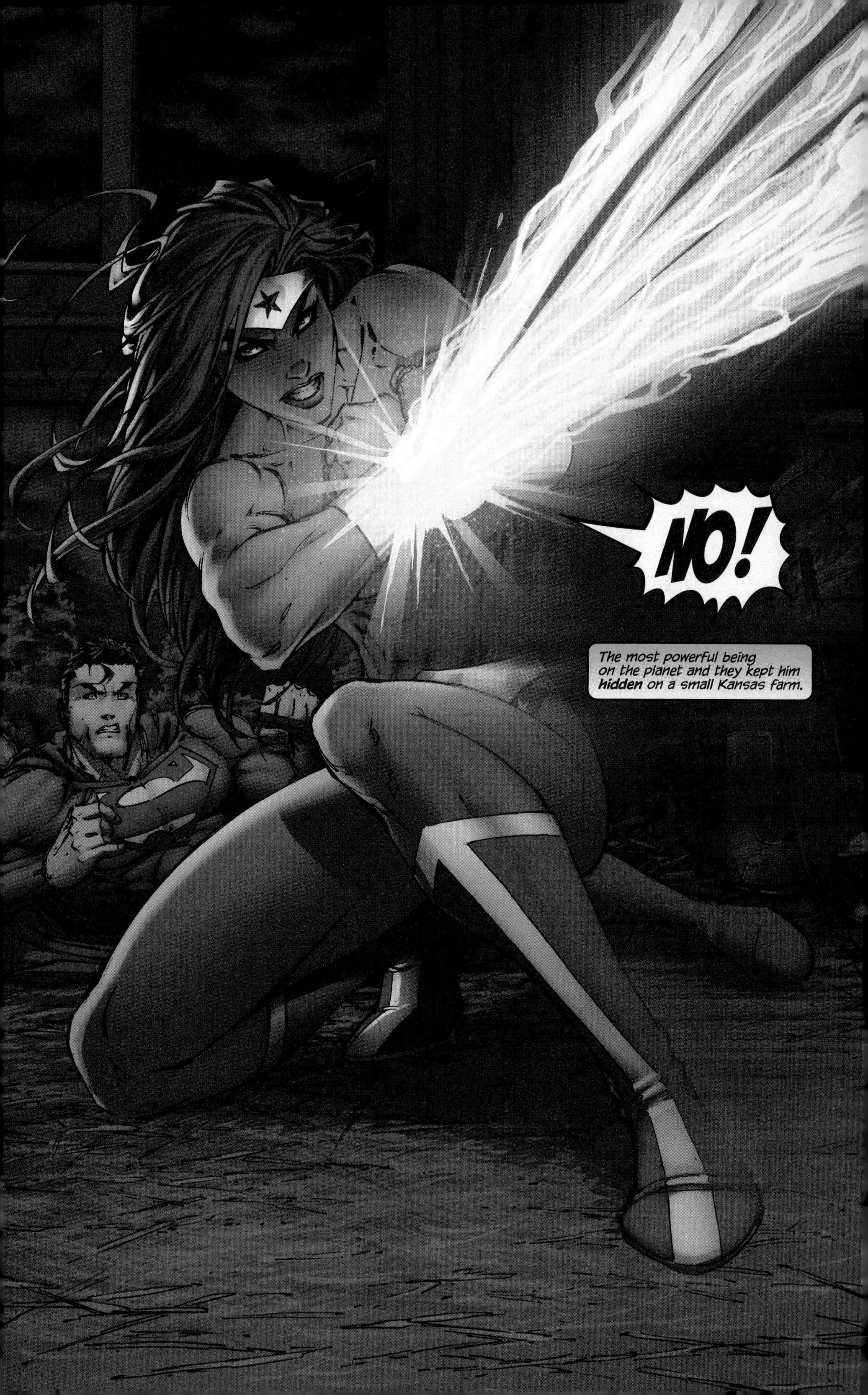
NO!
The most powerful being on the planet and they kept him **hidden** on a small Kansas farm.

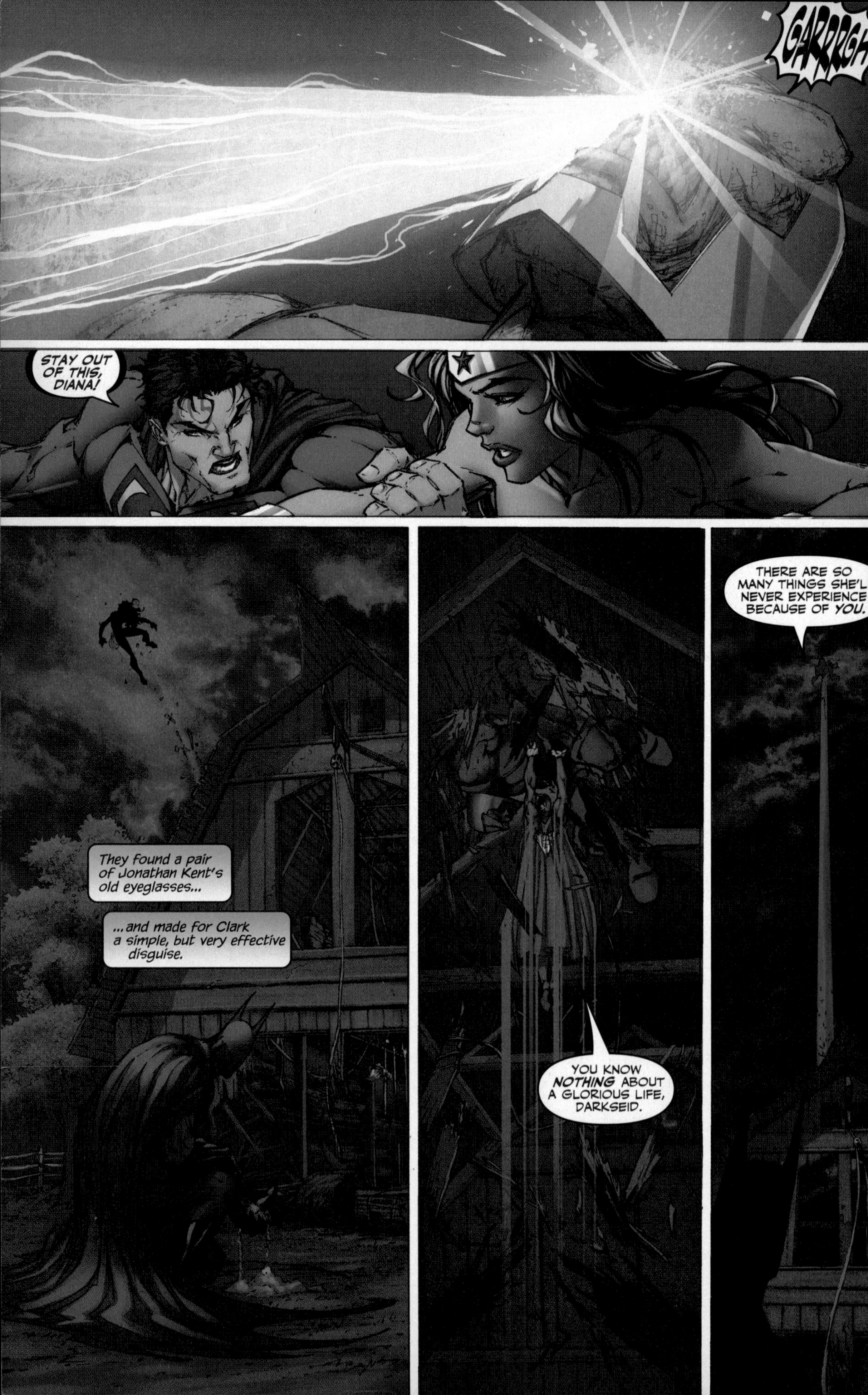
GARRRGH
STAY OUT OF THIS, DIANA!
They found a pair of Jonathan Kent's old eyeglasses...
...and made for Clark a simple, but very effective disguise.
YOU KNOW NOTHING ABOUT A GLORIOUS LIFE, DARKSEID.
THERE ARE SO MANY THINGS SHE'LL NEVER EXPERIENCE BECAUSE OF YOU.

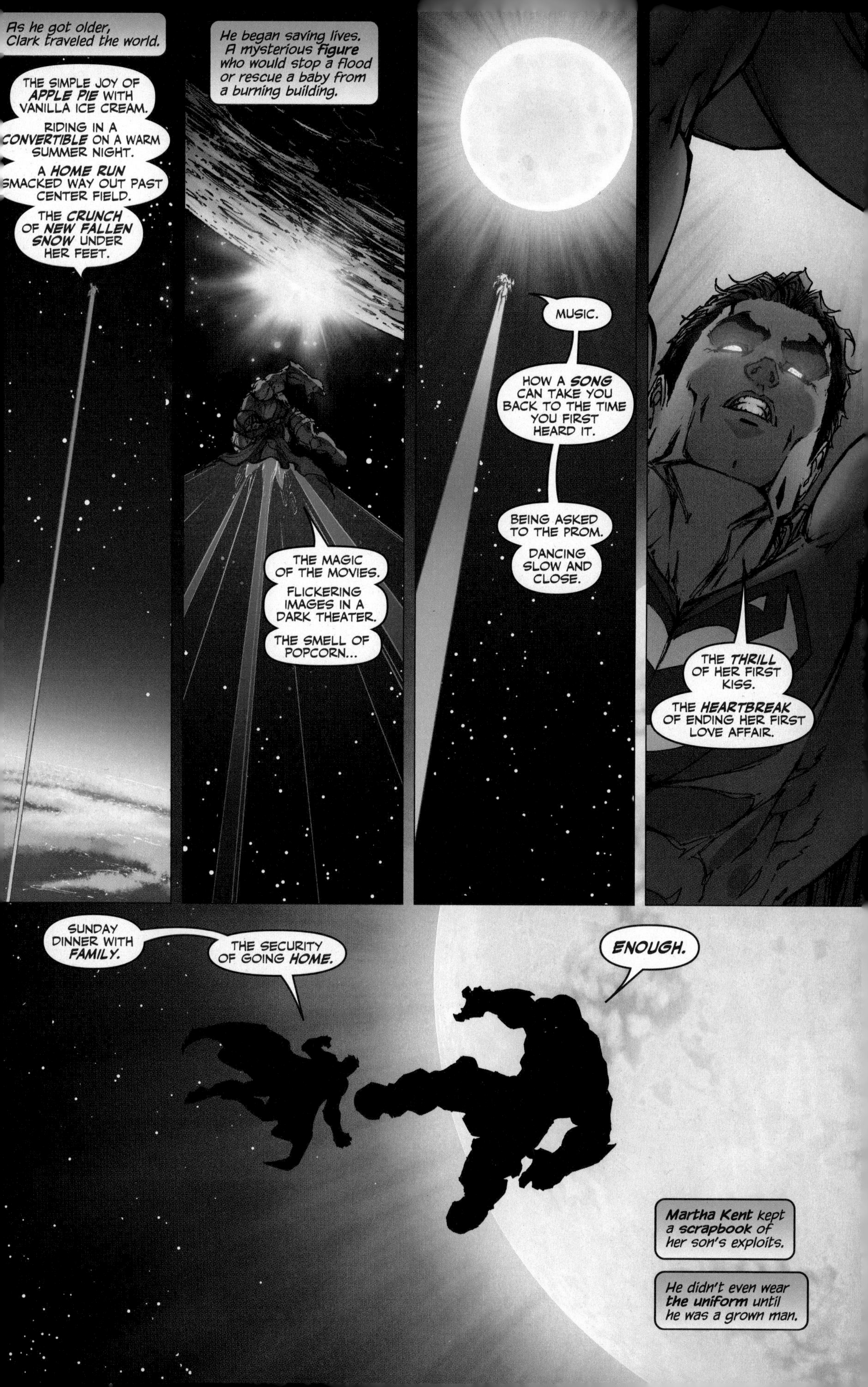
As he got older, Clark traveled the world.
THE SIMPLE JOY OF APPLE PIE WITH VANILLA ICE CREAM.
RIDING IN A CONVERTIBLE ON A WARM SUMMER NIGHT.
A HOME RUN SMACKED WAY OUT PAST CENTER FIELD.
THE CRUNCH OF NEW FALLEN SNOW UNDER HER FEET.
He began saving lives. A mysterious figure who would stop a flood or rescue a baby from a burning building.
THE MAGIC OF THE MOVIES.
FLICKERING IMAGES IN A DARK THEATER.
THE SMELL OF POPCORN...
MUSIC.
HOW A SONG CAN TAKE YOU BACK TO THE TIME YOU FIRST HEARD IT.
BEING ASKED TO THE PROM.
DANCING SLOW AND CLOSE.
THE THRILL OF HER FIRST KISS.
THE HEARTBREAK OF ENDING HER FIRST LOVE AFFAIR.
SUNDAY DINNER WITH FAMILY.
THE SECURITY OF GOING HOME.
ENOUGH.
Martha Kent kept a scrapbook of her son's exploits.
He didn't even wear the uniform until he was a grown man.

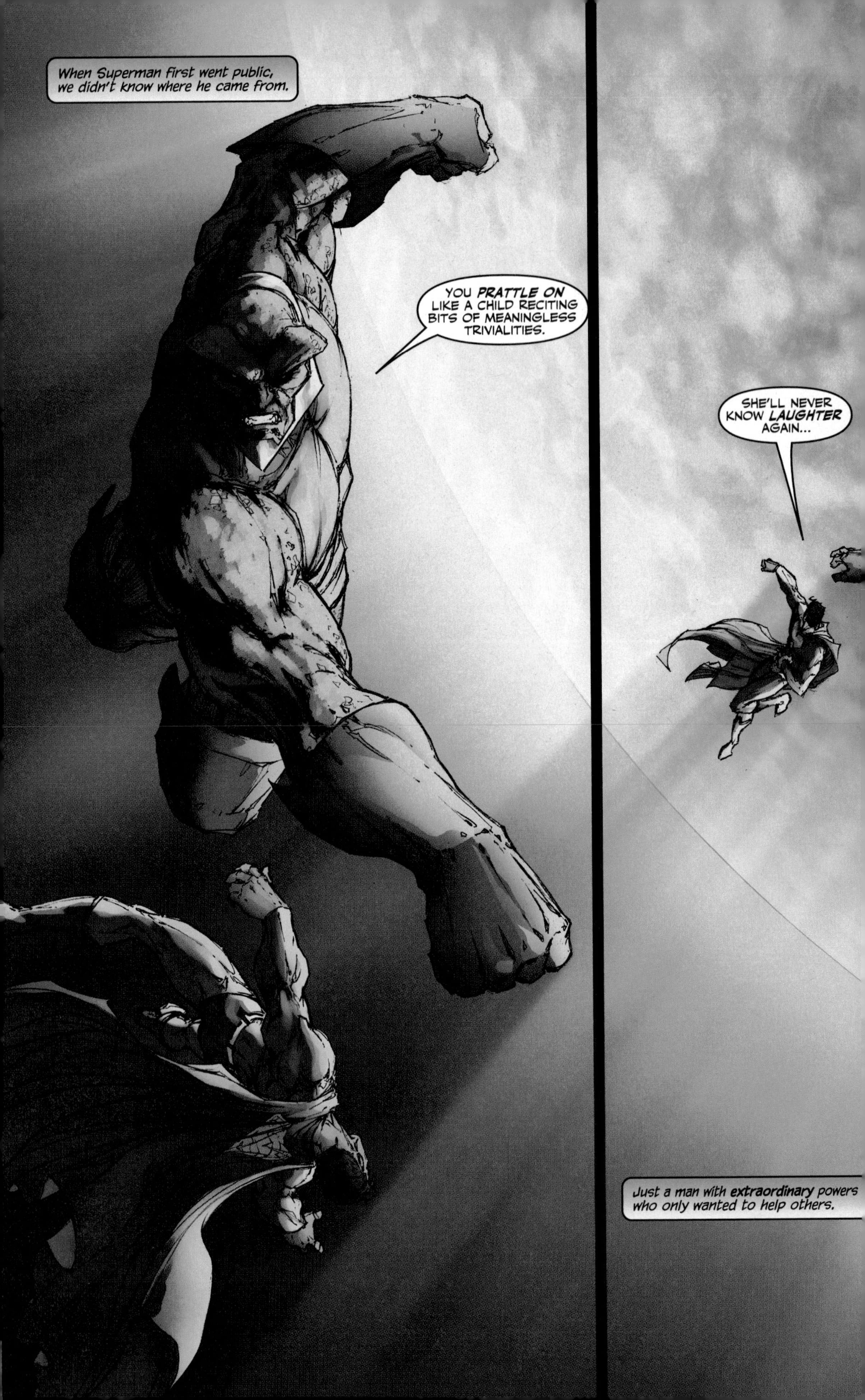
When Superman first went public, we didn't know where he came from.
YOU PRATTLE ON LIKE A CHILD RECITING BITS OF MEANINGLESS TRIVIALITIES.
SHE'LL NEVER KNOW LAUGHTER AGAIN...
Just a man with extraordinary powers who only wanted to help others.

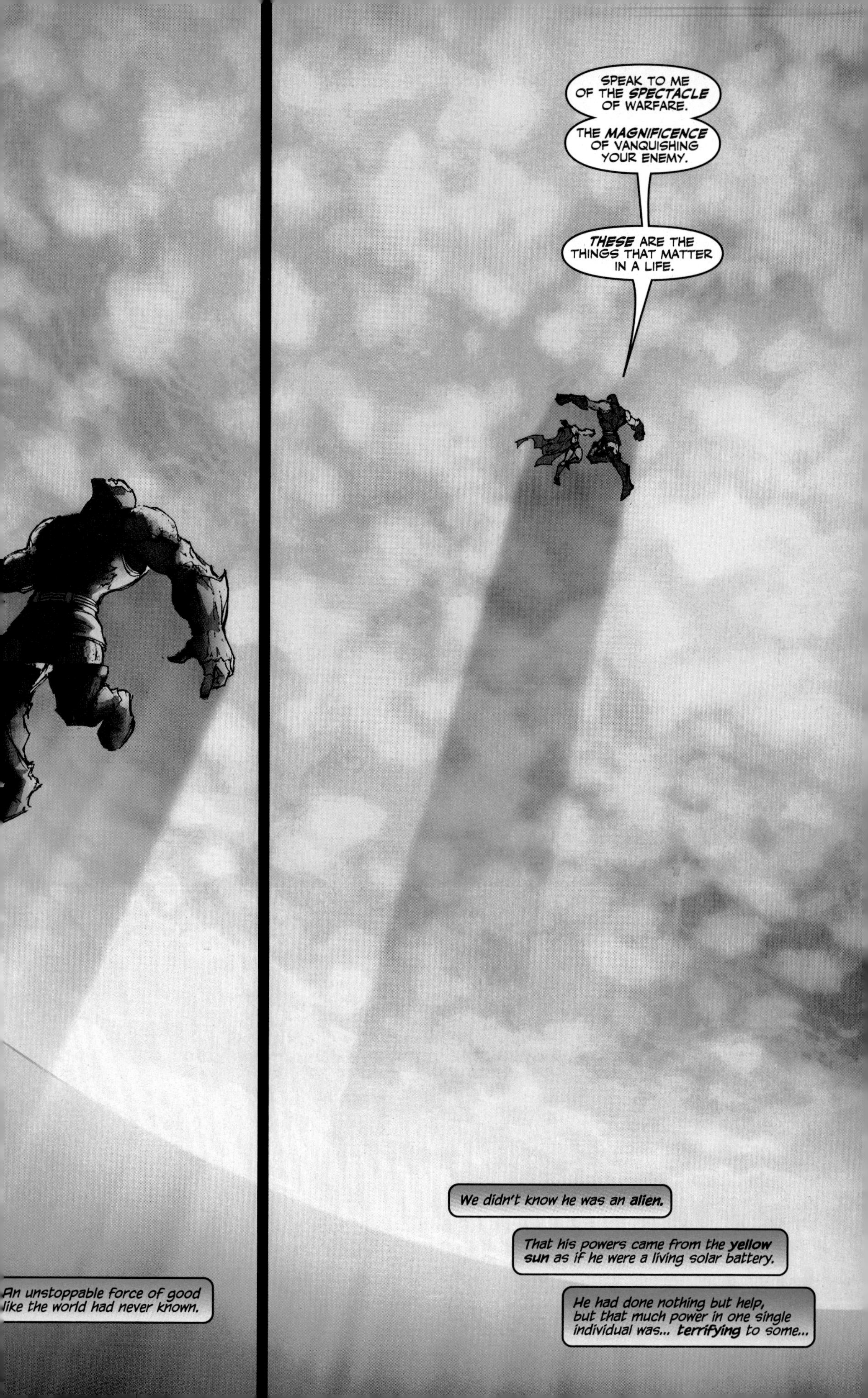

An unstoppable force of good like the world had never known.
SPEAK TO ME OF THE SPECTACLE OF WARFARE.
THE MAGNIFICENCE OF VANQUISHING YOUR ENEMY.
THESE ARE THE THINGS THAT MATTER IN A LIFE.
We didn't know he was an alien.
That his powers came from the yellow sun as if he were a living solar battery.
He had done nothing but help, but that much power in one single individual was... terrifying to some...

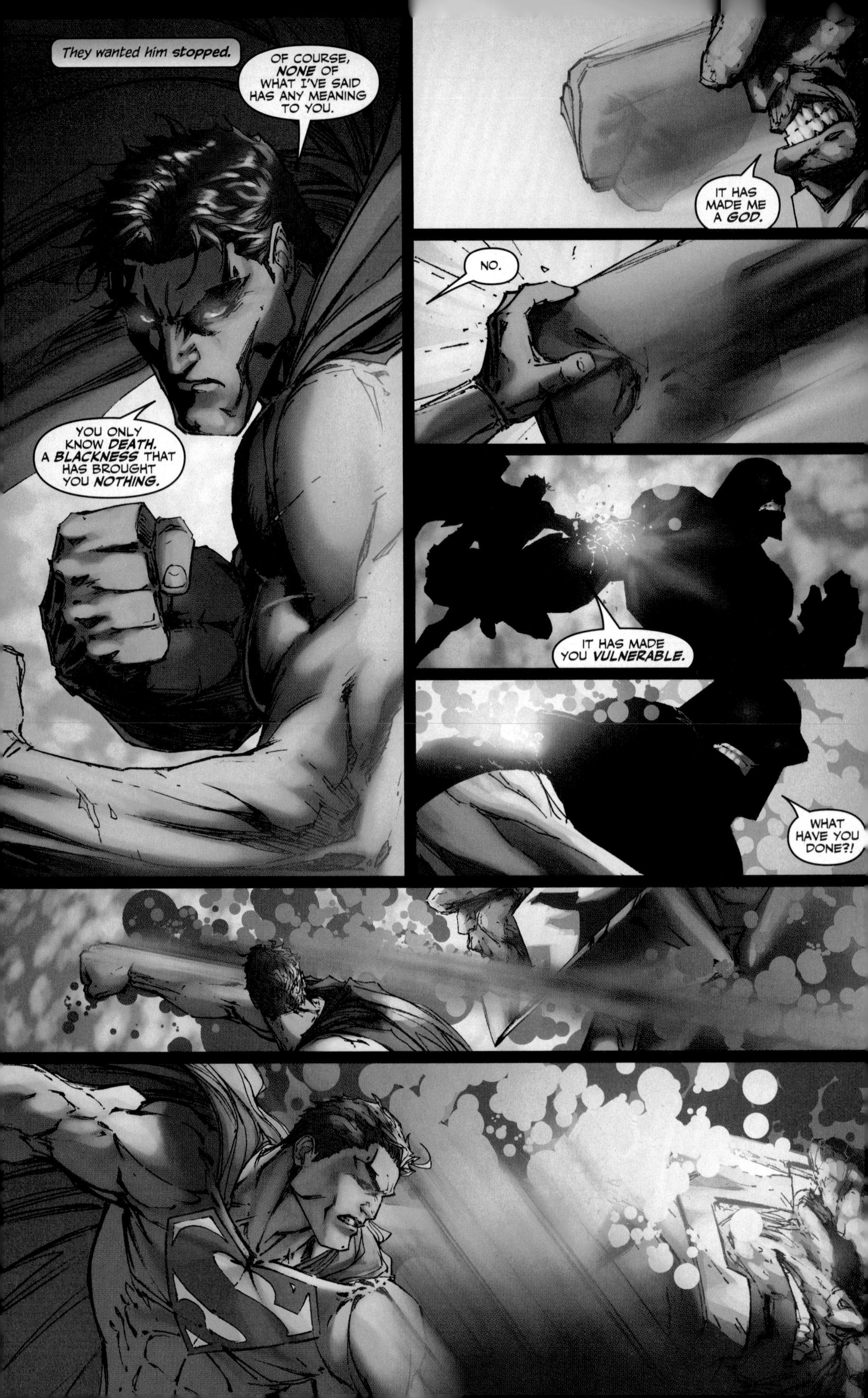
They wanted him stopped.
OF COURSE, NONE OF WHAT I'VE SAID HAS ANY MEANING TO YOU.
YOU ONLY KNOW DEATH. A BLACKNESS THAT HAS BROUGHT YOU NOTHING.
IT HAS MADE ME A GOD.
NO.
IT HAS MADE YOU VULNERABLE.
WHAT HAVE YOU DONE?!

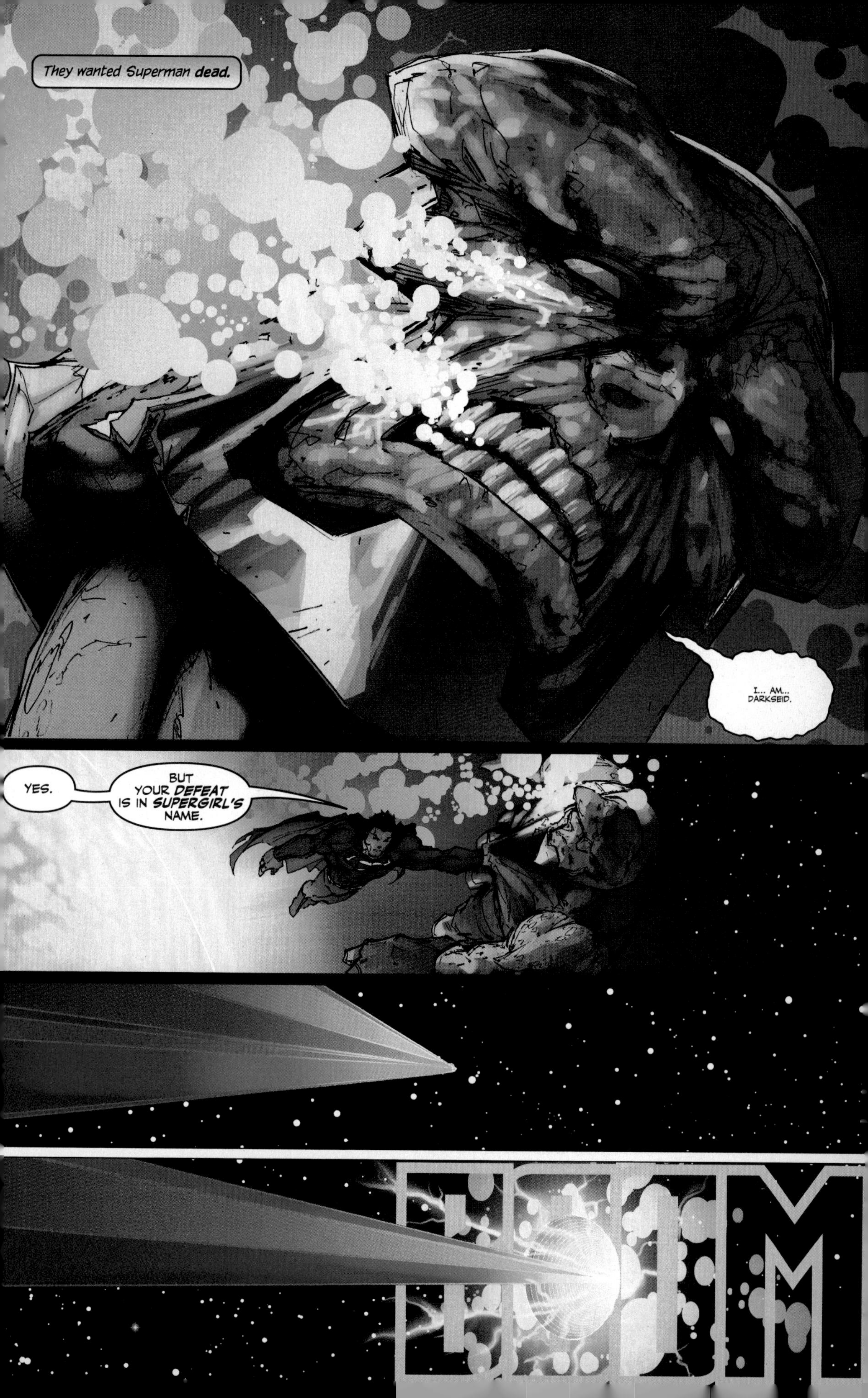
They wanted Superman dead.
I... AM... DARKSEID.
YES.
BUT YOUR DEFEAT IS IN SUPERGIRL'S NAME.

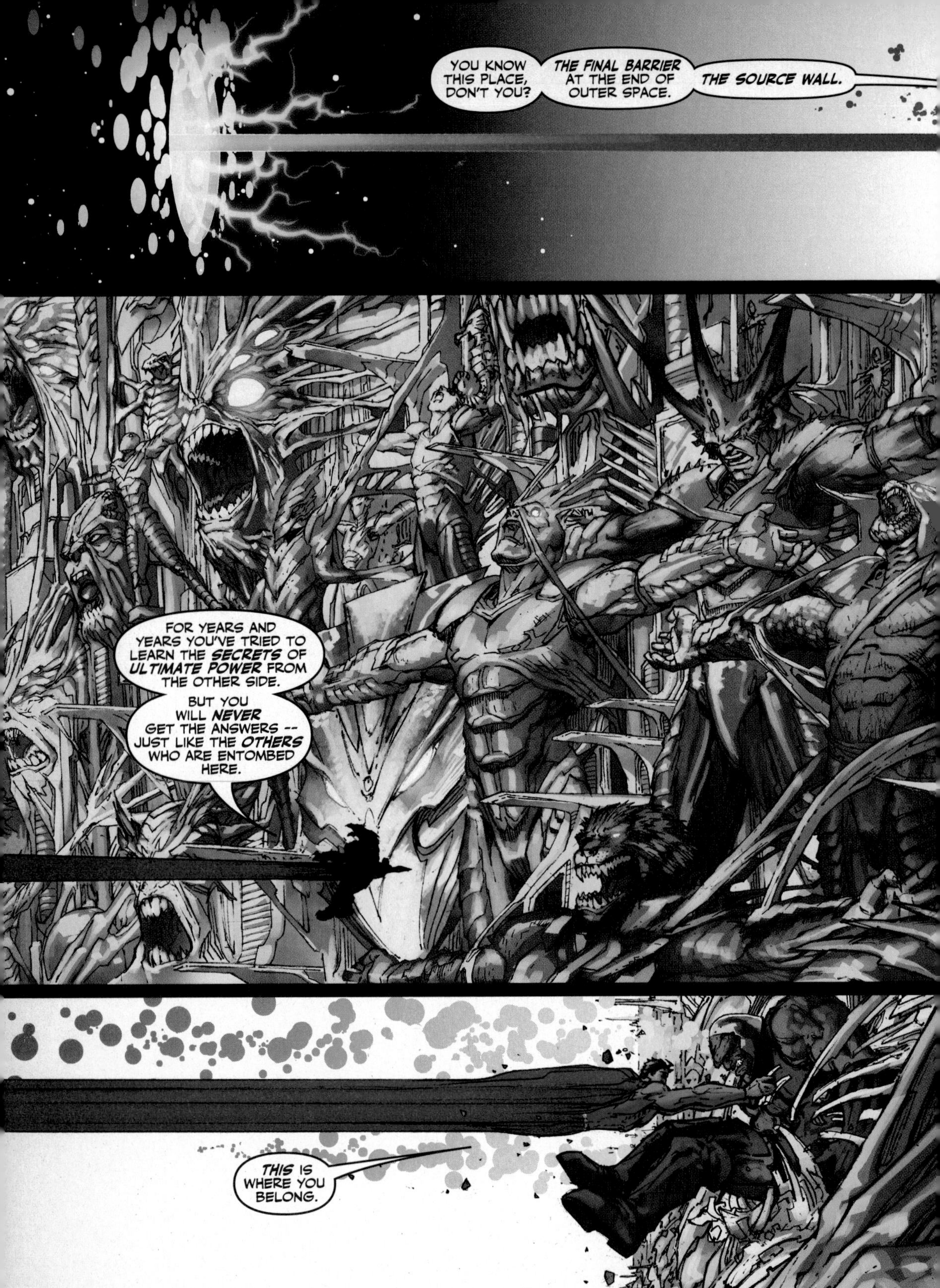
YOU KNOW THIS PLACE, DON'T YOU?
THE FINAL BARRIER AT THE END OF OUTER SPACE.
THE SOURCE WALL.
FOR YEARS AND YEARS YOU'VE TRIED TO LEARN THE SECRETS OF ULTIMATE POWER FROM THE OTHER SIDE.
BUT YOU WILL NEVER GET THE ANSWERS -- JUST LIKE THE OTHERS WHO ARE ENTOMBED HERE.
THIS IS WHERE YOU BELONG.

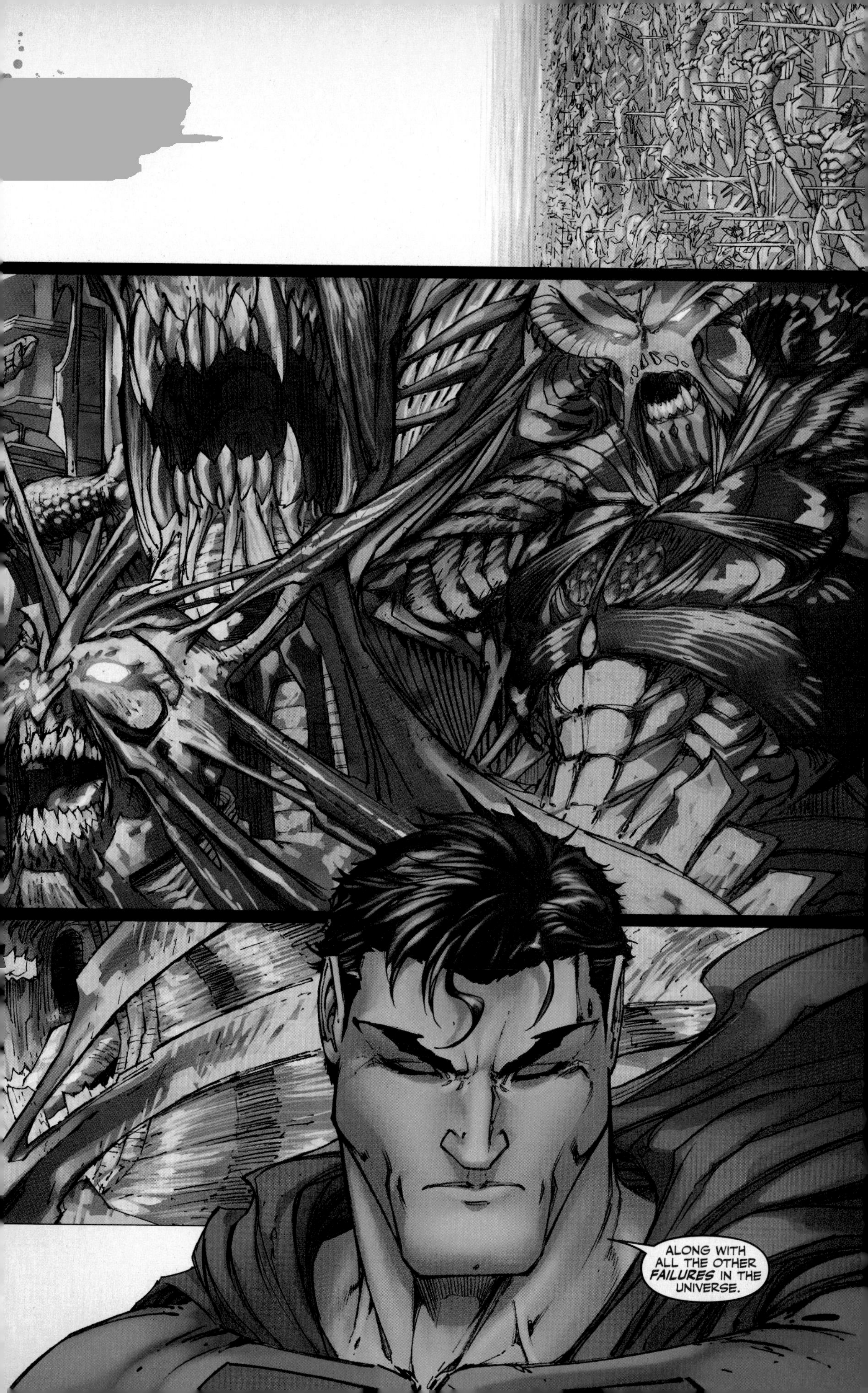
ALONG WITH ALL THE OTHER FAILURES IN THE UNIVERSE.

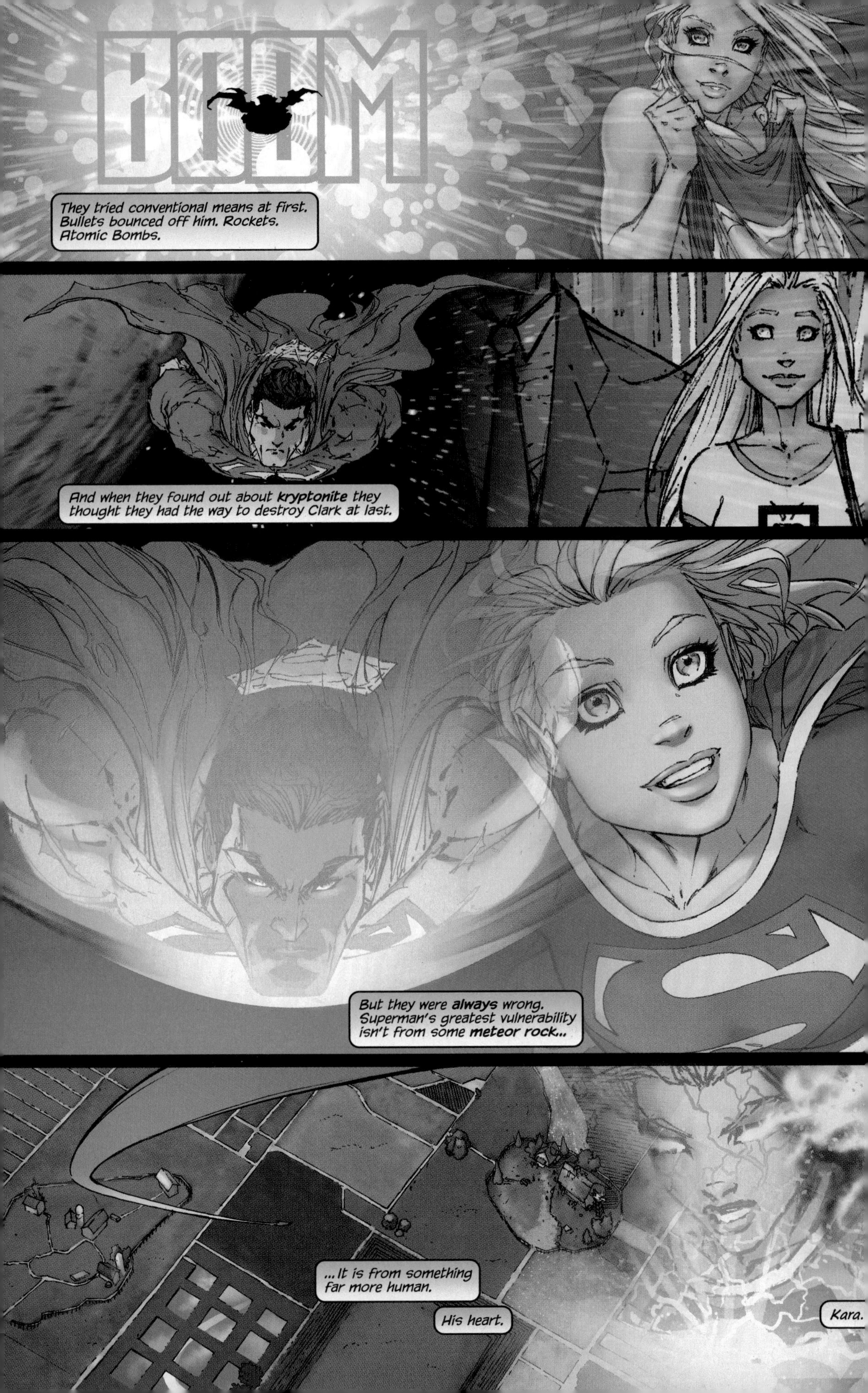
BOOM
They tried conventional means at first. Bullets bounced off him. Rockets. Atomic Bombs.
And when they found out about **kryptonite** they thought they had the way to destroy Clark at last.
But they were **always** wrong. Superman's greatest vulnerability isn't from some **meteor rock...**
...It is from something far more human.
His heart.
Kara.

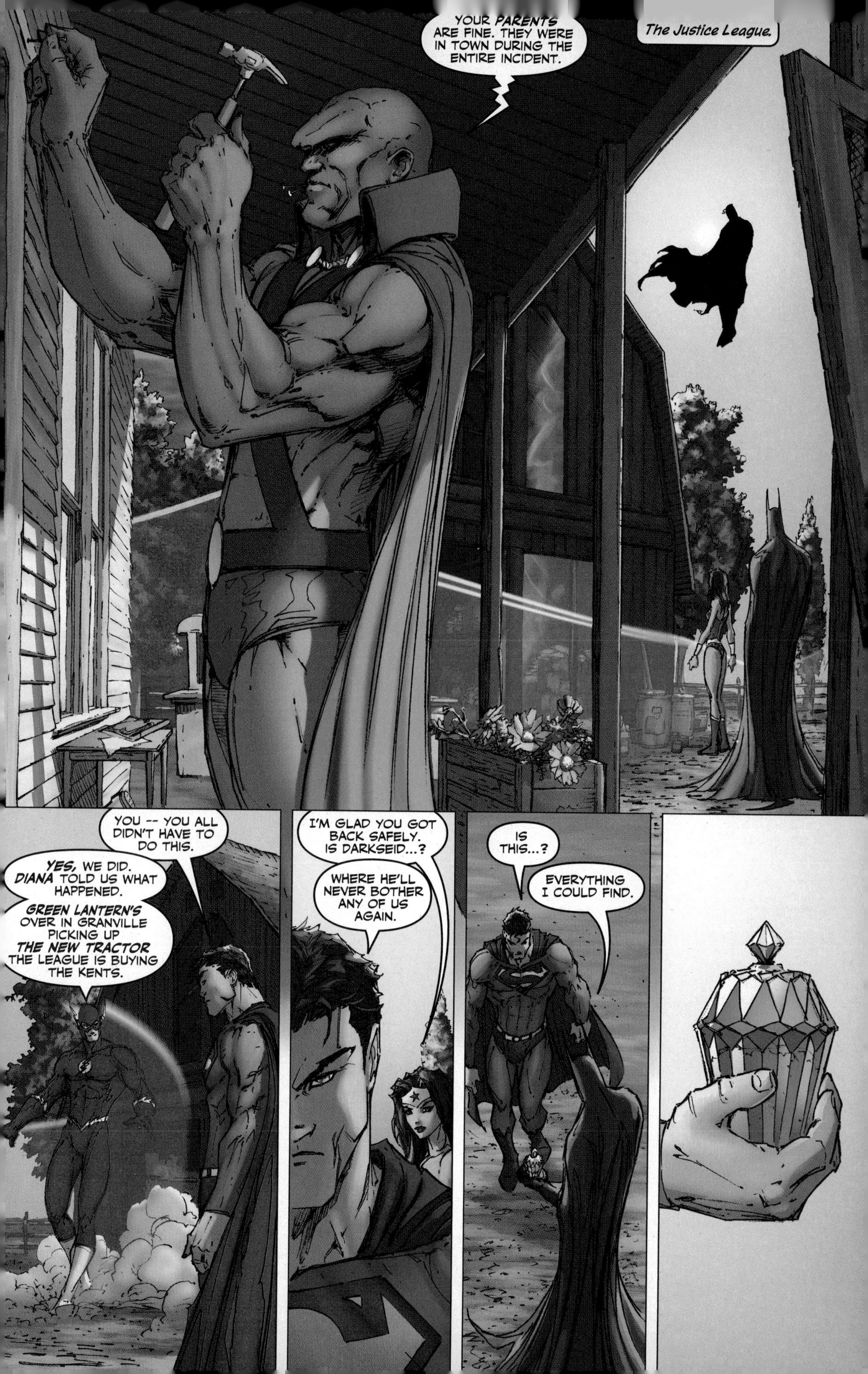
YOUR PARENTS ARE FINE. THEY WERE IN TOWN DURING THE ENTIRE INCIDENT.
The Justice League.
YOU -- YOU ALL DIDN'T HAVE TO DO THIS.
YES, WE DID. DIANA TOLD US WHAT HAPPENED.
GREEN LANTERN'S OVER IN GRANVILLE PICKING UP THE NEW TRACTOR THE LEAGUE IS BUYING THE KENTS.
I'M GLAD YOU GOT BACK SAFELY. IS DARKSEID...?
WHERE HE'LL NEVER BOTHER ANY OF US AGAIN.
IS THIS...?
EVERYTHING I COULD FIND.

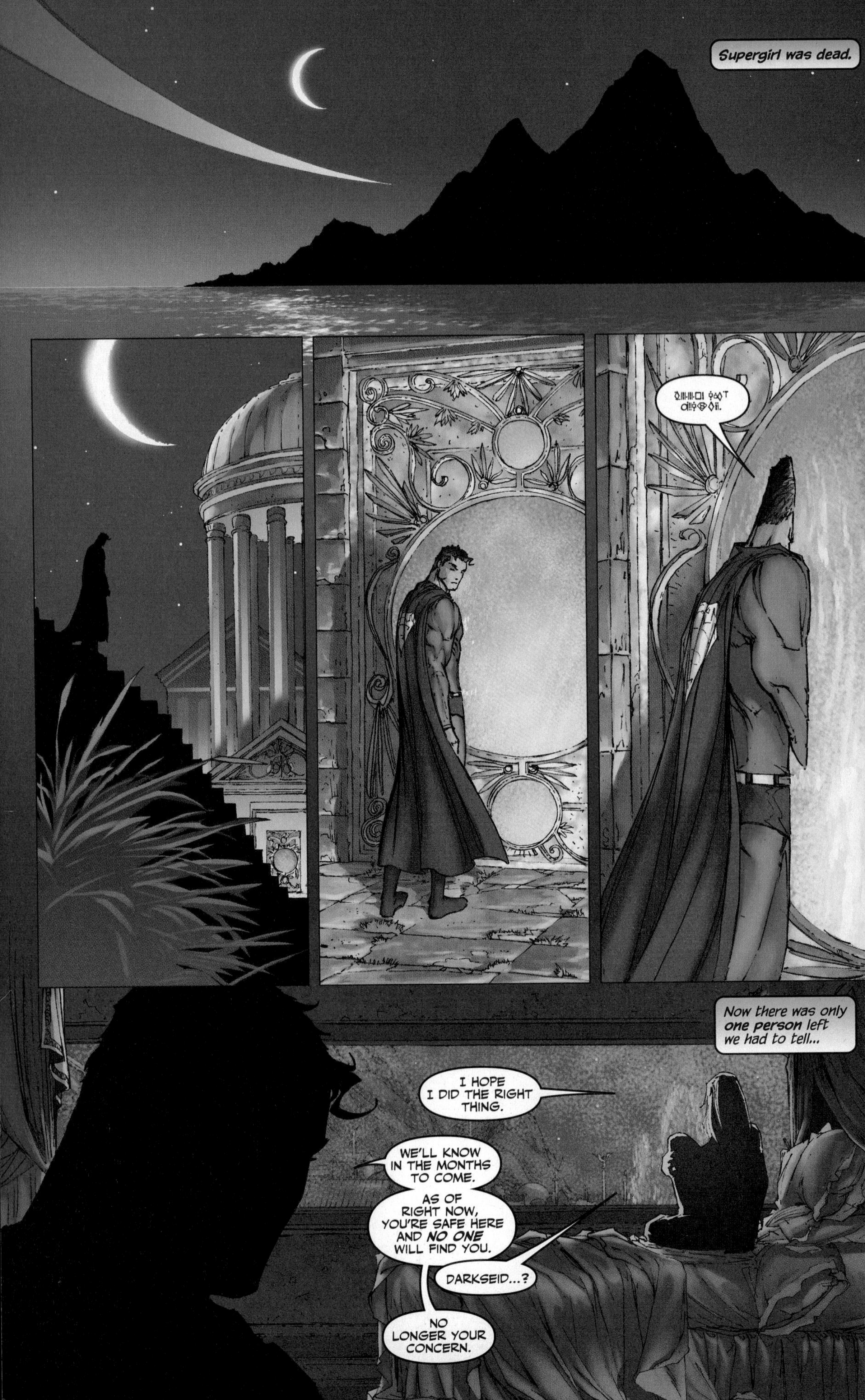
Supergirl was dead.
Now there was only **one person** left we had to tell...
I HOPE I DID THE RIGHT THING.
WE'LL KNOW IN THE MONTHS TO COME.
AS OF RIGHT NOW, YOU'RE SAFE HERE AND ***NO ONE*** WILL FIND YOU.
DARKSEID...?
NO LONGER YOUR CONCERN.

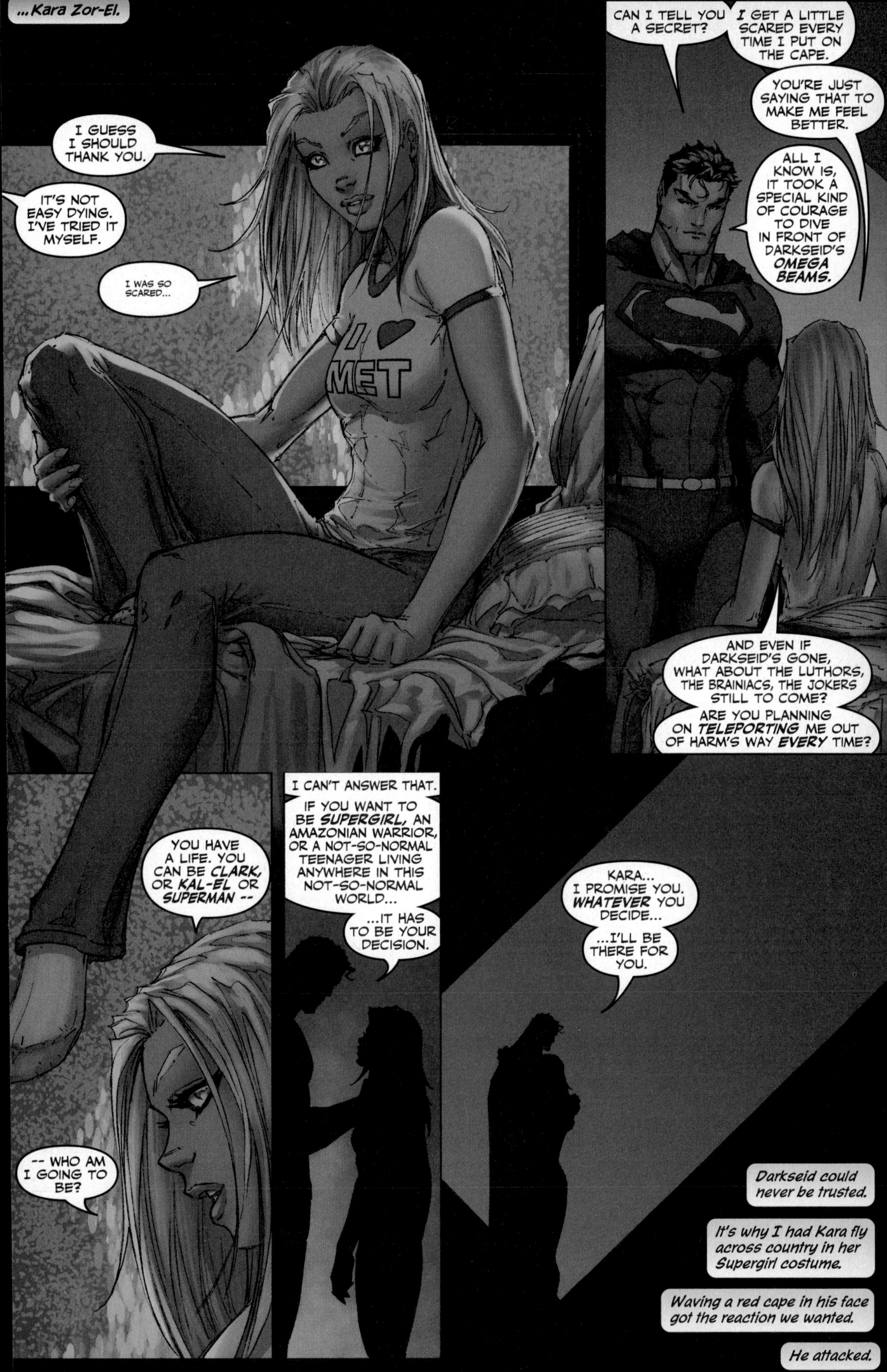

...Kara Zor-El.
I GUESS I SHOULD THANK YOU.
IT'S NOT EASY DYING. I'VE TRIED IT MYSELF.
I WAS SO SCARED...
CAN I TELL YOU A SECRET?
I GET A LITTLE SCARED EVERY TIME I PUT ON THE CAPE.
YOU'RE JUST SAYING THAT TO MAKE ME FEEL BETTER.
ALL I KNOW IS, IT TOOK A SPECIAL KIND OF COURAGE TO DIVE IN FRONT OF DARKSEID'S OMEGA BEAMS.
AND EVEN IF DARKSEID'S GONE, WHAT ABOUT THE LUTHORS, THE BRAINIACS, THE JOKERS STILL TO COME?
ARE YOU PLANNING ON TELEPORTING ME OUT OF HARM'S WAY EVERY TIME?
YOU HAVE A LIFE. YOU CAN BE CLARK, OR KAL-EL OR SUPERMAN --
-- WHO AM I GOING TO BE?
I CAN'T ANSWER THAT.
IF YOU WANT TO BE SUPERGIRL, AN AMAZONIAN WARRIOR, OR A NOT-SO-NORMAL TEENAGER LIVING ANYWHERE IN THIS NOT-SO-NORMAL WORLD...
...IT HAS TO BE YOUR DECISION.
KARA... I PROMISE YOU. WHATEVER YOU DECIDE...
...I'LL BE THERE FOR YOU.
Darkseid could never be trusted.
It's why I had Kara fly across country in her Supergirl costume.
Waving a red cape in his face got the reaction we wanted.
He attacked.

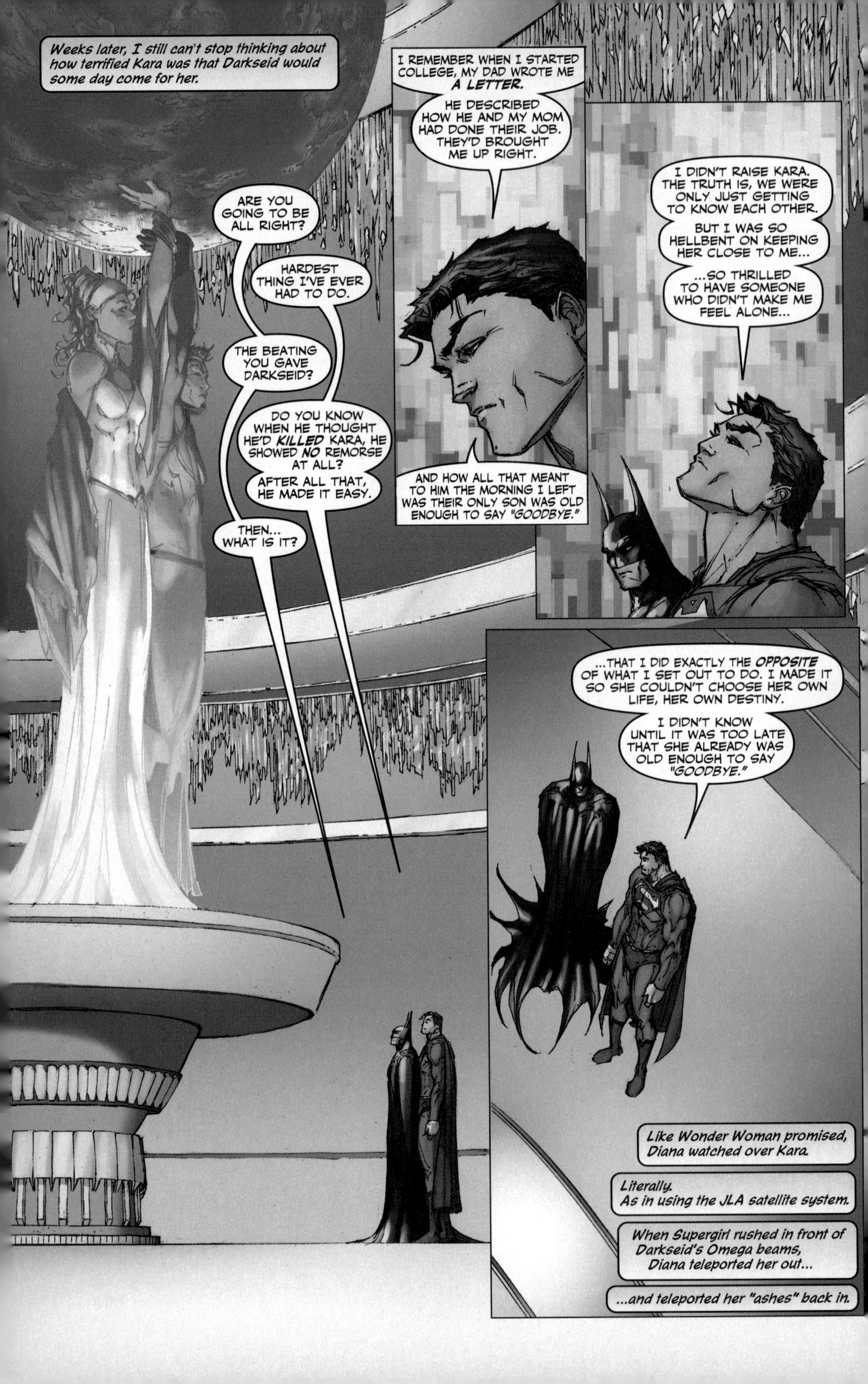

Weeks later, I still can't stop thinking about how terrified Kara was that Darkseid would some day come for her.
ARE YOU GOING TO BE ALL RIGHT?
HARDEST THING I'VE EVER HAD TO DO.
THE BEATING YOU GAVE DARKSEID?
DO YOU KNOW WHEN HE THOUGHT HE'D KILLED KARA, HE SHOWED NO REMORSE AT ALL?
AFTER ALL THAT, HE MADE IT EASY.
THEN... WHAT IS IT?
I REMEMBER WHEN I STARTED COLLEGE, MY DAD WROTE ME A LETTER.
HE DESCRIBED HOW HE AND MY MOM HAD DONE THEIR JOB. THEY'D BROUGHT ME UP RIGHT.
AND HOW ALL THAT MEANT TO HIM THE MORNING I LEFT WAS THEIR ONLY SON WAS OLD ENOUGH TO SAY "GOODBYE."
I DIDN'T RAISE KARA. THE TRUTH IS, WE WERE ONLY JUST GETTING TO KNOW EACH OTHER.
BUT I WAS SO HELLBENT ON KEEPING HER CLOSE TO ME...
...SO THRILLED TO HAVE SOMEONE WHO DIDN'T MAKE ME FEEL ALONE...
...THAT I DID EXACTLY THE OPPOSITE OF WHAT I SET OUT TO DO. I MADE IT SO SHE COULDN'T CHOOSE HER OWN LIFE, HER OWN DESTINY.
I DIDN'T KNOW UNTIL IT WAS TOO LATE THAT SHE ALREADY WAS OLD ENOUGH TO SAY "GOODBYE."
Like Wonder Woman promised, Diana watched over Kara.
Literally. As in using the JLA satellite system.
When Supergirl rushed in front of Darkseid's Omega beams, Diana teleported her out...
...and teleported her "ashes" back in.

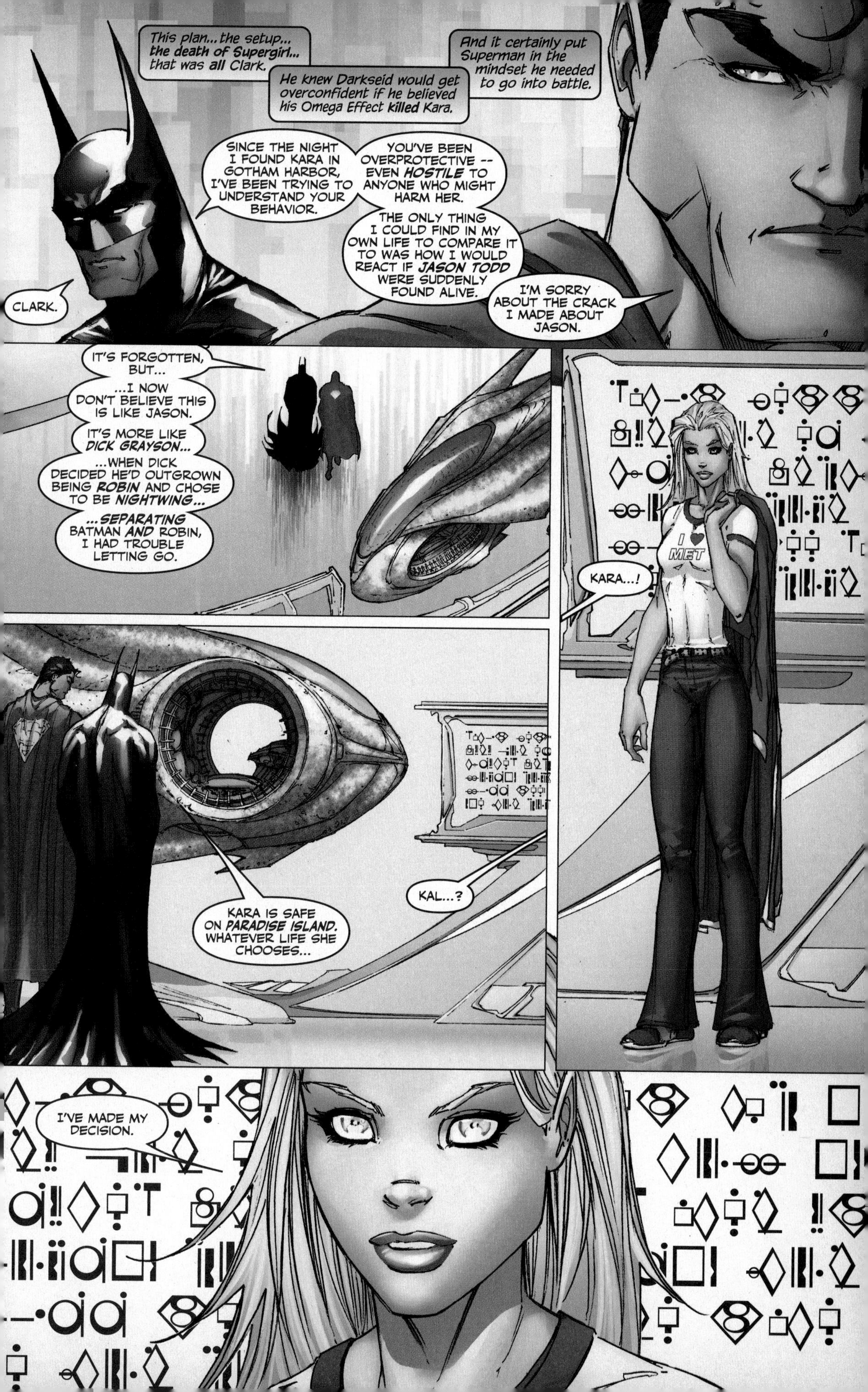
This plan... the setup... the death of Supergirl... that was all Clark.
He knew Darkseid would get overconfident if he believed his Omega Effect killed Kara.
And it certainly put Superman in the mindset he needed to go into battle.
CLARK.
SINCE THE NIGHT I FOUND KARA IN GOTHAM HARBOR, I'VE BEEN TRYING TO UNDERSTAND YOUR BEHAVIOR.
YOU'VE BEEN OVERPROTECTIVE -- EVEN HOSTILE TO ANYONE WHO MIGHT HARM HER.
THE ONLY THING I COULD FIND IN MY OWN LIFE TO COMPARE IT TO WAS HOW I WOULD REACT IF JASON TODD WERE SUDDENLY FOUND ALIVE.
I'M SORRY ABOUT THE CRACK I MADE ABOUT JASON.
IT'S FORGOTTEN, BUT...
...I NOW DON'T BELIEVE THIS IS LIKE JASON.
IT'S MORE LIKE DICK GRAYSON...
...WHEN DICK DECIDED HE'D OUTGROWN BEING ROBIN AND CHOSE TO BE NIGHTWING...
...SEPARATING BATMAN AND ROBIN, I HAD TROUBLE LETTING GO.
KARA...!
I ♥ MET
KARA IS SAFE ON PARADISE ISLAND. WHATEVER LIFE SHE CHOOSES...
KAL...?
I'VE MADE MY DECISION.

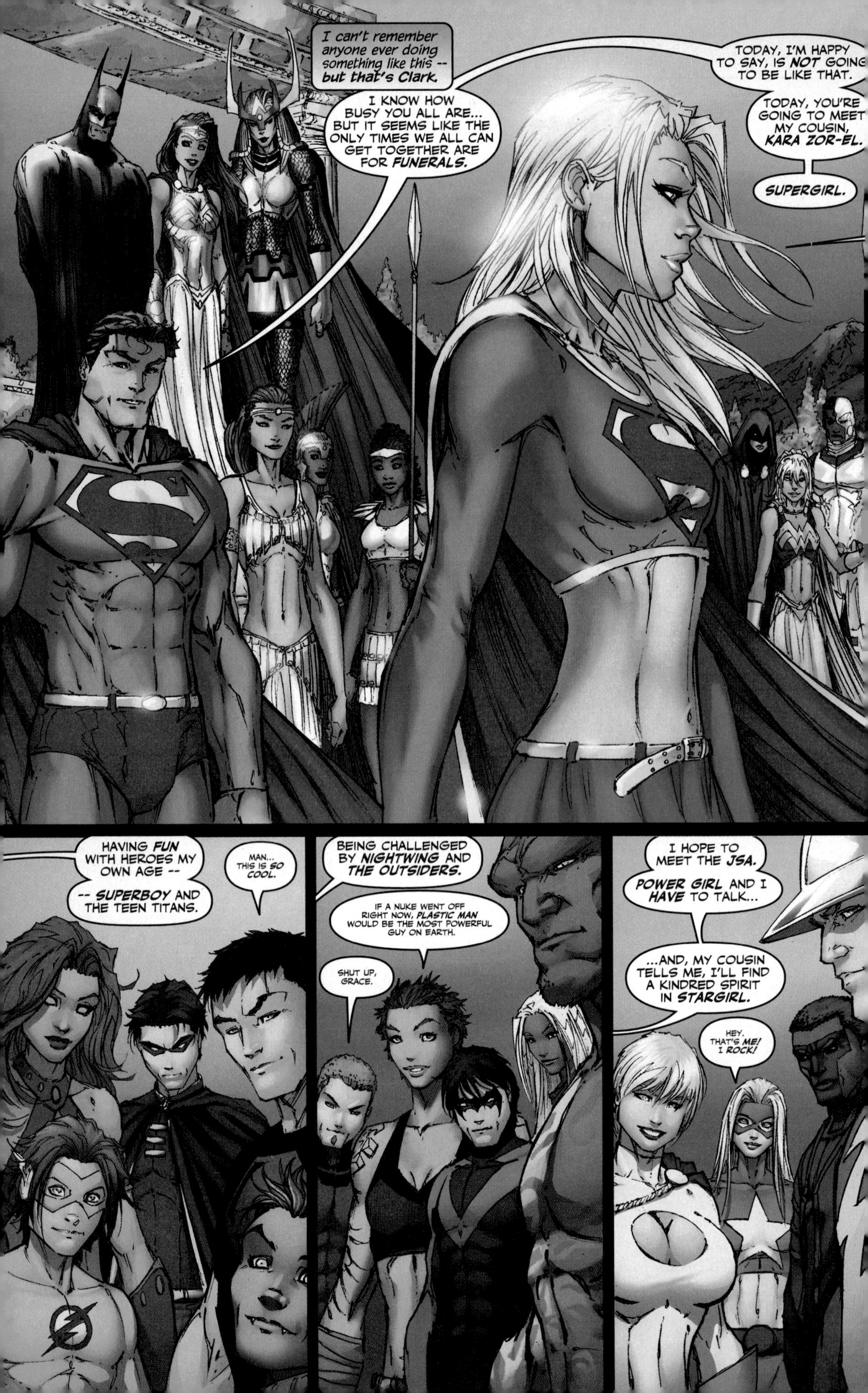
I can't remember anyone ever doing something like this -- but that's Clark.
I KNOW HOW BUSY YOU ALL ARE... BUT IT SEEMS LIKE THE ONLY TIMES WE ALL CAN GET TOGETHER ARE FOR FUNERALS.
TODAY, I'M HAPPY TO SAY, IS NOT GOING TO BE LIKE THAT.
TODAY, YOU'RE GOING TO MEET MY COUSIN, KARA ZOR-EL.
SUPERGIRL.
HAVING FUN WITH HEROES MY OWN AGE --
-- SUPERBOY AND THE TEEN TITANS.
MAN... THIS IS SO COOL.
BEING CHALLENGED BY NIGHTWING AND THE OUTSIDERS.
IF A NUKE WENT OFF RIGHT NOW, PLASTIC MAN WOULD BE THE MOST POWERFUL GUY ON EARTH.
SHUT UP, GRACE.
I HOPE TO MEET THE JSA.
POWER GIRL AND I HAVE TO TALK...
...AND, MY COUSIN TELLS ME, I'LL FIND A KINDRED SPIRIT IN STARGIRL.
HEY. THAT'S ME! I ROCK!

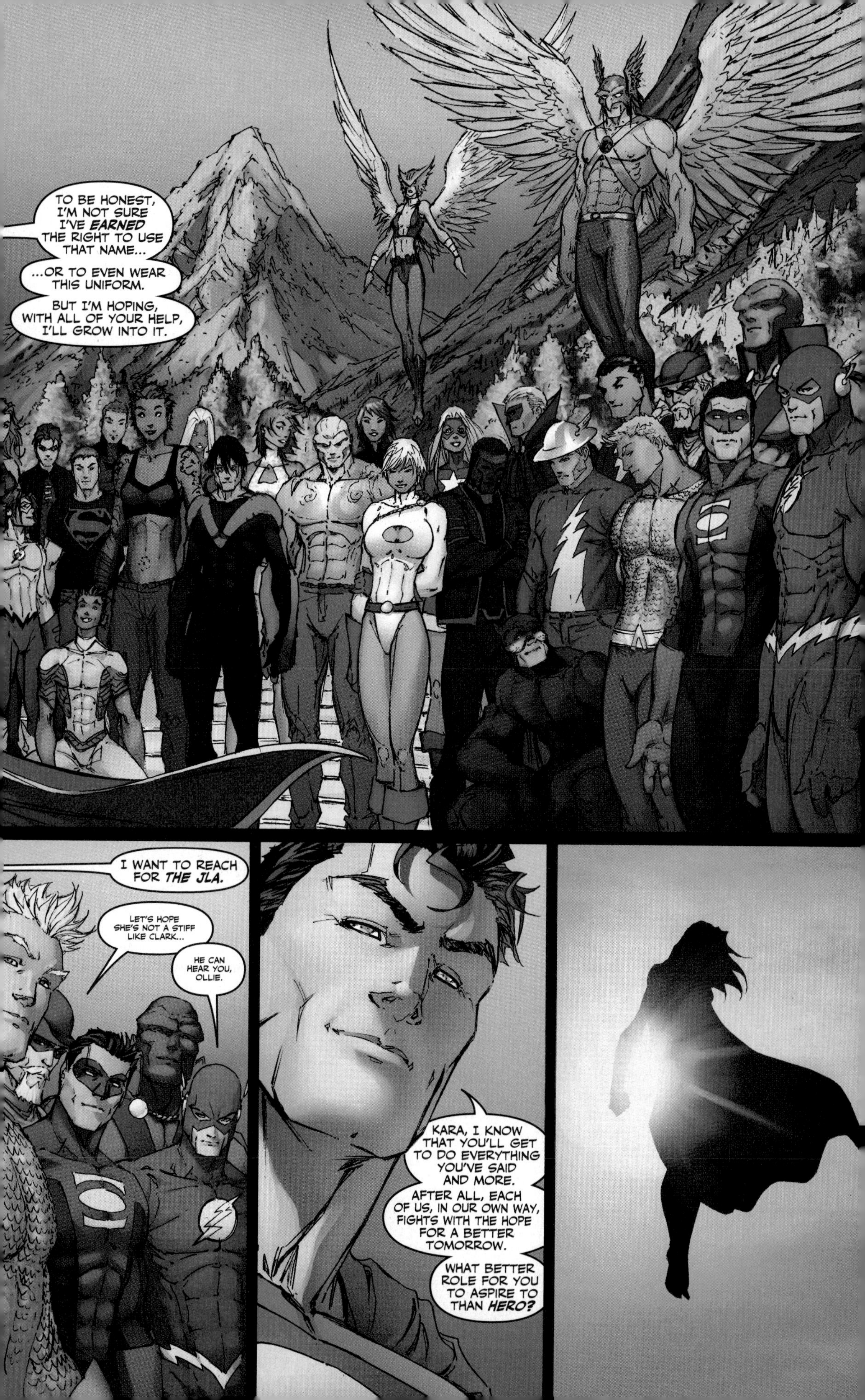
TO BE HONEST, I'M NOT SURE I'VE *EARNED* THE RIGHT TO USE THAT NAME...
...OR TO EVEN WEAR THIS UNIFORM.
BUT I'M HOPING, WITH ALL OF YOUR HELP, I'LL GROW INTO IT.
I WANT TO REACH FOR *THE JLA.*
LET'S HOPE SHE'S NOT A STIFF LIKE CLARK...
HE CAN HEAR YOU, OLLIE.
KARA, I KNOW THAT YOU'LL GET TO DO EVERYTHING YOU'VE SAID AND MORE.
AFTER ALL, EACH OF US, IN OUR OWN WAY, FIGHTS WITH THE HOPE FOR A BETTER TOMORROW.
WHAT BETTER ROLE FOR YOU TO ASPIRE TO THAN *HERO?*

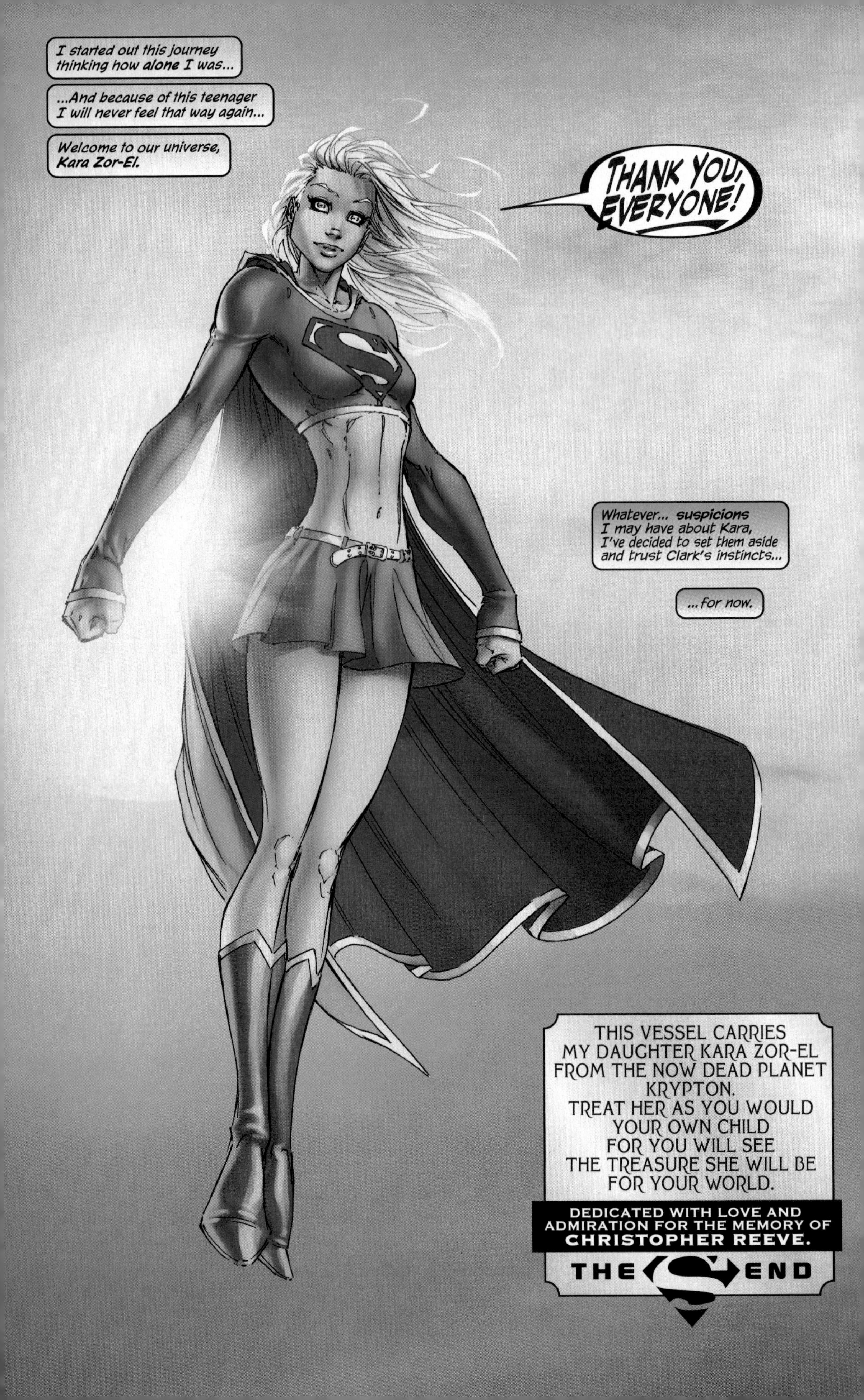
I started out this journey thinking how alone I was...
...And because of this teenager I will never feel that way again...
Welcome to our universe, Kara Zor-El.
THANK YOU, EVERYONE!
Whatever... suspicions I may have about Kara, I've decided to set them aside and trust Clark's instincts...
...for now.
THIS VESSEL CARRIES MY DAUGHTER KARA ZOR-EL FROM THE NOW DEAD PLANET KRYPTON. TREAT HER AS YOU WOULD YOUR OWN CHILD FOR YOU WILL SEE THE TREASURE SHE WILL BE FOR YOUR WORLD.
DEDICATED WITH LOVE AND ADMIRATION FOR THE MEMORY OF CHRISTOPHER REEVE.
THE END

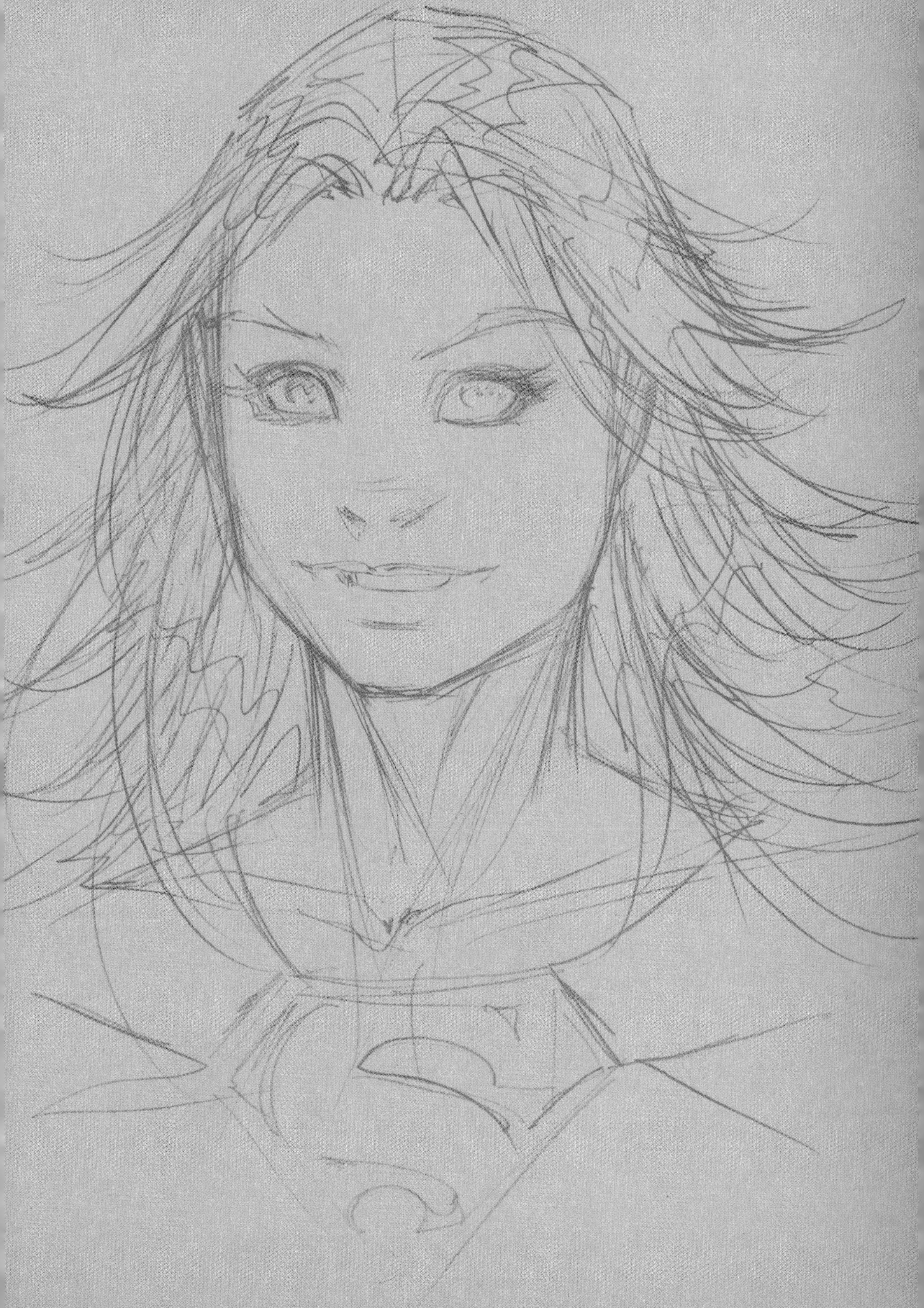

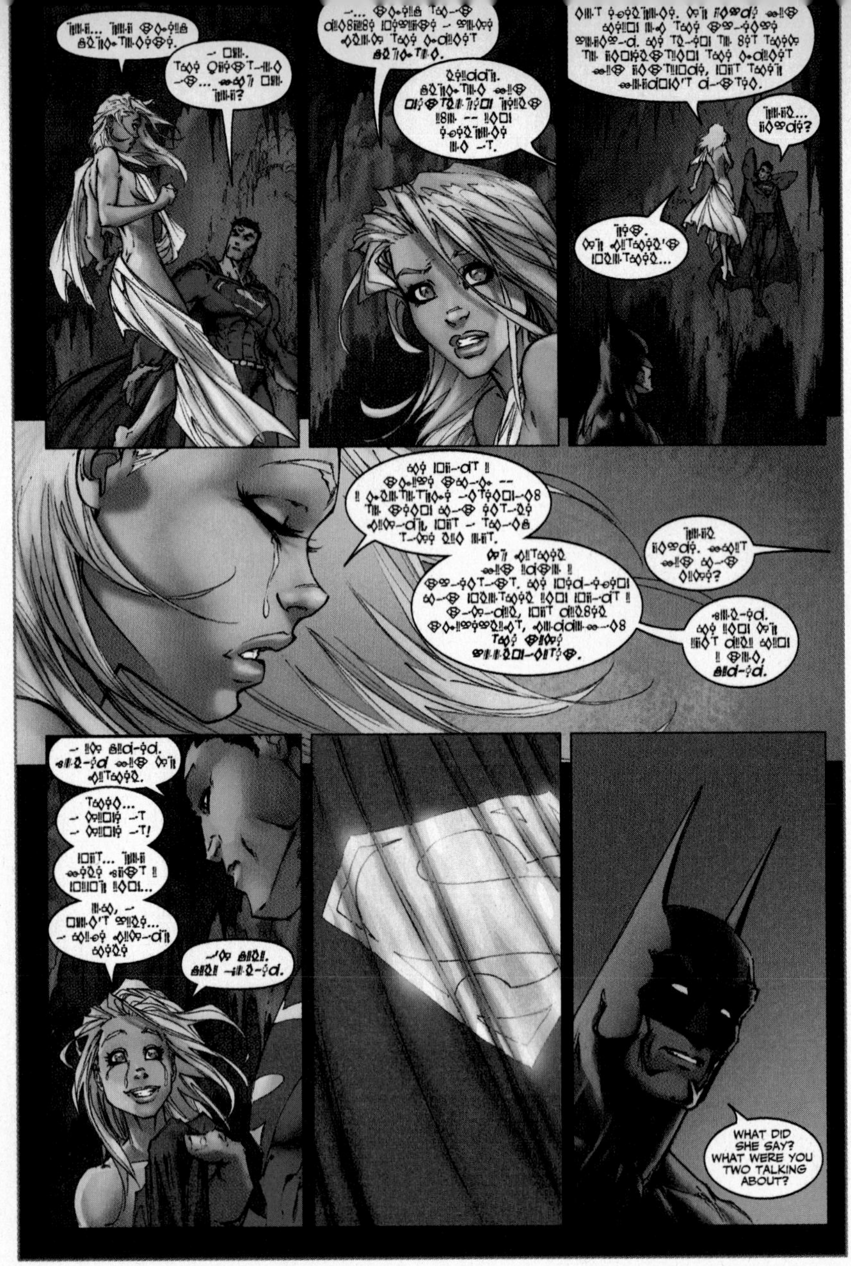
WHAT DID SHE SAY? WHAT WERE YOU TWO TALKING ABOUT?

Hey, Kids! Having trouble with your Kryptonese? We've made it easy by translating one of the story pages for you. Here's the original page.

KRYPTONIAN

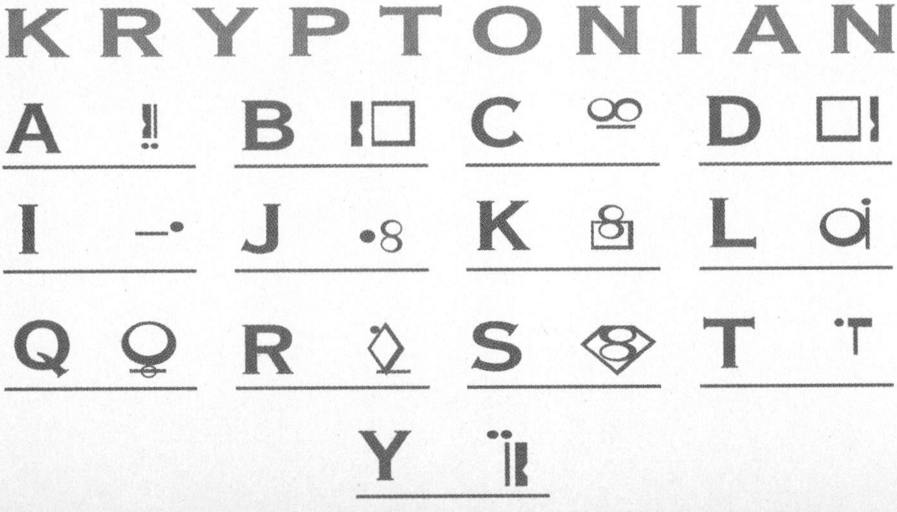
A
B
C
D
I
J
K
L
Q
R
S
T
Y

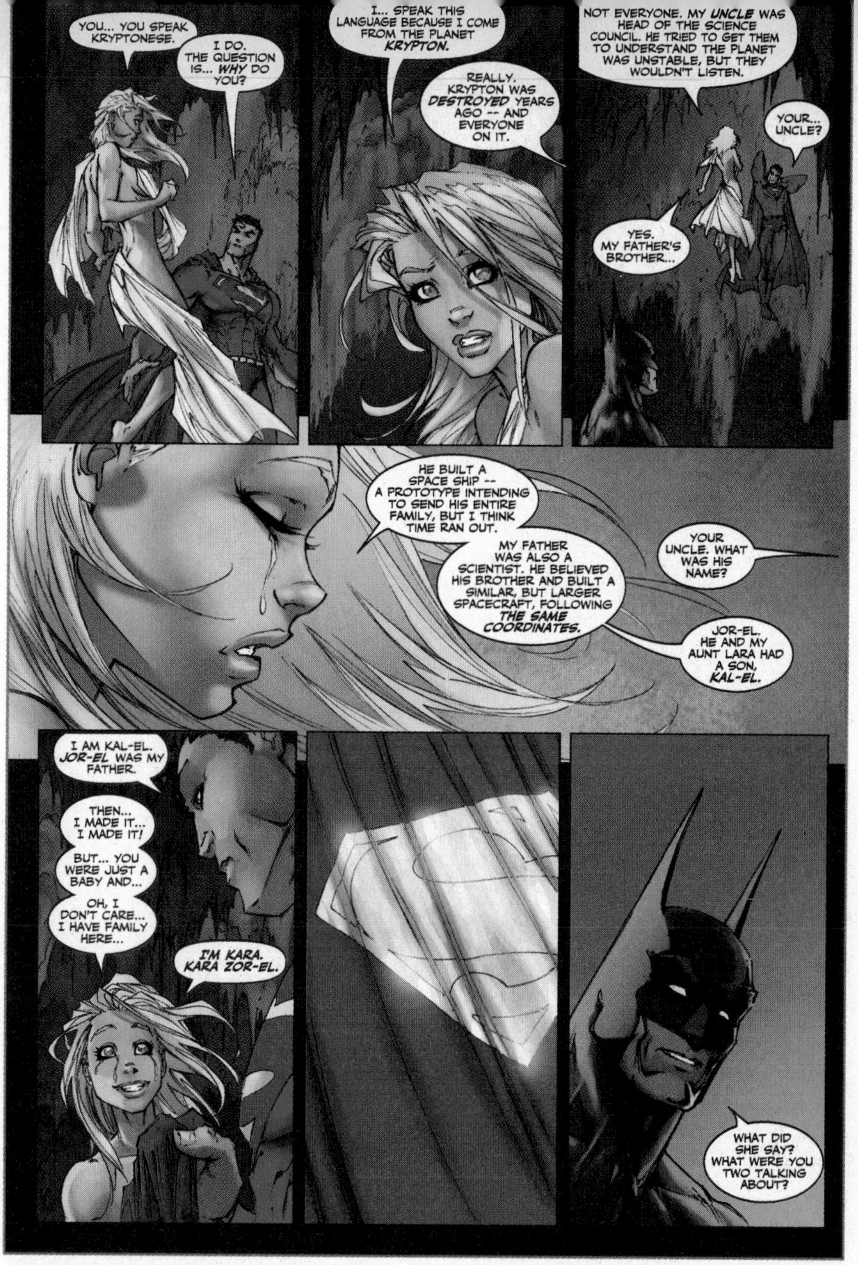
YOU... YOU SPEAK KRYPTONESE.
I DO. THE QUESTION IS... WHY DO YOU?
I... SPEAK THIS LANGUAGE BECAUSE I COME FROM THE PLANET KRYPTON.
REALLY. KRYPTON WAS DESTROYED YEARS AGO -- AND EVERYONE ON IT.
NOT EVERYONE. MY UNCLE WAS HEAD OF THE SCIENCE COUNCIL. HE TRIED TO GET THEM TO UNDERSTAND THE PLANET WAS UNSTABLE, BUT THEY WOULDN'T LISTEN.
YOUR... UNCLE?
YES. MY FATHER'S BROTHER...
HE BUILT A SPACE SHIP -- A PROTOTYPE INTENDING TO SEND HIS ENTIRE FAMILY, BUT I THINK TIME RAN OUT.
MY FATHER WAS ALSO A SCIENTIST. HE BELIEVED HIS BROTHER AND BUILT A SIMILAR, BUT LARGER SPACECRAFT, FOLLOWING THE SAME COORDINATES.
YOUR UNCLE. WHAT WAS HIS NAME?
JOR-EL. HE AND MY AUNT LARA HAD A SON, KAL-EL.
I AM KAL-EL. JOR-EL WAS MY FATHER.
THEN... I MADE IT... I MADE IT!
BUT... YOU WERE JUST A BABY AND...
OH, I DON'T CARE... I HAVE FAMILY HERE...
I'M KARA. KARA ZOR-EL.
WHAT DID SHE SAY? WHAT WERE YOU TWO TALKING ABOUT?

And here's the translated page.

Use this handy-dandy Kryptonese translation guide key (decoder ring not included) to decipher all the funny-looking symbols you see in other word balloons throughout this volume! Amaze your friends! Good luck!

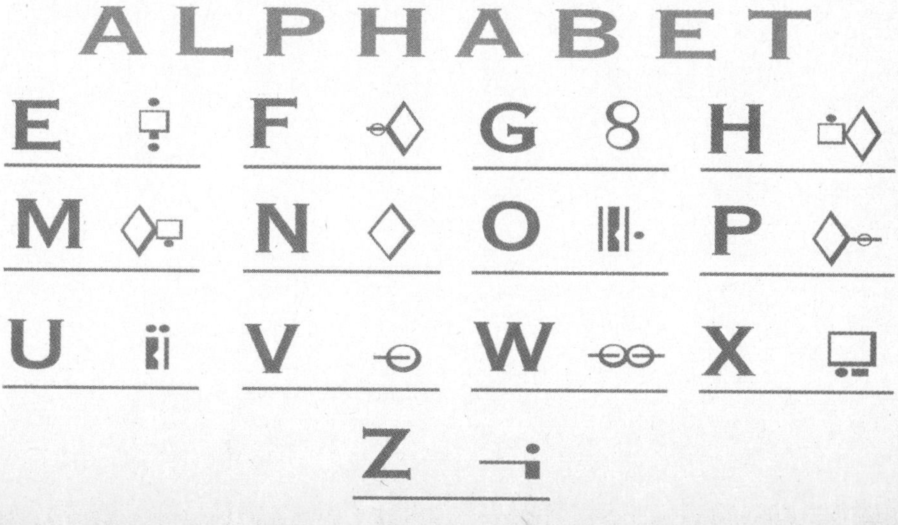
ALPHABET
E
F
G
H
M
N
O
P
U
V
W
X
Z

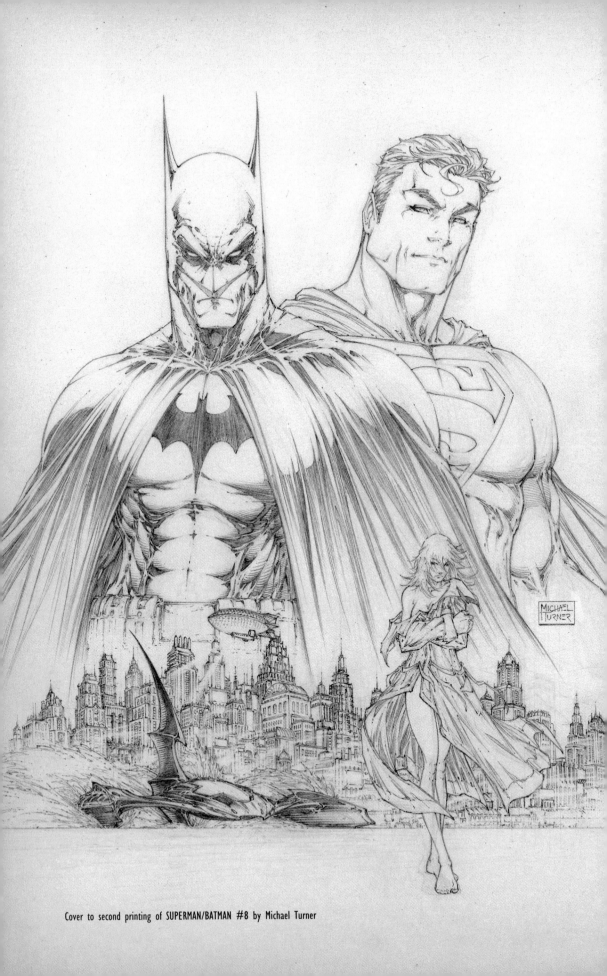

Cover to second printing of SUPERMAN/BATMAN #8 by Michael Turner

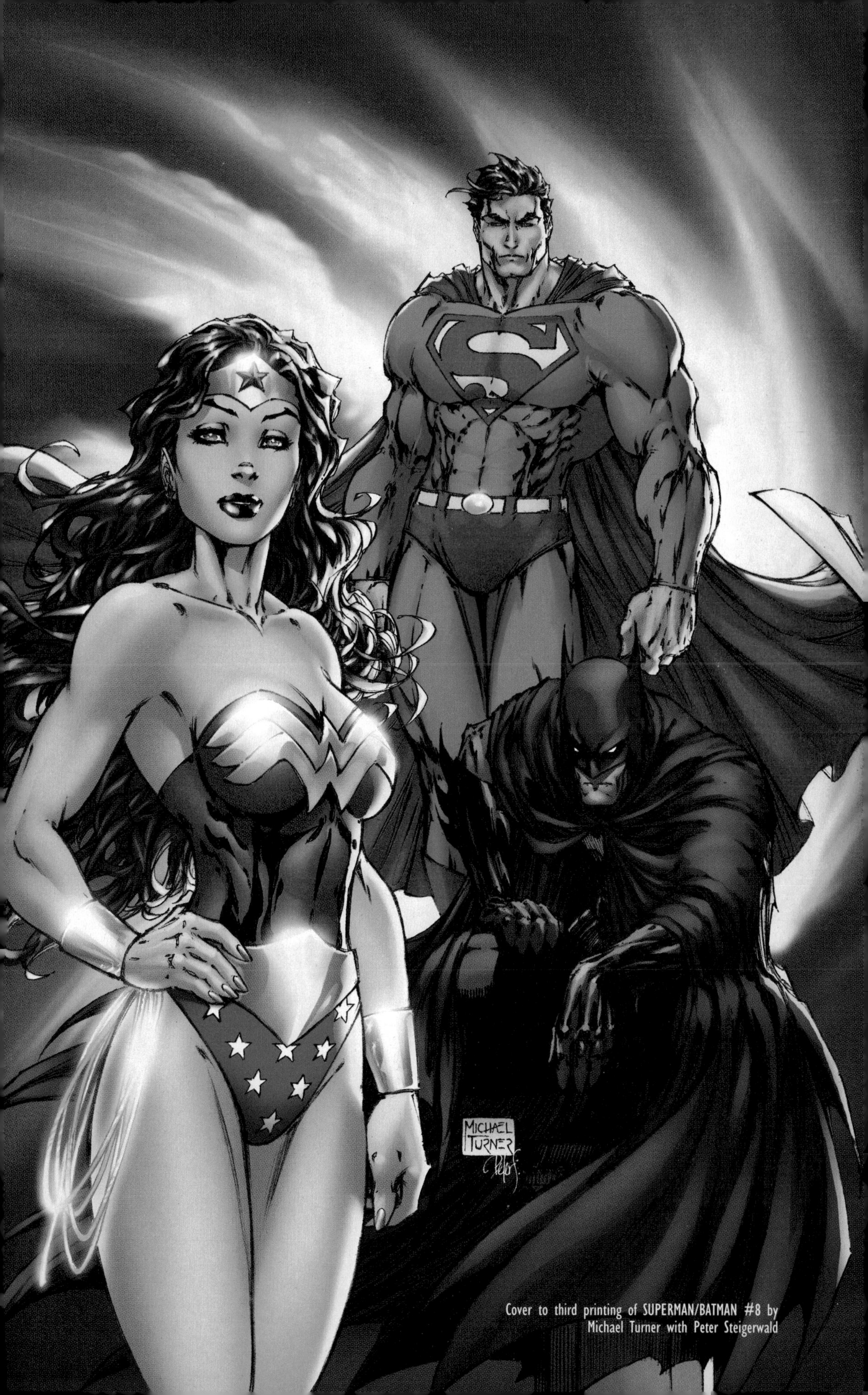
MICHAEL TURNER

Cover to third printing of SUPERMAN/BATMAN #8 by Michael Turner with Peter Steigerwald

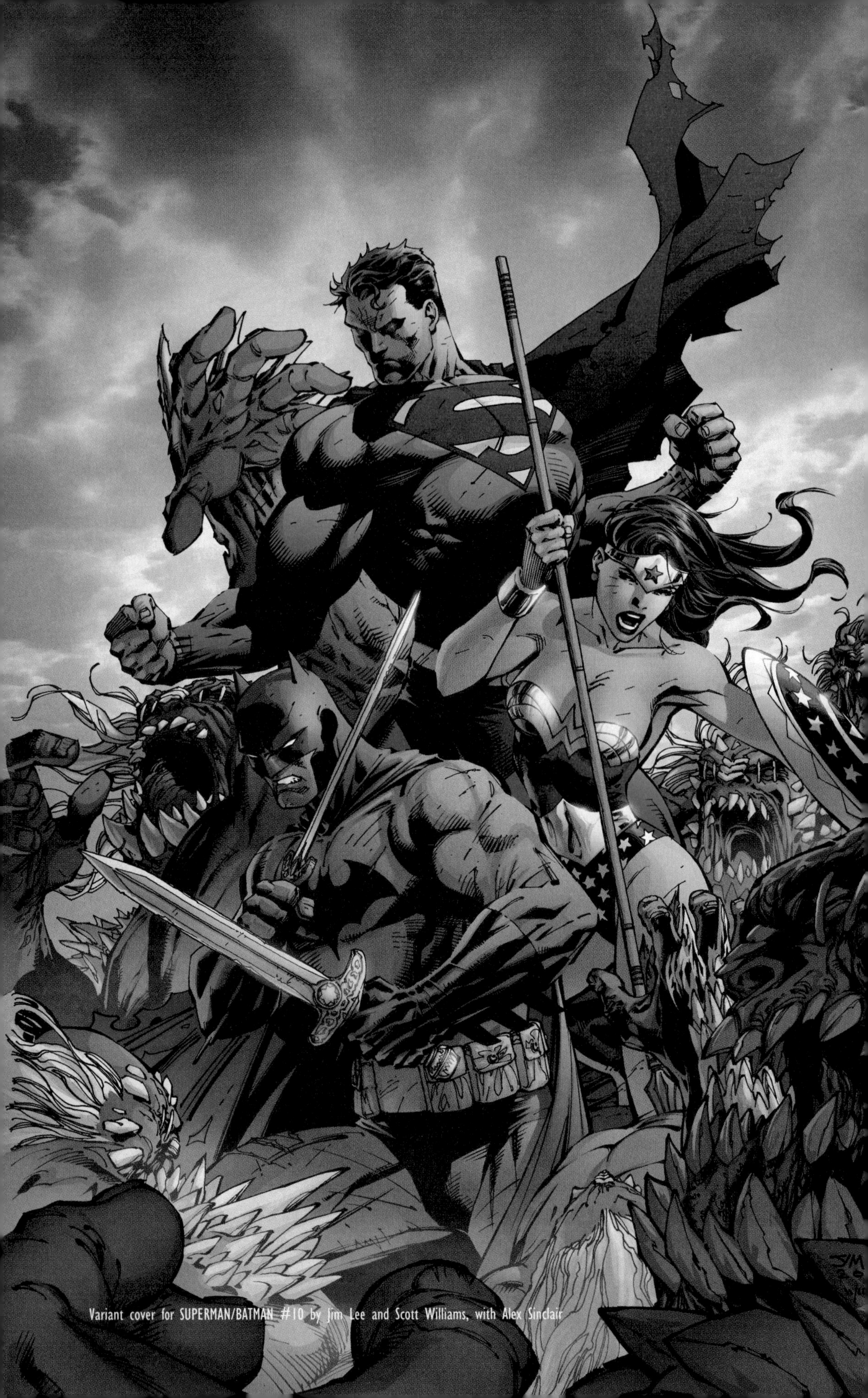

Variant cover for SUPERMAN/BATMAN #10 by Jim Lee and Scott Williams, with Alex Sinclair

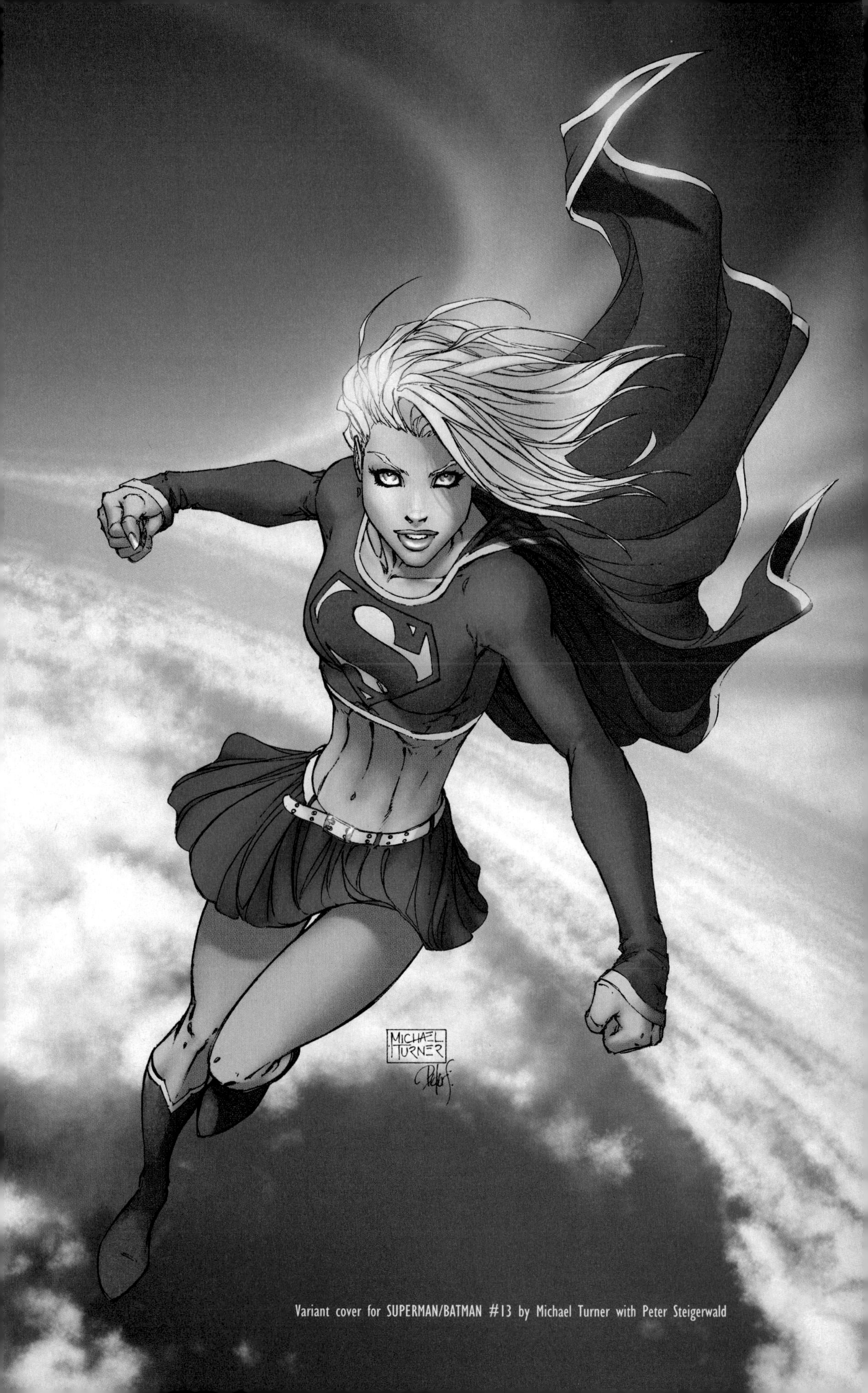
MICHAEL TURNER
Variant cover for SUPERMAN/BATMAN #13 by Michael Turner with Peter Steigerwald

SKETCHES MICHAEL TURNER

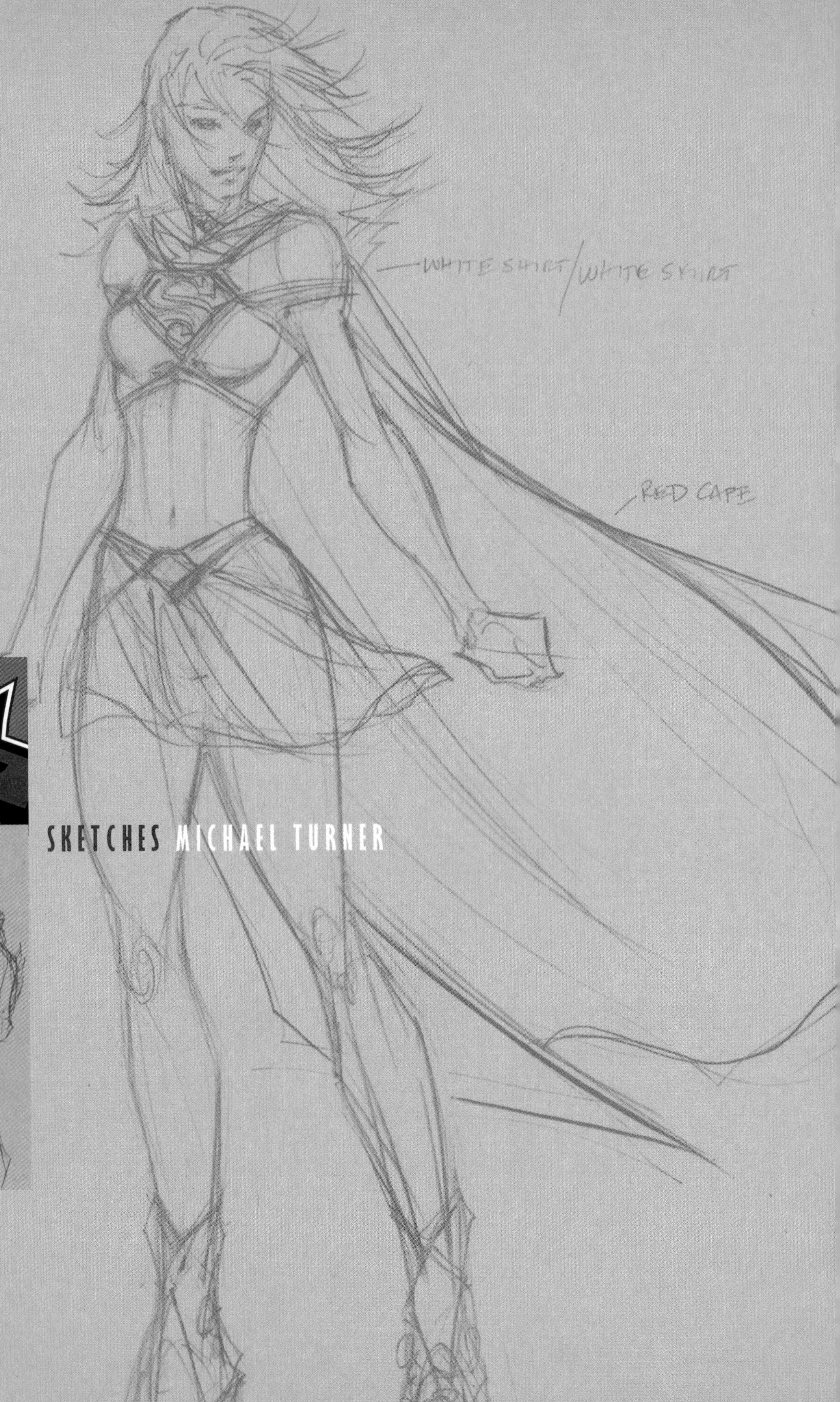
WHITE SHIRT/WHITE SKIRT
RED CAPE

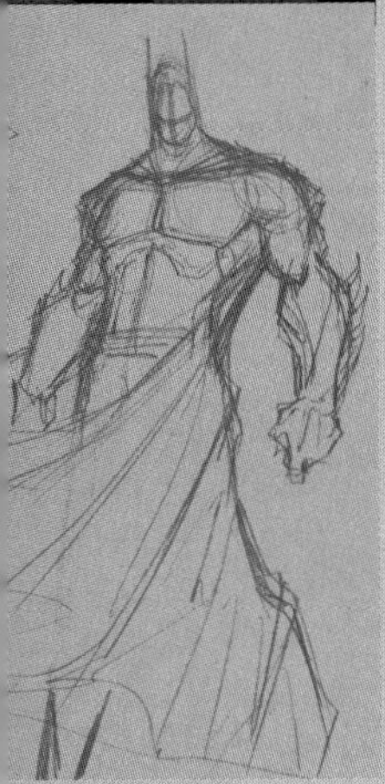

Character study of Supergirl.

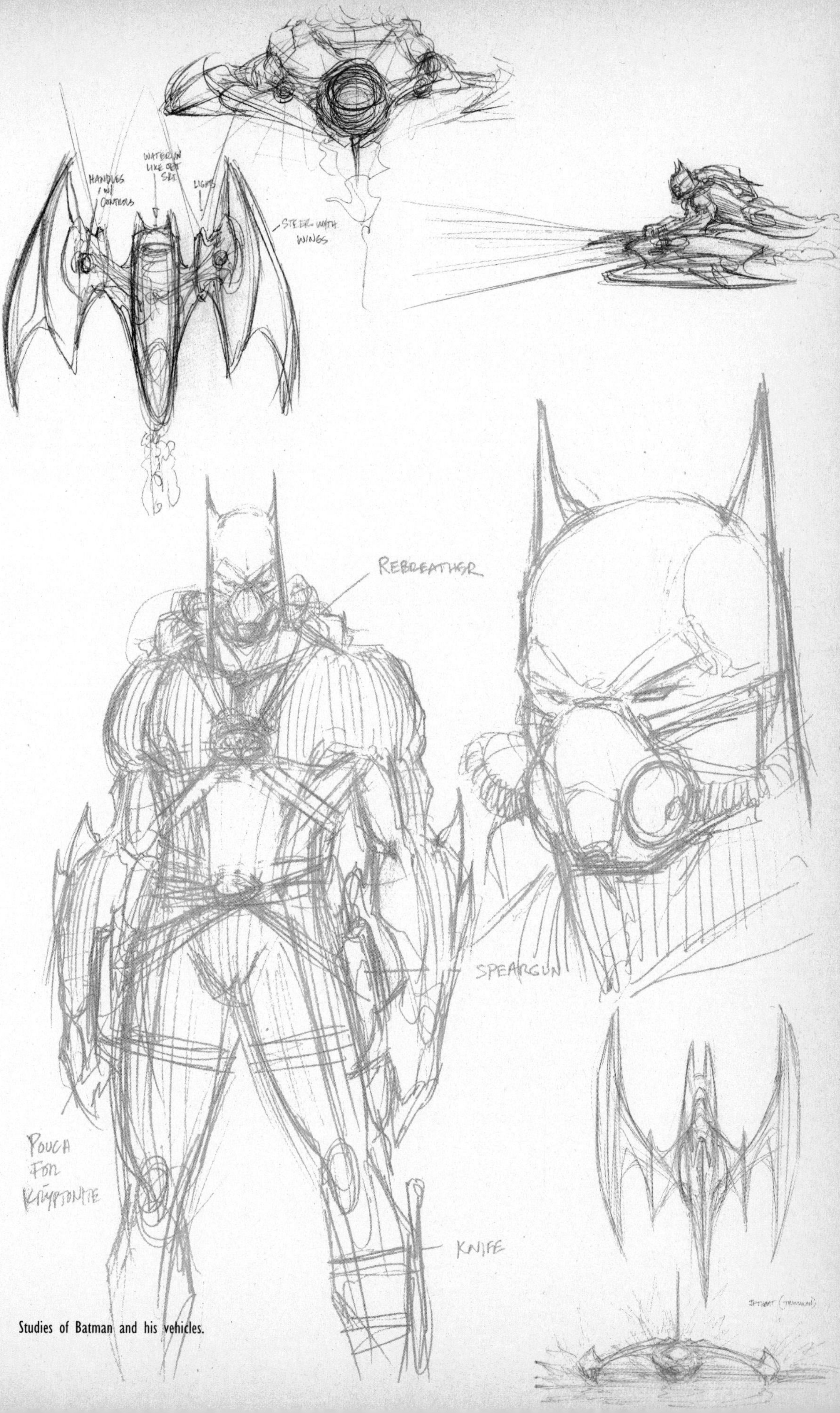
HANDLES W/ CONTROLS
WATERJET LIKE JET SKI
LIGHTS
STEER WITH WINGS
REBREATHER
SPEARGUN
POUCH FOR KRYPTONITE
KNIFE

Studies of Batman and his vehicles.

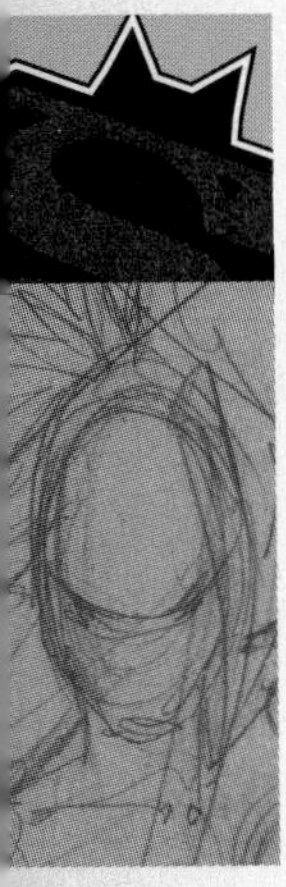

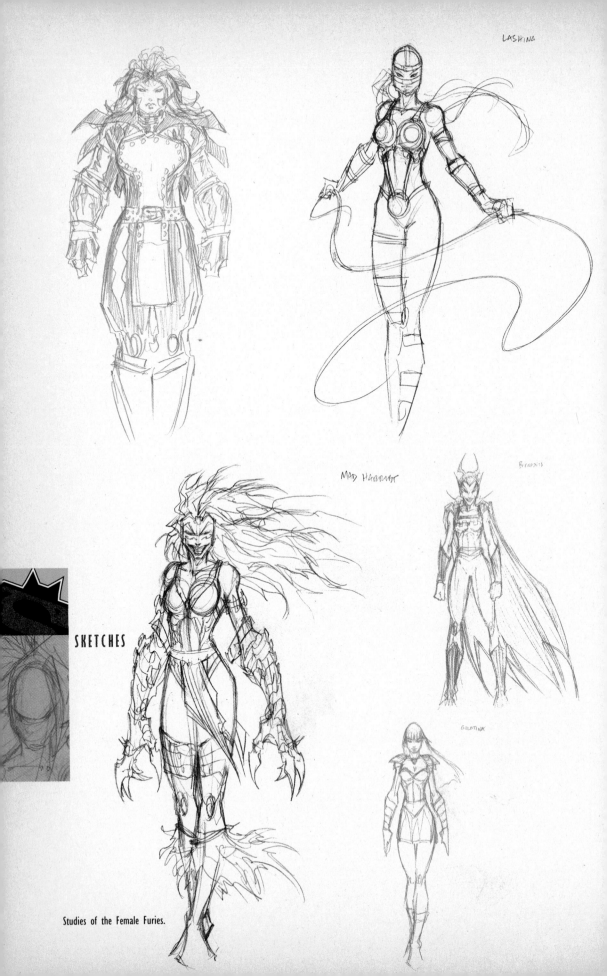

SKETCHES

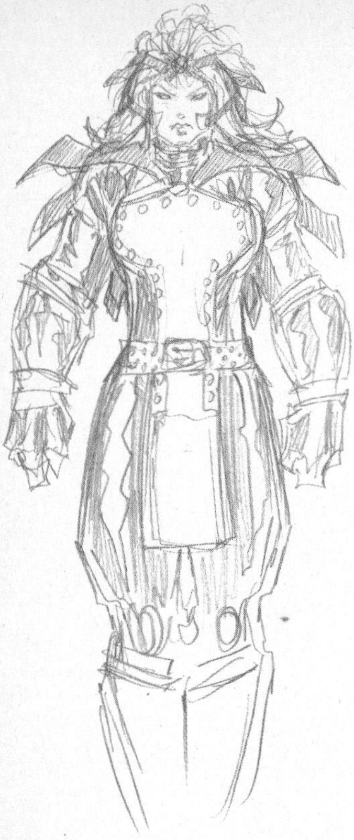

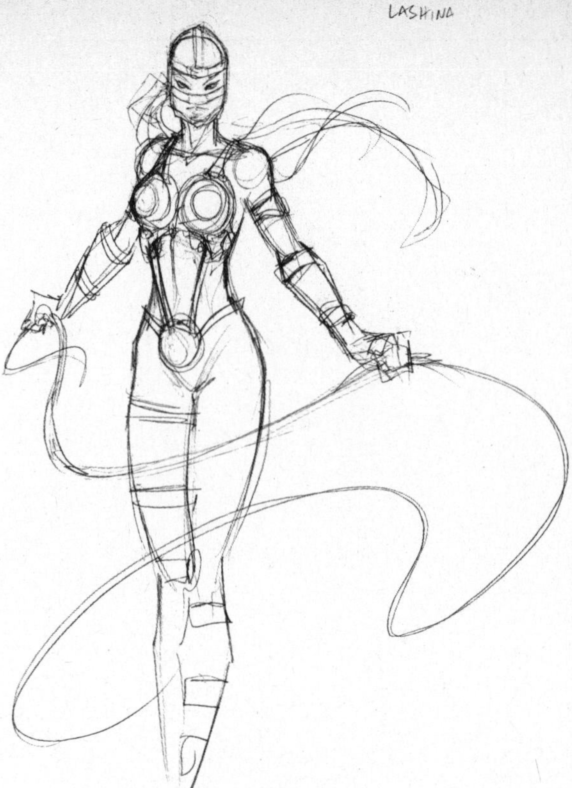
LASHINA

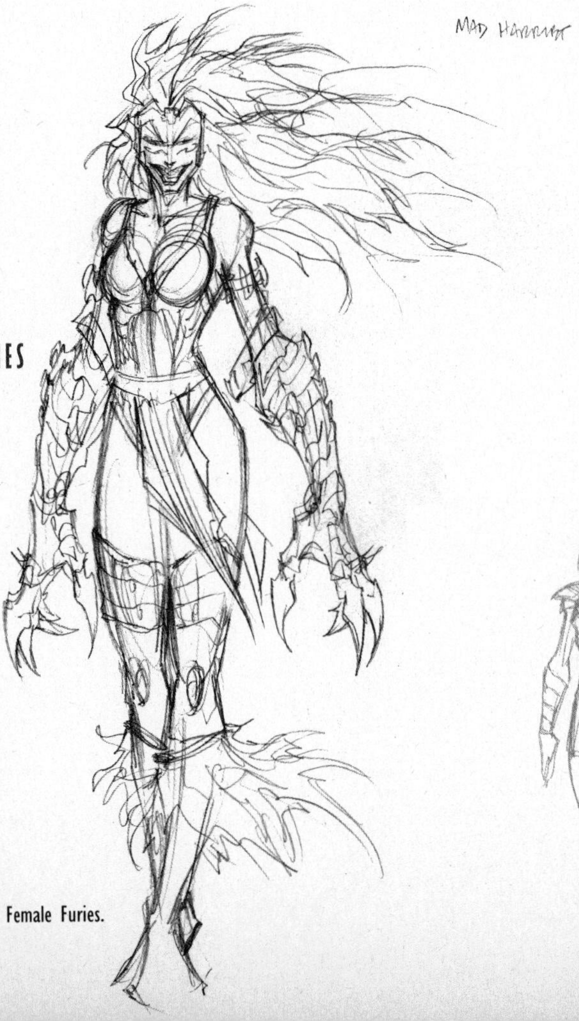
MAD HARRIET

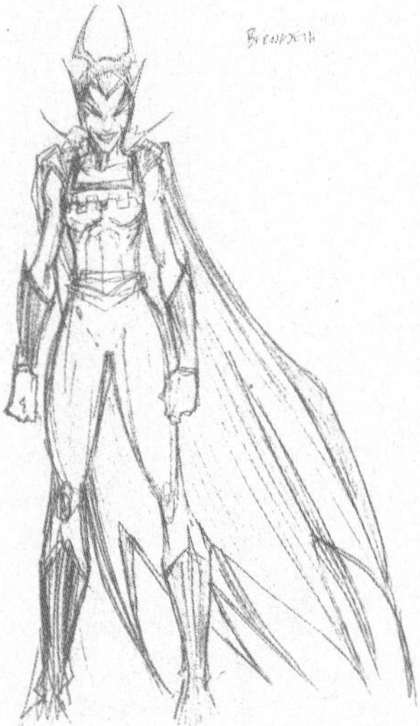

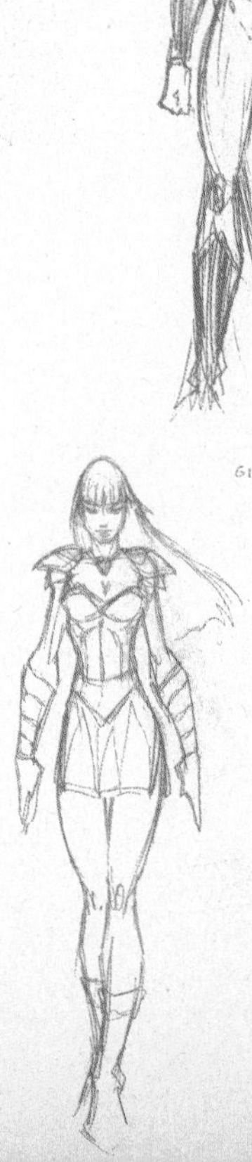
GILOTINA

Studies of the Female Furies.

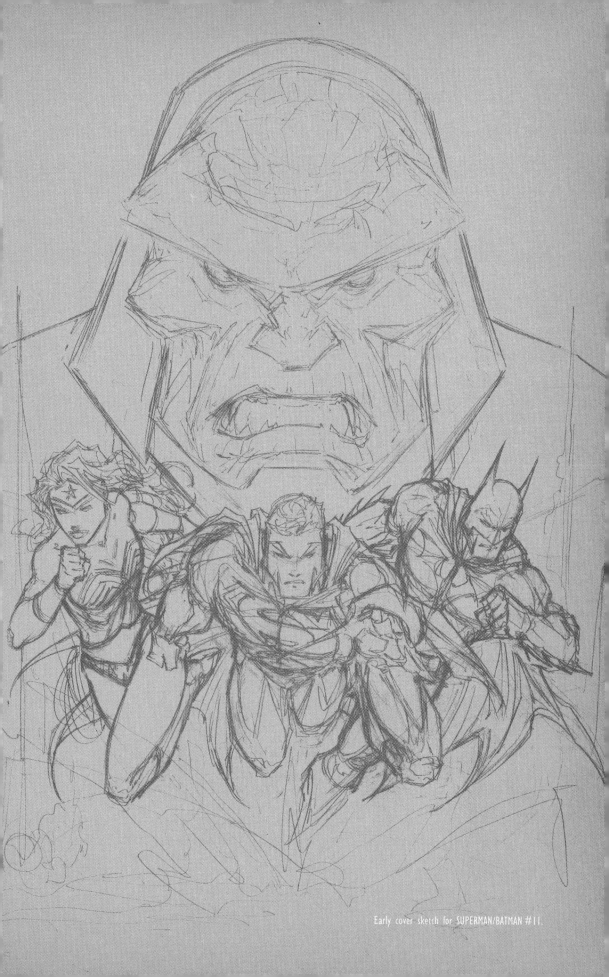

Early cover sketch for SUPERMAN/BATMAN #11.

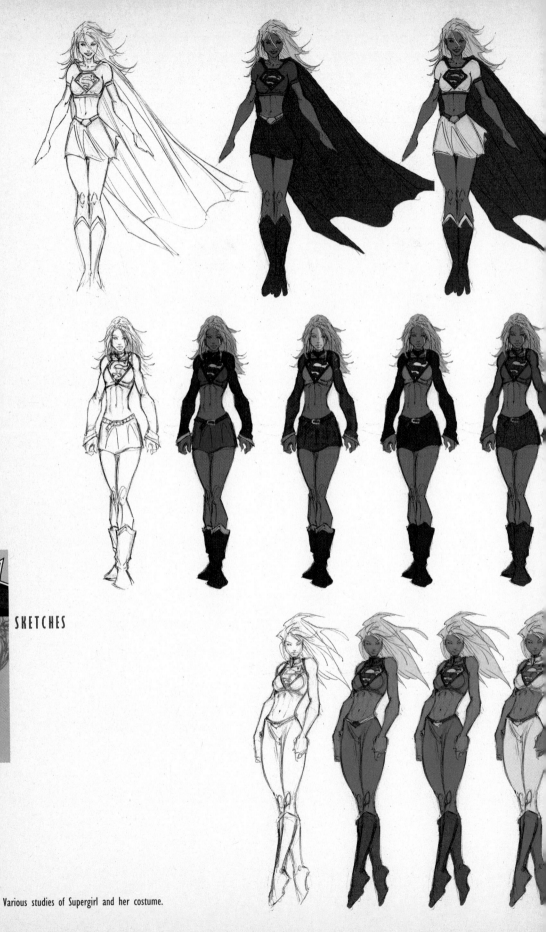

SKETCHES

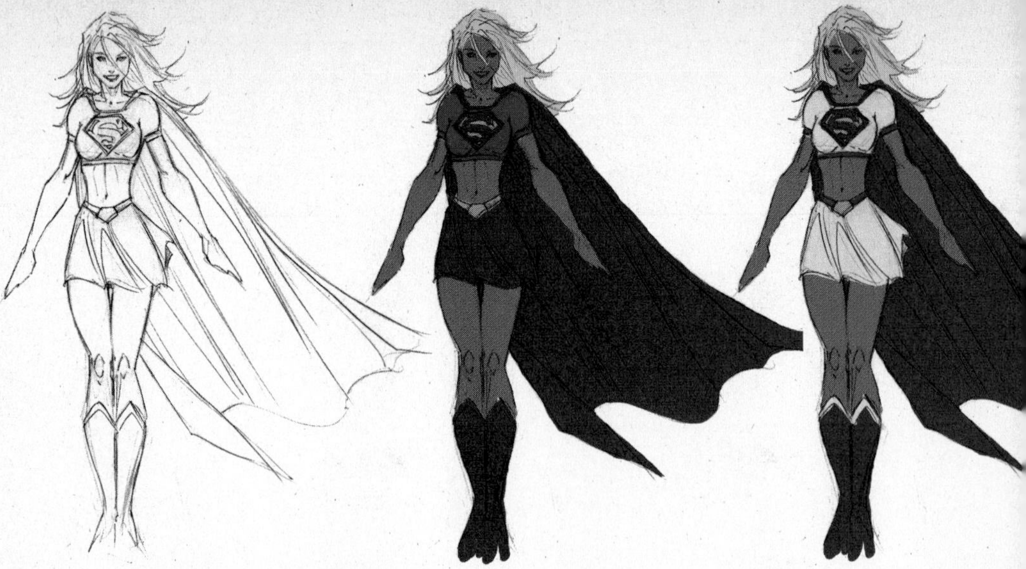

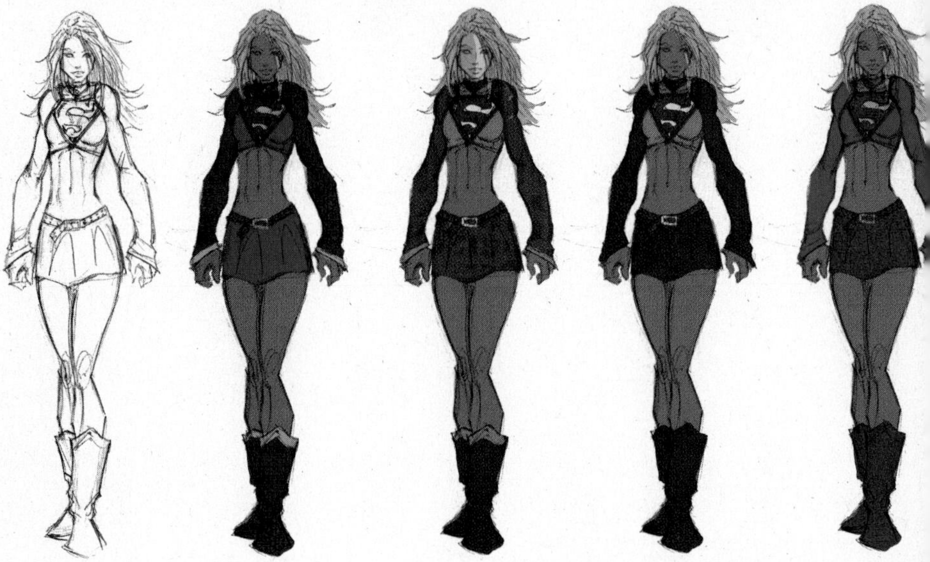

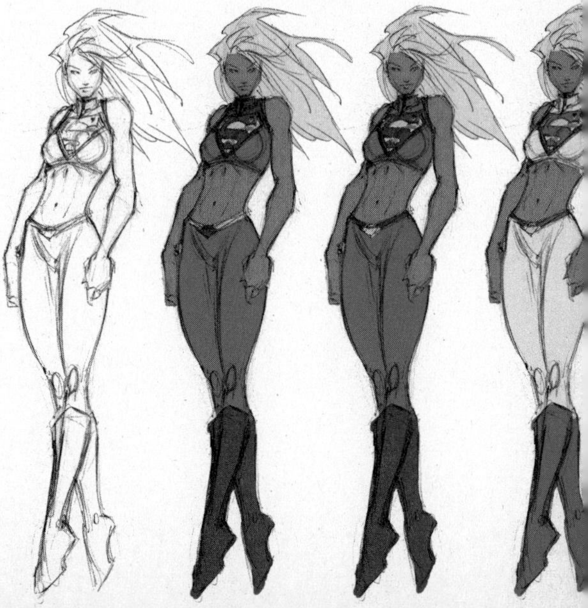

Various studies of Supergirl and her costume.

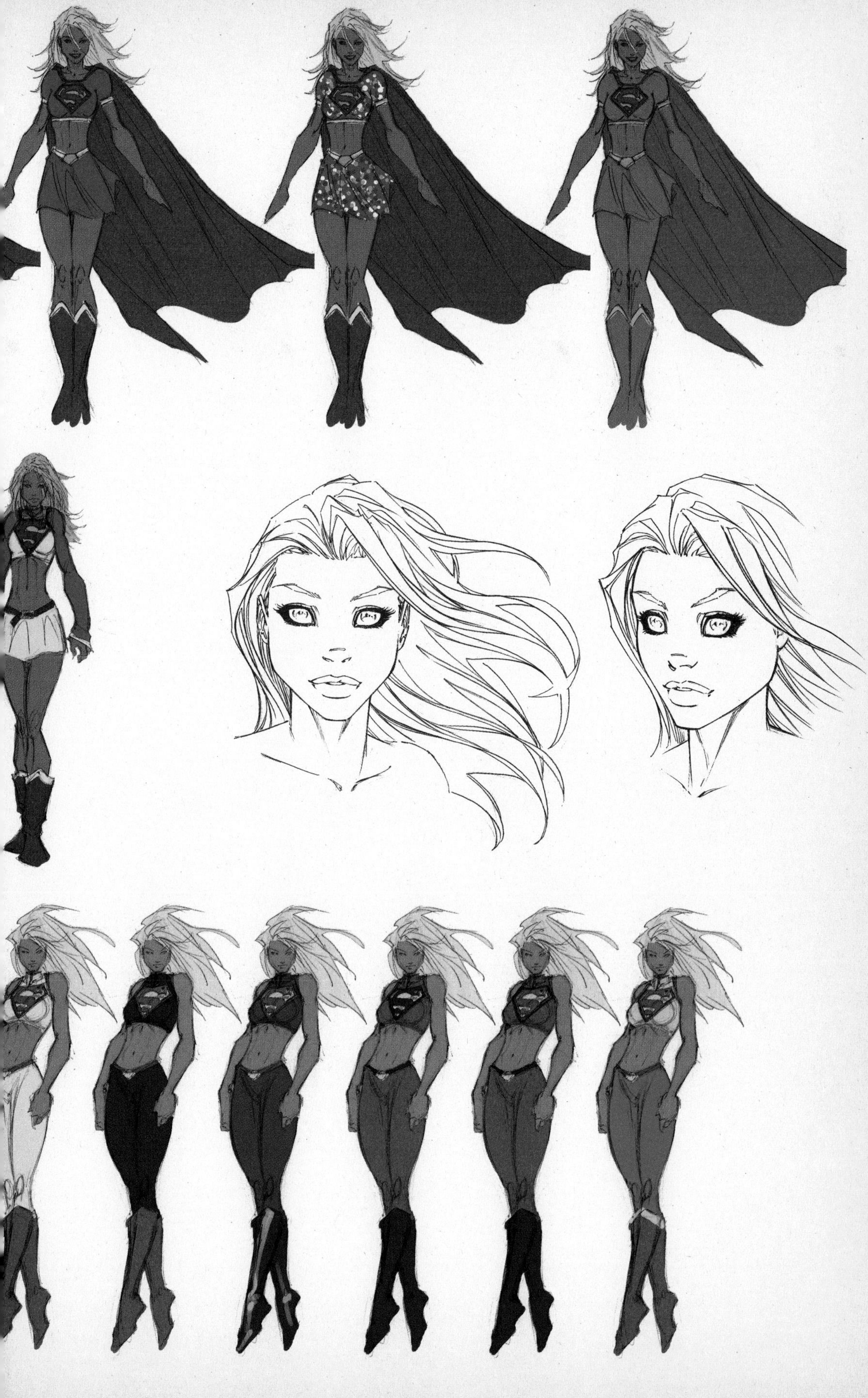

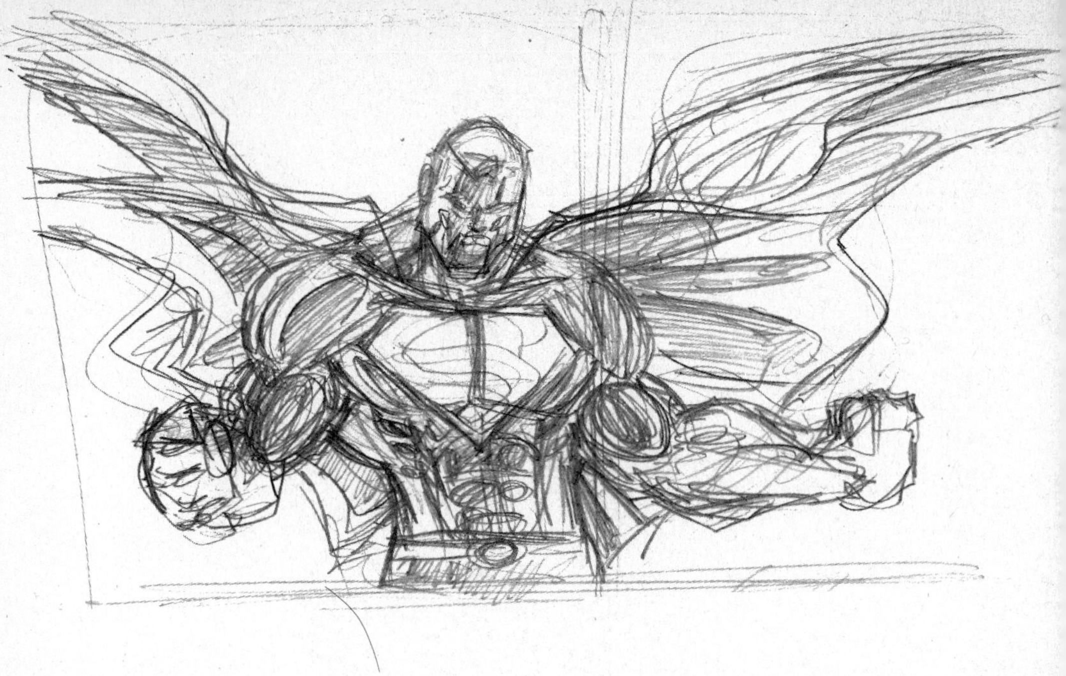

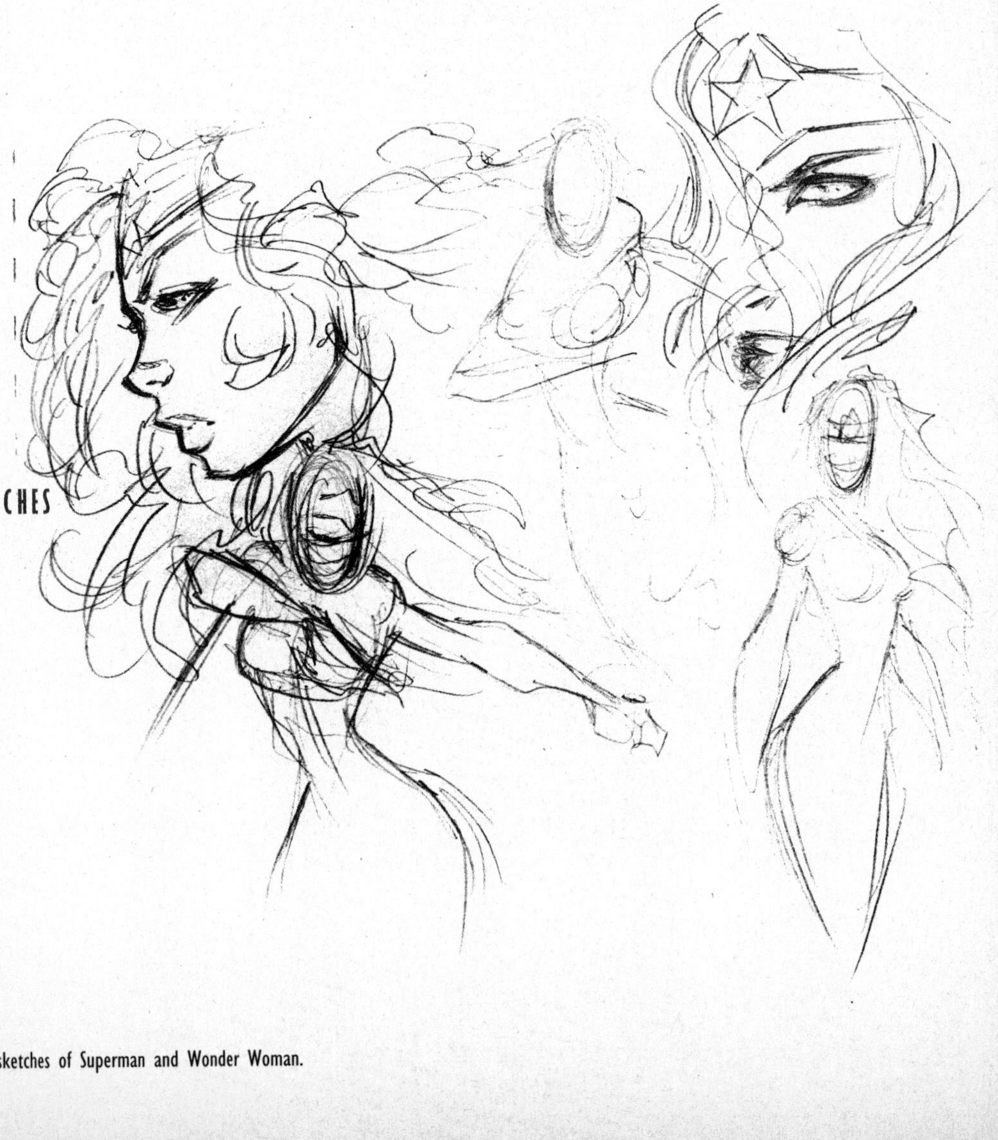

Character sketches of Superman and Wonder Woman.

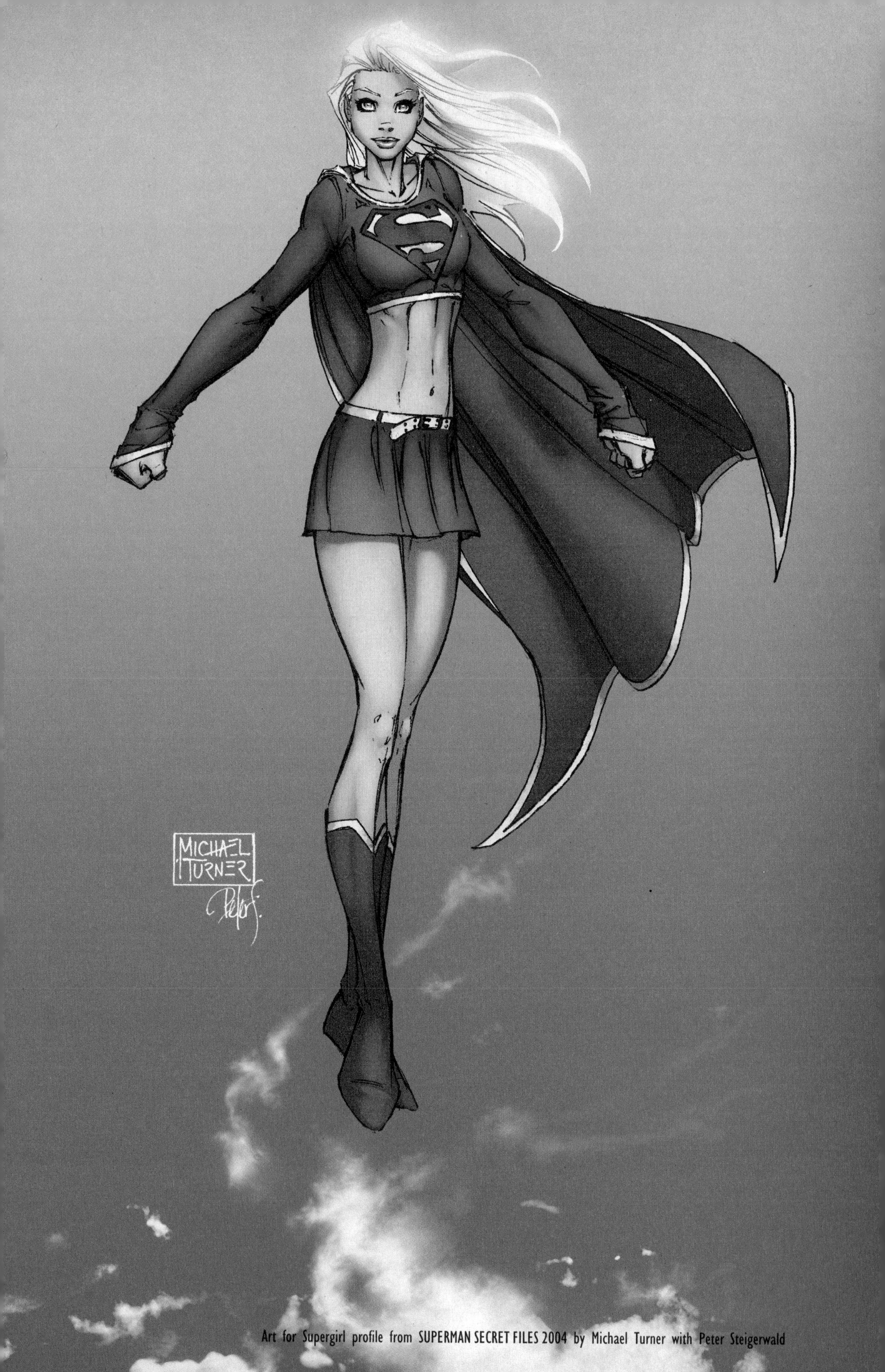
MICHAEL TURNER

Art for Supergirl profile from SUPERMAN SECRET FILES 2004 by Michael Turner with Peter Steigerwald

BIOGRAPHIES

JEPH LOEB is the author of BATMAN: THE LONG HALLOWEEN, BATMAN: DARK VICTORY, SUPERMAN FOR ALL SEASONS, CATWOMAN: WHEN IN ROME, CHALLENGERS OF THE UNKNOWN MUST DIE!, *Spider-Man: Blue*, *Daredevil: Yellow* and *Hulk: Gray* — all of which were collaborations with artist Tim Sale. He has also written SUPERMAN, THE WITCHING HOUR, *Cable*, *X-Man*, *X-Force*, and various other books. A writer/producer living in Los Angeles, his credits include *Teen Wolf*, *Commando* and *Smallville*.

MICHAEL TURNER began his comics career in 1994 with Top Cow Productions, helping to create and launch the successful *Witchblade* series — which quickly became one of the most successful titles of the '90s due to Michael's detailed art. A few years later, Michael created his own series, *Fathom*, which became an instant smash hit. Recently, his writing talents were put to good use by co-writing the SUPERMAN: GODFALL storyline. Michael now has his own publishing company, Aspen MLT Inc., which produces his two series *Soulfire* and *Ekos*.

PETER STEIGERWALD has worked on a number of books with Michael Turner and Aspen MLT Inc., including *Fathom*, *Soulfire* and *Ekos*, plus SUPERMAN: GODFALL for DC Comics. In addition to his coloring duties, Peter also doubles as Aspen's vice-president of publishing.

RICHARD STARKINGS is best known as the creator of the Comicraft studio, purveyors of unique design and fine lettering — and a copious catalogue of comic-book fonts — since 1992. He is less well known as the creator and publisher of *Hip Flask* and his semi-autobiographical cartoon strip, *Hedge Backwards*.

S U P E R M A N   C O L L E C T I O N S

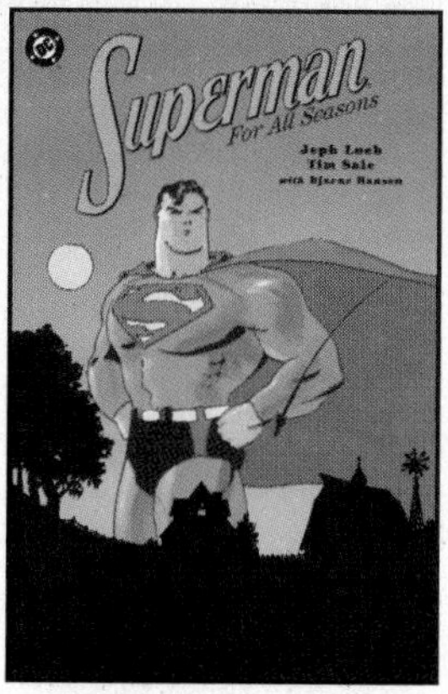
Superman
For All Seasons
Jeph Loeb
Tim Sale

SUPERMAN FOR ALL SEASONS
Jeph Loeb/Tim Sale

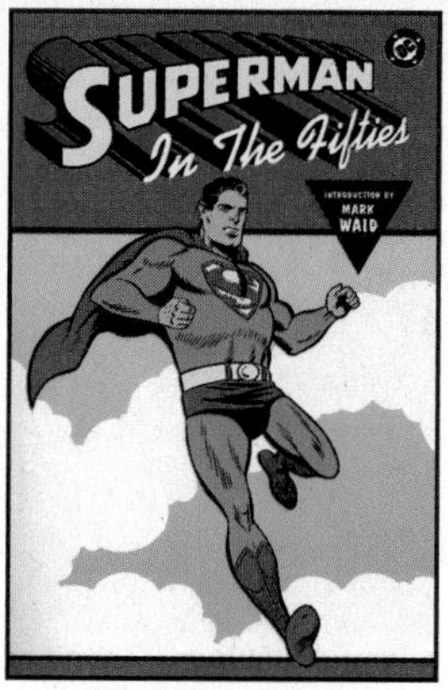
SUPERMAN
In The Fifties
INTRODUCTION BY
MARK
WAID

SUPERMAN IN THE FIFTIES
various

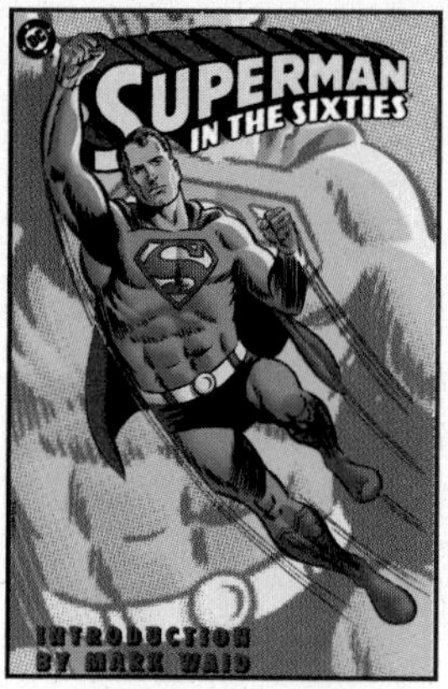
SUPERMAN
IN THE SIXTIES
INTRODUCTION
BY MARK WAID

SUPERMAN IN THE SIXTIES
various

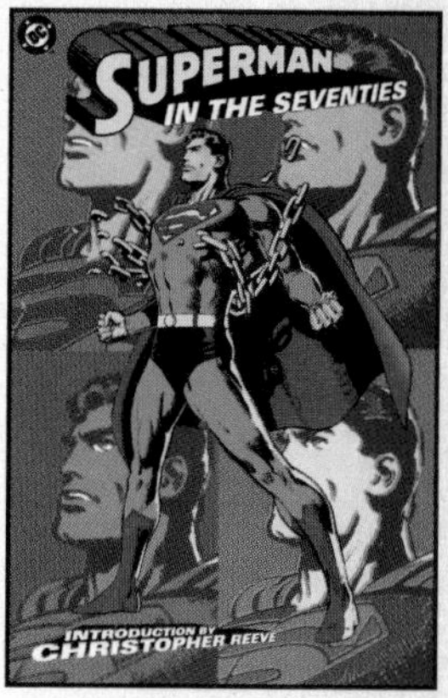
SUPERMAN
IN THE SEVENTIES
INTRODUCTION BY
CHRISTOPHER REEVE

SUPERMAN IN THE SEVENTIES
various

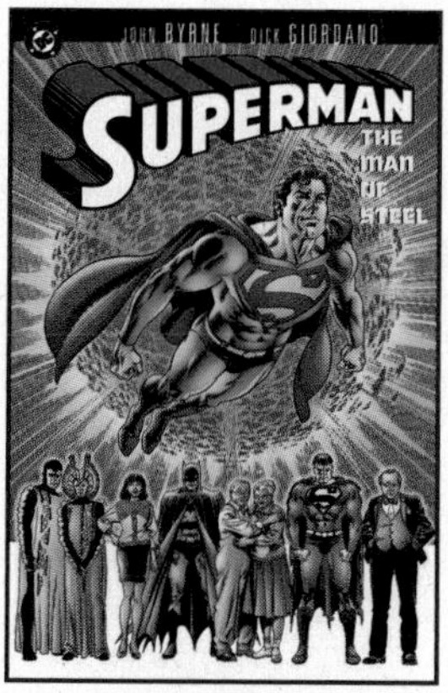
JOHN BYRNE
DICK GIORDANO
SUPERMAN
THE
MAN
OF
STEEL

SUPERMAN: MAN OF STEEL VOLUMES 1 - 3
John Byrne/Marv Wolfman/
Jerry Ordway

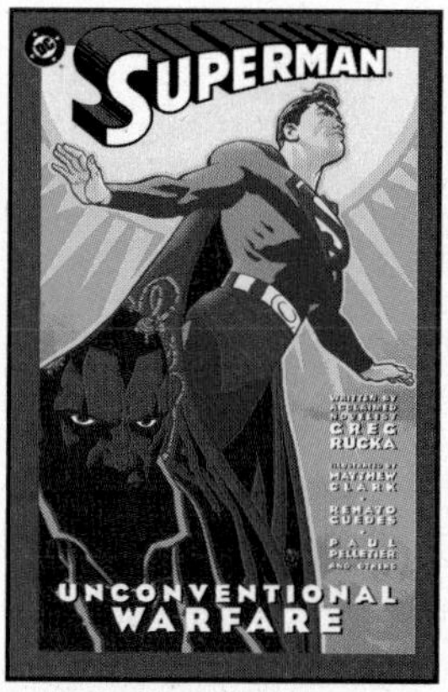
SUPERMAN
GREG
RUCKA
UNCONVENTIONAL
WARFARE

SUPERMAN: UNCONVENTIONAL WARFARE
Greg Rucka/various

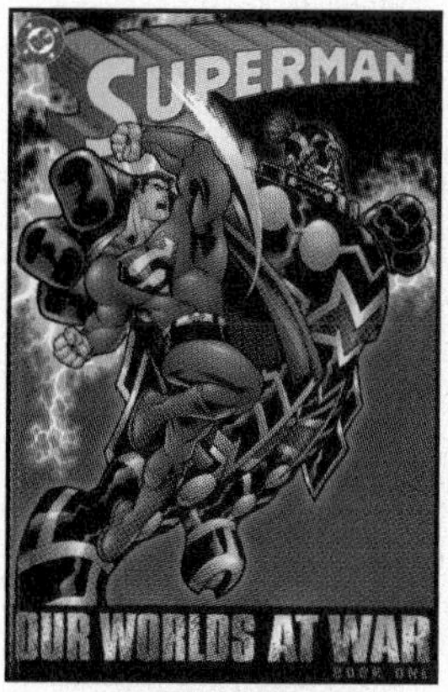
SUPERMAN
OUR WORLDS AT WAR
BOOK ONE

SUPERMAN: OUR WORLDS AT WAR VOLUMES 1 & 2
various

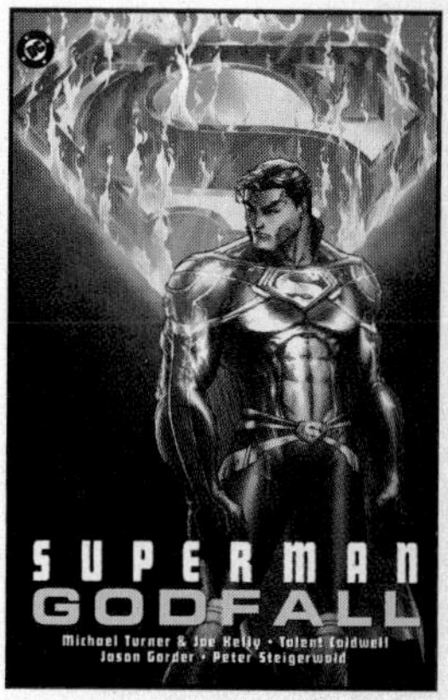
SUPERMAN
GODFALL
Michael Turner & Joe Kelly • Talent Caldwell
Jason Gorder • Peter Steigerwald

SUPERMAN: GODFALL
Michael Turner/Joe Kelly/Talent Caldwell/
Jason Gorder/Peter Steigerwald

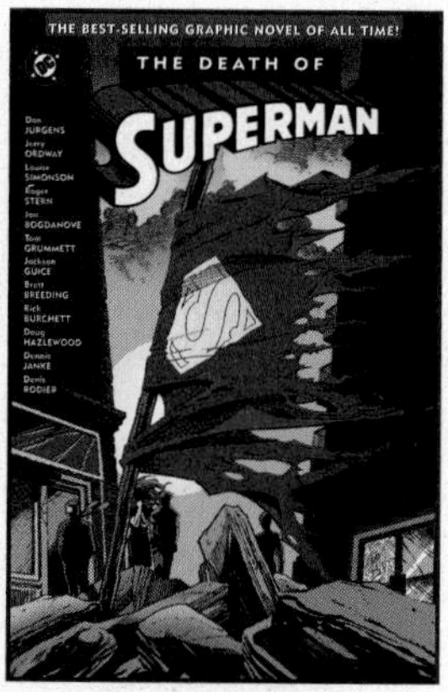
THE BEST-SELLING GRAPHIC NOVEL OF ALL TIME!
THE DEATH OF
SUPERMAN

DEATH OF SUPERMAN
various

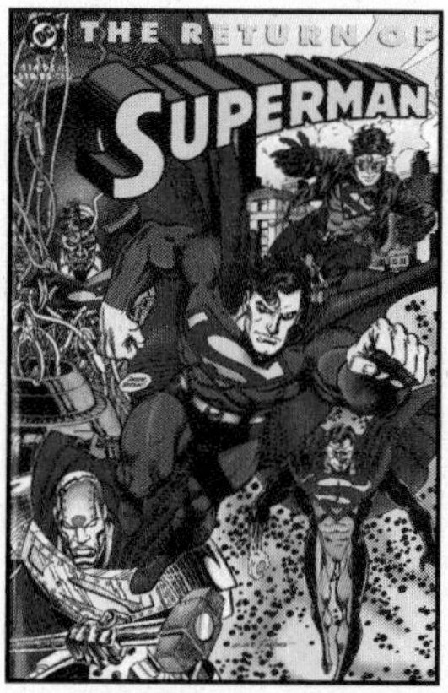
THE RETURN OF
SUPERMAN

RETURN OF SUPERMAN
various

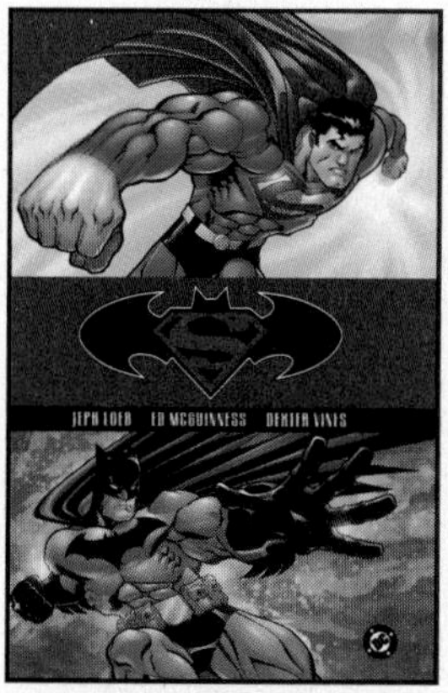
JEPH LOEB
ED McGUINNESS
DEXTER VINES

SUPERMAN/BATMAN: PUBLIC ENEMIES
Jeph Loeb/Ed McGuinness

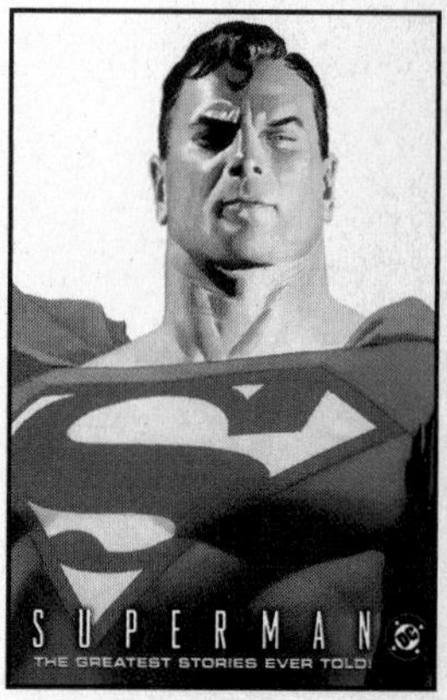
SUPERMAN
THE GREATEST STORIES EVER TOLD!

SUPERMAN: THE GREATEST STORIES EVER TOLD!
various

B A T M A N   C O L L E C T I O N S

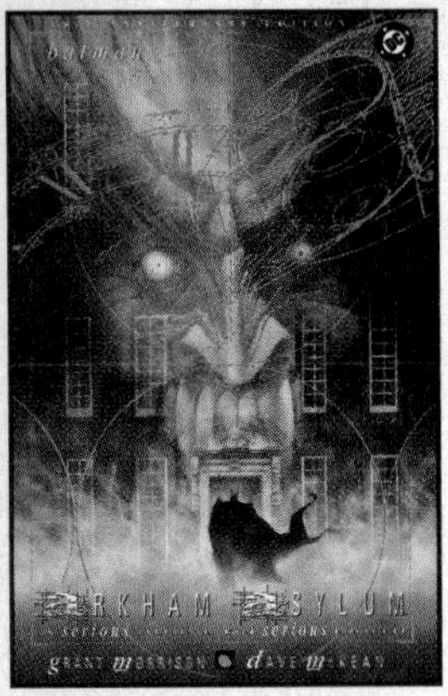
ARKHAM ASYLUM
GRANT MORRISON
DAVE McKEAN

BATMAN: ARKHAM ASYLUM

Grant Morrison/Dave McKean

suggested for mature readers

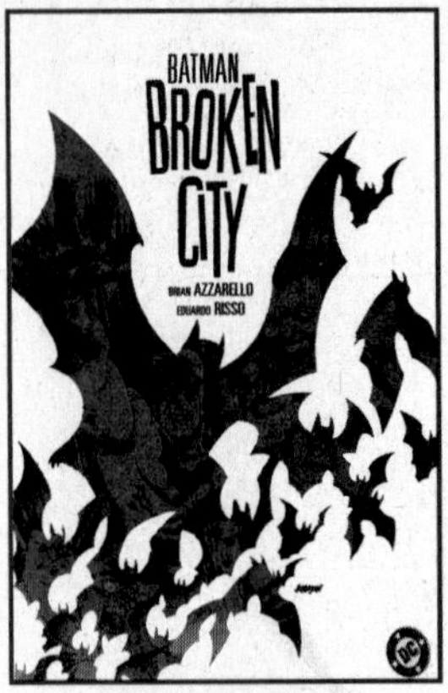
BATMAN
BROKEN CITY
BRIAN AZZARELLO
EDUARDO RISSO

BATMAN: BROKEN CITY

Brian Azzarello/Eduardo Risso

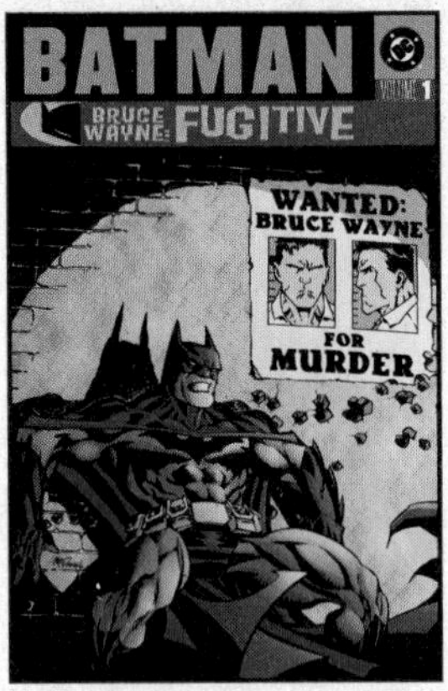
BATMAN
VOLUME 1
BRUCE WAYNE: FUGITIVE
WANTED:
BRUCE WAYNE
FOR
MURDER

BATMAN: BRUCE WAYNE — MURDERER?

BATMAN: BRUCE WAYNE — FUGITIVE VOLUMES 1-3

various

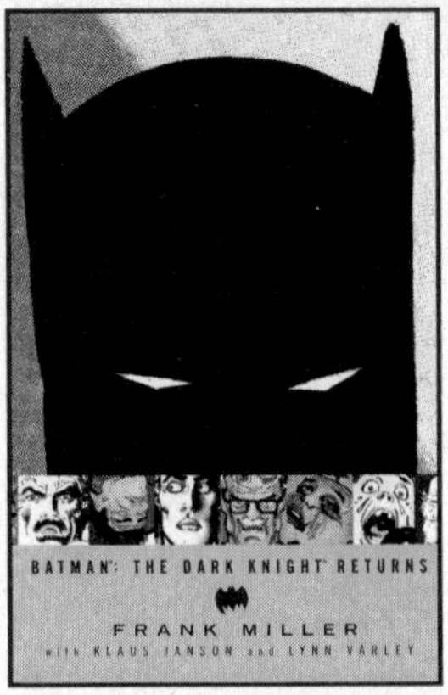
BATMAN: THE DARK KNIGHT RETURNS
FRANK MILLER
with KLAUS JANSON and LYNN VARLEY

BATMAN: THE DARK KNIGHT RETURNS

BATMAN: THE DARK KNIGHT STRIKES AGAIN!

Frank Miller

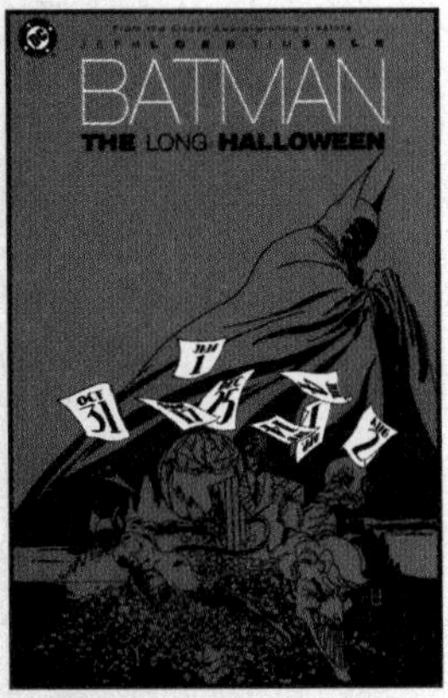
BATMAN
THE LONG HALLOWEEN

BATMAN: HAUNTED KNIGHT

BATMAN: THE LONG HALLOWEEN

BATMAN: DARK VICTORY

Jeph Loeb/Tim Sale

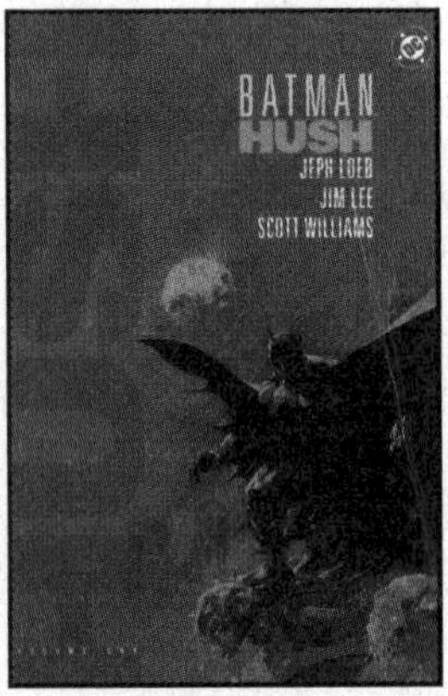
BATMAN
HUSH
JEPH LOEB
JIM LEE
SCOTT WILLIAMS

BATMAN: HUSH VOLUMES 1 & 2

Jeph Loeb/Jim Lee/
Scott Williams

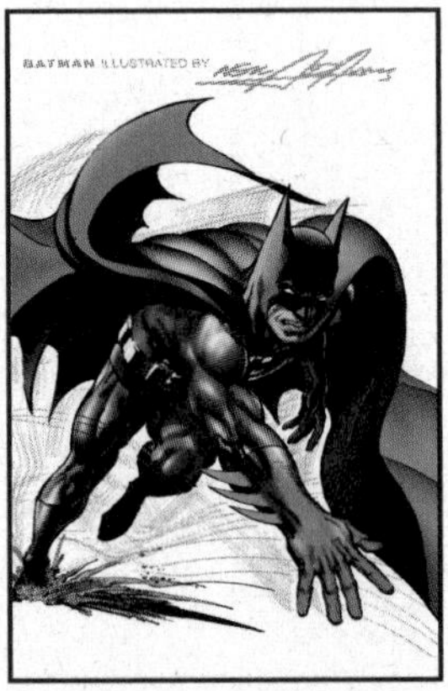

BATMAN ILLUSTRATED BY NEAL ADAMS VOLUMES 1-2

Dennis O'Neil/Neal Adams/various

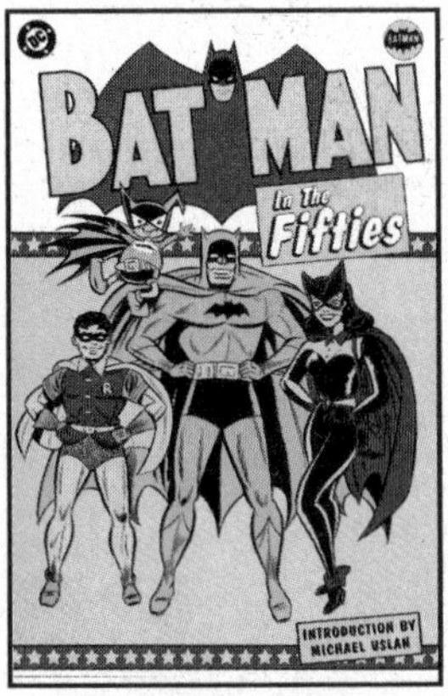
BATMAN
In the Fifties
INTRODUCTION BY
MICHAEL USLAN

BATMAN IN THE FORTIES

BATMAN IN THE FIFTIES

BATMAN IN THE SIXTIES

BATMAN IN THE SEVENTIES

BATMAN IN THE EIGHTIES

various

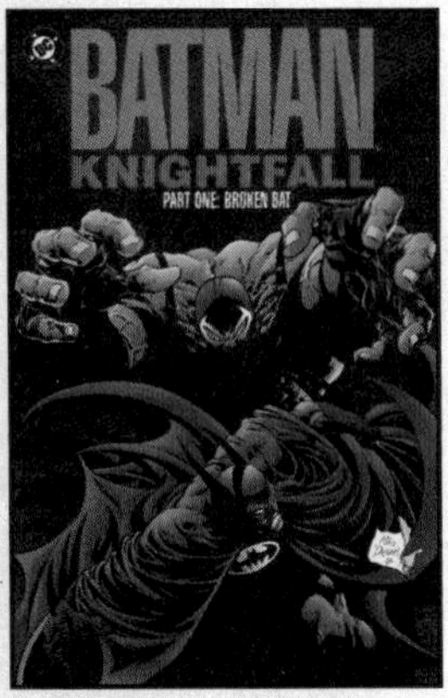
BATMAN
KNIGHTFALL
PART ONE: BROKEN BAT

BATMAN: KNIGHTFALL TPS

PART 1: BROKEN BAT

PART 2: WHO RULES THE NIGHT

PART 3: KNIGHT'S END

various

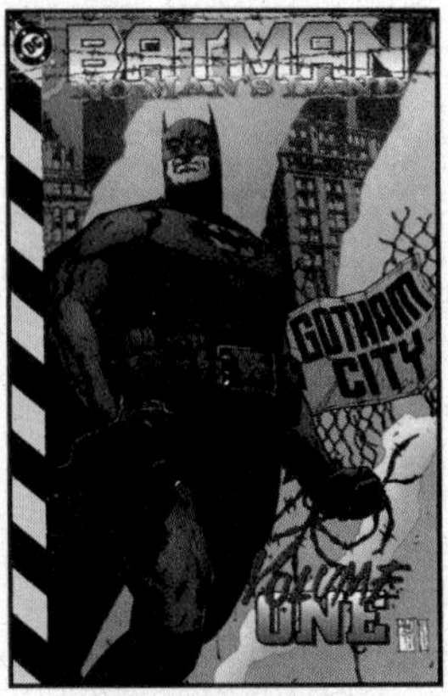
BATMAN
NO MAN'S LAND
GOTHAM CITY
VOLUME ONE

BATMAN: NO MAN'S LAND VOLUMES 1-5

various

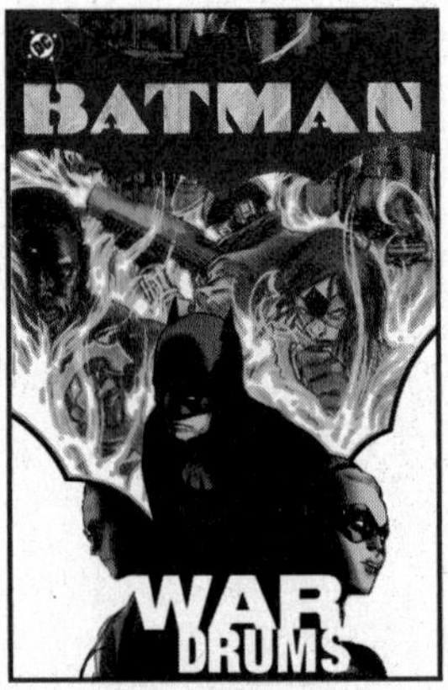
BATMAN
WAR DRUMS

BATMAN: WAR DRUMS

BATMAN: WAR GAMES VOL. 1

various

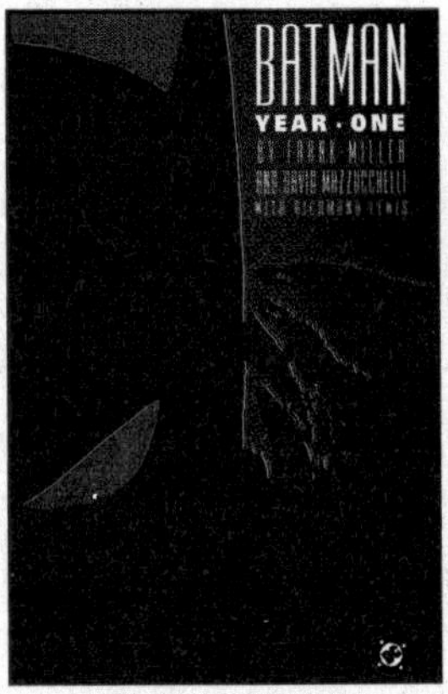
BATMAN
YEAR · ONE

BATMAN: YEAR ONE

Frank Miller/David Mazzucchelli